ADAB AS-SALAT

THE DISCIPLINES OF THE PRAYER

Imam Khomeini

*In the Name of Allah,
the Compassionate, the Merciful*

ADAB AS-SALAT

THE DISCIPLINES OF THE PRAYER

Imam Khomeini

The Institute for Compilation and Publication
of Imam Khomeini"s Works
(International Affairs Department)

Adab aS-Salat: The Disciplines of the Prayer

Publisher: International Affairs Department ,The Institute for Compilation and Publication of Imam Khomeini"s Works
Translated and edited by: Muhammad Jafar Khalili, Salar Manafi Anari,
Proofreaders: Sayyed Taher Shariat-Panahi and Mansoor L. Limba
Third Printing: 2008
Copies: 3,000
Price:
Address: No. 5 Sudeh Alley, Yaser Street, Bahonar Avenue, Jamaran,
P.C. 19778, P.O. Box 19575/614, Tehran, Islamic Republic of Iran
Tel: (009821) 22283138, 22290191-5
Fax: (009821) 22834072, 22290478

E-mail: international-dept@imam-khomeini.ir

کتاب آداب نماز به زبان انگلیسی

Table of Contents

APPENDIX
Photostat Pages of the Book in Imam Khomeini"s
Own Handwriting

Preface

THE DISCIPLINES OF *SALAT* (The Islamic Prayer), which was finished on Monday, the 2nd of Rabi ath-Thani, 1361 L.H. (Lunar Hijri Year) [30th of Farvardin, 1321 S.H. (Solar Hijri year)], is a detailed explanation of the *Salat*'s strict disciplines and moral secrets. Three years before the writing of this work, the Imam (*s*) [*salamullahi alayh* = may Allah's peace be upon him] had written a book under the title: *The Secret of the Salat*, which contained the same concepts, but it was concise and in the terms of the elect gnostics.[1] Nevertheless, the late Imam, believing that more people should benefit from the subjects of the book, set upon writing this book in a simpler language. He says:

> Before this, I prepared a paper in which I wrote on the secrets of the *Salat* as much as was feasible. But as it was not suitable for the common people, I decided to write parts of the cordial disciplines of this spiritual ascension, so that my brothers in faith may have a remembrance, and my hard heart may be affected by it.

Formerly, the folds [*matawi*] of the book *Adab as-Salat*, with explanations and revisions, had been published under the title: *Flying in the Heavenly Kingdom*. Then the book itself was published. The former editions, however, were not agreeable, for some reasons. One of the reasons might probably have been the lack of a manuscript. Therefore, The Institute for Compilation and Publication of Imam Khomeini's Works set forth to publish this work, with complete precision, faithfulness, and reference to the available copies, and collating them with the original MS (manuscript) copy which is within the reach of this Institute.

---

[1] The complete and revised text of *The Secret of the Salat*, including its photostatic copy, comments and different indexes, has already been published by this Institute.

The book includes two prefaces, which the Imam wrote in 1363 S.H., dedicating this work to his respected son, Hujjatul-Islam wal-Muslimin, Haj Sayyid Ahmad Khomeini, and to Mrs. Fatimah Tabatabai (wife of Haj Sayyid Ahmad Khomeini).

This edition is accompanied by footnotes and explanations, in which the sources and the references of the *hadith*s and statements are stated, and the Arabic texts are translated. All these marginations— except a few which the Imam himself had written down and are marked by an asterisk (*) (in the Persian copy)—as well as the different indexes of the book, have been prepared and arranged by this Institute.

Certain Islamic and gnostic terms have been printed in italics or in bold (beside the titles of the books). Some of these terms have been explained in English in the GLOSSARY at the end of the book. A thousand copies of the first edition of the book (in Persian) are accompanied with the photostatic copy of the complete MS (manuscript) to be sent to the libraries and those interested in keeping specimens of the Imam"s handwritten works. Other copies include only a printed sample of the MS.

We cordially thank the management and the staff of The Scientific and Educational Publishing Company for the help they accorded us.

Sending our greetings to the late Imam, we pray Allah, the Great, to bestow upon us His help to be more serviceable to Islam.

The Institute for Compilation and Publication of Imam Khomeini"s Works (International Affairs Department)

Foreword

In His Most Exalted Name

Surely the greatest characteristic of Imam Khomeini is that he was a God-centered and a Faith-pivoted man—a characteristic, which has its roots in his religious ideology. From the positive gnostic point of view[2] Allah, the Great, is the Ruler over the heavens and the earth, and men are to perform their duties, and to bow, in respect, their heads before the Divine Will. They are not to worship other than Him, and not to put foot on any path except on His, as this world is just a transit station, while the permanent abode of the servants is in the neighborhood of Allah, the Glorified. Man, in this world of matter, is to sow what he wants to harvest in the Hereafter. So, he should deservedly carry out what is incumbent upon him, and not to enter upon a course forbidden to him, so that he may prosper.

The Imam started his course in life with such an outlook, and when he rose, he was prompted only by the idea that it was his duty to rise, and when he issued his orders to wage the defensive war and to be steadfast, he issued them because he believed that to fight and be steadfast were religious duties. On the day when he decreed—to the astonishment of everybody—that Salman Rushdie was to be executed, it was only because it is the very judgment of Islam against such an apostate.

---

[2] The term "positive gnosticism" as against "negative gnosticism", means that the Gnostic would not break with the creatures of Allah nor would he take to live in seclusion and isolation, rather he prefers to live among the people and with them. He even believes that it is his duty to guide the people to the straight and true path.

As regards the negative gnostic person, he breaks with the people, lives in seclusion, dislikes attending meetings, and spends his life in an isolated place, engaging himself in worshipping Allah.

Consequently, the thinkers of the world and the well-versed politicians admit that (Imam) Khomeini was more of a religious leader than a politician, and he was engaged more in carrying out Allah's verdicts than in ruling on the basis of politics.

Only from this angle one may be able to cast a glance at the world-enlightening sun of the Revolution and get acquainted with his personality, and only with such a view in mind one may comprehend the depth of this expression in his will, where he says: " ...With a calm soul, a confident heart, a cheerful spirit and a conscience full of hope in Allah's favor, I take leave from my sisters and brothers to travel to the eternal abode..." **Peace be upon him the day he was born, the day he dies and the day he shall be raised up alive.**

The book which is before you covers a part of Imam Khomeini's looks into the valley of theoretical gnosticism. It is dedicated by that godly man to his efficient and gnostic son, the late Hujjatul-Islam wal-Muslimin Haj Sayyid Ahmad Khomeini, who, with a clear heart and a pure soul, spent his life walking along practical gnosticism, and who tried hard to carry out all the moral instructions of the Imam. It is dedicated to his daughter-in-law, too.

Now that the pen has inscribed the names of such great men, I feel ashamed of having my feeble fingers scribble an introduction to such a great book by such a great man. I request the people of knowledge, research and readings to pardon me, and extend their helping hands to me, who am lost on the road, trembling upon myself like the leaves of a willow!

At the end, I regard it necessary to offer my thanks to the respected Director of the International Affairs Department of the Institute for Compilation and Publication of Imam Khomeini's Works, his colleagues and the honorable translators who have translated this and other books of the Imam. I request all the translators in the country and those familiar with translating the gnostic works to assist this Institute in bettering such translations, since such an important question cannot be handled without their cooperation and heart-felt sympathy.

Sayyid Hasan Khomeini

Dedications

In the Name of Allah, The Beneficent, The Merciful

I dedicate *Adab as-Salat*—the book from which I had no benefit except regret because of my failure and negligence of the days on which I could have made myself, and except contrition and remorse during old age, being empty-handed, with a heavy burden, and a long way to go, with a lame leg, while the call of departure is ever resounding in my ears—to my dear son, Ahmad. He is in the prime of life, and thus, he may, *insha Allahu Taala* (if Allah, the Exalted, wills), avail himself of its contents, which are taken from the Glorious Book, the Noble Sunnah (The Prophet"s traditions) and the statements of the distinguished. Haply he will succeed in finding his way to the real ascension through the guidance of "the people of knowledge" [*ahl-i marifat*], and tear off his heart from this dark dungeon, and head for the original destination of humanity, along the road on which the great prophets, the noble "holy men" [*awliya*]—may Allah"s blessing and peace be upon them all—and the "people of Allah" [*ahlullah*] trod, and to which they invited the others.

O my son! Hasten to comprehend yourself, which is fermented in "the divine disposition" [*fitratullah*]. Save yourself from the ruining whirlpool of the formidable waves of self-conceit and selfishness. Get on board Noah"s Ark, which is the light of "Allah"s guardianship" [*wilayatullah*], because: "Whoever got on board it was safe, and whoever stayed behind it perished."

O my son! Try hard to be moving along the Straight Path—which is the path of Allah—even with a limping leg. Try to tinge the movements and the stillness of your heart and body with the divine spiritual tint, and to serve the creatures (just) because of their being Allah"s creatures. The great prophets and the close "friends" [*awliya*] of Allah, despite their daily works like others, were never on good terms with the world, because they worked with Allah and for Allah. The Last Messenger—may Allah bless him and his household and give them peace—is quoted to have said: "My heart is sometimes covered (as if with unmindfulness), so I ask forgiveness from Allah seventy times every day."[3] He probably regarded discerning Allah in multiplicity as opacity [with respect to Allah].

O my son! Prepare yourself, after me, to face unkindness from those who will burden you with the worries they had on my part. If you settle your accounts with Allah and take refuge in remembering Him, you need not fear any creature, as the reckoning of creatures is transitory, while the reckoning before Allah is eternal.

My son! After me you may receive an offer for service. If you intend to serve the Islamic Republic and dear Islam, then do not refuse it. But if your intention is—Allah forbid!—to serve your sensual desires or to satisfy your passions, eschew it, for the worldly positions are too trivial to deserve perishing yourself for their sake.

O Allah! Make Ahmad, his offspring and family, who are of your servants and of the offspring of the Holy Messenger, happy in this world and in the Hereafter, and cut off the hands of the accursed Satan, so that he may not hurt them!

O Allah! We are weak, unable and lagging behind the caravan of the devotees on the road to you. O Allah! You Yourself help us. O Allah! Treat us with Your grace and do not treat us with Your justice. Peace be upon the righteous servants of Allah.

Ruhullah al-Musawi al-Khomeini
23 Rabi al-Awwal 1405/ 25 Azar 1363 S.H.

---

[3] *Mustadrak al-Wasa'il*, "Book of *as-Salat*," sec. on "Invocations," ch. 22, *hadith* 1.

In His Most Exalted Name

Alas! My life has passed in vain,
Loaded with sins, with no devotional gain;
Tomorrow when I am brought to the Scene of Judgment,
They will say that repentance chance did not remain.

The book *Adab as-Salat*, which I present to my dear daughter [-in-law], Fati,[4] whom may Allah make one of the *musallin* (*salat* performers), was finished more than forty years ago. A few years before that, I had completed the book of *Asrar as-Salat* (The Secrets of the *Salat*). From that time till now more than forty years have elapsed, while I have neither perceived the secrets of the *Salat* nor applied its disciplines, for "perceiving" is other than "conceiving", and "forming" is different from "performing". These books are as a proof [*hujjat*] from the Lord on this poor servant. I take refuge in Allah from being among those referred to by these back-breaking noble *ayah*s (Quranic verses): **"O you who believe, why do you say what you do not do? It is most detested in the sight of Allah that you say what you do not do"** (*Surah* 61:2-3). I have no refuge but His vast mercy.

O my daughter, I hope you will be successful in applying the disciplines of this grand divine ascension, and be guided by this divine *Buraq* (the Prophet"s heavenly horse) through a migration from the dark room of the self to Allah. I entrust you to Allah"s custody lest reading these papers should increase your sensual longings, or make you—like the writer—a plaything in Satan"s hands.

Dear daughter, although I found in you, thank Allah, such a spiritual fineness that I hope you will be guided by Allah, the Glorified and High, favored with His patronage, and be saved from nature"s deep pit to the straight path of humanity, yet do not be heedless of the deceit of Satan, and of that of your own soul, which is even more

---

[4] Fatimah Tabataba"i, wife of Hujjatul-Islam wal-Muslimin Haj Sayyid Ahmad Khomeini.

dangerous. Take refuge in Allah, the Great, for He has mercy upon His servants.

My daughter, if there was no result from reading these pages— Allah forbid!—except self-conceit, pretence and intrusion, it would be better to forgo reading them, or rather beware of them, so that you may not, like me, be subject to remorse and regret. But if you—Allah willing—prepare yourself to be benefited by the subject-matters of this book, which have been taken from the Book, the Sunnah, the *hadith* of the infallible *Ahl al-Bayt* (The Prophet"s progeny) and the statements of the people of knowledge, and to make use of your delicate God-given talent, then here you are! Here is the ball and here is the ground! I hope you will, by this human ascent and divine mixture, empty your heart from others, rinse it with the water of life, say four *takbir*s (*Allahu Akbar* = Allah is Greater!) and release yourself from selfness in order to reach the Friend: "And whoever leaves his home migrating to Allah and His Messenger, and then death overtakes him, his reward is indeed with Allah" (*Surah* 4:100).

O Allah! Make us of the immigrants to You and to Your Messenger, and take us to "annihilation" [*fana*]. Grant Fati [Fatimah] and Ahmad Your assistance to serve (Your servants), and let them attain happiness.

Was-Salam.

Ruhullah al-Musawi al-Khomeini
2nd of Safar al-Muzaffar 1405 A.H.

Author"s Preface

Praise be to Allah, the Lord of the worlds, and may Allah send blessing onto Muhammad and his pure progeny, and may His curse be upon all their enemies, from now till the rise of the Day of Judgment.

O Allah! Our steps of traveling are too short to reach Your Sacred Court, and our demanding hand is unable to touch Your Skirt of Intimacy. The veils of desire and negligence have blocked our insight from Your Most Beautiful Beauty, and the heavy curtains of loving this world and devilry have secluded our hearts from attending to the Glory of Your Majesty. The road to the Hereafter is narrow, and the path of humanity is tortuous, while we, the helpless, like the spiders, think of the jerked meat. We, like the silkworms, are perplexed, tying ourselves with the chains of desires and hopes, completely closing our eyes against the unseen world and the sociable gathering, except for the divine brightness with which You may light our hearts, and for Your unseen firebrand with which You may take us into rapture.

O Allah! Grant me to be exclusively dedicated to You. Light the eyes of our hearts with the light of looking at You, until the eyes of the hearts penetrate through the partitions of light so as to reach the origin of greatness, and our souls become hanging onto the glory of Your Sanctity.[5]

Now then, some years ago, I prepared a paper,[6] in which I inserted as much as was possible of the secrets of the *salat*. But as it

---

[5] "Munajat-i Shabaniyyah," *Bihar al-Anwar*, vol. 91, p. 99.
[6] He refers to the book *Sirr as-Salat* (*Miraj as-Salikin wa Salat al-Arifin*). The author (may Allah sanctify his honorable tomb, at its beginning, after praising (Allah),

was not suitable for the common people, I decided to write parts of the cordial disciplines of this spiritual *miraj*, so that my brethren in faith may have a remembrance and my hard heart may be affected by it. I take refuge with Allah, the Blessed and Most High, from Satan''s conduct and from failure, for He is a powerful guardian. I have arranged in this book a preface, a few discourses and a conclusion.

Preface

Know that for the *salat*, beside its form, there is a meaning, and apart from its exterior it has an interior; and as the exterior has its disciplines, neglecting which would render the outer form of the *salat* invalid or incomplete, likewise its interior has cordial spiritual disciplines, neglecting which would render the spiritual *salat* invalid or incomplete; whereas observing them would inspire the *salat* with a heavenly spirit. It would be possible that after paying attention to and observing the cordial inner disciplines, the *musalli* would have a share of the divine secret of the *salat* of the "people of knowledge and of hearts"—the *salat* which is the delight of the people of *suluk*[7] and the reality of the *miraj* (ascension) to the proximity of the Beloved.[8]

Besides what was just said about the *salat*'s interior and unseen divine images, and in addition to its being in conformity with a kind of proof and the observations of the people of *suluk* and asceticism, there are many *ayah*s and narratives, in general and particular, which denote that, too, and we shall bless the following pages by relating some of them.

Among them is the saying of Allah, the Most High:

"On the day when every soul shall find present what it has done of good and what it has done of evil, it shall wish that there

---

sending blessings (to the Prophet) and invoking, has written: "Now then, I, the bewildered in the valley of perplexity and ignorance, and tied to the wishes of I-ness and egoism, indulged in the intoxicating selfness and egotism, knowing nothing of the spiritual stations and the kingdom of existence, have sincerely decided to write about some of the spiritual stations of the great guardians in this spiritual *suluk* (spiritual travel) and *miraj* (ascension) of faith ..." He has finished the said honorable book on the 21st of Rabi ath-Thani 1358 L.H. (19 Khordad, 1318 S.H.).

[7] It hints at some narratives, including one from the Messenger of Allah (*s*) saying, "My delight has been placed in the *salat*." *Furu' al-Kafi*, vol 5, "Book of Marriage", ch. on "Loving Women", *hadith* no.7, p. 321.

[8] It refers to a narrative from the Messenger of Allah (*s*) saying, "The *salat* is the *miraj* of the believer." Allamah al-Majlisi, *Itiqadat*, p. 29.

were a long duration of time between it and that [day]...”[9] This noble *ayah* says that everybody will see his good and bad deeds present and he will discern their unseen inner images. In another *ayah* He says: “... **and they shall find present what they have done,**”[10] and “**So, he who has done an atom's weight of good shall see it...,**”[11] which means that the soul shall see its deeds.

As regards the noble *hadith*s in this respect, they are too many to be contained in these pages. So, it suffices to state a few of them.

Among them, in the *Wasail*, quoting Imam as-Sadiq (*a*), it is said: “Whoever performed the obligatory *salat*s at the beginning of their times and observed their restrictions, the angel would raise them, white and pure, to heaven, and the *salat* would say (to the performer): “May Allah preserve you as you preserved me and entrusted me to a generous angel.” But whoever performed them after their times, with no excuse, and did not observe their restrictions, the angel would raise them, black and dark, while the *salat* shouting at the performer: “You have lost me, may Allah lose you, and may He not care for you as you did not care for me”.”[12]

It denotes that the *salat* is raised by Allah's angels to heaven, white and pure, when it is performed at the start of its time and its disciplines are observed. In this case it invokes good for the *musalli*; or it will be dark and black if it is delayed, without a reasonable cause, and its disciplines are neglected, in which case it will curse him. This *hadith*, besides denoting the fact that there are heavenly unseen images, it also denotes that they are alive, as evidenced by *ayah*s and narratives. Allah, the Most High, says: “... **and the next abode, most surely, is the life...**”[13] There are many *hadith*s to the same effect, relating which would lengthen the subject.

Imam as-Sadiq (*a*) is quoted to have said: “When a believing servant is put into his grave, the *salat* stands on his right and the *zakat* on his left, his good deeds stand shadowing over him and forbearance stands aside. When the two angels in charge of interrogation enter the grave, forbearance tells the *salat*, the *zakat* and good deeds: “You have

---

[9] *Surah Al-i Imran* 3:30.
[10] *Surah al-Kahf* 18:49.
[11] *Surah Zilzal* 99:7.
[12] *Wasa'il ash-Shi'ah*, vol. 3, *Kitab as-Salat*, sec. on “Times” ch. 3, *hadith* 17, p. 90 (with a slight difference).
[13] *Surah al-Ankabut* 29:64.

to help your friend. If you felt unable, I would be with him"." [14] This noble *hadith* is related in the noble *al-Kafi* through two channels. Shaykh as-Saduq (may Allah have mercy upon him) has related this *hadith* in *Thawab al-Amal*. It speaks clearly of the unseen images of the *barzakh*, and their life and common sense. The *hadith*s about the heavenly images of the Quran and the *salat* are numerous.

With regard to what has been said that the *salat* and other forms of worship have, besides their outward disciplines, other inward disciplines without which the *salat* would be incomplete or even unacceptable to Allah, the following pages will numerate and state those cordial (inward) disciplines, *insha Allah* (if Allah wills).

What one should know, however, in this stage, is that to satisfy oneself with the appearance and outer form of the *salat*, and to be deprived of its blessings and inner perfections which bring about eternal happiness, or rather, bring one to the proximity of the Lord of Might, and set up the ladder of ascent to the stage of meeting the Absolute Beloved—the Ultimate Goal of the godly men and the Final Hope of the people of knowledge and those who have "hearts", or rather, the Beloved of the Master of the Messengers (s)[15]—is one of the heavier losses, as it will be—after leaving this world and entering the reckoning (day) of Allah—the cause of so great regrets that our minds are incapable of comprehending them. As long as we are enwrapped in the veils of this world, and live in the covers of nature, we cannot have knowledge of the other world, and cannot keep warm by a remote fire. What regret, remorse and loss can be greater than that after forty or fifty years of toiling for the sake of attaining a thing which is the means of man's perfection and happiness, and the remedy for the pains of the cordial deficiencies, and it is, in fact, the image of the human perfection, we cannot be spiritually benefited by it, and rather, it becomes the cause of tarnishing the heart and brings dark veils, and what is the pleasure of the Messenger (s) causes the weakness of our insight: **"...Alas for me, for what I fell short of my duty to Allah..."**[16]

---

[14] *Usul al-Kafi*, vol. 3, "Book of Belief and Disbelief," ch. on "Forbearance," *hadith* 8, p. 143; *Thawab al-Amal*, "Thawab as-Salat waz-Zakat wal-Birr was-Sabr," *hadith* 1, p. 203.
[15] Refer to footnote 7.
[16] *Surah az-Zumar* 39:56.

So, dear, tuck up the skirt of aspiration, extend the hand of demand, bear every labor and hardship in order to reform your affairs and acquire the spiritual conditions of the *salat* of the people of knowledge, and make use of this divine mixture [*majun*], which is prepared with the complete understanding [*kashf*] of Muhammad (*s*) for the sake of soothing all the pains and deficiencies of the souls.

Since it is still not too late, try to break camp and leave this dungeon of darkness, regret and remorse, this deep pit, which is far away from the holy presence of the Lord, the Exalted and Most High. Release yourself and try to reach the ascension [*miraj*] of union [*wisal*] and the proximity of perfection. Beware! If this means were lost, other means would fit: "If it was accepted, other deeds would be accepted, and if it was rejected, other deeds would be rejected, too."[17]

We shall explain, as much as possible and necessary, the inner disciplines of this spiritual *suluk*, so that someone of the people of faith may have a share of it. This might as well be a cause for the divine mercy and the unseen care to be bestowed upon me, lagging as I am in the way to happiness and humanity, and chained in the prison of nature and selfishness. Surely Allah is the Patron of generosity and care.

---

[17] *Falah as-Sa'il*, p. 127, quoting *Man La Yahduruh al-Faqih*, in which the text is: "The first thing about which the servant is questioned is the *salat*, if it was accepted his other (devotional) acts would be accepted, and if it was returned to him, his other acts would be returned to him (too)." vol. 1. "The Merit of the *Salat*," ch. 30, *hadith* 5.

DISCOURSE ONE

Concerning the Disciplines which are
Necessary in All States of the *Salat*,
Or Rather in All Worships and Rituals

Discussed in Twelve Chapters

CORDIAL DISCIPLINES
Chapter One

One of the cordial disciplines of the worships and the spiritual duties of the traveler along the path to the Hereafter is paying attention to the Might of the Lord and to the humility of servitude. It is one of the important stages for the *salik* (traveler). The strength of everybody"s *suluk* (journey) is in proportion to the strength of this attention, or rather the perfection or the imperfection of humanity is connected to the perfection or imperfection of this matter. The more one is overwhelmed by egoism, egotism, self-conceit and selfishness, the farther he will be from the human perfection and from the nearness of the presence of Allah. The veil of self-conceit and egotism is thicker and darker than all other veils. To tear open this veil is more difficult than tearing all other veils, and tearing it is a preparatory step to tearing other veils. In fact, tearing off this veil is the master key for the invisible, the visible and the great door of the ascent to the perfect spirituality. As long as man has his eyes on his own self, his imagined beauty and perfection, he will be veiled and discarded from the absolute beauty and pure perfection. The first condition for traveling to Allah is to leave this house. Actually, it is the criterion for the struggle between right and wrong. So, every *salik*, who travels with the steps of selfishness and self-conceit, and is wrapped in the veils of egotism, his sufferings would be in vain and his journey would not be to Allah, it would rather be to his self: "The mother of the idols is the idol of your self."[18]

Allah, the Most High, says: **"And whoever leaves his house migrating to Allah and His Messenger, and then death overtakes**

---

[18] "The Mother of the idols is your self's idol,
As those are snakes, and this is a dragon-idol!"
Mawlawi

him, his reward is, indeed, with Allah.[19] The formal migration, or the form of migration, is the corporeal migration from the formal house to the *kabah* or to the shrines of the holy men [*awliya*] (*a*), but the spiritual migration is the going out of the house of the soul and the house of this world to Allah and His Messenger. To migrate to the Messenger and the guardian [*wali*] is also a migration to Allah. As long as one"s soul has an inclination to oneself and to egotism, it is not journeying. And so long as there are residues of I-ness in the *salik*"s eyes, and as long as the walls of his own town and the *adhan* announcing selfishness have not yet disappeared, he is regarded as a staying one, not a traveler or an emigrant.

It is stated in *Misbah ash-Shariah* that Imam as-Sadiq (*a*) said: "Servitude is a gem whose core is Lordship [*rububiyyat*]. Whatever is lost of servitude is found in the Lordship, and whatever is hidden of Lordship is obtained by servitude."[20]

The one who travels on the foot of servitude, and burns his forehead with the brand of the humility of serfdom, will reach the Glory of (His) Lordship. The way of attaining to the facts of Lordship is journeying along the footsteps of servitude, and what is lost of servitude because of egoism and egotism, can be recovered under the shadow of the Lordship"s patronage, until he reaches a stage in which the *Haqq* (Allah), the Most High, will become his ears (hearing), eyes (seeing), hands and legs, as is stated in the true and well-known *hadith* accepted by the two sects.[21]

When the *salik* forsook his conducts [*tasarrufat*] and completely submitted the kingdom of his existence to Allah, leaving the house to its Owner, and perishing in the Glory of (His) Lordship, the Owner of the house would Himself manage the affairs. Thus his conducts [*tasarrufat*] would become divine, and his eyes would be divine and he would see with the *Haqq*"s (Allah"s) eyes, his ears

---

[19] *Surah an-Nisa"*4:100.

[20] *Misbah ash-Shariah*, "On the Reality of Servitude," ch. 100.

[21] This is a reference to a narrative about "The Approximation by *Nawafil*", which reads: "...He (Allah"s servant) keeps trying to get closer to Me by means of the *nafilah* until I love him. Loving him, I will become his ears with which he hears, his eyes with which he sees, his tongue with which he speaks and his hand with which he strikes. When he asks Me I answer him, and if he demands from Me I will give him..." *Usul al-Kafi*, vol. 4, "Book of Faith and Infidelity," ch. on "One who Hurts and Despises the Muslims," *hadith*s 7-8, p. 53.

would become divine and he would hear with the *Haqq*'s (Allah's) ears. The more complete the lordship of the soul and the more its glory be cherished, the more, in the same proportion, the Glory of the (divine) Lordship decreases and becomes incomplete (in the *salik*'s kingdom of existence), because these two stand face to face: "This world and the next are like the two wives of a man."²²

Thus, the *salik* to Allah has to recognize his state of humility, and to place the humility of servitude and the Glory of the Lordship before his eyes. The stronger this viewpoint, the more spiritual his worship and the stronger the spirit of his worship, until, if, with the help of Allah and the perfect holy men [*awliya*] (*a*), he reaches the truth of servitude and its core, he will catch a glimpse of the secret of worship. In all the worships—especially (in) the *salat* which has a position of comprehensiveness [*jamiiyyat*], and is, among the worships, like the Perfect Man, and like the Greatest Name (of Allah), or rather it is the very Greatest Name—these two positions, i.e. the position of the Glory of Lordship, which is a fact, and the position of the humility of servitude, which accompanies it, are occult. Among the recommended acts the *qunut*, and among the obligatory acts the *sujud*, have particular peculiarities to which we shall refer later *insha Allah*.

It should be noted, however, that absolute servitude is of the highest degrees of perfection and of the loftiest positions of humanity, of which no one has any share except the most perfect of the creatures of Allah, Muhammad (*s*) at the top, followed by the perfect *wali*s (the Guardians). The others are limping in servitude, and their worshipping and servitude are endued with causes, only with the steps of servitude one can reach the real absolute *miraj*. That is why the noble *ayah* says: "**Glorified is He Who carried his servant by night...**"²³ It was the step of servitude and the attraction of (His) Lordship that carried that holy person to the *miraj* of proximity [*qurb*] and union [*wusul*]. In the *tashahhud* of the *salat*—which is a return from an absolute "annihilation" [*fana*] that was achieved in the *sujud* there is once again a tendency to servitude, before paying attention to the Messengership. It may also be a reference to the position of Messengership as a result

---

²² *Awaliy ul-Laali*, vol. 1, p. 277 and vol. 4, p. 115; *Nahj al-Balaghah*, edited by Fayd al-Islam, maxim 100.
²³ *Surah al-Isra"*17:1.

of the essence of servitude. This is a lengthy subject, which is out of the scope of these papers.

THE STAGES OF THE STATIONS
OF THE PEOPLE OF *SULUK*
Chapter Two

Know that there are for the people of *suluk*, in this station (i.e., paying attention to the humility of servitude and the Glory of His Lordship) and other stations, countless stages and degrees, only to a few of which we can generally refer, since comprehensively knowing all their aspects and counting all the stages are beyond the capacity of this humble creature: "The ways to Allah are as numerous as the breaths of the creatures."[24]

One of those stages is the stage of Knowledge [*ilm*], which is such that it proves, by scientific conduct [*suluk*] and philosophic argument, the humility of servitude and the Glory of (His) Lordship. This is a pure sort of knowledge, since it is clearly proved in the high sciences and supreme philosophy that the entire House of Realization [*dar-i tahaqquq*] and the complete circle of existence are mere relation and attachment and nothing but poverty. The Glory, Kingdom and Sovereignty belong to His Sanctified Essence of Majesty. No one can have any share of Glory and Majesty, while the humility of servitude and poverty is engraved on the forehead of everybody, and is registered in the innermost part of their truth. The truth of gnosis and vision [*shuhud*], and the result of suffering and *suluk*, are in lifting the veil off the face of the truth, and discerning the humility of servitude and the origin of poverty and lowliness in oneself and in all the creatures. The invocation ascribed to the master of all beings (the

---

[24] This *hadith* is ascribed to the Prophet (*s*) in *Jami al-Asrar wa Manba"al-Anwar* by Sayyid Haydar Amuli, pp. 8, 95 and 121. Also in the Lahiji's Commentary on *Gulshan-i Raz*, p. 153; *Naqd an-Nusus*, p. 185; *Minhaj at-Talibin*, p. 221; *Al-Usul al-Asharah*, p. 31.

Prophet of Islam) (*s*): "O Allah, show me the things as they are,"[25] may be a reference to this stage, i.e. wishing to see the humility of servitude which requires discerning the Glory of the Lordship.

Therefore, if the *salik* on the road of the truth, the traveler in the way of servitude, covers this distance with the steps of scientific *suluk* and the mount of intellectual advance, he will fall in the veils of knowledge and attain the first station of humanity. But this veil is a thick one, as it is said: "Knowledge is the greatest veil." The *salik* should not stay behind this veil. He is to tear it, since, should he be contented with this stage and keep his heart chained by it, he would fall into *istidraj* (being engaged in other than the *Haqq*). *Istidraj* in this stage, means becoming engaged in the numerous secondary branches of knowledge, presenting many arguments justifying his intellectual roamings in that field, and depriving himself of the other stages, because his heart is attached to this stage only, neglecting the wanted result, which is attaining annihilation in Allah. He, thus, would spend his life in the veil of argument [*burhan*] and its branches. The more these branches are, the thicker the veil and the greater the distance from the truth. The *salik*, therefore, should not be deceived, in this stage, by Satan, secluding himself from the truth and reality, and stopping his journey to the goal on the pretext of being a great scholar, a very learned person and a powerful man of argument. He must set to work briskly, be serious in his quest for the real demand, and take himself to the next stage, which is the second stage.

And that is such that he should write what (his) reason has understood through irrefutable proof and scientific conduct, with the pen of intellect on the tablet of the heart, to convey the truth of the humility of servitude and the Glory of Lordship to the heart and free himself from the chains and the veils of knowledge. We shall refer to this stage presently, *insha Allah*. So, the result of the second stage is acquiring belief in the facts.

The third stage is that of "tranquility and calmness of the soul," which is, in fact, the perfect stage of faith. Allah, the Exalted, said to his "friend" [*khalil*] Ibrahim: **"Have you not believed [yet]?"** He said:

---

[25] In *Awaliy ul-Laali*, vol. 4, p. 132, it is stated: "Oh Allah, show us the facts as they are." Commenting on the same, quoting *at-Tafsir al-Kabir* by al-Fakhr ar-Razi, vol. 6, p. 26, and in *Mirsad al-Ibad*, p. 309, it is stated as follows: "Show us the things as they are."

"I have, but just to have a calm heart."[26] A reference to this stage may come later.

The fourth stage is that of "vision" [*mushahadah*], which is a divine light and a divine manifestation, as a consequence of the manifestations of the Names and the Attributes appearing in the secret of the *salik*, and lightening his complete heart with the visionary light. This stage comprises many degrees that are out of the capacity of these pages. In this stage an example of the effect of the *nafilah*s: (I would be his hearing, sight and hand)[26a] will appear, and the *salik* will see himself drowned in limitless ocean, beyond which there is another very deep ocean, in which the secrets of "fate" are partly disclosed.

Each one of these stages has its special *istidraj* (being engaged in other than the *Haqq*) through which the *salik* is exposed to great perishing [*halakat*]. So, he will have to rid himself, in all stages, of egoism and I-ness. He should not be self-conceited or egotistic, both of which are the sources of most of evils, especially for the *salik*. However, we shall have another reference to this subject presently *insha Allah* [Allah willing].

---

[26] *Surah al-Baqarah* 2:260.
[26a] Refer to footnote 21.

CONCERNING SUBMISSIVENESS [*KHUSHU*]
Chapter Three

One of the things necessary for the *salik* in all his worships, especially in the *salat*, which is at the head of all worships and has a position of comprehensiveness [*jamiiyyat*], is submissiveness [*khushu*]. It is, in fact, a complete submission [*khudu*] mixed with love or fear. It is the result of comprehending the Greatness, Power and Majesty of Beauty and Glory. The detail of this generality is that the hearts of the people of *suluk* are different according to their disposition and nature:

Some of the hearts are amorous and of the manifestations of Beauty [*jamal*] and, driven by their nature, they are attracted to the Beauty of the Beloved. When, in the *suluk*, they comprehend the shadow of the Beautiful, or witness the origin of the Beauty, the Greatness hidden in the secret of the Beauty effaces them, and they go into rapture, for in every beauty there is a hidden glory, and in every glory there is a covered beauty. There is probably an allusion to this point in his saying when the guardian of the gnostics and of the *salik*s, Amir al-Muminin (Commander of the Faithful), may Allah bless him and all his offspring, says: **"Glory be to the One whose compassion is vast for His friends despite His severe revenge, and whose revenge is severe for His enemies despite His vast compassion,"**[27]

Thus, the Majesty, Greatness and Power of Beauty envelop them and they fall into a state of submission [*khushu*] before the Beauty of the Beloved. This state, at the beginning, causes agitation to the heart and engenders anxiety. Then, after submission [*tamkin*], it changes to a state of familiarity, and the agitation and anxiety, caused by the Greatness and Power, turn into familiarity and peace, and there

---

[27] *Nahj al-Balaghah*, sermon 90.

happens a state of tranquility, as was the state of the heart of *khalil ar-Rahman* (Allah's Friend = Ibrahim) (*a*).

Some other hearts are "fearing" and they are of the manifestations of Glory [*jalal*]. They are in continual understanding of the Greatness, Grandeur and Glory. Their submission is of fright, and the Subjugative and Majestic Names are manifested to their hearts, as was the state of Prophet Yahya (may Allah's peace be upon him and our Prophet and his progeny). So, submission is sometimes mixed with love, and sometimes with fear and fright, though in every love there is fear, and in every fear there is love.

The degrees of submission are according to the degrees of understanding the Greatness, Majesty and Beauty. Now as we, in our case, are deprived of the light of visions, we have but to indulge in acquiring submission by means of knowledge and faith [*iman*]. Allah, the Exalted, says: **"Successful, indeed, are the believers who are submissive in their** *salats*.**"**[28] Submission in the *salat* is regarded as a sign of faith [*iman*]. So, whoever is not submissive in his *salat*, will, according to Allah's saying, be excluded from the faithful [*ahl-i iman*]. Our *salat*s which are not accompanied by submission are caused by a deficiency of faith or by lacking it. Belief [*itiqad*] and knowledge are other than faith, our knowledge of Allah, His Names and Attributes and of other divine knowledge [*maarif*], is other than faith. Satan according to the testimony of Allah, has information about the Beginning and the Resurrection, yet, he is a disbeliever. He said: **"You have created me of fire, while You created him of dust,"**[29] So, he believes in Allah and in His being the Creator; and he says: **"Respite me until the day they are resurrected."**[30] So, he believes in the Day of Resurrection, too. He knows about the Books, the Messengers and the angels. Nevertheless, Allah addresses him as a disbeliever, excluding him from the group of the believers [*muminin*].

Thus, the people of knowledge are distinct from those of faith. Not every man of knowledge is a man of faith. Therefore, after acquiring knowledge, one has to join the believers, and to convey the Greatness, Majesty, Brightness and Beauty of Allah, the Most Exalted and High, to his heart, so that it may become submissive, since mere

---

[28] *Surah al-Mu'minun* 23:1-2.
[29] *Surah al-Araf* 7:12.
[30] *Ibid.*, 7:14.

knowledge does not result in submission. You can realize it in yourself: although you do believe in the Beginning and the Resurrection and in Allah''s Majesty and Glory, your heart is not submissive.

As to Allah''s saying: **"Has not the time yet come for those who believe that their hearts should be submissive when remembering Allah and what has come down of the truth,"**[31] it may be that it is the formal faith—the very belief in what the Prophet (s) has brought—which is intended here, for the true faith is accompanied by a degree of submission; or the submission in the noble *ayah* may refer to a submission at its complete degree, as sometimes they apply the word, *'alim* (erudite) to the one whose knowledge has reached the limit of faith. In the noble *ayah*: **"...verily only the erudite among Allah''s servants fear Him,"**[32] the reference may be to them. In the terms of the Book and the *Sunnah*, knowledge, faith and Islam refer to different degrees, the explanation of which is out of the scope of these papers.

Generally speaking, the *salik* on the way to the Hereafter—specially if with the *mi'raj* (ascending) step of the *salat*—will have to make his heart submissive by the light of knowledge and faith, so as to strengthen, as much as he can, this divine gift and the beneficent gleam, in his heart, trying to keep this state during the whole length of the *salat*. This state of consolidation and stability, though a bit difficult at the beginning for people like us, it becomes quite possible by practice and by exercising the heart.

My dear, acquiring perfection and the provision for the Hereafter requires demand and seriousness, and the greater the demand, the more it deserves being serious about it. Certainly, with such a state of weakness, laxity and carelessness, one cannot ascend to the divine proximity and to be in a place neighboring the Lord of Might. One has to manly set forth in order to reach what one wants. Since you do believe in the Hereafter, and find no way of comparability between that world and this—whether regarding their happiness and perfection, or their sufferings and calamities, as that world is eternal, with no death and perishing, where the happy live in comfort and dignity and in everlasting bliss, a comfort which has no

---

[31] *Surah al-Hadid* 57:16.
[32] *Surah Fatir* 35:28.

like in this world, a divine glory and sovereignty, the like of which cannot be found in this life, and a bliss which never occurs in anybody"s imagination, and similarly regarding the sufferings of that world, its pains, torments and evils can have no match in this world— you should know that the way to happiness runs through obeying Allah, the Lord of Might. None of the acts of worship and obedience can be on the same footing as that of the *salat*, which is a comprehensive [*jami*] divine mixture [*ma'jun*] undertaking the happiness of humanity. If it is accepted, all other acts (of worship) will be accepted. So, you are to exert utmost seriousness in obtaining it, never to feel tired in the quest, and to bear whatever hardship there may be, though there will be none. Actually if you continued it for a while and got cordially familiar with it, you would get, in this very world, so much pleasure out of your talk with Allah—a pleasure which cannot be compared with anyone of this world"s pleasures. This will be quite obvious if we study the states of the people supplicating to Allah.

In general, to sum up our discussions in this chapter, we may say that, having comprehended the Greatness, the Beauty, and the Majesty of Allah, either by means of reasoning and proofs, or through the explanations of the prophets (*a*), one must remind his heart of it, and then, by gradual remindings, cordial attention and continual remembering Allah"s Greatness and Majesty, he has to bring about the state of submission in his heart, so as to attain the required result. At any rate, the *salik* should not suffice himself with his present station, as any station which we may obtain is not worth a farthing in the market of the people of knowledge, nor is it worth a grain of mustard in the bazaar of "the people of heart". The *salik* must, in all situations, remember his own faults and deficiencies, so that he may find, through this, a way to his happiness. And praise be to Allah.

TRANQUILITY
Chapter Four

Of the important cordial disciplines of worships, especially the invoking worships, one is tranquility [*tumaninah*], which is not the same tranquility as demanded by the jurisprudents (may Allah be pleased with them) in the *salat*. It is that the *salik* should perform his worship with a quietude of the heart and a tranquility of the mind, because if the worship was performed in a state of anxiety and with shaky heart, the heart would not have any reaction, and no effects of worship would appear in the dominion of the heart, and the reality of the worship would not become an inner image of the heart.

One of the significances of the repetition of worships and the increase of supplications and invocations is that the heart is affected by them and there will be an emotion until, gradually, the reality of worship and supplication forms the innermost part of the *salik*, and his heart unites with the spirit of worship. Should the heart lack tranquility [*itminan*], quietude and serenity, there would be no effect of the supplications and the rituals on it, and they would not pass from the outer appearance and limits of the body to the dominion of the inner soul, and the cordial parts of the truth of worship would not be effected. This is one of the clear matters that need no explanation, as it could be understood by a little contemplation. If a worship was such that the heart could have no information whatsoever about it, and there was no effect at all in the interior, it would not be kept in other dominions, nor would it ascend from the kingdom of this world to the kingdom of the heavens. And it may be that at the time of the throes of death and its horrible agonies, and the terrors and calamities of after death, the image of such a worship may completely be effaced—God forbid!—from the plane of the heart, and that man may stand at the sacred presence of Allah empty-handed. For example, if one recites the noble supplication: *La ilaha illallah, Muhammadun Rasulullah* (There is no god but Allah; Muhammad is the Messenger of Allah) with a calm and tranquil heart and teaches his heart to repeat it, the tongue of the heart will gradually become talking, and the outer tongue will be a follower of the heart"s tongue, and then the heart will supplicate first, and the tongue will follow it. This is referred to by Imam as-Sadiq (*a*) as is stated in *Misbah ash-Shariah* (the Torch of the Islamic Law). He said: "Let your heart be your tongue"s *qiblah*, and do not move it except by the heart"s order, the reason"s assent and the faith"s consent."[33]

At the beginning, before the tongue learns talking, the *salik* on the way to the Hereafter is to teach it and to instruct it, in tranquility and quietude, with the supplications. As soon as the heart finds its tongue, it becomes the *qiblah* (the focus of attraction) of the mouth"s tongue and of the other organs of the body. When it starts supplication, the whole kingdom of the human existence becomes supplicant. But if the noble supplication is recited without the tranquility and calmness of the heart, but with haste, trouble, and unbalanced senses, it will have no effect on the heart, and will not pass the limits of the animal tongue and ear of the outer body to the interior and the human hearing, and its truth will not be implemented in the core of the heart, nor will it become a perfect and non-transitory image of the heart. Thus, when there are terrors and difficulties, especially the terrors of the agonies of death and the difficulties of the throes of the last breaths, one completely forgets supplication and it will be erased from the plane of the heart. Even the name of Allah the Exalted, the Seal of the Prophets (*s*), the noble religion of Islam, the divine sacred Book, the Imams of guidance (*a*) and other knowledge [*maarif*] which have not been conveyed to the heart, will be forgotten, and when he is questioned in the grave, he cannot answer, and the *talqin* will be of no avail, because he does not find in himself any trace of the truth of Lordship, prophethood or other knowledge [*maarif*], and that what he used to chatter about, and had no image of in his heart, vanishes from his memory, and thus he will have no share of testifying the Lordship, prophethood and other knowledge [*maarif*].

It is stated in a *hadith* that a group of the people [*ummah*] of the Messenger of Allah (*s*), on being entered into Hell, forget the name

---

[33] *Misbah ash-Shariah*, ch. 5, "On Supplication"; *Mustadrak al-Wasa'il*, "Book of as-Salat," sec. on "Supplication," ch. on "Rarities," *hadith* 2.

of the Prophet because of the fearfulness of the Hell-keeper, despite the fact that the same *hadith* states that they are of the believers and their hearts and features glitter brightly because of the light of faith.[34]

The great narrator, the late Majlisi, in *Mirat al-Uqul* explaining the expression: "I will be his hearing and his seeing," says: "One who does not dedicate his eyes, ears and other organs to the way of obeying Allah, will not obtain spiritual eyes and ears, as his corporeal eyes and ears will not go to the other world, and so he will be without ears and eyes in the worlds of the grave and the Resurrection, whereas the criterion for the questionings of the grave is those spiritual organs (the end of the sum of his translation)."[35]

In short, the noble *hadith*s about this kind of tranquility and its effects are many. The Glorious Quran orders that it (the Quran) should be recited in *tartil*, and it is stated in the noble *hadith*s: "Whoever forgets a *surah* from the Quran, it will appear before him in Paradise in a most beautiful image. When he looks at it he says: "What are you? How wonderful you are! I wish you were mine." It will reply: "Do you not know me? I am so-and-so *surah*. If you had not forgotten me, I would have lifted you to this high rank"."[36]

In another *hadith* it is stated: "Whoever learns the Quran as a young man, it will mix with his flesh and blood." This is because the heart of a young man is less engaged and less tarnished, and so, it is affected quicker and easier, and the effect remains longer.

There are many *hadith*s in this respect, to which we shall refer when we discuss "recitation," *insha Allah*. In a noble *hadith* it is said: "Nothing is more loved by Allah than a deed which is done persistently, no matter how small the deed may be."[38] Its important point may be that such a deed becomes the inner image of the heart, as it has already been noted.

[34] *Ilm al-Yaqin*, vol. 2, p. 1039.
[35] *Mirat al-Uqul*, vol. 10, p. 392.
[36] *Usul al-Kafi*, vol. 4, p. 410, "Book of the Merit of the Quran," ch. "One who Learnt the Quran then Forgot it," *hadith* no. 2.
[38] *Ibid.*, vol. 3, p. 137, "Book of Faith and Infidelity," ch. "Economy in Worshipping," *hadith* 2.

PROTECTING THE WORSHIPS FROM SATAN"S INTRUSION
Chapter 5

One of the important cordial disciplines of the *salat* and other worships which is of the chief cordial disciplines, and to implement it is one of the great affairs and minute problems, is protecting the worships against the intrusion of Satan. The noble *ayah*: **"And those who keep guard on their *salats*"**[39] probably refers to all degrees of keeping guard, a degree of which, or rather the most important one of them, is to guard against Satan"s intrusion.

To go into details, we say that it is quite explicit to the people of knowledge and the men of heart that as bodies require material food for nourishment, and that the food should be suitable for their disposition so that they may be brought up corporeally and have vegetable growth, similarly the hearts and the souls require a particular food to suit them both, so that they may be educated with it, and feed on it to grow up spiritually and progress inwardly. The nutrition suitable for the growth [*nashah*] of the souls is the divine knowledge [*maarif*] from the beginning of existence till the ultimate end of the system of existence. It is expressed in defining philosophy by the great experts that: "It is man"s development into a mental world matching the material world in its form and perfection."[40] This is an indication of the said spiritual nutrition, as the hearts feed on spiritual merits and divine rites.

It must be noted that each one of these foods, if kept away from Satan"s intrusion and prepared by the hands of the guardianship of the Seal of the Prophets and Allah"s great friend (*s*), the soul and the heart

---

[39] *Surah al-Maarij* 70:34; *Surah al-Mu'minun* 23:9.
[40] Mulla Sadra and his disciples used this expression to define philosophy, to which some added the phrase: "in its image and perfection."

would be nourished by them and would attain the perfection becoming of humanity and ascend to the proximity of Allah. Getting rid of Satan's intrusion, which is a preliminary step to sincerity, cannot really be brought about, unless the *salik* is in quest of Allah in his *suluk*, and tread upon his selfishness and self-conceit, which are the origin of all evils and the inner diseases. This, in its full meaning, is not possible except by the Perfect Man, or, rather, by the sincere holy men [*awliya*] (*a*). But the *salik* must not despair of the inner kindness of Allah, because to despair of Allah's mercy is the beginning of all coldnesses and weaknesses, and it is one of the great sins. That which is possible for the common people, too, is the delight of eyes of "the people of knowledge" [*ahl-i ma'rifat*].

So, it is a must for the *salik* on the road to the other world to act very seriously to rid his knowledge [*ma'arif*] and rites [*manasik*] of the intrusion of Satan and the commanding soul [*nafs-i ammarah*], and to go deep into his doings, quests and desires, with strictness and examination, so as to find out the ultimate objective of his journey, learning the principles of his inner activities and spiritual nutrition. He is not to neglect the tricks of the soul and Satan, as well as the snares of the commanding soul and *Iblis*. He is always to distrust his self in all his doings and activities, and never to let it go willfully. It is quite possible that, with a little negligence, it may overcome man, knock him down and drive him to perdition and annihilation. If the spiritual foods were not free from Satan's intrusion, and if he shared in preparing them, the souls and hearts would not be educated with them nor can they reach their becoming perfection, let alone the irreparable insufficiency that would befall them. Such foods may probably cause man to join the group of Satans or the quadruped and beasts of prey. Then whatever is the capital of happiness, the source of the human perfection and the means of attaining to high ranks, results in the opposite, and drives man to the dark abyss of misfortune. Actually we did come across some of the so-called gnostics who had been led astray because of their deep indulgence in the gnostic terminology, such that their hearts became inverted and their interiors were darkened. Their gnostic practices strengthened their selfishness and I-ness, and they uttered improper allegations and abnormal expressions. Similarly, among the ascetics and the devotees there were persons who practiced asceticism and self-purification, yet their exercises only aggravated their hearts' impurity and their interiors' darkness. This is because they did not keep on their divine spiritual journey and migration to Allah, and their scholarly and ascetic *suluk* (journey) was subject to the intrusion of Satan and the self's desire, and so, it was to Satan and self. We also noted that among the students of religious sciences there were some who had badly been affected by their studies, which increased their moral corruption; and knowledge, which should have guided them to success and salvation, had driven them to annihilation and led them to ignorance, hypocrisy, arrogance and deception. Likewise, it is seen that among the people of worship and ceremonies, who persist in observing disciplines and traditions, there were those whose worship and sacrifices—which are the source of reforming the conditions and souls—had affected their hearts with impurity and darkness, causing them to be conceited, egotistic, arrogant, pampered, slanderous, ill-tempered and distrusting the servants of Allah. These are also caused by neglecting to observe those divine mixtures [*ma'ajin*].

Naturally, the mixture [*ma'jun*] prepared by Satan"s filthy hand and the meddling of the obstinate self can give birth to nothing but Satanic character, and since the heart gets its nourishment from them, in any case, and they become the inner image of the soul, after a while of man"s continuing so, he becomes an offspring of Satan, and will be brought up under his patronage. And when the visible eye of such a man is closed and his invisible eye is opened, he will see himself among the Satans. Thus, the result will be nothing but a loss, and his regret and repent will avail him to nothing.

Consequently, the traveler on the road to the Hereafter, notwithstanding his religious branch or divine method, has, firstly to be on the alert, like a kind doctor or a compassionate nurse, to take full care of his moods, looking for the faults of his conduct with strictness, and secondly, as he does so, he is not to neglect seeking refuge in the Sacred Essence of Allah, the Glorified and Most High, in his privacy, and supplicating in the presence of His Sanctity and Majesty.

O Lord! You do know our weakness and helplessness. You do know that without Your helping hand we cannot find our way out of the hands of such a powerful enemy who covets the great prophets and the perfect and high holy men. Without Your spark of kindness and mercy, this strong-handed enemy will knock us down on the ground of annihilation and hurl us into the pit of darkness and wretchedness. We adjure You by Your distinguished favorites and intimate confidants to extend Your helping hand to us, the bewildered in the valley of error and the fallen down in the desert of seduction. Purge our hearts of rancor, deceit, polytheism and doubt. Surely You are the Patron of Guidance!

ON VIVACITY AND CHEERFULNESS
Chapter Six

Of other cordial disciplines of the *salat* and other worships, one, which has good results, or rather it opens some doors and uncovers some secrets of worships, is that the *salik* is to try to worship with vivacity, cheerfulness of heart and gaiety of mind, and to avoid laziness and reluctance in performing worships. He is to choose for worship a time in which he is quite prepared to perform it with animation and freshness, feeling no tiredness or lassitude. Should one force oneself to worship in times of laziness and tiredness, it would probably bring about bad consequences, such as feeling tired of worshipping and of taking the trouble and bearing difficulty. Then, gradually, one may feel disgusted with worshipping. Furthermore, it may possibly turn man completely away from remembering Allah, and give pains to the spirit from the state of servitude, which is the source of all happiness. Such worship will bring no luminosity to the heart, and the inside of the soul will not have any reaction, and the image of servitude will not become the image of the inner heart. It has already been said that the aim of worship is that the inner soul should become the image of servitude.

We now say that one of the secrets and results of worships and austerities is that the will of the soul becomes operative on the realm of the body, and its authority is overcome by the majesty of the soul and is annihilated, and the forces and soldiers spread in the kingdom of the body can no longer revolt, disobey and be obstinate and selfish. They actually surrender to the inner kingdom of the heart, or rather those forces gradually dissolve in the invisible heavenly domain, and its command is effective on the visible dominion. The will of the soul gets stronger and takes the reins of the kingdom from Satan and the commanding soul, and the soldiers of the soul are driven to submission, from submission to contentment, and from contentment to annihilation. In this situation the soul will get to discover some secrets of worship and some actual manifestations will appear. But all these cannot be implemented unless the worships are performed cheerfully and actively, away from every sort of laziness and carelessness, so that a mood of affection and love towards remembering Allah, the Exalted, and the state of servitude, with familiarity and consistency, happen. Loving Allah and remembering Him is one of the great affairs, which is very much cared for by the people of knowledge, and is a subject of competition among the people of *suluk*. Physicians believe that if food is eaten with cheerfulness and gaiety, it will be digested much easier. Similarly, psychiatrists stress that if the spiritual nutrition is taken cheerfully and enthusiastically, and with avoiding laziness and affectedness, its effect will appear very quickly in the heart and the inner heart will be purified more quickly, too.

This discipline is referred to in the Glorious Divine Book, the upright Lordly pages, as it, in defiance of the disbelievers and the hypocrites, says: **"...And they do not come to the *salat* unless they are sluggish, and they do not spend unless they are reluctant..."**[41] and the noble *ayah*: **"O you who believe! Do not approach the *salat* when you are drunk..."**[42] The word "drunkenness" is explained in a *hadith* to mean "sluggishness". Some narratives refer to this discipline. By relating some of them we shall give pride to these papers.

Muhammad ibn Yaqub quoted Abu Abdullah (Imam as-Sadiq) (*a*) to have said: "Do not force yourselves to worship."[43]

Abu Abdullah (as-Sadiq) (*a*) is (also) quoted to have said: "The Messenger of Allah (*s*) said: "O Ali, this religion is firm, get into it mildly, and do not cause yourself to hate worshipping your Lord."[44]

Imam al-Askari (*a*) is quoted to have said: "When the hearts are active, confide in them, and when they are reluctant, bid them farewell."[45] This is a general instruction to deposit in your hearts any information you may when they are lively and gay, and leave them alone when they are restive. So, in acquiring knowledge [*maarif*] and

---

[41] *Surah at-Tawbah* 9:54.

[42] *Surah an-Nisa"* 4:43.

[43] *Usul al-Kafi*, vol. 3, "Book of Belief and Disbelief," ch. on "Equality (moderateness) in Acting and its Persistence," *hadith* 3, p. 129.

[44] *Ibid.*, ch. on "Economy in Worshipping," *hadith* 6, p. 138.

[45] *Bihar al-Anwar*, vol. 75, "Book of *ar-Rawdah*," ch. 29, *hadith* 3, p. 377.

sciences this discipline must also be applied, and the hearts must not be forced when they are irresponsive.

It can be deduced from this and other *hadith*s that there is another discipline, which is also an important chapter of asceticism. This discipline is "considerateness" [*mura'at*]; that is, the *salik*, in whatever stage he is, in scholarly or in spiritual and practical austerities and strivings, must consider his conditions, treat his soul with kindness and care, and avoid burdening himself with more than it can bear, especially the young people and the inexperienced, to whom this discipline is quite important. If the young people do not treat themselves considerately and kindly, and if they do not meet the needs of (their) nature through lawful ways, they will be subject to a great danger, which cannot be compensated. The danger is that when one is too severe with his self and pulls the reins too hard, they will break off, and then the will gets out of control, and the accumulated natural needs and the sharp fires of desire, under unlimited pressure of austerity, burn out the whole kingdom. If a *salik*'s reins break off— God forbid!—or an ascetic person becomes unable to control himself, he will fall so deep in a precipice that he can never see the face of rescue, nor can he ever return to the road of happiness and righteousness.

Thus, a *salik*, like a clever physician, has to feel his own pulse during his progress on the journey and to treat his self according to the requirements of the conditions of the journey. When the flames of desire, which are the vanity of youthfulness, blaze high, one is not to completely prevent his nature from getting satisfaction, but one has to resort to lawful ways to put out the flames of his desire, as gratifying the desire, according to the divine command, is a complete help along the journey to Allah. So, he is to marry, as it is one of the great divine laws, which, besides being the base of the survival of the species, has a great effect on the journey to the Hereafter, too. For this reason, the Messenger of Allah (s) said: "He who marries will keep half of his religion."[46] Another *hadith* says: "He who desires to meet Allah pure,

---

[46] *Ibid.*, vol. 100, p. 220, "Book of *al-Uqud wal-Iqaat* (Contracts and Agreements)," sec. on "Marriage," ch. 1, *hadith* 14, p. 220, as quoted from *Amali* by Shaykh at-Tusi, vol. 2, p. 132.

let him meet Him with a wife."[47] The Messenger of Allah (s) is quoted to have said: "Most of the people of Hell are singles."[48] A *hadith* from Amir al-Muminin (Ali) (a) says: "A group of the companions abstained from women (their wives), and from eating in daytime and sleeping at night. The Messenger of Allah (s) was informed about them by Umm us-Salamah (his wife). He came to them and asked them: "Do you reject women (your wives)? I do go into women (my wives), eat in daytime and sleep at night. Whoever disregards my tradition is not of me. Allah, the Exalted, has revealed: **"O you who believe! Do not forbid the good things which Allah has made lawful for you, and do not transgress. Surely Allah does not love the transgressors. And eat of what Allah has provided you as lawful and good, and fear Allah in Whom you believe." "**[49]

Generally speaking, the traveler along the road to the Hereafter is to be considerate with respect to the ups and downs of the soul. And, while he is never to curb the needs (of his nature) which, otherwise, would cause big mischief, he is also not to be severe nor to exert pressure upon himself with respect to worship and practical austerities, especially during his youth and on starting the journey, as otherwise this will also cause the soul to feel exasperated and bolt away, and perhaps, lead him to abandoning remembering Allah.

This point is frequently referred to in the noble *hadith*s. The noble *Al-Kafi*, quoting Imam as-Sadiq (a), says: "During my youth I was seriously and earnestly doing my worshipping. My father told me: "My son, act less on that, as when Allah, the Exalted, loves someone, He will accept his little." "[50] Another *hadith* goes almost the same.[51]

The same course relates another *hadith* to the effect that Abu Jafar (Imam al-Baqir) (a), quoting the Messenger of Allah (s), said: "Surely this religion is firm, so go deep in it with mildness, and do not cause Allah's servants to hate worshipping Him; otherwise, you will be like the one whose mount was too tired to go on, so he neither

---

[47] *Ibid.*, *hadith*s 18 and 35, quoting *Rawdat ul-Wa'izin*, p. 373, and *Nawadir ar-Rawandi*, p. 12.
[48] *Wasa'il ash-Shi'ah*, "Book of Marriage," ch. 2, *hadith* 6, p. 15.
[49] *Surah al-Ma'idah* 5:87-88; *Ibid.*, *hadith* 8.
[50] *Usul al-Kafi*, vol. 3, "Book of Faith and Disbelief," ch. on "Economy in Worshipping," *hadith* 5.
[51] *Ibid.*, *hadith* 4.

finished the journey nor preserved the mount."[52] Another *hadith* says: "Do not cause yourselves to hate worshipping Allah."[53]

However, the criterion for being "considerate" is that one should be observant of his soul"s conditions and act according to its strength and weakness. When one"s soul is strong and able to perform worships and bear hardship with good endurance, he should, then, try to perform the acts of worship. As to those who have crossed the prime of life, and the fires of their desires have subsided to some extent, it is suitable for them to increase their ascetic austerity, and to set foot on the road of self-discipline with manly vigilance and industry. The more they accustom themselves to ascetic practices, the more doors will be opened to them, until the soul gradually overcomes the forces of (their) nature, which will be subjugated to them under the majesty of the soul.

Concerning the noble *hadith*s which urge the people to strive earnestly in worshipping and praise the people who do so with reference to the worships and austerities of the Imams of (the Islamic) guidance (*a*), as well as the noble *hadith*s which recommend economy in worshipping and praise it, both categories are based on the different people of *suluk* and the ranks and conditions of the soul. The general criterion is the vivacity and the strength of the soul or its weakness and aversion.

---

[52] *Ibid.*, *hadith* 1.
[53] *Ibid.*, *hadith* 2.

ON INFORMING THE HEART
Chapter Seven

A cordial discipline of worship, especially the invoking worship, is "informing" [*tafhim*]. It is to take the heart, at the beginning, as a child not yet able to speak, and is wanted to be taught. So, each of the invocations, recitations, facts and secrets of worship is to be taught to the heart with strict accuracy and effort, and whatever the degree of perfection, one has to teach to the heart the facts which he has so far recognized. Even if one was unable to understand the meanings of the Quran and the invocations, and had no share of the secrets of worship, he, nevertheless, would have to teach his heart the very general meanings, such as telling it that the Quran is the words of Allah, that the invocations are remembrance of Allah, and that worship is obeying the Creator. He has to teach his heart such general information. Should he be of those who understand the apparent meanings of the Quran and the invocations, such as the promises, warnings, biddings and forbiddings, as well as the information about the Source [*mabda*] and Resurrection [*maad*], he must inform his heart of whatever has been understood from them by him. Should a fact of knowledge or a secret of worship be exposed to him, he is to inform it to his heart carefully and strictly. The result of such information is that after a period of perseverance the tongue of the heart will open to speaking and will become an invoker and a reminder. At the beginning the heart is a learner and the tongue a teacher. Whenever the tongue invokes, the heart also becomes an invoker, and so the heart is a follower of the tongue. But after that the heart''s tongue learns to speak, the contrary happens: the heart becomes invoker and the tongue follows it in invocation and in movement. Rather, sometimes it happens that even when man is sleeping, his tongue starts invoking in pursuit of his heart''s invocation, as the heart''s invocation is not confined to the state of wakefulness, and when the heart remembers, the tongue, having become its follower, starts invocating after it, and it leaks out from the dominion of the heart: **"Say: Every one acts according to his own manner..."**[54]

In short, at the beginning man must observe this discipline, that is, "informing," so that the tongue of the heart starts speaking, which is the real objective. The sign denoting that the heart's tongue has been released is that the tiredness and the hardship of the invocation are removed and replaced by animation and pleasure. It is like a baby, who has not yet started talking, its tutor feels tired and bored before it speaks. No sooner the baby starts prattling than his tutor's fatigue goes away and the teacher follows up the child's utterances without tiredness or trouble. Similar is the heart. It is a mere infant at the start, knowing not how to speak. It is to be taught, and the invocations and the recitations are to be placed on its tongue. Then, as it begins talking, man begins to be its follower, and there will remain neither pain of teaching nor any tiredness of invocating. This discipline is quite necessary for the beginners.

It must be noted that one of the secrets of repeating the invocations and benedictions and continuing the remembrance and worshipping is that the heart's tongue gets untied, and the heart becomes an invoking devotee. Without observing this discipline the tongue of the heart would remain tied up.

Some noble *hadith*s refer to this. The noble *al-Kafi*, quoting Imam as-Sadiq (*a*), who quoted Imam Ali (*a*) who, referring to some disciplines of recitation, said: "...But strike with it (the Quran) your hardened hearts, and do not be eager to get to the end of the *surah*."[55]

In another *hadith* in *al-Kafi*, Imam as-Sadiq (*a*) told Abu Usamah: "O Abu Usamah, call your hearts [*qulub*] to remember Allah, and avoid what displeases Him."[56]

Even the most perfect godly men (*a*) used to observe this discipline. A *hadith* relates that Imam as-Sadiq (*a*) (once) was subject to a fit during the *salat* and fainted. When he came to his senses and he was asked about the reason, he said: "I kept repeating this *ayah* to my

---

[54] *Surah al-Isra"* 17:84.
[55] *Usul al-Kafi*, vol. 4, Book on "The Merit of the Quran," ch. on "Reciting the Quran in a Melodious Voice," *hadith* 1, p. 418.
[56] *Al-Kafi*, (*Rawdah*), vol. 8, p. 167; *Bihar al-Anwar*, vol. 67, Book on "Faith and Disbelief," ch. 44, *hadith*, 38, p. 59.

heart until I heard it from the one Who spoke it, and so, my body could not bear to see His power."[57]

Abu Dharr is quoted to have said that the Messenger of Allah (*s*) was one night repeating this Quranic verse: **"If You should torment them, then they are, indeed, Your servants, and if You should forgive them, then You are, indeed, the Mighty, the Wise."**[58]

In short, the reality of invocation and remembrance is the invocation of the heart, without which the invocation of the tongue will be futile and worthless. This is referred to in a number of *hadith*s. The Messenger of Allah (*s*) informed Abu Dharr: "O Abu Dharr, two *rakat*s of *salat* in contemplation are better than spending the whole night with an inattentive (or forgetful) heart."[59]

The Messenger of Allah (*s*) is also quoted to have said: "Allah, the Exalted, would not look at your faces, but at your hearts."[60]

In the *hadith*s concerning the presence of heart it is stated that the more the presence of heart in the *salat*, the better it is accepted, and the more the negligence of the heart, the less it is acceptable. As long as the said discipline is not observed, no cordial invocation will happen, and the heart will not come out of its being inattentive and negligent.

It is narrated that Imam as-Sadiq (*a*) said: "Make your heart a *qiblah* to your tongue and do not move it except by a sign from the heart."[61] But the heart would not become a *qiblah* nor would the tongue and the other organs follow it unless the said discipline was observed. Should it happen without the observance of this discipline, it would be a rarity, and one must not take pride in it.

---

[57] *Al-Mahajjat ul-Bayda'*, vol. 1, Book on "The Secrets of the *Salat*," ch. on "The Merit of Submission and its Meaning," p. 352.

[58] *Surah al-Ma'idah* 4:118. *Ruh ul-Maani fi Tafsir al-Quran* by Allamah al-Alusi vol. 7, p. 70, quoted from the *Sunans* of an-Nasa'i and al-Bayhaqi.

[59] *Bihar al-Anwar*, vol. 74, Book of *"Ar-Rawdah"* ch. on "The Prophet's Admonitions," *hadith* 2, p. 82, quoted from *Makarim al-Akhlaq*, p. 465.

[60] *Ibid.*; *Bihar al-Anwar*, vol. 67, p. 248, quoted from *Jami al-Akhbar*, p. 117 (with a slight addition).

[61] Refer to footnote 33.

ON THE PRESENCE OF HEART
Chapter Eight

One of the important cordial disciplines, which many other disciplines may be its preliminaries, and worship without it would be lifeless, and it is the key to the lock of perfections and the door of the doors of felicities, and the noble *hadith*s seldom attach so much importance to a discipline other than that, is the "presence of heart." Although we have sufficiently explained this topic, together with its ranks and degrees in the thesis *The Secret of the Salat*[62] and in *Forty Hadiths*,[63] nevertheless, we shall allude to it once again, to complete the benefit, and to avoid reference.

It has already been explained that worships, ceremonies, invocations and benedictions can have their results only when they become the inner image of the heart, and the interior of the essence of man is mixed with them, and his heart takes the form of servitude, renouncing disobedience and obstinacy. It has also been noted that one of the secrets and advantages of worship is that one"s will gets stronger, the soul overcomes (one"s) nature, the forces of nature become subjugated by the soul"s power and sovereignty, and the will

---

[62] Refer to footnote 6.

[63] *Forty Hadiths* is one of Imam Khomeini"s works, which he finished in the month of Muharram 1358 L.H. In its preface, after praising, blessing and invocation, he says: "...I, a poor and weak servant, have, for sometime, been thinking to collect forty *hadith*s of the *hadith*s of the infallible and pure *Ahl al-Bayt* (a) out of the reliable books of the Companions and *ulama* (may Allah be pleased with them), and to explain each in a way suitable for the common people. I, thus, wrote it in Persian so that the Persian-speaking people may benefit from it, and, *insha" Allah* (Allah willing), I may be covered by the noble *hadith* of the Seal of the Prophets (*s*) who said: "Whoever preserved for my *Ummah* forty *hadith*s that may benefit them, Allah would resurrect him on the Day of Resurrection as a learned jurist." I was, thanks to God, successful, with Allah"s good help, in starting it. I ask Allah, the Exalted, to help me in finishing it. Surely He is the Giver of success!"

of the invisible soul overrules the visible body, such that the forces turn like the angels with regard to Allah, the Exalted, i.e. **"...they do not disobey Allah in what He commands them, and do as they are commanded."**[64]

Now we add that one of the important secrets and advantages of worship, to which everything is a preliminary, is that the entire inside and outside kingdom becomes subservient to Allah"s will and moves at Allah"s command, and the soul"s visible and invisible forces become Allah"s soldiers, and all of them get the post of being Allah"s angels. This is regarded as one of the low degrees of the annihilation of the forces and wills in Allah"s will. Then, gradually, big consequences appear, the physical man becomes divine, and the soul practices servitude to Allah. The soldiers of *Iblis* will totally be defeated and abolished, and the heart and its powers surrender to Allah, and in it appear some inner stages of Islam. The result of this submitting of the will to Allah in the Hereafter will be that Allah, the Exalted, will enforce (make effective) the will of such a servant in the invisible worlds and make him His "sublime similitude" [*mathal-i ala*]. And, like His Sacred Self when at His mere Will everything He wants is created, He makes this servant"s will like His; as some of the people of knowledge, quoting the Messenger of Allah (*s*), concerning the people of Paradise, say that an angel comes to them, and, after asking permission from them, he enters and after conveying Allah"s greeting to them he delivers a letter from Allah, the Exalted. The letter says to whomsoever it is addressed:

"From the Ever-Living, the Everlasting, Who never dies, to the ever-living, everlasting, who never dies. Now then, I tell a thing: Be! And it is. I made you tell a thing: Be! And it is." The Messenger of Allah (*s*) said: "Hence, no one of the people of Paradise says to something: "Be!" unless it will be."[65]

This is the divine sovereignty bestowed upon the servant, because of his forsaking his own will and his desires" sovereignty, and because of his disobeying *Iblis* and his soldiers. None of the said results may take place except with the complete "presence of heart." If the heart were negligent and forgetful during the *salat*, his worship would not be real, but more like a play and sporting. Such a worship,

---

[64] *Surah at-Tahrim* 66:6.
[65] *Ilm ul-Yaqin*, vol. 2, p. 1061 (with a slight difference).

as a matter of fact, will have no effect whatsoever on the soul, and the worship will never sublime from its outer form to the inside and the invisible world [*malakut*]. This fact is referred to by many narratives. The powers of the soul would not surrender, through such worship, to the soul itself, nor can the sovereignty of the soul be seen on them. Similarly, the outward and inward powers will not surrender to Allah"s will, and the kingdom will not be subdued to Allah"s Majesty, as is quite clear. That is why you can see no effect from forty or fifty years of worship on us. On the contrary, the darkness of the heart and the obstinacy of the powers increase day after day, since our longing for nature, our obedience to our desires and to the satanic whispers, increase, too. These mean nothing but that our worships are empty and their interior and exterior disciplines are not observed. Otherwise, the Quranic text denotes that: **"...the *salat* forbids lewdness and vice."**[66] Naturally, this forbidding is not something superficial. A torch should be lighted in the heart, and a light must shine in one"s interior so as to guide him to the invisible world, and there appears a divine preventer, which prevents man from disobedience.

We do regard ourselves among the *musallin*, and we have been engaged in this great worship for decades, without seeing such a light, nor discerning such a preventer in our interior. So, woe to us on the day when the images of our deeds and the list of our acts are handed to us in that world and we are told to check our own accounts.[67] See if such deeds can be accepted by His Majesty, and whether such a *salat*, in such a deformed and darkened form, can bring one nearer to His Presence. Is it right to treat this great divine trust and the advice of the prophets and *awsiya* (executors of the prophets" wills) in such a way, and to let the treacherous hand of the accursed Satan, the enemy of Allah, meddle in it? The *salat*, which is the *miraj* of the believer and the means of proximity of the pious,[68] why should it keep you away from the sacred proximity to the Divine Presence? What would be our share on that day except regret, remorse, helplessness, wretchedness, shame and disgrace—a regret and a remorse which have no equal in

---

[66] *Surah al-Ankabut* 69:45.
[67] It refers to the *ayah*: "Read your book; your soul suffices as a reckoner against you this day." *Surah al-Isra"* 17:14.
[68] *Itiqadat*, p. 29. by the late Majlisi; *Furu al-Kafi*, vol. 3, "Book of *as-Salat*," ch. on "The Merit of *as-Salat*," *hadith* 6, p. 265.

this world, and a shame and disgrace which cannot be imagined? This world"s regrets, are, at any rate, mixed with a thousand kinds of hope, and the shamelessness here is transitory, while there is nothing there except regret and remorse day after day. Allah, the Exalted, says: **"And warn them of the day of regret, when the matter shall have been decided."**[69] What has passed cannot be returned and the life which has been wasted cannot be restored. **"O woe to me! For what I fell short of my duty to Allah..."**[70]

My dear, this day is the day of opportunities and the grace period for actions. The prophets came and brought Books, and they proclaimed their calls, with a lot of celebrities, enduring pains and hardships, in order to wake us up from the sleep of negligence and to sober us from the nature"s intoxication, and to take us to the world of light and the source of joy and pleasure, and to introduce us to the eternal life, the everlasting bliss and the unlimited delights, and to deliver us from annihilation, misery, fire, darkness, regret and remorse. All these are for our own benefit, without there being any profit for them, as those sacred personalities are in no need of our faith and deeds. Despite all that, they had not the least effect on us, as Satan was so firmly closing the ears of our heart, and exerted such a strong control over our inside and outside that none of their admonitions could ever have an effect on us, nor could any of the *ayah*s and *hadith*s pierce the ears of our hearts, going to no farther than our outer animal ears.

In short, O respected reader who read these papers, do not be, like the writer, void of all lights, and empty-handed of all good deeds, entangled in the sensual desires. Have mercy on yourself, and get a fruit from your life. Carefully look into the lives of the prophets and the perfect godly men [*awliya*], and cast away the false desires and Satan"s promises. Do not be deceived by Satan"s fraud, nor by the deceptions of the commanding soul, as their trickery is very clever, and they are able to dress every wrong as right in the eyes of man in order to deceive him. Sometimes they fool man by making him think that he will repent at the end of his life, and thus, drag him into wretchedness, despite the fact that repenting at the end of life, after the accumulation of the darkness of sins, and the numerous acts of

---

[69] *Surah Maryam* 19:39.
[70] *Surah az-Zumar* 39:56.

injustice against the people and against Allah's right, is a very difficult task. Now, when man is still strong and in the prime of life, and the tree of sin is still frail and the influence of Satan has not yet become widespread in the soul, and the soul is still new to the invisible world and very near the God-given disposition, and the conditions for an acceptable repentance are easy, they do not let man repent and uproot this frail tree and overthrow the dependent kingdom. They suggest old age, when, on the contrary, the will is weak, the powers have given way, the trees of different sins are strong and deep rooted, the kingdom of *Iblis*, inwardly and outwardly, is independent and firm, the familiarity with nature is strong, the distance from the invisible world is great, the light of innate disposition is extinguished, and the situation for repentance is difficult and bitter. This is nothing but delusion.

In another instance the promise of the intercession of the intercessors (*a*) drives man out of their sacred realm and deprives him of their intercession, because indulgence in disobedience gradually darkens and upsets the heart and drags man to a bad end. Satan's aim is to rob man's faith, and he makes committing sins a preliminary step to that aim so as to attain it. If a man covetously thinks of intercession, he must try hard in this world to keep his connection with his intercessors, and think of the status of those who will intercede on the Day of Resurrection to see how their state of worship and devotion was. Suppose that you died a faithful man, but if the load of the sins and injustices was heavy, it is possible that concerning the different pains and tortures in the *barzakh* there would be no intercession for you, as Imam as-Sadiq was quoted to have said: "Your *barzakh* is with yourselves."[71] The tortures of the *barzakh* cannot be compared with the tortures of this world, and the length of the period of the *barzakh* is unknown except to Allah. It will probably last for millions and millions of years. It is possible that in the Hereafter and after long periods of diverse and unbearable kinds of torture, we get the intercession, as it is also related in the *hadiths*.[72]

---

[71] This concept is understood from the narrative of Amr ibn Yazid in *Furu al-Kafi*, vol. 3, p. 242, and in *Ilm ul-Yaqin*, vol. 2, p. 1051.

[72] As in *Bihar al-Anwar*, vol. 8, "Book of Justice and Resurrection," ch. 12, *hadiths* 35 and 36, p. 362.

Thus, the satanic deception stops man from good deeds, and causes him to leave this world either faithless or loaded with heavy burdens, afflicting him with wretchedness and misfortune. In some instances, Satan, by giving man hope in the vast mercy of the Most Merciful, cuts his hand off the skirt of mercy, while he is careless of the fact that raising up so many prophets, revealing the Books, descending the angels, and the revelations and inspirations to the prophets, and their showing the right path, are all of the mercy of the Most Merciful. The whole world is enveloped in the vast mercy of Allah, while we, at the fringe of the spring of life, die of thirst.

The greatest of the divine mercies is the Quran. If you are looking greedily for the mercy of the Most Merciful, hoping for His vast mercy, do benefit from the Quran, the vast mercy. It has opened to you the way to happiness, and has distinguished for you the pit from the paved road. But you fall over into the pit by yourself, because you deviate from the right path. So, what has mercy to do with that? Had it been possible to show the road of good and happiness to the people in a different way, it would have been done, according to the vastness of the mercy. Had it been possible to force the people into happiness, it would have been done. But alas! How far it is! The road to the Hereafter is a road, which cannot be trodden except at one"s free will. Happiness cannot be attained forcibly. Piety and righteous deeds are not so if not done voluntarily. This is probably the very meaning of the noble *ayah*: **"There is no compulsion in religion"** (2:256).

Yes, what can be made compulsory and forcible is the appearance of the divine religion, not its reality. The prophets (*a*) were enjoined to impose the appearance, in any possible way, on the people, so that the appearance of the world might become the appearance of the divine justice, and to guide the people to the interior, so that they themselves might march on their own feet towards happiness.

In short, this is also a satanic delusion, which cuts, by coveting mercy, man"s hand short from mercy.

HADITHS CONCERNING
THE PRESENCE OF HEART
Chapter Nine

There are many *hadith*s from the infallible and pure *Ahl al-Bayt* (*a*) concerning urging the "presence of heart". It suffices to translate some texts of those narratives:

The Messenger of Allah (*s*) is quoted to have said: "Worship Allah as if you see Him. If you do not see Him, He does see you."[73]

From this noble *hadith* two of the degrees of the presence of heart can be realized:

The first is that the *salik* discerns the Beauty of the Beautiful, and is absorbed in the manifestations of the Beloved [*hadrat-i mahbub*] such that all the ears of his heart will be closed to all other creatures, while the eye of his insight opens to the pure Beauty of the Lord of Majesty, discerning nothing else. That is, he is engaged in the Present [*hadir*], neglecting the presence [*hudur*] and company [*mahdar*].

The second degree, which is lower in rank, is that the *salik* sees himself present in His Presence [*mahdar*] and observes the discipline of the Presence [*hudur*] and Company [*mahdar*]. The Messenger of Allah (*s*) says: "If you can be of those who are in the first degree, then worship Allah accordingly, or else, do not neglect the fact that you are in the Presence [*mahdar*] of the Lord." Naturally, there is a discipline for being in the Presence [*mahdar*] of Allah, which should not be neglected in respect of the state of servitude. In a *hadith*, Abu Hamzah ath-Thamali narrates: "I saw Ali ibn al-Husayn (*a*) performing his *salat*. His cloak slipped off his shoulders, but he did not try to

---

[73] *Bihar al-Anwar*, vol. 74, "Book of *ar-Rawdah*, ch. 4, hadith 3, p. 74; *Makarim al-Akhlaq*, p. 459.

rearrange it until he finished the *salat*. When I asked him about that, he said: "Woe unto you! Do you know at whose service I was?" "[74]

The Messenger of Allah (s) was quoted to have said: "Two of my *Ummah* stand for the *salat*, and, although their *ruku* and *sujud* are the same, the difference between the two *salat*s is like that which is between the earth and the sky."[75]

He also said: "Is the person who turns his face in the *salat* not afraid that it may turn into the face of an ass?"[76]

He further said: "Whoever performs a two-*rakat salat* without paying attention to any worldly matter, Allah, the Exalted, will forgive him his sins.[77]

In another *hadith* he said: "A *salat*, half of it may be accepted, or one-third, or a quarter, or one-fifth, or even one-tenth. Another *salat* may be folded, like an old dress, and be thrown back at the face of its owner."

"No part of the *salat* is yours except that part which you perform with an attentive heart."[78]

Imam al-Baqir (a) has quoted the Messenger of Allah (s) as saying: "When a believing servant stands for the *salat*, Allah, the Exalted, looks at him (or he said: He turns to him) until he finishes, and mercy shadows over his head, the angels surround him from all sides up to the horizon of the heaven, and Allah assigns an angel to stand at his head, saying: "O *musalli*, if you know who is looking at you, and to whom you are supplicating, you will look to nowhere, nor will you leave your position." "[79]

Imam as-Sadiq (a) is quoted to have said: "Eagerness and fear will not get together in a heart unless Paradise is his. So, when you perform your *salat*, turn with your heart to Allah, the Glorified, the Almighty, because there would be no believing servant who would turn with his heart to Allah, the Exalted, during the *salat* and

---

[74] *Wasa'il ash-Shiah*, vol. 4, "Book of *as-Salat*," sec. on "The Acts of *as-Salat*," ch. 3, *hadith* 6, p. 688.

[75] *Bihar al-Anwar*, vol. 81, "Book of *as-Salat*," ch. 16, *hadith* 41, p. 249.

[76] *Mustadrak al-Wasa'il*, "Book of *as-Salat*," sec. on "The Acts of the *Salat*," ch. 2, *hadith* 20.

[77] *Ibid.*, *hadith* 13.

[78] *Bihar al-Anwar*, vol. 81, "Book of *as-Salat*," ch. 16, *hadith* 59, p. 260.

[79] *Mustadrak al-Wasa'il*, "Book of *as-Salat*," sec. on "The Acts of the *Salat*," ch. 2, *hadith* 22.

invocation, unless Allah would turn to him the hearts of the believers, and with their love He would back him and lead him to Paradise."[80]

It is narrated that Imams al-Baqir and as-Sadiq (*a*) said: "Nothing of your *salat* is yours except that which you did with an attentive heart. So, if one performed it completely mistaken, or neglected its disciplines, it would be folded and thrown back at its owner"s face."[81]

Imam Baqir al-Ulum (the cleaver of knowledge) (*a*) is quoted to have said: "Of a servant"s *salat* ascends half, one-third, one-fourth or one-fifth to his account. That is, of his *salat* will not ascend except that part which is performed with an attentive heart. We have been commanded to perform the *nafilah* so as to make up for the shortcomings of the obligatory *salats*."[82]

Imam as-Sadiq (*a*) is quoted to have said: "When you wear the *ihram* for the *salat* (i.e., when you prepared for the *salat*), pay attention to it, because when you pay attention to it, Allah will pay attention to you. If you do not care for it, Allah will not care for you. So, sometimes, does not ascend of the *salat* except one-third, one-fourth or one-sixth, according to the amount of attention the *musalli* pays to it. Allah grants nothing to the negligent."[83]

The Messenger of Allah (*s*) is quoted to have said to Abu Dharr: "Two moderate *rakats* of *salat* with contemplation are better than worshipping a whole night with a negligent heart."[84] The *hadith*s on this are many, but those which have been related are enough for those whose hearts are awake and attentive.

---

[80] *Wasa'il ash-Shiah*, vol. 4, "Book of *as-Salat*", sec. on "The Acts of the *Salat*," ch. 3, *hadith* 3, p. 678.
[81] *Ibid.*, *hadith* 1.
[82] *Ilal ash-Sharai'*, vol. 2, ch. 22, *hadith* 2, p. 327.
[83] *Mustadrak al-Wasa'il*, "Book of *as-Salat*," sec. on "The Acts of the *Salat*," ch. 3, *hadith* 7.
[84] Refer to footnote 59.

ON CALLING TO ACQUIRING THE PRESENCE OF HEART
Chapter Ten

Now that you have understood the rational and traditional merits and characteristics of the presence of heart, as well as the disadvantages of neglecting it, (you should know that) understanding alone is not enough, though it strengthens the evidence. So, use all your endeavors and try to acquire what you have understood, and turn your understanding into practice in order to be benefited by it and get its advantage. Think a little, as, according to narratives from the infallible *Ahl al-Bayt* (*a*)—who are the sources of revelation, and all their knowledge and utterances are of divine inspirations and Muhammadan intuition [*kashf*]—the acceptance of the *salat* (by Allah) is the condition for the acceptance of other acts of worship. If the *salat* is rejected, they will not pay attention to the other acts at all.[85] The acceptance of the *salat* is conditioned by the presence of heart. Without the presence of heart in the *salat* it would be worthless and not becoming of being in the Presence of Allah and cannot be accepted, as had been explained by formerly mentioned *hadith*s. Thus, the key to the treasury [*ganjinah*] of deeds and the entrance to the doors of all kinds of happiness is the presence of heart, with which the door of happiness is opened to man, and without it all worships are degraded and worthless.

Now, with a look of regard, contemplate a little, and with the eye of insight look at the importance and the greatness of the situation, and carry it out with complete seriousness. The key to the door of happiness and the doors of Paradise, as well as the key to the door of wretchedness and the doors of Hell are in this world, in your own pocket. You can open the doors of Paradise and happiness to yourself,

---

[85] See footnote 17.

and you can do the contrary. The reigns are in your hands. Allah, the Exalted, has completed the evidence for you, showed you the roads to happiness and wretchedness, and has offered you the outward and the inward successes. What was needed on the part of Allah and His friends [*awliya*], has been done. Now it is our turn for action. They are the guides and we are the treaders. They did their work as best as possible without the least negligence, such that there remained no excuse whatsoever. So, you, too, wake up from your sleep of negligence and tread upon the road to happiness and make use of your years and powers, since, if you waste your cash of years and youth, and your treasure of power and ability, no compensation can make up for them. If you are young, do not let yourself reach old age, because old age has its particular shortcomings, which are known to the elderly people, and you do not know. To reform oneself in old age and in weakness is quite difficult. If you are old, do not let the rest of your years be waste, because, at any rate, as long as you are alive, you still have a way to happiness, and a door of happiness is open to you—God forbid its being closed and the road being blocked, as in that case you lose your free will and there remains nothing but regret, remorse and repentance of the past, of which you have no portion.

So, my dear, if you believe in what has been said, which is the sayings of the prophets (*a*), and if you prepare yourself for attaining happiness and for the journey to the Hereafter, and find it necessary to obtain the presence of heart, which is the key to the treasure of happiness, the way to obtain it is to remove, first, the obstacles which prevent the presence of heart and to uproot the thorns from the road of the journey, and then to practice it. The obstacles, which prevent the presence of heart in worship, are the dispersion of the mind and too many engagements of the heart. They happen most frequently from outside and through the outer senses, such as the ear hearing some sound during worship and the mind is, thus, distracted, stirring the imagination and inner thoughts, which fall under the effect of fancy, flying from one branch to another. Or a person's eye may see something, which disturbs the mind and distracts the thoughts. Likewise, other senses may be attracted, causing imaginative transitions.

Regarding the doing away with these obstacles, they have said that it is done by removing the causes, such as standing in a dark place, or in a privacy, when performing the *salat*, and closing the eyes during the *salat*, and refraining from performing it in places causing mental distraction. The late prosperous martyr (the Second Martyr) (may Allah be pleased with him), quotes some devotees to have said that they used to worship and perform their *salat*s in a small dark room barely large enough for worshipping.[86] Yet, it is obvious that this would not remove the obstacle, nor would it uproot the cause, because the principal hindrance is the imagination, which, with even a little motive, does its job. It may sometimes happen that in a very small, dark and private room, the activities of imagination and fancy become greater, and they cause more (mental) plays, and jests. So, uprooting the whole matter is done by reforming one"s imagination and fancy. Later on we shall return to this point. However, this type of treatment is sometimes effective and helpful in some souls, but we are looking for a decisive cure and uprooting the real cause, and it cannot be done that way.

Sometimes the disturbance of mind and absence of heart are caused by inner matters, which, generally speaking, are originated by two big causes to which return most of the matters:

One is the dissoluteness and volatility of the bird of imagination. Imagination is, indeed, an extremely slippery power. It flies from one branch to another and from one peak to another. This is not connected to loving the world or paying attention to worldly matters, wealth or position. Actually, the volatility of imagination is, in itself, a calamity that afflicts even the ascetics. Acquiring calmness of mind, peace of soul and repose of imagination are of the important affairs, which, if acquired, can bring about the final remedy. This shall be referred to later on.

The other cause is the love of the world and the attraction of mind to mundane matters. This cause is at the top of the sins and it is the mother of the inner diseases, the thorn of the road of the people of *suluk* and the source of disasters. As long as the heart loves this world and is indulged in it, the way to reforming the heart is closed and the door of all happiness is shut in the face of man. We shall, within two chapters, refer to these two big origins and strong obstacles, if Allah wills.

---

[86] *At-Tanbihat ul-Illiyyah ala Waza'if is-Salat il-Qalbiyyah*, p. 110 (printed within a collection of the statements of the Second Martyr, lithographed in 1313 L.H. by the handwriting of Muhammad Hasan Jarfadaqani).

ON CURING
THE WANDERING IMAGINATION
Chapter Eleven

Concerning Showing an Effective Cure for the Treatment of the Wandering and Escaping Imagination that Brings about the Presence of Heart

Know that each one of the inner and outer powers of the soul can be educated and taught by way of practicing a particular austerity. For example, human eye is unable to gaze at a point or at an intense light, such as the disk of the sun, for a long time, without blinking. But if a man educates his eye, such as that which is done by some of the people of false asceticism for certain purposes, he can look into the sun for several hours without blinking or getting tired. Similarly, he can gaze at a certain point for hours without any movement. This is also true of the other faculties, like stopping breathing, which, as they say, is seen among the people of false asceticism, as there are some who can stop breathing for an extraordinary period.

Of the faculties that can be educated are the faculties of imagination and fancy. Before educating them, they are like two ever-jumpy and restless birds flying from a branch to another, and from one thing to another. If one tries to watch them for a single minute, he will see their many successive movements of very slight and far-fetched connections. Many think that to control the bird of imagination and tame it is out of the limits of possibilities, and falls within the realm of the common impossibilities. But, as a matter of fact, it is not so. With hardship, practice and time-taking education, it can be tamed, and the bird of imagination can be put under one"s control and will be such that it can be confined for several hours and for a certain purpose, according to one"s will.

The principal way of taming it is to act to its contrary. That is, at the time of the *salat* one is to prepare himself to control the imagination during the *salat* and confine it to action, and, as soon as it tries to slip out of his hand, to recapture it. One should carefully watch it in all the actions, recitations, invocations, etc. of the *salat*, observing it so as not to be obstinate. At the beginning, this seems to be a difficult task. But after a while of strict practice and treatment, it will certainly become tame and obedient. You should not, of course, expect yourself, at the beginning, to be able to control the bird of imagination along the *salat* completely. Actually, this is impossible. Perhaps those who stressed this impossibility had such expectations. The situation requires deliberateness, careful patience and gradual training. It is possible that you can first control your imagination during only one-tenth of the *salat* or even less than that, in which you can have the presence of heart. Then, if one pays more attention, and if he feels himself in need of that, he can attain a better result, and can gradually overcome the Satan of fancy and the bird of imagination, such that they come under his control in most of the *salat*. However, you should never despair, as despair is the origin of all weaknesses and inabilities, whereas the flash of hope guides man to his complete happiness.

The important thing in this respect, however, is to feel being in need—a mood that is little felt by us. Our heart does not believe that the source of the happiness in the Hereafter, and the means of a long-lasting life, is the *salat*. We take the *salat* to be an additional burden on our lives. We think it an imposition and an obligation. The love of a thing is seen from understanding its consequences. We understood its consequence and the heart believes in it, and, therefore, we are not in need of any advice or admonition in acquiring it.

Those who think that the message of the Seal of the Prophets, the Hashimite Messenger (*s*), has two dimensions: one belonging to this world and the other to the Hereafter, and take this to be a pride of the bringer of the *Shariah* and the perfection of prophethood, know nothing of the religion and are unaware of the message and far from understanding the purpose of the prophethood. Inviting to worldly things is quite alien to the objectives of the great prophets, since desire, sense of anger and the interior and exterior Satans, are sufficient for such an invitation and it does not need the sending of messengers. The administration of desire and anger is in no need of a Quran or a prophet. The prophets, actually, have come to keep people back from this world to curb the release of the desire and anger, and to limit the sources of worldly interests. An ignorant person thinks that they invited the people to this world. They say: "Do not acquire wealth by whatever means. Do not satisfy your desire in whatever way available—there should be marriage, and there should be (lawful) trade, industry and agriculture though the door of the center of desire and anger is opened by letting them free." So, the prophets demand them to be chained, not to be set free, and they do not invite to worldly things. They ask for a lawful business so as to prohibit the unlawful ones. They call to marriage in order to curb the nature and prevent debauchery and releasing the power of desire [*shahwat*]. As a matter of fact, they are not absolutely against them, because it would be against the perfect system.

In short, as we feel we need this world, regarding it to be the capital of life and the source of pleasure, we get ready to attend to it and to acquire it. But if we believe in the Hereafter-life and feel we are in need of that life, and regard worship, especially the *salat*, to be the capital for living there, and the source of happiness in that world, we, naturally, will try to do our best to acquire it, and we will not feel any difficulty and fatigue in ourselves; or rather, we will hurry to acquire it with complete eagerness and craving, and endure every hardship and undergo all circumstances for that purpose.

Now, this coldness and weakness, which are manifest in us, are caused by the coldness of the radiance of our faith and the weakness of its foundation. Had all the news of the prophets and holy men [*awliya'*] (*a*) and the arguments of the elite and learned men (may Allah be pleased with them) created "sufferance" [*ihtimal*] in us, we could have done better in our attempts and acquirements. So, we have to regret a thousand times for letting Satan overcome our inside and conquer the whole of our heart and the hearings of our interior, preventing us from hearing the sayings of Allah and His Messengers, and those of the scholars, as well as the admonitions of the divine Books. Such being the case, our ears are changed to those of worldly animals, and the divine admonitions would not go beyond the apparent and the animal ear to the inside **"Most surely there is a reminder in this for him who has a heart or he gives ear and is a witness."** (Q 50:37)

One of the great duties of the traveler to Allah and the striver for the sake of Allah is to completely give up self-reliance during the striving and *suluk*, and, by nature, to pay attention to the Cause of the causes, and by disposition, to belong to the Origin of the origins, asking from His Sacred Existence protection and immunity from sin, and depending on the help of His Sacred Essence. In his privacy he is to implore Him and very seriously request Him to improve his condition, for there is no refuge save Him. And praise be to Allah!

EXPLAINING THAT LOVING THIS WORLD CAUSES DISTRACTION OF THE MIND
Chapter Twelve

A Reference to that Loving this World is the Origin of the Distraction of the Imagination and Prevents the Presence of Heart, and Explaining its Remedy as Much as Possible

It must be noted that the heart, according to its nature and disposition, looks at what it loves and is inclined to that beloved to have it as its *qiblah*. If an affair distracted the heart from thinking of the beauty of its cherished beloved, no sooner the engagement slackens and the distraction stops than the heart flies towards its beloved and clings to his skirt. Should the people of knowledge and the divinely attracted enjoy strength of heart and be firm in absorption and love, they would recognize the Beauty of the Beloved in every mirror, and would discern the wanted perfection in every being: "I discerned nothing unless I recognized Allah in it and with it,"[87] and if their leader [the Prophet (*s*)] says: "Sometimes my heart is enveloped by a cover of dust, and I ask Allah's forgiveness seventy times every day,"[88] it is because to see the Beauty of the Beloved—especially in an impure mirror like the Abu Jahl mirror—is in itself a sort of impurity with respect to the perfect ones. If their hearts are not strong enough, and their engagement in multiplicity prevents the presence (of heart), no sooner the engagement lessens than their hearts' birds fly back to their sacred nests and cling to the Beauty of the Beautiful.

As to those who look for other than Allah—who, in the eyes of the people of knowledge, all seek for this world—they are also

---

[87] A quotation from Amir al-Mu'minin [Ali] (a) in *Ilm al-Yaqin*, vol. 1, p. 49.
[88] *Mustadrak al-Wasa'il*, "Book of *as-Salat*," sec. on "Invocations," ch. 22, *hadith* 1.

attracted to their want and cling to it. If they, too, are extremely in love with their quest, and the love of this world has completely possessed their hearts, they will never relax in their attraction towards it, and, whatever the situation, they remain beside the beauty of their beloved. Should their love be less, their hearts would return, in their leisure time, to their beloved. Those who cherish in their hearts the love of wealth, rule and position, dream of them in their sleep, too, and, in their wakefulness, they live thinking of their beloved. As long as they are engaged in worldly matters, they live hugging their beloved, and when the time of the *salat* arrives, the heart feels a kind of vacancy and sticks to its beloved, as if the *takbirat ul-ihram* (the first *Allahu akbar* uttered aloud at the start of the *salat*) is the key to the shop, or the remover of the curtain between it and its beloved. So, he comes to himself only when he has just uttered the *taslim* (the finishing words of the *salat*), whereas he had paid no attention to the *salat* itself, and during it he had been engaged in thinking of this world. That is why our *salat*s for forty or fifty years have no result whatsoever in our hearts except darkness and impurity, and what should have been a cause for ascension to the proximity of Allah's presence and a means of becoming familiar with His sanctity, has, on the contrary, driven us out of His proximity and taken us miles away from ascending to be familiar with His presence. Had our *salat* a smell of servitude, its result would have been modesty and humility, not self-conceitedness, ostentation, arrogance and pride, each one of which can possibly be a separate cause of man's misfortune and perdition.

In short, when one's heart becomes mixed with the love of this world, with no objective or aim except building it up and developing it, this love will inevitably prevent the heart from being vacant and present in the presence of Allah. This deadly disease and ruinous corruption can be cured by useful knowledge and good deed.

The useful knowledge suitable for this ailment is to think of the fruits and outcomes of curing it, and compare them with the harmful and destructive consequences resulting from it. In my commentaries on the *Forty Hadiths* in this respect I have explained this topic in details as was possible. Here I will suffice myself with explaining some *hadiths* of the infallible *Ahl al-Bayt* (*a*):

In *Al-Kafi*, Abu Abdullah (As-Sadiq) (*a*) is quoted to have said: "The origin of every sin is the love of this world."[89] Other *hadith*s on this subject, though in different wordings, are plenty.[90]

Yet, this noble *hadith* is quite enough for the wakeful man, and it is enough for this big and pernicious sin to be the source of all sins and the root and basement of all corruptions. By a little contemplation it can be realized that almost all moral and practical corruptions are the fruits of this vile tree. No false religion was established in the world, and no corruption has ever happened, unless it stemmed from this grave sin. Murders, plunders, injustice and transgressions are of the offspring of this sin. Debauchery, atrocities, theft and other crimes are the outcomes of this germ of corruption. The man who is afflicted with this love is void of all moral virtues. Courage, chastity, generosity and equity, which are the origin of all the spiritual virtues, are not compatible with the love of this world. Divine knowledge [*maarif*], unity of Names, Attributes, Actions and Essence, truth-seeking and truth-discerning are contrary to the love of this world. Tranquility of the soul, calmness of the mind and repose of the heart, which are the spirit of happiness in both worlds, cannot come along with loving this world. Richness of the heart, greatness, self-respect, freedom, and manliness are of the requisites of ignoring this world, whereas poverty, humility, covetousness, greed, servitude and flattery are of the requisites of loving this world. Kindness, mercy, observing kinship relations, affection and amity are not in harmony with the love of this world. Hatred, rancor, despotism, severing kinship relations, hypocrisy and other evil characters are of the progeny of this "mother of diseases".

As-Sadiq (*a*), as stated in *Misbah ash-Shariah*, said: "This world is like a portrait: its head is arrogance, its eye is greed, its ear is covetousness, its tongue is pretence, its hand is desire, its leg is conceit, its heart is negligence, its being is perishing and its destiny is decline. Whoever loves it, it gives him arrogance, whoever approves of it, it grants him greed, whoever demands it, it drives him to covetousness, whoever praises it, it clothes him with pretence, whoever wants it, it offers him conceit, whoever trusts it, it neglects

---

[89] *Usul al-Kafi*, "Book of Faith and Infidelity," ch. on "Loving this World and Being Attached to it," *hadith* 1.
[90] *Ibid.*, *hadith*s 1-17.

him, whoever admires its properties, it ruins him, and whoever accumulates it and does not spend it, it turns him down to its dwelling place, the Fire."[91]

Daylami, in *Irshad al-Qulub*, quoting Amir al-Muminin (Ali) (*a*), says that the Messenger of Allah (s) said: "On the night of the *miraj*, Allah, the Exalted, said: "O Ahmad, if a servant performs the *salat* as much as that of the people of the earth and the heaven, and fasts as much as that of the people of the earth and the heaven, and refrains, like the angels, from food, and wears the apparel of a devotee, then I see in his heart a bit of love for this world or for worldly reputation, leadership, celebrity and ornaments, he will not be in an abode in My neighborhood and I will drive My love out of his heart and make it dark until he forgets Me. I will not let him taste the sweetness of My love." "[92] It is quite clear that loving this world and loving Allah cannot meet together. In this respect there are too many *hadith*s to be contained in these pages.

Now as it has become clear that the love of this world is the origin of all evils, it becomes incumbent on a man of reason, who cherishes his happiness, to uproot this tree from his heart. The practical way to treat it is to do the contrary, i.e., if he has a longing for wealth and position, he can get rid of it by way of being open-handed and spending obligatory and recommended alms and charities. By the way, one of the characteristics of alms-giving is lessening the love of this world. That is why it is recommended to give charity out of what you love most, as stated in the Glorious Quran: **"You shall not attain goodness until you spend out of what you love"** (3:92). If he desires pride, priority, authority and power, he is to act against that, to turn the nose of the evil-commanding soul into the dust to reform it.

Man should know that the world is such that the more one is attached to it and in pursuit of it, the more his affection to it and the more his regret for parting company with it. It seems as if one is in quest of something, which is not in his possession. Man thinks he is in need of a certain portion of the world, which he pursues, no matter what difficulties and risks he will have to endure to attain his goal, and, as soon as he obtains it, it loses its attraction and becomes an ordinary matter, and his love and attachment turn into something else

---

[91] *Misbah ash-Shariah*, ch. 32 "On This World's Attribute(s)".
[92] *Irshad al-Qulub*, vol. 1, p. 206.

more sublime than the previous one, and he starts his toil and endeavors anew. In this way his anxiety will never be subdued. Actually, his love gets ever stronger, and his hardships ever increase. This natural disposition never stops. The people of knowledge use this inborn nature to prove a lot of disciplines, which are out of the scope of these papers to explain. This subject is referred to by some noble *hadith*s, such as that which is stated in the noble *al-Kafi*, quoting. Imam al-Baqir (*a*) who said: "The parable of a man greedy of this world is the parable of the silk worm: the more it winds the thread round itself the farther it becomes from salvation, until it dies of grief."[93]

Imam as-Sadiq (*a*) is quoted to have said: "This world is like sea-water; the more a thirsty man drinks from it the thirstier he gets, until it kills him."[94]

---

[93] *Usul al-Kafi*, vol. 3, "Book of Faith and Infidelity," ch. on "Dispraising this World and Neglecting it," *hadith* 20, and ch. on "Loving this World and being Greedy of it," *hadith* 7, p. 202.

[94] *Ibid.*, *hadith* 24.

ON TURNING THE SOUL AWAY FROM THE WORLD
Completion

So, O seeker of the truth and traveler to Allah, as you have tamed the bird of imagination, chained the Satan of fancy, given up the love of wife, children and other worldly affairs, got familiar with the attraction of the fire of the natural divine love and said: **"Lo! I see a fire [afar off],"**[95] seen yourself with no barriers in the way and prepared the requirements of the journey, get up, then, leave this dark room of nature and the narrow passage of the world, break off the chains of time, save yourself from this prison and let the bird of sanctity fly to "the meeting place of intimacy." [*mahfil-i uns*].

A whistle is calling you from the turret of the *Arsh*,
I wonder what keeps you into this place of traps![96]

So, be resolute and strengthen your will, since the first condition of *suluk* is resolution [*azm*], without which no distance can be covered and no perfection can be reached. The great Shaykh, Shahabadi[97] (may my soul be his ransom) called it as the core of

---

[95] A part of Moses'' conversation with his people. **"When he saw a fire, he said to his people: "Stay here! Lo! I see a fire [afar off]." "** *Surah Ta-Ha* 20:10 and *Surah an-Naml* 27: 7.
[96] A poem by Hafiz Shirazi.
[97] The late Ayatullah Mirza Muhammad-Ali Isfahani Shahabadi, a jurist, methodist, gnostic and prominent philosopher, son of the late Ayatullah Mirza Muhammad Jawad Husaynabadi Isfahani, was born in Isfahan in 1292 L.H. After finishing his preliminary learning in Isfahan and Tehran, he traveled to study in the theological circles of Najaf al-Ashraf and Samirra''(in Iraq). There his tutors were great scholars, such as the late writer of *Al-Jawahir*, Akhund Khurasani and Shariat Isfahani. He soon attained the degree of *ijtihad*. He reached a high position in *fiqh*, philosophy and gnosticism, and he taught these branches of knowledge. His class was one of the

humanity. It can also be said that one of the great points of fearing Allah, avoiding the desires of the appetitive soul, the lawful austerities, and the divine worship and rituals, is strengthening the resolution and defying the worldly powers under the sovereignty of the soul, as has already been mentioned. We now close this discourse with praising and glorifying the Sacred Essence of Allah, the Exalted, and with praising the attributes of the Chosen Master, the elected Prophet, and his pure offspring (*a*). We ask the help of the holy souls of those sacred personalities in our spiritual journey and faithful ascension.

---

most powerful scholarly circles in Samirra". After returning from Iraq, he settled first in Tehran, and then he moved to the sacred town of Qum, where he dwelt for seven years. During his stay in Qum, Imam Khomeini (may Allah be pleased with him and send peace upon him) benefited so much from his lessons on ethics and gnosticism. The Imam of the nation, in many places in this book and in his other books and writings, refers to his great teacher with utmost respect and esteem, and relates his scholarly emissions. Besides teaching different branches of knowledge and educating his distinguished disciples, the late Shahabadi wrote many books in different fields. At the age of seventy-seven, that man of knowledge and action died in 1369 L.H. in Tehran, and was buried in the neighborhood of the shrine of Abd al-Azim al-Hasani, in the graveyard of the late Shaykh Abu 'l-Futuh ar-Razi. May Allah resurrect him together with the Prophet Muhammad and his pure progeny.

DISCOURSE TWO

ON THE PRELIMINARIES OF THE *SALAT* AND SOME OF ITS CORDIAL DISCIPLINES

Discussed in Five Objectives

OBJECTIVE ONE

On Purification

Explained in Seven Chapters

ON PURIFICATION IN GENERAL
Chapter One

As it has already been said, besides the outer appearance of the *salat*, it has a reality, and apart from its exterior it has an interior. And as its outer form has its formal disciplines and conditions, its interior has its disciplines and conditions, too, which are to be observed by the *salik*. Thus, purification has also its outer form and formal disciplines, the explanation of which is out of the scope of these pages. The *faqihs* (jurists) of the Jafari school (may Allah make high their words and raise their ranks) have explained them. As regards the inner disciplines and purifications, they shall be explained in general:

It should be noted that the reality of the *salat* is ascension to the Proximity, and reaching the Presence of Allah, the Almighty and Most High. Thus, to attain this great objective and ultimate goal, one should practice certain purifications, which are other than the outer purifications. The thorns of this road and the obstacles in the way of this ascension are such impurities that if the *salik* were marked by one of them, he would be incapable of ascending to the peak and completing the ascension. Such impurities are the hindrances in the way of the *salat* and the plagues of Satan. But what is a help to the *salik* in his journey and is a discipline of the Presence is the condition of this reality. The traveler to Allah has first to remove the obstacles and impurities so that he may be purified and attain purity which belongs to the world of light. Unless all the impurities, outer and inner, open and hidden, are purified, the *salik* will have no chance of attending the Presence (of Allah).

Thus, the first kind of impurities is that of the outer instruments and powers of the soul which may be polluted with obstinacies and acts of disobedience to "the Benefactor" [*waliyy un-niam*] This is an apparent snare of *Iblis*. As long as man is trapped in this snare, he is deprived of being in Allah's Presence and attaining His Proximity. No one may have the notion that without purifying the outside of his kingdom he can reach the state of the truth of humanity, or he can purify his inner heart, as this will be a Satanic vanity and of *Iblis"*big tricks. This is because the heart"'s impurity and darkness will be increased by disobediences, which mark the triumph [*ghalabah*] of nature over spirituality. Unless the *salik* conquers the kingdom of the outside, he will remain deprived of inner conquests, which are the big objective, and no way will be opened for him to happiness. Thus, one of the big obstacles of this *suluk* is the impurities of the acts of disobedience, which must be purged and purified with the water of sincere repentance.

It should also be noted that all the external and internal powers which Allah, the Exalted, has bestowed upon us from the invisible world are divine deposits free from all impurities and are purged and purified, and even illuminated with the light of the God-given disposition, and excluded from Satan"'s dark and impure influence. Yet, since they have descended in the dark abode of the world of nature, and the influential hands of the devil of imagination and fancy have reached them, they have deviated from the original purity and primary disposition, and got polluted with diverse Satanic filths and impurities. So, if the *salik* to Allah could, by adhering to the care of Allah"'s *Wali*, repel Satan"'s influence, purge the kingdom of the outside and return the divine trusts as they had been given to him with no treason, he would be forgiven and protected, and, as far as the outside is concerned, he need not worry, and then he would turn to the inside to purge it from the impurities of corrupt moralities. This is the second kind of impurity, which is more corrupt and more difficult to cure, and thus, it is more important to the people of austerity, because as long as the inner moralities of the soul are corrupt and encircled by spiritual impurities, it will not deserve the state of holiness and "the private place of intimacy" [*khalwat-i uns*], as the origin of the corruption of the exterior kingdom of the soul is its corrupt morals and its vile habits. And, unless the *salik* changes his vile habits to good ones, he will not be safe from the evil acts. If he is successful in repentance (while still having vile habits), its stability—which is a matter of grave importance—cannot be achieved. So, the outer purification depends on the inner purification, besides the fact that the interior impurities cause deprivation of happiness, and originate the Hell of morals, which, as the people of knowledge say, is worse and more intense in burning than the Hell of deeds. This question has frequently been mentioned in the *hadith*s of the infallible *Ahl al-Bayt* (a).

Therefore, it is a must for the *salik* to Allah to carry out this purgation. After he has cleansed his soul of the corrupting impurities of the morals with the pure water of useful knowledge and lawful, good austerity, he will have to set upon purifying the heart, the capital which, if reformed, all kingdoms will be reformed, and if it is corrupt, all will be corrupt. The impurities of the world of the heart are the origin of all impurities, such as being attached to other than Allah, to oneself and to this world. This is originated by the love of this world, which is at the head of all sins, and by self-love, which is the mother of all diseases. As long as the roots of this love are still deep in the heart of the *salik*, he will see no marks of the love of Allah in it, and he will find no way to his destination and objective. So, as long as there are remnants of this love in the heart, his journey will not be to Allah, but to the self, to the world, and to Satan. So, being purged of the love of self and of the world is the first stage of purifying the journey to Allah in reality, because before this purgation the journey would not be to Allah, and it would be a sort of carelessness to refer to *salik* and *suluk* in this instance.

After this stage there are other stages, after which there will appear a model of Attar''s *Seven Cities of Love*, the reciter of which, as a *salik*, could see himself at the bend of a lane, while we remain behind walls and thick veils, and think that those "cities" and "kings" are nothing but of the weavings of our presumption. I have nothing to do with Shaykh Attar or Maytham at-Tammar, but I do not deny the original (gnostic) stations, and I cordially love their owners, and, by this love, I hope to be relieved. You yourself be whom you may, and bind yourself to whom you like.

The pretender wanted to come to look at the Beloved [Friend], The hand of the invisible came and pushed off the stranger.[98]

But I do not approve of disloyalty by brethren in faith and by spiritual friends to the gnostic friends, and I will not refrain from offering advice, which is the right of the believers to one another.

---

[98] A poem by Hafiz. In the printed copies it is stated: "...to come to the show place of the Secret."

At the top of the spiritual impurities, which cannot be purged even with the seven seas, and which caused despair to the great prophets (*a*), is the impurity of "the compound ignorance" [*jahl-i murakkab*], which is the origin of the incurable disease of denying the stations of the people of Allah and of knowledge, and is the source of doubting the people of the heart. As long as man is polluted with such impurities, he will not take a step towards knowledge [*maarif*], or rather, this impurity so often extinguishes the inborn light [*nur*] of disposition, which is the light [*chiragh*] for the road of guidance, and puts out the fire of love, which is the heavenly horse [*buraq*] for ascending to high stations, causing man to eternally stick to the earth of nature.

Therefore, it is necessary for man, through thinking about the status of the prophets and the perfect holy men [*awliya*] (*a*), and by contemplating their stations, to wash those impurities away from his heart, and not to be satisfied with the status he is in, because this satisfaction with the knowledge [*maarif*] one has, and remaining stagnant, are of the great tricks of *Iblis* and the evil-commanding soul. We take refuge in Allah from them. Now, as this thesis is written according to the taste of the common people, I refrain from the three purifications of the holy men [*awliya*]. And praise be to Allah.

CONCERNING THE STAGES
OF PURIFICATION
Chapter Two

Know that as long as man is in the world of nature and in the abode of the primary [*hayulani*] matter, he is under the rule of the divine soldiers and the Satanic soldiers. The divine soldiers are the soldiers of mercy, safety, happiness, light, purity, and perfection. The soldiers of *Iblis* are on the opposite side. But as the divine aspects have mastery over the satanic aspects, at the beginning, man"s disposition possesses natural divine light, safety and happiness, as is openly stated in the noble *hadith*s and hinted at in the noble divine Book.[99] As long as man is in this world, he can, on his own free will, put himself at the disposal of either of the two. So, if from the beginning of the God-given disposition till the end, Satan had no way of intruding, man would be divine, luminous from head to foot with purity and happiness, his heart being the light of Allah, observing nothing but Allah. His inward and outward powers would be luminous and pure, and no one would use them but Allah, and Satan would have no share in them, nor would his soldiers be able to control him. Such an honorable being is absolute purity and pure light, and his past faults and the future ones are forgiven.[100] He is an absolute conqueror, enjoying the station of original "great infallibility" [*ismat-i kubra*], and the other infallibles have the same station as the followers of that sacred essence. He is the Seal of the Prophets and possesses the station of absolute perfection. His vicegerents, though of separate substance,

---

[99] For example, the noble verse: **"So set your face to the religion, as a man of pure faith—Allah"s nature upon which He originated mankind."** (*Surah ar-Rum* 30:30). See the *hadith*s in *Bihar al-Anwar*, vol. 3, p. 276; vol. 64, p. 130, and in *At-Tawhid*, ch. 53, p. 321.

[100] A hint at the noble verse: **"...That Allah may forgive your past faults and those to come."** (*Surah al-Fath* 48:2).

join him in disposition and completely follow him in absolute infallibility. As to some of the infallible prophets and holy men [*awliya*] (*a*), they have no absolute infallibility and are not protected against Satan's intrusion, such as Adam's act with respect to the "tree," which was one of the intrusions of the great *Iblis*, the chief of the *Iblis*es, and despite the fact that the "tree" was a paradisiac divine tree, yet it was marked by a multiplicity of names, which is contrary to the state of complete humanity. This is one of the meanings, or of the ranks, of "the forbidden tree".

If the light of the divine disposition was polluted with the formal and spiritual impurities, it would be at a distance from the court of the Proximity and "the Presence of Love" [*hadrat-i uns*] in proportion to its pollution, until the light of disposition completely goes out, and the kingdom becomes altogether Satanic, and its inside and outside, secret and open, are put at the disposal of Satan. Thus, Satan becomes its heart, ear (hearing), eye (seeing), hand, and leg, and all his other organs become Satanic. If somebody reaches this stage— Take refuge in Allah from it—he becomes absolutely wretched and will never see the face of happiness. Between these two limits there are so many stages which only Allah, the Exalted, knows. Whoever is nearer to the horizon of prophethood, is of "those on the right hand" [*ashab-i yamin*], and whoever is nearer to the satanic horizon, is of "those on the left hand" [*ashab-i yasar*].

It should be noted, however, that even after the pollution of the inborn disposition, it is possible to purify it. As long as man is still in this world he can get out of Satan's domain and can easily join the party of Allah's angels, who are the soldiers of the divine mercy. The reality of *jihad-i nafs* [self-struggle]—which, according to the Messenger of Allah (*s*), is more meritorious than struggling against the enemies of the religion, and is the greater *jihad*[101]—is this getting out of Satan's domain and entering the domain of Allah's soldiers.

So, the first stage of purity is the observance of divine laws and the obedience to Allah's commands.

The second stage is to be adorned with virtuous morals and faculties.

The third stage is the purity of the heart, which means submitting the heart to Allah, after which the heart becomes luminous,

---

[101] *Bihar al-Anwar*, vol. 67, p. 65; vol. 19, p. 182.

or rather it becomes of the world of light and a degree of divine light. The luminosity of the heart flows to other organs and inner powers, and the whole kingdom turns into light, and light upon light, till the heart becomes divine and godly and the Divinity [*hadrat-i lahut*] manifests in all the inner and outer stages. In this case, servitude completely vanishes and is annihilated, and Lordship explicitly appears, in which case, the heart of the *salik* is overcome by a state of tranquility and familiarity, and he loves the whole world, and experiences divine trances, and the sins and faults become forgivable to him, and will be covered by the shelter of "love manifestations" [*tajalliyat-i hubbi*, and primary holiness [*wilayat*] begins to appear in him, and he becomes worthy of attending "the Presence of Intimacy" [*mahdar-i uns*]. Then, there are other stages, mentioning which does not suit these papers.

THE CORDIAL DISCIPLINES OF THE *SALIK* WHEN COMING TO WATER FOR PURIFICATION
Chapter Three

In this chapter we translate a noble *hadith* from *Misbah ash-Shariah* so that the pure hearts of the people of faith may get from it some lumination.

It is stated in *Misbah ash-Shariah* that Imam as-Sadiq (*a*) said: "When you intend purification and *wudu* [ritual ablution], proceed to the water as you proceed to Allah''s mercy, because Allah has made water the key to His proximity and supplication, and a guide to the court of His service. And, as Allah''s mercy purifies the sins of the servants, similarly the outer filths are purified by water and by nothing else. Allah, the Exalted, says: **"And He it is Who sends the winds as good news heralding His mercy, and We send down purifying water from the sky"** (*Surah al-Furqan* 25:48). He also says: **"And We made every living thing of water. Will they not then believe?"** (*Surah al-Anbiya* 21:30). So, as He has given life with water to everything of the blessings of this world, likewise, He has made obedience the life of the hearts, out of His mercy and grace. Think of the clarity, softness, purity and blessing of water and of its tender mixing with everything. Use it to purge the organs that Allah has ordered you to purify, and observe their disciplines in His obligations and advantages. So, if you use them respectfully, the springs of the advantages will burst out for you presently. Then, mix with the creatures (servants) of Allah like the mixture of water with things: It gives to everything its due without any change in its own meaning. And learn a lesson from the Messenger of Allah (*s*) (who said): "A sincere believer is like water." Let your clearness with Allah, the Most High, be like the clearness of water as He sent it down from the sky and called it "purifier" [*tahur*]. Purify your heart with fear of Allah [*taqwa*] and certitude [*yaqin*] as you cleanse your organs with water."[102]

In this noble *hadith* there are delicate points and facts, which enliven the hearts of the people of knowledge, and bestow animation on the clear souls of "the people of heart" [*ashab-i qulub*].

Describing water, in this *hadith*, as Allah''s mercy, or interpreting it to be so, denotes that water is one of the great manifestations of Allah''s mercy, which He sent down to the world of nature, and made it the source of life for the beings. Rather, the vast divine mercy, which descended from the high heaven of His Names and Attributes, and with which the lands of the individual entities [*taayyunat-i ayan*] were revived, is called "water" by the people of knowledge. And as the vast divine mercy is more obvious in the apparent substance of water than in other things, Allah, the Exalted, has assigned to it the task of purifying the outer filths, and made it the key to the door of His proximity and of the supplications to Him, and the guide to the court of His service, which is the door of the doors of the inner mercies. Actually, the water of Allah''s mercy descends and appears in every growth [*nashah*] of existence and in every visible and invisible scene to purify the sins of Allah''s servants according to that growth [*nashah*] and suitable to that world. So, the invisible sins of the individual entities are purified with the water of mercy which descends from the heaven of His Oneness [*ahadiyyat*], and the sins of the non-existence of "the outer quiddities" [*mahiyyat-i kharijiyyah*] are purged with the water of the vast mercy descending from the heaven of His Unity [*wahidiyyat*] in every stage of existence according to that stage. In the stages of human growths [*nashaat*], too, the water of mercy has different manifestations, as with the water descending from His Essence onto "the purgatorial collective individuations" [*taayyunat-i jamiyyat-i barzakhiyyah*] the sins of the "existential secret" [*sirr-i wujudi*] are purified: "Your existence is a sin incomparable with any other sin." With the water descending from His Names and Attributes and the manifestation of Act, the vision of the attribute and the act is purged. With the water descending from the sky of His "Decree of Justice" [*hukm-i adl*] the inner moral impurities are purified. With the water descending from the sky of His Forgiveness the sins of the servants are purged. And with the water descending from the sky of

---

[102] *Misbah ash-Shariah*, ch. 10, on "Purification".

"the kingdom of heaven" [*malakut*] the formal impurities are purged. So, it is clear that Allah, the Exalted has made water the key to His proximity and the guide to His court of mercy. Then, in the noble *hadith* there is another instruction, which opens another way to the people of *suluk* and of observance. It says: "...Think of the clarity, softness, purity and blessing of water and of its tenderly mixing with everything. Use it to purge the organs, which Allah has ordered you to purify, and observe their disciplines in His obligations and traditions, as under each one there are many advantages. So, if you use them respectfully, the springs of the advantages will burst out for you presently."

This noble *hadith* refers to the degrees of purity in general and puts it in four general degrees, of which one is that which is mentioned so far in the noble *hadith*, i.e. purifying the organs. It also notes that the people of observance and the *salik*s to Allah should not stop at the apparent form of the things. They have to regard the appearance as a mirror reflecting the inside, to detect the facts from the forms and not to be satisfied with formal purification, which is a satanic snare. So, in the purity of water they discover the purity of the organs, which they have to purge and clarify by way of performing the obligatory duties and the divine laws, whose fineness is to be used to make fine the organs and to take them out of the coarseness of disobedience, and to let purity and blessing flow into all the organs. And, from the tenderly mixing of water with things, they realize how the divine heavenly powers are mixed with the world of nature, preventing the impurities of nature from affecting them. When the organs are clothed with the divine obligations and laws and their disciplines, the inner advantages gradually appear, the springs of the divine secrets burst out and a part of the secrets of servitude and purity uncover themselves for the *salik*. After explaining the first stage of purification and its instruction, the *hadith* gives the secondary instruction, saying: "...then mix with the creatures (servants) of Allah like the mixture of water with things: It gives to everything its due without any change in its own meaning. And learn a lesson from the Messenger of Allah (*s*) (who said): "A sincere believer is like water." "

The first instruction concerns the *salik*'s managing his organs and inner powers. The second instruction mentioned in this noble *hadith* concerns man's relation with Allah's creatures. This is a comprehensive instruction telling how the *salik*'s behavior with the creatures should be, which is also an implication of the reality of privacy [*khalwat*]; that is, the traveler to Allah, while treating each group of the people with kindness, giving them their natural dues, and dealing with anyone of them according to his disposition, is to strictly observe the divine rights, and never to lose his own meaning, which is servitude and attending to Allah. At the same time of being in multiplicity [*kathrat*], he is to be in privacy [*khalwat*], and his heart—which is the lodging of the Beloved—is to be free from others and empty of all designs and paintings. Then the *hadith* refers to the third instruction, which concerns the *salik*'s connection with Allah, the Exalted. It says: "Let your clearness with Allah, the Most High, be like the clearness of water when He sent it down from the sky and called it „purifier" [*tahur*]."

That is, the traveler to Allah should be free from the intrusion of nature, and its impurity and darkness should not be allowed into his heart, and all his acts of worship should be free from all external and internal polytheism. As the water is pure when descending from the sky, and the hands of impurity have not extended to it, the heart of the *salik*, which has descended pure from the heaven of the invisible, is to be protected against the intrusion of Satan and nature, and to be prevented from being polluted with the impurities. After this instruction, the *hadith* comes to the last and the comprehensive instruction for the people of austerity and of *suluk*. It says: "Purify your heart with fear of Allah and certitude as you cleanse your organs with water."

Here is a reference to two lofty stations of the people of knowledge: one is "God-fearing," which is perfected by abandoning everything other than Allah. The other is certitude, which is perfected by discerning the Presence of the Beloved.

CONCERNING THE PURIFIER
Chapter Four

The "purifier" is either water—which is, in this respect, basic—or "earth".

Know that the traveler to Allah, generally speaking, has two ways to take him to the loftiest goal, the station of proximity to the Divinity: The first of them, which is the principal and original one, is the journey to Allah by turning towards the Absolute Mercy, especially the compassionate mercy, which is the compassion that takes every being to its appropriate perfection. It is of this kind of compassionate mercy that the prophets (a) were sent to lead on the roads and to help those lagging behind. To the people of knowledge and the people of heart, the House of Realization is the form of divine mercy. The creatures are perpetually and completely drowned in the oceans of Allah"s mercy, yet they do not make use of it. The Great Divine Book—which has descended from the divine invisible world and the proximity of the Lord, and has appeared in the form of words and speech so that we, the deserted, the prisoners in the jail of nature and put in the fetters of the crooked chains of the soul"s desires and whims, make use of it and rescue ourselves—is one of the greatest manifestations of the absolute divine mercy, of which, we, the blind and deaf, have in no way made use. The Messenger—the Seal of the prophets, the honorable absolute guardian, who came from the Sacred Presence of the Lord and the company of the divine proximity and familiarity to this abode of estrangement and dread, where he had to keep company with the people like Abu Jahl (the Prophet"s uncle and his bitter enemy) or even worse, and whose sigh: "...My heart is enveloped by a cover of dust..."[103] has burnt the hearts of the people of knowledge and friendship—is Allah"s vast mercy and the divine

---

[103] Refer to footnote 88.

absolute generosity, who had come into his (worldly) body as an all-embracing mercy for the dwellers of this lower world, in order to take them out of this abode of terror and estrangement, like a "ring-dove"[104] which throws itself into the net of blight to save its flock.

The traveler to Allah should take the purification with the water of mercy as a form of using the descending divine mercy, and to make use of it as long as it is possible for him to do so. Should his hand become short of it, because of inertia or negligence, and be bereaved of the water of mercy, he would have but to pay attention to his own humility, indigence, poverty and destitution. When he has in full view of his humility of servitude and is aware of his need, his poverty and his own potentiality, and discards his haughtiness, conceit and selfishness, a door of mercy opens to him, and the earth of (his) nature changes into the white earth of mercy, and becomes the dust which is one of the "two purifiers",[105] and becomes the object of Allah's mercy and kindness. The stronger this state in man, i.e., his awareness of his humility, the more he receives of mercy. Should he decide to depend on himself and on his action in his journey, he would perish, since there might be no one to extend help to him, like an infant which boldly starts walking alone, taking pride in its own steps, and depending on its own ability, without its father offering it any help, rather leaving it to itself. But when it recognizes its inability and inefficiency, it turns to its affectionate father, distrusting its own power, and entrusts itself to the care of its father, who offers his help, hugs it and guides it step by step to walking. So, it is better for the traveler to Allah to break the leg of his journey and completely renounce his self-confidence, austerity and action, and abolish himself, his power and ability. He should always remember his mortality and dependence in order to become an object of Allah's care, and to cover a hundred-year distant road in a single night by the attraction of the Lord, and the tongue of his inside and his state say, in the Presence of the Lord's Sanctity, imploringly and helplessly: **"Oh, Who responds**

---

[104] See *Kalilah wa Dimnah*, ch. "Ring-Dove."

[105] It refers to a narrative related by the late Akhund Khurasani (may Allah sanctify his soul) in *Kifayat al-Usul*, vol. 1, p. 130, to the effect that: "Dust is one of the two purifiers, and is enough for you for ten years."

to the distressed, when he calls unto Him, and removes the evil...?"[106]

---

[106] *Surah an-Naml* 27: 62.

SOME DISCIPLINES OF THE *WUDU* (RITUAL ABLUTION) IN RESPECT OF THE INTERIOR AND THE HEART
Chapter Five

Imam ar-Rida (*a*) is quoted to have said: "The servant has been commanded to perform the *wudu* (ritual ablution) so as to be pure when standing before the All-Powerful and supplicating, and by obeying Him, to be purged from filth and impurity, beside his removing laziness, expelling sleep and purifying the heart to stand in the Presence of the All-Powerful. Confining it (the *wudu*) only to the face, the two hands, the head and the two feet, was because when the servant stands before the All-Powerful, the parts which are exposed are those which are ordered to be washed in the *wudu*: as with his face he performs the *sujud* (prostration), with his hands he requests, desires, dreads and supplicates, with his head he inclines to Him in his *ruku* (bowing down) and his *sujud*, and with his legs he stands and sits..."[107]

Up to here he explained the principal point in the *wudu*, informing the people of knowledge and *suluk* that to stand in the holy Presence of Allah, the Glorified and Most High, and to offer supplication to the Provider of Needs, require certain disciplines which should be observed. One must not appear in His Presence even with the external filths and impurities and with a sleepy eye, let alone with a heart, which is filled with dirts, and it is afflicted with spiritual impurities, which are the origin of all impurities. Despite the fact that a narrative says: "Allah, the Exalted, does not look at your faces, but He looks at your hearts,"[108] and despite the fact that the means with which man attends to Allah, the Exalted, and what is, in the worlds of

---

[107] *Uyunu Akhbar ar-Rida*, vol. 2, ch. 34, *hadith* 1, p. 104.
[108] *Bihar al-Anwar*, vol. 67, p. 241, quoting *Jami al-Akhbar*, p. 117 (with a slight difference).

creation, worthy of looking at His Majesty, Greatness and Glory, is the heart, while the other organs have no share in it, yet, they did not neglect the outer cleanliness. So, they decided the external purification for cleaning man"s exterior, and the inner purification for cleaning his interior. In this noble *hadith*, it is clear from assigning the purification of the heart to be a result of the *wudu* that the *wudu* has an interior with which man"s interior is purified, and meanwhile it appears that there is a connection between the exterior and the interior, the visible and the invisible. Similarly, it becomes clear that the outer cleanliness, the outside *wudu*, is the act of worship, and of obeying the Lord. Therefore, the purification of the outside results in the purification of the inside, and purging the exterior leads to the purity of the interior. Generally, the traveler to Allah must, at the time of *wudu* be aware of his being about to stand in the Presence of Allah, the Almighty, as with such states of heart as he has, he does not deserve to be in His Presence, or he may even be dismissed from the Presence of the Lord, the Most High. Thus, he must get ready to have his outer purification transferred to his interior, and to purify his heart—which is the object of Allah"s attention, or, actually, is the lodging of His Sanctity—from all that is other than Allah, and to take out from his head any notion of arrogance and I-ness, which is the origin of the origins of the impurities, so as to become worthy of His Presence. After that, Imam ar-Rida (*a*) explains the reason for specifying certain organs to *wudu*. He says:

"Confining it only to the face, the two hands, the head and the two feet, was because when the servant stands before the All-Powerful, the parts which are exposed are those which are ordered to be washed in the *wudu*: as with his face he performs the *sujud* (prostration), with his hands he requests, desires, dreads and supplicates, with his head he inclines to Him in his *ruku* (bowing down) and his *sujud*, and with his legs he stands and sits..."

The gist of his discourse is that these organs take part in worshipping Allah, and it is through these organs that worship is manifested. Consequently, it is necessary to purify them. Then he refers to those acts of worship which appear from them, opening the way of their being valid and useful to the deserving people, and making the people of knowledge familiar with these secrets that the organs on which servitude appears in Allah"s Blessed Presence, should be clean and purified, as the outer limbs and organs of the body, which have a deficient share of those meanings, would not be worthy of that station without purification. Although submission is not, actually, a character of the face, and none of requesting, desiring, dreading, supplicating and facing the *qiblah* belongs to any of the tangible organs, yet, as these organs are the manifestations of those meanings, they must be purified. Therefore, purifying the heart, which is the real place of servitude, and the actual center of those meanings, is more necessary. Without its purification, the external organs will never be purified even if they are washed in the seven seas, and it (the heart) will not deserve being in the Presence of Allah. Actually, Satan will have a hand in it, and it will be dismissed from His Glorious Presence.

Connection: In an authorized narrative in *Ilal ash-Sharai* it is thus related: "A group of Jews came to the Messenger of Allah (*s*) and asked him questions. Among their questions they asked: "Tell us, O Muhammad, why are these four organs given the *wudu*, while they are the cleanest parts of the body?" The Messenger of Allah (*s*) said: "When Satan whispered to Adam (*a*) and he came near the „tree" and looked at it, he lost face. He stood up and walked to it—the first step taken towards sinning. He took with his hand some of what was on it and ate it. Off his body flew what were on him of jewelry and apparel. He put his hand on the top of his head and wept. Allah accepted his repentance, but made it incumbent upon him and his offspring to purify those four organs. So, Allah ordered the face to be washed, because it looked at the „tree". He ordered the hands to be washed to the elbows, because he took with them (the fruit of the tree). He ordered the head to be wiped (with the hand wet with water), as he put his hand on the top of his head, and He ordered the feet to be wiped because with them he walked to sin."[109]

Concerning the reason for imposing fasting, there is also a noble *hadith* to the effect that the Jews asked him: "What caused Allah to impose on your people to fast for thirty days?" He said: "It was Adam (*a*), because what he had eaten from that „tree" remained in his stomach for thirty days. So Allah made it incumbent upon him and his offspring to endure hunger and thirst for thirty days, and He allowed them, out of His kindness, to eat and drink at the nights."[110]

---

[109] *Ilal ash-Shara'i*, vol. I, ch. 191, *hadith* 1, p. 280.
[110] *Ibid.*, vol. 2, ch. 109, *hadith* 1, p. 378.

These noble *hadith*s give the people of allusion and the people of heart to understand many points: Although Adam"s sin was not like the sins of the others, as it might have been a natural one, or a sin of being inclined to multiplicity, the tree of nature, or of attending to multiplicity of names after the attraction [*jadhibah*] of self-annihilation [*fana-i dhati*], yet it was not expected from one like Adam (*a*) who was Allah"s chosen one [*safiyy*] and distinguished by proximity [*qurb*] and self-annihilation. Therefore, according to the love-zeal [*ghayrat-i hubbi*] of His Sanctified Essence, He announced his disobedience and going astray to all the worlds and on the tongues of all the prophets (*a*). He, the Exalted, said: "And Adam disobeyed his Lord, so he went astray."[111] Thus, so much cleaning and purification were needed for him (Adam) and his offspring who were hidden in his loin and (so) participated in the sin, though they did participate (in it) after coming out of the loin, too.

Therefore, the sin committed by Adam and his offspring has many degrees and manifestations. The first of those degrees is paying attention to multiplicity of names, and the last of those manifestations is eating from the forbidden tree, the invisible [*malakuti*] form of which is a tree that carries diverse sorts of fruits. And its visible [*mulki*] form is its nature and affairs, and the love of this world and the self, as seen now in his offspring, is of the affairs of the same inclination to that tree and eating from it. Similarly, for their cleaning, purifying, cleansing, *salat* and fasting—for the redemption of the father"s sin, which is the origin—there are many degrees in proportion to the degrees of the sin. From this explanation it is understood that all kinds of disobedience of the children of Adam are related to eating from the „tree", and are purified in a certain way. All their sins of the heart are also related to that tree, and are purified in a certain way. Then, all kinds of spiritual sins are related to it, too, and are purified in a certain way.

Purifying the external organs is the „shadow" [*zill*] of the purity of the heart and spirit for the perfect. It is an order, and a „means" to them, for the people of *suluk*. As long as man is within the veil of the individuation [*taayyun*] of the organs and their purification, and he lingers there, he cannot be of the people of the *suluk*, and is still in the sin. But if he engaged himself in passing through the stages of external

---

[111] *Surah Ta-Ha* 20:121.

and internal purifications, and used the formal and outer purifications as a means of purifying the spirit and the heart, and in all the acts of worship and rites he observed their spiritual aspects and was benefited by them, or better, if he gave more importance to the internal aspects and regarded them to be the highest objective, he would be admitted through the door of the *suluk* along the road of humanity, as is referred to in a noble *hadith* in *Misbah ash-Shariah*: "...And purify your heart with *taqwa* (fear of Allah) and *yaqin* (certitude) when you cleanse your organs with water."[112]

So, a *salik* man needs first a scientific *suluk* so as to distinguish, with the blessings of "the people of remembrance" [*ahl-i dhikr*] (a), the stages of servitude, and regard the formal worship inferior to the spiritual and inner worship. Then the practical *suluk*, which is the reality of the *suluk* has started. The aim of this *suluk* is to free the soul from other than Allah, and adorn it with the manifestations of His Names and Essence. Getting to this stage, the *salik* would be at the end of his journey, attaining the goal of his progress to perfection, and acquiring the secrets of austerity and worship, as well as the delicacies of *suluk*. Those are the manifestations of Majesty, which are the secrets of purity, and the manifestations of Beauty, which are the objective of other worships. To give the details is beyond the capacity of these pages.

---

[112] *Misbah ash-Shariah*, ch. 10 on "Purity".

CONCERNING THE *GHUSL* AND ITS CORDIAL DISCIPLINES
Chapter Six

"The people of knowledge" [*ahl-i marifat*] say that the (state of) *janabah* (major ritual impurity) is getting out of the homeland of servitude and entering exile [*ghurbat*]. It is "declaring lordship" [*izhar-i rububiyyat*] and claiming I-ness and entering within the frame [*hudud*] of the Patron [*mawla*] and acquiring the quality of mastery [*siyadat*]. The *ghusl* (ritually washing the whole body) is a purification of this filth and a confession of the shortcoming. One of the religious personalities has enumerated one hundred and fifty states, in ten chapters, saying that the *salik* should purify himself from them during his practicing the *ghusl*. Most of them, or rather all of them, stem from might [*izzat*], power [*jabarut*] and haughtiness of the soul, selfishness, and self-conceit.[113]

The writer says that the (state of) *janabah* is vanishing [*fana*] in nature and neglecting spirituality. It is the ultimate end of the complete sovereignty of animality and bestiality, and falling down to the lowest of the low. The *ghusl* is purging from this sin, turning away from the rule of nature, and attaining the divine authority and power. This is brought about by cleansing the whole kingdom of the soul, which has vanished in nature and been afflicted with Satan"s conceit.

So, its cordial disciplines are that the traveler to Allah, at the time of *ghusl*, should not stop at the outer purification and washing the body, as it is a low superficial crust and belongs to this world. His paying attention to the *janabah* of the inside of the heart and the secret of the spirit and purifying them from that impurity should be more important to him. Therefore, he must avoid letting his bestial soul and

---

[113] He refers to Shaykh Muhyi "d-Din ibn al-Arabi in his *al-Futuhat al-Makkiyyah*, vol. 1, p. 363.

animal concern [*shan*] overpower the human soul and the divine concerns [*shuun-i rahmani*], and to repent of Satanic impurity and arrogance, and to purify the inside of the spirit which is a divine blow breathed in him by "the Breath of the Compassionate" [*nafas-i rahmani*], from Satanic tastes, which mean paying attention to other than Allah, being the root of the forbidden tree, so that he may deserve his father Adam''s Paradise. He must also know that eating of this tree of nature, desiring this world and attending to multiplicity are the origins of *janabah*, and, unless he purifies himself from this *janabah* by immersion in, or by complete purification with, the water of Allah''s mercy, which flows from the pillar [*saq*] of the Divine *Arsh* and is free from Satan''s intrusion, he will not be fit for the *salat*, which is the reality of ascension to (Allah''s) proximity, as there can be no *salat* without purification.[114] This is referred to in the noble *hadith* in *al-Wasail*, quoting Shaykh as-Saduq (may Allah be pleased with him), who said with authorities:

"A group of Jews came to the Messenger of Allah (*s*). The most learned among them asked him some questions. Among his questions was: "What for did Allah command that one should perform *ghusl* because of the *janabah*, but He did not command it after relieving oneself from feces and urine? The Messenger of Allah (*s*) said: "When Adam (*a*) ate from the (forbidden) tree, it crept into his veins, hair and skin." During sexual intercourse water would come out of every vein and hair in his body. So, Allah made it incumbent upon his offspring to perform the *ghusl* of the *janabah* till the Day of Resurrection...["115] as the narrative goes.

In another narrative, Imam ar-Rida (*a*) said: "They were ordered to perform the *ghusl* because of the *janabah*, but they were not ordered to do it after the *khala* (relieving oneself from feces and urine), though it is filthier than the *janabah*, because the *janabah* pertains to the soul of man, and what comes out is something from the whole body, while the *khala* does not pertain to the soul of man, and

---

[114] *Wasa'il ash-Shiah*, vol. 1, "Book of Purification," sec. on "*Wudu*'," ch. 4, *hadith* 1, p. 261.

[115] *Ibid.*, sec. on "*Janabah*," ch. 2, *hadith* 2, p. 466, quoted from *Man la Yahduruh al-Faqih*, vol. 1, p. 22; *Al-Majalis*, p. 115; *Al-Ilal*, p. 104.

what comes out is the food that goes in through an inlet and comes out from an outlet."[116]

The appearance of these *hadith*s to "the people of the appearance" [*ashab-i zahir*] denotes that as the semen is from the whole body, the whole body needs the *ghusl*, and this coincides with the opinion of a number of physicians and natural philosophers. But giving it the cause of eating from the tree, as in the first *hadith*, and ascribing the *janabah* to the soul, as in the second *hadith*, open a way to information for the people of knowledge and allusion, because the question of the „tree" and Adam"s eating of it are of the secrets of the sciences of the Quran and the infallible *Ahl al-Bayt* (*a*), in which many sciences are occult. For this reason in the noble *hadith*s the causes of legislating many rituals are ascribed to the said case of the „tree" and Adam"s eating of it, such as the *wudu, salat, ghusl*, fasting during the month of Ramadan and its being thirty days, and many of the *hajj* rituals. The writer has for many years been thinking of writing a thesis on this subject, but other engagements have prevented that. I ask Allah, the Exalted, success and happiness.

Generally speaking, you are an offspring of Adam, a seed for meeting (Allah) and created for knowing (Him). Allah, the Exalted, has chosen you for Himself and has shaped you with His two hands of Beauty and Majesty, and told the angels to fall down bowing to you, and caused *Iblis* to envy you. So if you want to get out of the state of the *janabah* of your father, who is your origin, and to be worthy to meet the Beloved [*hadrat-i mahbub*] and to become ready to attain "the state of familiarity" [*maqam-i uns*] and "the Presence of the Divine Sanctity" [*hadrat-i quds*], you are to ritually wash the interior of your heart with the water of mercy, and to repent from attending to this world, which is of the manifestations [*mazahir*] of the forbidden tree, and to completely wash your heart, which is the meeting place of the Beautiful and the Beauty of the Majestic, from loving the world and its evil affairs, which are Satanic impurities, for the paradise of meeting the *Haqq* (Allah) is a place for the pure: "No one enters Paradise except the pure."[117]

---

[116] *Ibid., hadith* 4, quoted from *al-Ilal*, vol. 1, p. 281 and *Uyunu Akhbar ar-Rida*, p. 291.
[117] "Paradise is not entered except by the good." *Usul al-Kafi*, vol. 3, "Book on Faith and Disbelief," sec. on "Sins," *hadith* 7, p. 371.

"Wash yourself, then walk to the tavern."[118]

---

[118] *Wash yourself, then walk to the tavern,*
That this ruined convent may not be polluted by you.

Hafiz Shirazi

SOME CORDIAL DISCIPLINES FOR REMOVING FILTH AND PURIFYING IMPURITIES
Chapter Seven

Be aware that removing the *hadath* (impurity), as already stated, is getting out of I-ness and selfishness and parting with carnality [*nafsiyyat*] or rather it is complete separation from the house of the soul, since, as long as there are remnants of a servant"s self, he will be polluted with *al-hadath al-akbar* (the major impurity) and the worshipper and the worshipped in him are Satan and the soul. If the stages of the journey of the people of the Road and *suluk* were for getting ranks and ascension to high degrees, they would not be out of the intrusion of Satan and the soul, and the journey and *suluk* are justified [*muallal*]. Thus, the *suluk* is within the stages of the self, and the journey in the very inside of the house. Such a *salik* is not a *salik*, not a wayfarer, nor is he an emigrant to Allah and His Messenger, and he has not yet been purged from the major impurity, which is "the servant himself" [*ayn-i abd*]. Should he become completely purified from this *hadath*, the worshipper and the worshipped would be the *Haqq* [Allah], and "I would be his ear (hearing) and his eye (seeing),"[119] which is the result of the proximity by the *nafilah* (supererogatory act of worship), would take place. Therefore, as far as purification from the *hadath* is concerned, the *ghusl* of the whole body is necessary, because as long as "the very servant" [*ayn-i abd*] is still there in a way, the *hadath* is not yet removed, as "under each hair there is a *janabah*."[120]

---

[119] Refer to footnote 21.
[120] *Bihar al-Anwar*, vol. 78, "Book of Purification," sec. on "The Incumbency of the *Ghusl* of Janabah," *hadith* 23, p. 51.

So, purification from the *hadath* is purification from the *huduth* [novelty] and perishing in the sea of ancientness [*qidam*]. Its perfection is in getting out of the multiplicity of names, which is the interior of the „tree". By this getting out he will get out of Adam"s infectious sin, which is the origin [*asl*] of the offspring.

So, the *hadath* is of the spiritual impurities, and its purification is of the inner invisible affairs and is a light. *Wudu* is a limited light, while the *ghusl* is an absolute light. "Which *wudu* is purer than the *ghusl*?"[121]

But removing the external filth and impurities has no such position, because it is a superficial cleaning and an external purification. Its cordial discipline is that the wayfarer servant, who wants to be present in the Presence of Allah, is to know that with Satanic filth and impurity one cannot find his way there, and unless he comes out from the big moral dispraised acts, which are the source of the corruption of the human utopia, and the origin of the external and internal sins, he will have no way to the wanted goal.

Satan, who was in the neighborhood of the world of sanctity and was regarded of the cherubim, yet, at last, because of evil inclinations, he was dismissed from the position of the favorites, and was cursed by: **"Then get out of it, for surely you are accursed."** (*Surah Sad* 38:77 and *Surah al-Hijr* 15:34).

So, we, the survivors of the caravan of the invisible world, the sinking ones in the deep pit of nature, and the returned to the lowest of the low, how can we, with our Satanic, evil inclinations, deserve being in the Presence of His Sanctity and in the neighborhood of the godly and the companions of the favorites? Satan became self-conceited, recognized his being of fire, then said: **"I am better than him..."**[122] This self-admiration led to self-worship and arrogance, which drove him to despise and insult Adam (*a*), and said: **"...and him You created of dust,"** and made a false analogy. He did not see Adam"s goodness or his perfect spirituality. He looked only at Adam"s appearance, his being of clay and of dust, while of himself he looked at his being of fire, disregarding his polytheism of egoism and

---

[121] *Jami Ahadith ash-Shiah*, "Book of Purification," sec. on "The *Ghusl* and its Regulations," ch. 12.

[122] **"I am better than him. You have created me of fire, and him You created of dust."** (*Surah Sad* 38:76).

egotism. Self-love prevented him from discerning his shortcomings and hid his faults from his eyes. This selfishness and self-conceit led him to self-love, arrogance, ostentation, hypocrisy, obstinacy, and disobedience, driving him from the sacred ascension down to the desert of the abode of darkness of nature.

So, it is on the wayfarer to Allah, as he cleans himself from external filth, to purify himself from the origins of vileness and internal Satanic impurities, and thoroughly cleanse, with the divine water of mercy and lawful austerity, his utopia, his virtuous city, and purify his heart, the place of divine manifestation, and to take off the shoes of ambition and loving pomposity, so as to become worthy of entering the sacred valley of *ayman* and of being a place for the Lord''s manifestation. Unless he is cleaned from evil filths, purification from impurities [*ahdath*] cannot take place, as purifying the exterior is a preliminary step to the purification of the interior. Unless a complete, mundane and visible *taqwa* according to the instructions of the pure *shariah* happens, no cordial *taqwa* will take place; and unless the cordial *taqwa* is brought about by the already named affairs, no real, secret and spiritual *taqwa* can happen. All the stages of *taqwa* are preliminaries to this stage, which is neglecting everything other than Allah.

As long as there are in the *salik* remnants of selfishness, his heart will not discern Allah''s manifestation. It is, however, possible that sometimes, owing to the precedence of (Allah''s) mercy and the prevalence of the "near-to-Allah" [*yalillahi*] aspect, invisible help is extended to the *salik* such that the remnants of his I-ness are burnt out by the Divine firebrand [*jadhwah*]. It is probable that in the way Allah manifested His glory to the mountain, crushing it to pieces and in the falling down of Moses senseless, there are references to what has been said; and there is a similar difference between the *salik-i majdhub* (the *salik* attracted by Divine Grace), and the *majdhub-i salik* (the attracted one who is traveling to Allah). The people of truth understand from this an important point worthy of knowing, since knowing nothing about it would be the cause of many errors, goings astray and deviations from the right path. No one of those who are in quest of truth is to ignore it or be unaware of it. It is this: The *salik* who is in quest of truth must declare himself innocent from the extremities of some ignorant Sufis and some negligent phenomenalists, so that it may become possible for him to travel to Allah. As a matter of fact, some sects of the first group believe that the external knowledge and act are formal, and stuffed moulds, intended for the ignorant and the common people, and that those who are the people of the secret, heart and truth, and are of good background, need not practice such acts, and that the external acts are required for the purpose of acquiring cordial truths and attaining the looked-for destination, and so, when the *salik* reaches his destination, practicing those preliminaries will be departing, and engaging in the multiplicities will be a veil. The second group, on the other hand, rose to face the first group and went to the other end of extremity by denying all the spiritual stages and divine secrets, and rejected all affairs, except the mere external appearance and the superficial form, alleging that everything else is nothing but imagination and fancy. These two groups are still in dispute and argument, each one accusing the other of being against the *shariah*. In fact, both groups have somewhat exceeded the limits and they have gone to the extremes. In my *Sirr as-Salat* I have referred to this point, and I show, here, a moderate and middle way, which is the straight path.

It should be noted that the formal rituals and the external worships are not only for acquiring perfect spiritual characters and cordial truths, but that is actually one of their fruits. To the people of knowledge and of heart, all worships transfer the divine knowledge from the inside to the outside and from the secret to the public. And as the blessing of mercy of the Beneficent [*ar-rahman*], or rather of the Compassionate [*ar-rahim*], covers all human cordial and formal growths [*nashaat*] and each one of these stages has a share of the general divine blessings, each has to do a part of praising Allah, and thanking Him for the beneficent and merciful favors of His Absolute Necessary Being. As long as the soul has a share of the formal mundane growth [*nashaat*] as well as of the visible life, the carpet of multiplicity will not be completely rolled away, and the shares of nature will not be done with. As the traveler to Allah must not engage his heart with other than Allah, he is also not to make use of his bosom, imagination and nature in other than Allah's way, so that his *tawhid* (monotheism) and glorification may become firm in all the growths [*nashaat*]. And if the spiritual attraction has any result other than serving Allah and submission to Him, it will indicate that there are still some remnants of selfishness, and the *salik*'s journey is inside the house of the soul, and not to Allah.

The goal of the journey of the people of Allah is to color the nature and the kingdom of the body with Allah's color. There is a noble *hadith* in which Allah, the Great and Almighty, says: "I am Allah! I am *ar-Rahman* (the Beneficent)! I created *rahim* (the womb, relationship) and derived its name from Mine. So, whoever observed it (i.e., observed kinship relations), I would observe him, and whoever severed it, I would sever him."[123] One of the interior concepts of this *hadith* is, perhaps, this severing the nature, which is the mother of the spirits, off the original homeland, and observing (connecting) it is its austerity and returning it to its homeland of servitude. Abu Abdullah (as-Sadiq) (*a*) is quoted to have said: "I advise you to take care of your aunt, the date-palm, as it was created of Adam"s clay."[124] This noble *hadith* refers to that kinship relations mentioned before.

In short, taking out the kingdom of the exterior from the homeland of servitude, and leaving it to itself, is a deep ignorance of the stations of the people of knowledge, and is of the temptations of the accursed Satan who deviates each group from Allah, the Exalted, in a particular way. At the same time, denying the stations and blocking the way to knowledge, which is the delight of the eye of the holy men [*awliya*] (*a*), and confining the divine laws to the exterior, which is the world"s share, the kingdom of the self and the animal state, and disregarding the inner secrets and disciplines of worship—which result in purifying the inside, reforming the heart and developing the interior—are utmost ignorance and negligence. Both of these two groups are far away from the way of happiness and the straight path of humanity, and both are cut off from the stations of the people of knowledge. The one who is aware of Allah and knows the stations, must observe all the inner and outer rights and help everyone who has a right to get it. He must purify himself of exaggeration, fault and going to the extremes, remove the filth of denying the outside of the *shariah*, which is, in fact, limitation, and remove the filth of denying the inside of the *shariah*, which is restriction, and both of which are of the temptations of Satan and his treacheries, so that the road of traveling to Allah and attaining the spiritual stations become easy for him.

---

[123] *Bihar al-Anwar*, vol. 71, p. 95, quoted from *Maaniy al-Akhbar*, p. 302.
[124] *Ibid.*, vol. 66, p. 129, quoted from *al-Mahasin*, p. 528.

Thus, one of the stages of removing filth is removing the filths of the false fancies, which prevent Allah's proximity, and the ascension of the believers. One of the concepts and positions of the universality of the ultimate prophethood, or rather, of the proofs of the finality of the prophethood, is that he (the Last Prophet) attained, in all the spiritual states to all their rights and shares as regards all the affairs of the *shariah*. As in the knowledge of the affairs of the Lordship, the Glorified, He is known in the highest height and in the nearest nearness to the state of universality: **"He is the First and the Last and the Manifest and the Hidden,"**[125] **"Allah is the light of the heavens and the earth...,"**[126] "If you are lowered down with a rope to the lowest of the earth, you will come down onto Allah,"[127] and **"...Wherever you turn, there is Allah's Face...,"**[128] etc., through which the knower of the divine knowledge, attracted by the divine attractions, feels invisible delight and divine ecstasy. Similarly the practical-cordial monotheism is permeated into the last stage of the horizon of the nature and the corporeal body, and no being is deprived of a share of knowing Allah.

In short, the people of Sufism unknowingly speak of Isa's (Jesus') wisdom, while the phenomenalists speak of the wisdom of Moses. The *Muhammadan*s, however, are, by limitation, innocent of both of them. To expand on this brief is out of the question and does not suit these pages.

Connection:

Quoting Imam as-Sadiq (*a*) it is narrated in *Misbah ash-Shariah*, thus: "The *mustarah* (washing closet or toilet where one relieves oneself) is called so because the people are relieved there from the weights of the filths, and they clear out there the dirts and impurities. The believer learns from this that the pure of the ephemeral things of this world (i.e., food) will finally have such an (impure) end. Then, he will be relieved by abandoning this world and turning away from it. He empties his soul and his heart from being engaged with it, and disdains collecting and possessing it, as he disdains the impurities,

---

[125] *Surah al-Hadid* 57:3.
[126] *Surah an-Nur* 24:35.
[127] *Ilm al-Yaqin*, vol. 1, p. 54.
[128] *Surah al-Baqarah* 2:115.

the feces and filth. He thinks, of himself, how he is honored in an instance and feels humiliated in another. He then realizes that adhering to contentedness and *taqwa* gives him relief in both worlds, that comfort is in neglecting this world, in refraining from enjoying it and in removing the impurity of (wanting) the unlawful and the doubtful, and so, he closes the door of arrogance to himself after knowing it, runs away from sins, opens the door of modesty, remorse and shyness, strives to carry out His commands and to refrain from the forbidden, hoping for a good return and a delightful proximity. He imprisons himself in the prison of fear, patience and abstinence from (satisfying) the desires until he arrives, with Allah's custody, in the eternal abode, and tastes His pleasure, as this is what is reliable (counted), and everything else is nothing."[129] This is the end of his noble speech.

In this noble speech there is a comprehensive order for the people of knowledge and *suluk*, and it is that a conscious person, on his journey to the Last Abode, must, in whatever state he may be, demand all the spiritual pleasures, and not neglect, in any condition, to remember his ultimate goal and return. That is why the wise men have said: "The Prophet serves the (divine) decree [*qada*] as the physician serves the body." As the great prophets and holy men [*awliya*] (*a*) have no care whatsoever except for Allah's decree [*qada*] and the "near-to-Allah" [*yalillahi*] aspect, and the heavenly Kingdom [*malakut*] of the divine decree governs their hearts, they believe that the management of all affairs is in the hands of Allah's angels, who are the divine soldiers, while the physical physician, being far from this stage and discarded from this valley, ascribes the running of the affairs of nature to the natural powers.

In brief, a *salik* should, in all conditions, make use of all the aspects of his *suluk*. So, as he sees that the trivial matters and the pleasures of the visible world are destined to annihilation and change, and realizes that their fate is corruption and vanishing, he will easily have his heart turn away from them and free his heart from thinking of them and being engaged with them, and he will be disgusted with them as he is with filths. The inside of the world of nature is filthy. Filth and dirt seen in a dream—which is a door of revelation [*mukashafah*]—are interpreted to mean worldly positions and wealth, and, according to the

---

[129] *Misbah ash-Shariah*, ch. 9, on "Privy".

revelations [*mukashafah*] of Ali (*a*), this world is but a carrion.[130] So, as the believer empties himself from the loads and excretions of nature and relieves the natural town from their harm, he is also to relieve his heart from being attached to it (nature) and getting engaged with it. He is to remove from his heart the burden of loving the world and position, and empty the spiritual utopia and relieve it from those impurities. Let him think how being engaged in the world will, after few hours, humiliate the honorable soul and force it to undergo the worst and most disgraceful state. Let him know that to busy the heart with the world, after a while, when the curtain of visibility is drawn up and the veil of nature is pushed aside, will humiliate man and bring him to the reckoning and punishment. He is to know that adherence to *taqwa* and contentment brings comfort in both worlds—a comfort which is a result of neglecting the world, by slighting it and rejecting its pleasures and entertainments. Having purged himself of the formal filths, he is also to purify himself from the impurities of the *haram* (the unlawful) and the doubtful cases.

Having understood himself and recognized the humility of his need, he has to close to himself the door of arrogance and haughtiness, to run away from recalcitrance and sin, and to open to himself the door of modesty, remorse and shyness. He is to strive to obey Allah and refrain from disobedience, so as to return to Allah good and well, and to attain Allah's proximity with purity and serenity of the soul. He is to imprison himself in the prison of fear and patience and curb his soul of its desires, so as to be saved from the prison of Allah's punishment, and to join Allah's custody in the eternal abode, and, thus, to taste Allah's contentment. This is the ultimate hope of the people of *suluk*, and everything else is nought.

---

[130] *Nahj al-Balaghah*, edited by Fayd al-Islam, sermon 108: "They fell upon a carrion by eating of which they were exposed." Or as in sermon 151: "They are falling upon an easy carrion."

OBJECTIVE TWO

Some Disciplines Concerning the Clothes

Covered under Two Stations

GENERAL DISCIPLINES
FOR THE CLOTHES
Station One

Know that man's rational soul is a reality which at the same time of its unity and perfect simplicity, has diverse aspects (growths = *nashaat*), the principal ones of which are, generally, three:

The first aspect (growth = *nashah*) is the external mundane visible aspect, displayed in the apparent senses, and its lowest surface is the body.

The second is the aspect [*nashah*] of the *barzakh* world (the Isthmus, or the intermediate, world) displayed in the internal senses, the *barzakhian* (intermediate) body and "the mould of the ideal" [*qalib-i mithali*].

The third is the invisible internal aspect [*nashah*], displayed in the heart and in its affairs.

The relation of each of these aspects to the other is that of the external to the internal, and of the manifestation to the manifested. This is the reason for the effects, the characteristics and the reactions of each of these aspects to permeate into the other aspects. For example, if the sense of seeing discerns something, it will have an effect on the *barzakh*ian sense of seeing according to its aspect [*nashah*]. Then the effect is transmitted to the internal seeing sense of the heart according to its aspect [*nashah*]. In the same way the effects of the cordial aspect appear in the other two aspects. This, besides being proved by a strong and firm evidence, coincides with the conscience, too. Consequently, all the formal disciplines of the Shar have their effect, or effects on the interior; and each of the good characters—which belong to the *barzakh*ian status of the soul also has its effects on the exterior and interior. All the divine knowledge [*maarif*] and the true beliefs also have their effects on the two *barzakh*ian and external aspects. For example, this belief that to have control over the kingdom of existence as well as the invisible and visible worlds belongs to Allah, and no other being has any control over them, except that permitted shadowy control, brings about so many spiritual perfections and good human moralities, such as depending on Allah and trusting Him, and pinning no hope on any creature. This is the mother of perfections and the cause of so many good deeds and commendable acts, and prevents one from committing evil practices. Likewise other sorts of knowledge, which are so numerous that these pages, as well as the broken pen of the writer, have no patience to count them nor to relate the effects of each one of them, since it needs writing a huge book which can be expected only from the powerful pen of the people of knowledge, or from a warm soul of "the people of ecstasy" [*ahl-i hal*]: "My hand is short, while the dates are (high) on the date-palms."[131]

Similar is, for example, contentment [*rida*] as a character, which is one of the human moral perfections. It is effective in purifying and polishing the soul, rendering the heart a place for special divine manifestations, elevating faith to a perfect faith, the perfect faith to tranquility [*tumaninah*], tranquility to its perfection, its perfection to vision [*mushahadah*], the vision to a perfect vision, its perfection to "reciprocal love" [*muashaqah*] (with the Beloved), the reciprocal love to its perfection, its perfection to courting [*murawadah*], the courting to its perfection, its perfection to union [*muwasalah*], the union to its perfection, and to what neither you nor I can imagine. The character of contentment has a surprising effect on the kingdom of the body and on the formal marks and acts, which are leaves and branches. It changes hearing, seeing and other powers and organs into divine ones, and the secret of "I will be his hearing and seeing"[132] is somewhat manifested. As those stages have an effect, or rather, effects, on the appearance, they are also affected so surprisingly by the outer shape, all the ordinary and extraordinary movements and pauses, and all the acts and abstentions, so that it sometimes happens that a scornful glance by a

---

[131] *My leg is lame, while the destination is so far,*
My hand is short, while the dates are (high) on the date-palms.

Hafiz Shirazi

[132] Refer to footnote 21.

salik at a servant of Allah causes the *salik* to fall from his high status to the lowest of the low, and this will need him years to make up for it.

Now, as our helpless hearts are weak and shaky, like the weeping willows, losing their stillness, by every gentle breeze, it would be, therefore, necessary, even in ordinary situations—one of which is the instance of choosing one"s clothes—to observe the conditions of the heart and to take care of it. As the soul and Satan have quite firm snares and clever delusions which we are unable to understand, we have to do our best, as much as we can and is in our capacity, to resist them, and to ask, in all cases, Allah"s help and support for success.

So, we say that as it has become clear that the exterior and the interior have reciprocal effects, the seeker for the truth and spiritual elevation has to avoid choosing such clothes and models which have bad effects on the spirit, deviate the heart from perseverance and remembering Allah, and turn the soul"s direction to worldly matters. Do not think that Satan"s delusions and the tricks of the evil-commanding soul are confined only to expensive and nice clothes and luxurious articles. Actually even by old and worthless clothes they may disgrace a man. Therefore, one should avoid seeking fame through clothes, or rather he should avoid all conducts contrary to the normal and the customary. He is to abstain from wearing highly luxurious clothes made of expensive materials and attractively and notoriously tailored, because our hearts are very weak and inconstant, and they slip by slightest distinction and deviate from moderation. It may often happen that a wretched, helpless man, devoid of all degrees of honor, humanity, dignity and perfection, just because of a few meters of silk or woolen cloth, well tailored in a foreign style, and which might have been obtained through shameful and dishonorable bargains, looks down upon the servants of Allah with scorn, arrogance and haughtiness, devaluating the people. This is caused only by a completely powerless soul with so small a capacity that it takes the spit of a worm or the apparel of a sheep to be a cause of honor and dignity for itself.

O helpless man! How wretched and indigent you are! You should be the pride of the world of possibility, and the gist of space and place. You are the offspring of Adam, and you should teach the names and the attributes. You are the child of (Allah"s) vicegerent; so, you should be of the brilliant signs (of Allah). "A whistle calls you from the turret of the *Arsh*.[133] You, unfortunate degenerate! You have usurped a handful of remnants and apparels of helpless animals, by which you take pride. This pride of yours is that of a silk worm, a sheep, a camel, a squirrel or a fox. Why do you feel proud of others" clothes, and show arrogance by others" pride?

In short, as the quality, the value and the decoration of the clothes have their effects on the souls, Amir al-Muminin (*a*), as quoted by the late Qutb al-Rawandi, said: "Whoever wears luxurious clothes, he will be, inevitably, arrogant, and the Fire is inevitably for the arrogant."[134] There are effects in their fashion and tailoring. It sometimes happens that the one who wears the clothes cut similar to those of the foreigners, gets a feeling of ignorant attachment to them, and thus, he repulses and abominates the friends of Allah and His Messenger, and loves their enemies. In this respect, Imam as-Sadiq (*a*) is quoted to have said: "Allah, the Exalted and Most High, inspired one of the prophets, commanding him: "Tell the believers not to wear the clothes of My enemies, not to eat like My enemies, and not to walk like My enemies, so as not to be My enemies as they are My enemies." "[135]

As the too luxurious clothes affect the souls, similarly, low and shabby clothes, both in material and quality, also affect them. It is most probable that this is more corruptive, by many degrees, than the exquisite clothes, as the soul can have quite crafty plots. When one sees himself distinguished from others by wearing rough, denim clothes, while others wear fine, soft clothes, he tries, as he loves himself, to neglect his defects, regarding this accidental and irrelevant affair as a matter of pride. He may probably get to admire himself and look down at the servants of Allah, alleging that the others are out of Allah"s holy sanctum, thinking himself to be among the most sincere and favorite servants of Allah. It is also most probable that he will be afflicted with hypocrisy and other big corruptions. So wretched he is that, out of all the degrees of knowledge, *taqwa* and spiritual perfections, he suffices himself with rough, shabby wears, unaware of

---

[133] Refer to footnote 96.

[134] *Mustadrak al-Wasa'il*, "Book of *as-Salat*," sec. on "The Rules on the Clothes," ch. 16, *hadith* 5, quoted from Qutb al-Rawandi, *Lubb al-Albab*.

[135] *Al-Jawahir as-Saniyyah*, ch. on "Abu Abdullah Jafar ibn Muhammad as-Sadiq," *hadith* 60.

thousands of his big faults, the biggest of which is this very bad effect resulting from these clothes. He thinks himself, who is of Satan's friends, of the people of Allah, regarding the servants of Allah as nothing and worthless. It also happens that the style and the way he wears his clothes throw him into many mischiefs, such as wearing them in such an arrangement as to make him famous as an ascetic and a holy man.

In short, to wear clothes for distinction, on either side of the extremities, is a matter that shakes the weak hearts, and deprives them of good moralities, and causes conceit, hypocrisy, arrogance and pride, each one of which is a mother of spiritual vileness. They further lead to being attached to this world and loving it, which is the head of all sins and the source of all evils. Many *hadith*s also refer to many of the said affairs, as is stated in the noble *al-Kafi* quoting Imam as-Sadiq (*a*) saying: "Allah, the Exalted, becomes angry with one's getting famous through clothes."[136]

He is also quoted to have said: "The famous, good or bad, is in the Fire."[137]

He is further quoted to have said: "Allah becomes angry with two fames: the fame of clothes and the fame of the *salat*."[138]

A *hadith* is quoted from the Messenger of Allah (*s*), saying: "Whoever wears an apparel of fame, Allah will make him wear, in the Hereafter, an apparel of humility."[139]

---

[136] *Wasa'il ash-Shiah*, vol. 3, "Book of *as-Salat*," sec. on "Rules Concerning the Clothes," ch. 12, *hadith* 1, p. 354.
[137] *Ibid.*, *hadith* 3.
[138] *Mustadrak al-Wasa'il*, "Book of *as-Salat*," sec. on "The Rules on the Clothes," ch. 8, *hadith* 2.
[139] *Ibid.*, *hadith* 1.

STATION TWO

Some Disciplines Concerning the *Musalli*'s *Clothing*

Explained in Two Chapters

THE SECRET OF THE PURITY
OF CLOTHING
Chapter One

Know that the *salat* is the state of ascension to the state of Proximity and being present in "the Presence of Intimacy" [*mahdar-i uns*], and the *salik* has to observe the disciplines of being present in the Holy Presence of the King of kings. As from the lowest of the degrees and stages of the appearance of the soul—which is most superficial (the crust of the crust) and is its formal and visible body—to the highest of its stages and realities—which is the innermost and the secret state of the heart—all are present in the Sacred Presence of Allah, likewise the *salik* must prepare himself to display all the internal and external soldiers of the overt and covert kingdoms in the Presence of Allah, the Exalted and Most High, and to return back to His Holy Presence all the trusts which His Sanctified Essence has bestowed upon him with complete purity, clarity, without the intrusion of any being, and with His hand of Power, Beauty and Majesty. He has to return the deposits as they have been given to him out of Kindness.

Therefore, there are many dangers in the discipline [*adab*] of the Presence, which the *salik* must take care not to neglect. He is to take the purity of the clothes—which cover the crust, or rather, the crust of the crust—as a means for the purity of the internal clothes, and to know that as these formal clothes cover the visible body, the body itself covers the isthmus body, which is actually existent, but is hidden within the curtains of the corporeal body which covers it. The isthmus body is the cover, the clothes and the veil of the soul, which covers the heart, and the heart is the cover of spirit, and the spirit is the cover of the secret, which covers the hidden *latifah* (the real essence), and other stages. Each low stage is the cover of its higher stage, and though all these stages exist in the most pure people of Allah, and the others are void of them, yet only some of these stages are mentioned because all people have them.

So, it must be noted that as the external form of the *salat* is not proved to be correct without the purity of the clothes and the body, and as impurities— which are of Satan's vile acts and cause repellence from the Presence of the Beneficent [*ar-rahman*]—block the way of attending the Presence, the *musalli* with clothes and body polluted with Satan's vileness is expelled from the divine Presence and prevented from attending the station of familiarity [*maqam-i uns*]. Similar is the vileness of disobeying Allah, which is also of Satan's practices and of the filths of that foul creature. It also prevents one from entering the Presence [*mahdar*]. So, the red-handed disobedient one, with an impure cover of the isthmus body, cannot be admitted to Allah's Presence [*mahdar*]. Purifying this cover is among the conditions for the realization and correctness of the internal *salat*. As long as man is in the veil of this world, he cannot know about the invisible body, the purity and filth of its clothes and the condition of its being pure and without filth. The day he comes out of this veil, and the sovereignty of the interior and of the day of gathering [*yawm al-jam*] twists aside the extensive disunion of the exterior, and the sun of truth rises out of the dark mundane veils, and the eye of the invisible interior opens, and the eye of the visible animality closes, thereupon, with the eye of insight, he will understand that his *salat*, had been, till the end of life, void of purity and surrounded by thousands of obstacles, each one of which was an independent cause for expelling one from the Holy Presence of Allah. Alas! A thousand alas! For on that day there will be no way for indemnity and there will be no cure. There will be nothing but regret and remorse—endless regrets and continuous remorse: **"And warn them of the day of anguish when the matter shall have been decided..."**[140]

After that the clothes of the interior body became pure, it would be necessary for the very invisible body to be purified from Satan's filths, that is, purification from the filths of the dispraised characters, as each one of them is apt to pollute the interior and to expel man from the Presence [*mahdar*] and prevent him from the Proximity. Such characters are of the filths of Satan who is deprived of (Allah's) mercy. The origins of all the dispraised acts are self-conceit,

---

[140] *Surah Maryam* 19:39.

selfishness, ostentation, and obstinacy, each of which is the origin of many dispraised characters, and is at the head of many sins

Having completed this purification, and purified the clothes of *taqwa* with the water of sincere repentance and lawful austerity, the *salik* will have to busy himself with the purification of the heart, which is the real concealer [*satir*] and into which Satan"s intrusion is greater, and its impurities spread to other clothes and concealers. So, without purifying the heart other purifications will not be easy. The purification of the heart passes through several stages, some of which will be referred to in these pages.

One of them is purging the heart from loving this world, which is at the head of all sins and it is the origin of all corruptions. As long as man has this love in his heart, it will not be possible for him to be admitted to the Presence of Allah; and divine affection, which is the mother of purities, is not accomplished with this impurity. Perhaps in the Book of Allah and in the advices of the prophets and holy men (*a*), particularly Amir al-Muminin [Ali] (*a*), importance is the least given to other than abandoning this world, neglecting it and avoiding it, all of which are of the realities of *taqwa*. This stage of purification is not achieved except by useful knowledge, strong cordial austerities, concentrating one"s thoughts on the beginning [*mabda*] and the return (to Allah) [*maad*], engaging the heart in taking lessons from the decay and the destruction of the world, and the excellence and happiness of the invisible worlds: "May Allah have mercy upon the one who knows where he has come from, where he is and where he is going."[141]

Another purification is to be purged from dependence on the creatures, which is a concealed polytheism; yet, to the people of knowledge, it is a manifest polytheism. This purification is accomplished through (the belief in) Allah"s Unity of Acts, which is the source of all cordial purifications. It must be noted that mere demonstrative knowledge and contemplative step concerning the Unity of Acts do not have the required result. It sometimes happens that too much indulgence in the experimental sciences brings darkness and displeasure to the heart, and hinders man from attaining the higher objective. In this respect it is said: "Knowledge is the greatest veil." The writer believes that all sciences, even the science of *tawhid* (monotheism), are functional [practical = *amali*]. Perhaps the

---

[141] Mulla Sadra, *Mafatih al-Ghayb*, ed. Khajawi, p. 50.

grammatical etymology of the word *tawhid*, which is *tafil*, proves that, as according to its etymological function it means advancing from multiplicity to oneness, and annihilating and abolishing the aspects of the multiplicity in "the Essence of Union" [*ayn-i jam*]. This idea cannot be proved with evidence, as with cordial austerity and instinctive inclination towards the Owner of the hearts, the heart is to be informed about what proofs say, so that the truth of *tawhid* can be understood. Yes, proof tells us: "There is no effecter [*muaththir*] in the (world of) existence except Allah,"[142] which is one of the meanings of "There is no God but Allah." By the blessing of this proof we cut short the intruding hands of beings from the realm of the Majesty of existence, and return the invisible and visible worlds to their Owner, and display the truth of **"His is what is in the heavens and the earth,"**[143] **"And in His Hand is the Kingdom of everything,"**[144] and **"He it is Who in the heaven and in the earth is God."**[145] But unless this proved subject reaches the heart and becomes an internal form [*surat*] of the heart, we will not cross the limit [*hadd*] of knowledge to the limit of faith; and of the light of faith, which illuminates the kingdom of the interior and the exterior, we shall have no share and no profit. This is the reason that although we have the proof supporting this divine, lofty subject, we are still in multiplicity and know little of *tawhid* which is the pleasure of the eyes of the people of Allah—we do ring the bell of "There is no effecter [*muaththir*] in the (world of) existence except Allah," yet we look with the eye of greed, and extend the hand of demand to everybody:

The legs of the inferentialists are wooden,
Legs will be very much infirm, if wooden.[146]

This purification is of the great stations of the wayfarers to Allah. There are, however, further stations, which are beyond our limit, though probably we may refer to some of them within these papers, when the occasion arises, *insha Allah* (Allah willing).

---

[142] It is ascribed to the theologian philosophers, as is related by Mirza Abu l-Hasan Sharani in the Preface of his *The Secrets of the Maxims*, p. 32.
[143] *Surah an-Nahl* 16:52.
[144] *Surah Ya-Sin* 36:83.
[145] *Surah az-Zukhruf* 43:84.
[146] A poem by Mawlawi.

CONCERNING CORDIAL CONSIDERATIONS OF COVERING THE NAKEDNESS
Chapter Two

The traveler to Allah finds himself present in the Holy Presence [*mahdar*] of Allah, the Almighty and Most High, or rather, he sees that his interior and exterior, his covertness and overtness are the very presence [*hudur*], as it is narrated in *al-Kafi* and *at-Tawhid* that Imam as-Sadiq (*a*) said: "The spirit of a believer is more connected to the spirit of Allah than the connection of the sunbeam to the sun."[147] Yet, strong evidential arguments in the high sciences stress that the entire circle of existence, from the highest invisible stages to the lowest visible ones, is the very connection and mere dependence and want (poverty) in its relation to the Absolute Self-Existent, the Glorified and Most High. It is probable that the reference is to this in the *ayah*: **"O men! It is you who are in need of Allah, and it is Allah Who is the Self-Sufficient, the Praised One."**[148] because if a being among the beings, in a state of states, in a moment of the moments and in an aspect of the aspects, had no connection to the Might of the Holy Lord, it would be out of the spot of self-potentiality and poverty, and into the sanctuary of Self-Necessity and Self-Sufficiency. The one who knows Allah and is journeying to Him will have to engrave this true evidential subject, this divine gnostic delicacy, by way of cordial austerities, disregarding the limits of reason and argument, on the face of the heart, in order to bring it to the borders of gnosis [*irfan*], so that the truth of faith and its light become manifest in his heart. The people of heart and of Allah step past the limit of faith onto the stage of revelation [*kashf*] and vision [*shuhud*]. This would be possible through

---

[147] *Usul al-Kafi*, vol. 3, "Book of Faith and Infidelity," ch. on "The Believers" Brotherhood to One Another," *hadith* 4, p. 242.
[148] *Surah Fatir* 35:15.

intense self-mortification [*mujahadah*], privacy with Allah and loving Him. It is stated in *Misbah ash-Shariah* that Imam as-Sadiq (*a*) said:

"The informed one (the gnostic), his person is with the people and his heart is with Allah. Should his heart be inattentive of Allah for a twinkle of an eye, he would have died of craving for Him.

"The informed one (the gnostic) is the entrusted with Allah's trusts. He is the treasure of His secrets, the source of His light, the evidence of His mercy on His creatures, the mount of His knowledge, and the criterion of His favor and justice. He is not dependent on the people, nor is he in need of them for his wants and the world. He feels intimate only with Allah, and gives no utterance, makes no gesture and draws no breath except by Allah, for Allah, from Allah and with Allah."[149]

In short, when the *salik* finds himself, in all aspects (affairs, states = *shuun*), being the very Presence [*hudur*], he covers all his internal and external kinds of nakedness [*awrat*] in order to observe the Presence and the discipline of Presence. He realizes that the exposure of the internal nakedness in the Presence of Allah is much more hideous and disgracing than the exposure of the external nakedness, as in the *hadith*: "Allah does not look at your forms, but He looks into your hearts."[150] The internal kinds of nakedness [*awrat*] are the dispraised characters, vile customs and immoralities, which deprive man of being worthy of the Presence [*mahdar*] and of the discipline of Presence [*hudur*]. This is the first stage of violating the covers and the exposure of the nakedness [*awrat*].

It must be noted that if one does not cover himself with Allah's veiling and forgiveness, and if he does not put himself under the Names of "the Concealer" and "the Forgiver," demanding concealment and forgiveness, it frequently happens that when the visible curtain is rolled up, and the worldly veil is removed, they cause his exposure in the presence of the favorable angels and the appointed prophets (*a*). Allah alone knows how much the exposed internal nakedness is ugly, disgraceful, stinking and scandalous.

O dear, do not compare the conditions of the Hereafter with this world, as this world can never have the capacity of the appearance

---

[149] *Misbah ash-Shariah*, ch. 95, on "Knowledge".

[150] *Bihar al-Anwar*, vol. 67, p. 248, quoting *Jami al-Akhbar*, p. 117 (with a slight addition).

of a single blessing or punishment of that world. This world, with all its vast heavens and kingdoms [*awalim*], cannot take in the appearance of a low invisible world such as the world of the grave, let alone the high kingdom of heaven, of which the resurrection world is a sample. In a detailed *hadith* narrated by the Shaykh ash-Shahid ath-Thani (may Allah be pleased with him) in *Munyat al-Murid* quoting Fatimah as-Siddiqah (*a*), who, quoting the Messenger of Allah (*s*), said: "The Messenger of Allah (*s*) said: "The scholars of our followers will be resurrected wearing coats of honor according to their knowledge and to their efficiency in guiding the servants of Allah, such that some of them are given thousands of coats of light." Then he added: "Some of those gifts are better than the best thing on which the sun may shine, by thousands of times"."[151] So much for its blessings. As to its punishments, Fayd (may Allah have mercy upon him), in *Ilm al-Yaqin*, has quoted a *hadith* from the late as-Saduq, on his authority, quoting Imam as-Sadiq (*a*) who said that in a *hadith* Gabriel said to the Messenger of Allah (*s*): "If a single link of the chain, whose length is seventy cubits, is placed on the world, the world will melt by its heat. Or if a drop of the *Zaqqum* and *Dari* (repulsive stinking drink) is dropped into the waters of this world, the people will die of its bad smell."[152] We take refuge with Allah from the wrath of *ar-Rahman*.

Therefore, the traveler to Allah has to replace his bad characters and evil habits with the perfect ones, and to vanish them in the stormy and endless sea of Allah's perfect attributes, and to change the dark Satanic land of (his) nature [*tabiat*] to a white and bright land, and to find out in himself: **"And the earth shines with the light of its Lord,"**[153] and to bring about the state of the names of Beauty and Majesty of the Holy Essence in the kingdom of his existence. In this state he will be under the shelter of Beauty and Majesty, and will acquire the divine moralities; and the vices of "personal individuations" [*taayyunat-i nafsiyyah*] and the darkness of fancy will be completely concealed. Having attained this state, he will be favored with the special care of Allah, the Most High, Who will help him with His special secret protection (kindness) [*lutf*], and conceal him under the cover of His Majesty such that no one, except Himself will know

---

[151] *Munyat al-Murid*, p. 24.
[152] *Ilm al-Yaqin*, vol. 2, p. 1033.
[153] *Surah az-Zumar* 39:69.

him, and he will know none but Allah: "My friends are under My *qibab* (domes); no one knows them except Me."[154] The sacred Book of Allah has many references to this point for those worthy of it, such as: **"Allah is the Protector of those who believe. He brings them out of the darkness into the light..."**[155] The people of knowledge and of past good records know that all the creational individuations [*taayyunat-i khalqiyyah*] and the essential multiplicities [*kathurat-i ayniyyah*] are darkness [*zulumat*], and the absolute light cannot happen except by discarding the annexations and breaking the individuations which are the idols in the way of the *salik*. When the darkness of the actual and participial multiplicities is effaced and vanished in "the Essence of Union" [*ayn-i jam*], all the nakedness will be covered, and the absolute presence and the complete attainment will take place, and the *musalli*, being concealed by the *Haqq* (Allah), will be performing the *Haqq*'s (Allah's) *salat*. The ascending *salat* of the Seal of the Messengers (*s*) was probably of this type, in its particular states and stages. Allah knows better.

Connection:

It is stated in *Misbah ash-Shariah* that Imam as-Sadiq (*a*) said: "The most decorative clothing for the believer is the clothing of *taqwa*, and the finest one is faith. Allah, the Almighty and Glorified, said: **"And the clothing of *taqwa*, that is the best."** As to the exterior clothing, it is a blessing from Allah, as it covers the nakedness of the children of Adam (*a*). It is a grace granted by Allah to His servants, the children of Adam, which He did not grant to other than them. To the believers, it is a means to perform the duties imposed by Allah upon them. The best of your clothing is that which does not distract you from Allah, the Almighty and Glorified, rather it brings you nearer to thanking, remembering and obeying Him, and it does not bear you to conceit, hypocrisy, decoration, taking pride and boasting, as these are among the pests of the religion and bring cruelty to the heart. When you put on your dress, remember Allah, the concealer of your sins by His mercy. Clothe your interior with truthfulness, as you dressed your exterior with your dress. Let your interior be under the protection of

---

[154] A *hadith al-qudsi* (divine saying) in *Ihya" Ulum ud-din*, vol. 4, p. 256. In the MS (manuscript) both the words *qibabi* and *qiba'i* are stated.
[155] *Surah al-Baqarah* 2:257.

fear, and your exterior under the protection of obedience. Take a lesson from the favor of Allah, the Almighty and Glorified, as He created the means for making clothes to conceal the apparent nakedness, and He opened the doors of repentance and imploring in order to cover the internal sins and evil characters. Do not uncover anyone"'s faults, as Allah has covered your greater faults. Attend to your own faults, and forgive that whose state and affair do not concern you. Beware of perishing your life for the action of others, letting the others trade with your capital, while you destroy yourself. Forgetting the sins is of the gravest punishments from Allah in this world, and of the most effective causes for the punishments in the Hereafter. As long as the servant is engaged in his obedience to Allah, the Exalted, in recognizing his own defects and abandoning what is disgraceful in the religion of Allah, he will be isolated from the plagues, plunging in the sea of the mercy of Allah, the Almighty and Glorified, and will win the gems of the advantages of wisdom and expression. But as long as he is forgetting his sins, unfamiliar with his defects, resorting to his own might and force, he will never be successful."[156]

---

[156] *Misbah ash-Shariah*, sec. 7, on "Clothing".

OBJECTIVE THREE

**On the Cordial Disciplines
Concerning the Place of the *Musalli***

Discussed in Two Chapters

ABOUT KNOWING THE PLACE
Chapter One

Know that the wayfarer to Allah has, according to his existential growths [*nashaat-i wujudiyyah*], certain places, each of which has its particular disciplines. The *salik* have to know them before attaining the *salat* of the people of knowledge.

The first is the natural growth and the apparent mundane stage, and its place is the earth of nature. The Messenger of Allah (*s*) said: "The earth is made for me a place for prostration and a purifier."[157] The *salik*'s discipline [*adab*] at this stage is to make his heart understand that his descending from the invisible growth [*nashah*] and the coming down of the soul from its high and lofty place to the lowest earth of nature and his being reduced from "the best stature" [*ahsan-i taqwim*] to the lowest of the low are for the voluntary journey to Allah and the ascension to the *miraj* of Proximity and reaching the Court of Allah and the Threshold of His Lordship, which is the objective of creation and the final end of the people of Allah. "May Allah have mercy upon one who knows where he has come from, where he is and where he is going."[158]

The *salik* must realize that he has come from the house of Allah's munificence [*karamat*], and is now in the house of worshipping Allah, and will go to the house of Allah's recompense. The gnositc says: "From Allah, in Allah and to Allah." So, the *salik* must tell himself, and his spirit, that the house of nature is a mosque for worshipping Allah, and that he has been brought to this world for this purpose, as Allah, the Almighty and Glorified, says: **"And I have not created the *jinn* and the *ins* [mankind] except that they should**

---

[157] *Wasa'il ash-Shiah*, vol. 3, "Book of *as-Salat*," sec. on "What One can Prostrate upon," ch. 1, *hadith* 8, p. 593.
[158] Refer to footnote 141.

worship Me.[159] After realizing that the house of nature is the mosque for worship, and finding himself in seclusion [*mutakif*] in it, he is to observe the relevant disciplines and abstain from remembering other than Allah. He is not to leave the mosque of worship, unless there is a need, such as for relieving himself, and then to return, and not to be familiar except with Allah, nor to have any affiliation with others, as these are contrary to the disciplines of cleaving to the door of Allah. In this stage the knower of Allah will have certain moods [*halat*] which cannot be written down, and as the writer is out of "the innate disposition of humanity" [*fitrat-i insaniyyat*], indulging in the overflowing darkened sea of nature, void of truth and reality, as well as of all the stations of the *salik*s and of the gnostics, the best thing for him is not to disgrace himself in the Presence of Allah, the Almighty, and his close friends, but to go past this stage and take his complaint against the evil-commanding soul to the Sacred Threshold of the Lord of Majesty, as perhaps He would extend to him a helping hand out of His general kindness and all-embracing mercy, and thus he would compensate during the rest of his life for what has passed: **"Our Lord! We have been unjust to ourselves, and if You forgive us not and have not mercy on us, we shall certainly be of the losers."**[160]

The second stage is the state of the external and internal powers, which are the visible and invisible soldiers of the soul, whose place is the ground (earth = *ard*) of man's nature, i.e., his structure and body. The *salik*'s discipline in this respect is to inform the inmost of the heart that the ground (*ard*) of his nature is the mosque of divinity and the place for the prostration of the soldiers of the Beneficent [*ar-Rahman*]. Therefore, the mosque should not be smeared with the filths or *Iblis*' intrusion, and the divine soldiers should not be put under the influence of *Iblis*, so that the ground [*ard*] of the nature is illuminated with the Lord's light, and be freed from the darkness and the impurity of being away from the Court of the Lord. So, let him believe that his visible and invisible powers are in seclusion in the mosque of the body, and he is to treat his body as he treats a mosque, and to look at his powers as being in seclusion in the Court of Allah. In this stage, the obligations of the *salik* are more, because it is his own responsibility to undertake cleaning and purifying the mosque, as he also is to observe

---

[159] *Surah adh-Dhariyat* 51:56.
[160] *Surah al-Araf* 7:23.

the disciplines of seclusion on the part of those (visible and invisible powers) that are in seclusion in this mosque.

The third stage is the *salik*"s cordial invisible growth [*nashah*], whose place is the invisible *barzakh*ian body of the soul, which is created and developed by the soul itself. The *salik*"s discipline, in this instance, is to make himself realize that this stage greatly differs from other ones, and to preserve it is of the *salik*"s important duties, because the heart is the leader of those in seclusion in the Court (of Allah), and with its corruption all of them will be corrupted: "If the scholar is corrupt, the world will be corrupted."[161] The heart of a scholar is a small world, while the scholar is the heart of the big world. In this stage the *salik*"s duties increase, because the building of the mosque is also added to his responsibilities, and it maybe that—God forbid!—his mosque will be a mosque of harm [*dirar*], disbelief and disunity of the Muslims. In such a mosque it is not allowed to worship Allah, and it must be pulled down. Having established the divine invisible mosque with the hand of the Beneficent and of the guardianship, and purified it from all impurities and satanic intrusions, and begun his seclusion therein, the *salik* is to strive to take himself out of his seclusion in the mosque in order to seclude in the Court of the Owner of the mosque. And, after purging himself from self-love and getting out of his own fetters, he himself will become the house of Allah, or better to say, he will become the mosque of the Lord, and Allah will glorify Himself through Manifestation of Action, then of Names and of Essence in that mosque, and this glorification is the *salat* of the Lord, saying: *Subbuhun quddus, rabb ul-malaikati war-ruh* (All-Glorious, All-Holy, the Lord of the angels and the spirit).[162]

The traveler to Allah has, in all the stages of the journey, another duty to perform, neglecting which is not permissible at all, for actually it is the core of the cores and the objective of the *suluk*. This duty is not to forget to remember Allah in any situation or stage, and to seek to know Allah from all rituals and worships, and to see Him in all phenomena, and not to let the blessings and munificence prevent him

---

[161] In *Ghurar al-Hikam* Vol. 7, p. 269, it is said: "A scholar's slip corrupts the world."

[162] "...[Y]our Lord prays...He says: "All-Glorious, All-Holy, I am the Lord of the angels and the Spirit"," *Usul al-Kafi*, vol. 2, "Book of the Proof," sec. on "Histories," ch. on "The Birth of the Prophet (*s*) and his Death," *hadith* 13, p. 329.

from the company [*suhbat*] and privacy, as this is a kind of *istidraj* (being engaged in other than the *Haqq*). In short, he is to take the spirit and the interior [*batin*] of the worships and rituals to be knowing Allah, and to look into them for the Beloved so that the attachment of loving and being loved becomes fixed in his heart, and he may be favored with hidden graces and secret associations.

Connection:

It is stated in *Misbah ash-Shariah* that Imam as-Sadiq (*a*) said: "When you arrive at the door of the mosque, know that you have come to the door of a great King. No one may walk into His Courtyard save the purified, and no one is admitted to His Company [*mujalasah*] but the truthful. So, attach reverence to your coming to the ground of serving the King, as you would be exposed to a great danger if you were negligent.[163] Know that He is capable of doing what He likes of justice and grace with you and by you. So, if He were kind to you with His mercy and favor, He would accept from you little worship and give you much reward for it. But if He demanded from you a share of truth and sincerity, to be just with you, He would block you and reject your worship, even if it is much. He is the doer of what He wants. Confess to His Presence your inability, shortcoming, humility and poverty, as you have come to Him to worship and to get His Intimacy [*muanasah*]. Expose your secrets to Him, knowing that nothing, covert and overt, of the entire universe, is hidden from Him. Before Him, be the poorest of His servants. Empty your heart of all occupants that keep you away from your Lord, as He does not accept except the pure(st) and the (most) sincere. Find out in which register your name is recorded. If you tasted the sweetness of supplication and the delight of addressing Him, and drank from the cup of His mercy and generosity out of His good reception of you and response to you, then you would become suitable for His service. So, enter, as you will have permission and protection. Otherwise, stop, like the one whose rope has snapped, whose hope has come short, and time has got the better of him. So, if Allah found in your heart true recourse to Him, He would look at you with the eye of kindness, mercy and leniency, and cause you to be successful in attaining what He likes and is pleased with, since He is

---

[163] Hafiz says: *O the wayfarer in the lane of our Beloved,*
Be aware that head breaks its wall.

generous and loves generosity for His servants who distressfully resort to Him and burn out at His door for the want of His pleasure. Allah, the Most High, says: **"Or, Who answers the distressed one, when he calls upon Him, and removes the evil...?"** "[164]

I have related the complete text of this noble speech because it is a comprehensive set of instructions for the people of knowledge and the wayfarers to Allah, who, by contemplating on it may acquire a different state.

---

[164] *Misbah ash-Shariah*, ch. 12, on "Entering the Mosque". The Quranic verse at the end of the *hadith* is verse 62 of *Surah an-Naml* (chapter 27).

ON SOME DISCIPLINES CONCERNING PERMISSIBILITY [*IBAHAH*] OF PLACE
Chapter Two

Having understood the stages of the place according to his states and existential growths [*nashaat*], the salik is to exert his effort, in respect with the cordial disciplines of their permissibility, so that his *salat* may come out of the usurping intrusions of the evil *Iblis*. In the first stage he is to perform the formal disciplines of worship and servitude, and to fulfill his former promises of the world of pre-existence and the Day of Covenant, cutting Satan's intruding hand from the kingdom of his nature, so as to establish amicable relations with the Owner of the House, and his actions [*tasarrufat*] in the world of nature may not be usurping. Some of the people of good aptitude say that the inner meaning of the noble *ayah*, **"O you who believe! Fulfill the obligations. The cattle quadruped are allowed to you,"**[165] is that allowing the cattle quadruped is conditioned by the fulfillment of the guardianship obligation. Noble *hadith*s relate that all land is the Imam's, and that other than the *Shiah*s are its usurpers.[166] People of knowledge regard the *wali al-amr* (the religiously legal authority) as the owner of all kingdoms of the existence, and the stages of the visible and the invisible, and regard using them without the Imam's permission to be wrong.

The writer says: The accursed *Iblis* is the enemy of Allah, and his conducts and all the satanic intrusions in the world of nature are tyrannical and usurping. So, if the wayfarer to Allah could bring himself out of the control of that wicked one, his conduct would be divine, and his place, clothing, food, and matrimony would be permissible and clean. And as much as he remains under Satan's

---

[165] *Surah al-Ma'idah* 5:1.
[166] *Usul al-Kafi*, vol. 2, "Book of the Proof," narratives in ch. "Concerning that All Land is the Imam's," p. 266.

control, his permissibilities become less, and satanic polytheism [*shirk*] will affect them. So, if man's external organs become under Satan's control, they will be Satanic organs, usurping Allah's kingdom, as the seclusion of the invisible powers in the mosque of the body can only be permissible and right when those powers are of the soldiers of Allah, in which case *Iblis''* soldiers will not have the right to intrude into the kingdom of the human body, which is the property of Allah, the Exalted. Having cut the intruding hand of Satan short off the kingdom of the heart, which is the private residence of Allah, and cleared his heart for Allah's manifestation, and excluded other than Allah, such as *Iblis*, from it, the external and internal mosques and the visible and invisible places become permissible for him, and his *salat*s become like those of the people of knowledge, and consequently, the purity of the mosque is realized, too.

OBJECTIVE FOUR

On the Cordial Disciplines of the Time

Discussed on Two Chapters

TIMES OF *SALAT*
Chapter One

Know that the people of knowledge and of observance pay attention to, and take care of, the times for the *Salat*s according to the depth of their knowledge of the Sacred State of the Lord, and according to their longing for supplication with the Creator, Honored be His Name, as these times are for supplication and meeting Allah.

Those who are attracted by the Beauty of the Beautiful, and are fond of the beauty of eternity, and are drunk with the cup of affection, and are in a state of ecstasy by (drinking) a goblet from *alastu* (Am I not...?),[167] are delivered from both worlds, closing their eyes against the regions of existence and joining the Majesty of the Sanctity of Allah's Beauty. To them the Presence is continual, and they do not forget, even for a single moment, remembrance, contemplation, perception and observance.

The people of knowledge, virtues and honorable learned souls, and of good disposition, would prefer nothing to supplication to Allah. They demand supplication and privacy with Allah. They take glory, honor, virtue and knowledge to be in supplication and remembering Allah. Should they look at the universe and the world, their look would be gnostic. In the world they are in quest of Allah and want Him. To them, all beings are the manifestations of Allah and the charms of the Beautiful: "I love the whole world as the whole world is from Him."[168] They watch for the times of the *Salat*s with all their hearts, and eagerly wait for the time of supplication to Allah, preparing themselves to be present at a fixed time to meet Him. Their hearts are present, and from

---

[167] This is a reference to the *ayah*: **"And made them bear witness against their own souls: "Am I not your Lord?" They said: "Yes, we bear witness." "** (*Surah al-Anam* 6:172).

[168] "By the world I am pleased, since the world is pleasant by Him, I love the whole world, as the whole world is from Him." Sadi

the Presence [*mahdar*] they demand the Present, as they respect the Presence [*mahdar*] for the sake of the Present. They believe that servitude is association and sociability with the Absolute Perfect, and their eagerness for worship is due to this fact.

And those who believe in the invisible and the other world, and are fascinated by the generosity of Allah, the Exalted, and who would not change the eternal heavenly blessings and the everlasting pleasures and the permanent cheerfulness for mundane perishing chances and the temporal, incomplete and suspected delights, at the times of worship—which is the seed of the blessings relating to the other world—they prepare their hearts and perform it whole-heartedly and anxiously. They wait for the times of the *Salats*—which are the times for getting the results and winning the treasures—and take nothing for the eternal blessings. As their hearts are aware of the invisible world and they cordially believe in the eternal blessings and the continual pleasures of the Hereafter world, they fully utilize their time and do not waste it. Those are the owners of Paradise and the lords of grace in which they will remain forever.

Those groups that have been mentioned, and the others which have not been mentioned, obtain pleasure from worshipping itself, in proportion to their ranks and their knowledge. They never feel the heaviness of the obligations, but it is we, the helpless, who are in the chains of hopes and desires, and in the fetters of whims and wishes, drowned in the overflowing dark sea of the world of nature, where neither a smell of affection and love has reached the sense of smell of our spirit, nor has our heart's sense of taste tasted any delicacies of knowledge and virtue. We are neither of the people of gnosticism and vision, nor of the people of faith and tranquility. We take the divine worship to be a heavy obligation, and regard supplication unto Allah a burden. We trust nothing but this world, which is a manger for animals, and are attached to nothing except to this house of nature, which is the seclusion place of the unjust. The eye of our heart's insight is blind to the Beauty of the Beautiful, and the taste of our spirit is void of the taste of gnosticism.

The master of the circle of the people of knowledge, and the gist of the people of affection and truth says: "I spend the night with my Lord Who feeds me and gives me drink."[169] O Lord! What a night which Muhammad (s) spent in the House of Private Intimacy with You! What food and drink were those, which You, with Your own hand, fed that honorable being and freed him from all worlds! It is proper for that master to say: "I have with Allah a time which is not within the capacity of any favorable angel and prophet."[170] Was that time of the times of this world and the other world? Or was it the time of the Privacy of *qaba qawsayn* (the distance of two bows" length) and discarding the two worlds? Moses, the interlocutor with Allah, fasted for forty days and could attain a meeting with Allah, and Allah said: **"So, the appointed time of his Lord was complete forty nights."**[171] Yet, he could not attain a meeting like Muhammad's, and it cannot be compared with that of him. In the meeting place Moses was told: "Take off your shoes,"[172] which is interpreted to mean "affection to family," while the Seal of the Prophets was told to love Ali. In my heart, of this secret, there is a firebrand, of which I would not talk. You yourself, from this brief, read its detailed talk.

---

[169] *Wasa'il ash-Shiah*, vol. 7, p. 388, with a slight difference; *Sahih al-Bukhari*, vol. 4, "Book of Wishes," p. 251. Mawlawi, in a couplet says: "As I spend the night with my Lord" became knowledge, He feeds and give drinks" afterwards became porridge."

[170] *Awaliyy ul-Laali*, vol. 4, *hadith* 7, p. 7; *Bihar al-Anwar*, vol. 18, "Book of the Prophet's History," ch. on "Proving the *Miraj*," p. 360.

[171] *Surah al-Araf* 7:142.

[172] "I am your Lord; take off your shoes," *Surah Ta-Ha* 20:12.

ON WATCHING OVER THE TIME
Chapter Two

Dear, you too, are to seize this opportunity for supplication, as available and according to the possible measure, and apply its cordial disciplines, informing your heart that the origin [*mayah*] of the eternal Hereafter life, the source of the spiritual virtues and the capital of the unlimited generosities are in the Proximity to, and Intimacy with, Allah, the Exalted, and in supplication to Him, especially in the *salat* which is a spiritual mixture [*majun*] prepared by the hand of Allah''s Beauty and Majesty. It is the most comprehensive and perfect worship among all types of servitude. So, take care, at your best, to keep its times, and select its virtuous times, for in them is a sort of luminosity not found in other times. In those times you are to lessen, or even sever, your heart''s engagements, and this can be achieved by arranging your times and assigning special times for the *salat*, which guarantees the eternal Hereafter life for you, such that in those assigned times you would have nothing else to do, and the heart could have no other attachments that might rival the *salat*, and the heart can be prepared and made present with ease.

Now I am going to relate some of the *hadith*s about the conditions of the infallibles [the Imams] (*a*), as needs be, so that contemplating their conditions may lead to being awake, and perhaps the importance of the situation and seriousness of the state can be recognized by the heart and it can be awakened from its sleep of negligence.

Some wives of the Messenger of Allah (*s*) were quoted to have said: "The Messenger of Allah (*s*) used to talk to us and we used to talk to him. But when the time for the *salat* arrived he appeared as if he did not know us and we did not know him, as his attention was completely directed to Allah."[173] It is said that Amir al-Muminin Ali (*a*), when it was time for the *salat*, used to writhe and tremble. Asked once about his uncommon state, he said: "The time has come for the trust which Allah, the Exalted, offered to the heavens and the earth and the mountains, but they refused to carry it and were afraid of it."[174] Sayyid Ibn Tawus (may his soul be sanctified) says in *Falah as-Sail*, that when Imam Husayn (*a*) used to perform the *wudu*, he changed colors and his joints trembled. Asked about the reason, the Imam said: "When one is going to stand before the Owner of the *Arsh*, his color is ought to turn pale and his joints to tremble."[175] Imam Hasan had a similar condition.[176] It is narrated that Imam as-Sajjad (the fourth Imam) (*a*) used to get pale at the arrival of the time of the *wudu*. He was once asked: "What is this state which happens to you whenever you want to perform the *wudu*?" He said: "Do you not know before whose presence I am to stand?"[177]

If we, too, think a little and tell our veiled and discarded heart that the times of the *salat*s are the times of being present at the Holy Threshold of the Owner of Majesty, the times in which Allah, the Exalted, the Master of the Kings and the Absolute Great, invites His helpless and worthless servant to supplication, admitting him to His House of Generosity, so that he may win the eternal happiness and permanent pleasures and cheerfulness, we will have pleasure and cheerfulness, according to our level of knowledge when the time of the *salat* arrives. If the heart understands the greatness and the importance of the situation, there will be fear and dread in proportion to the extent of its understanding of the greatness. But as the hearts of the holy men [*awliya*] and their conditions are different, according to the gracious and the overpowering manifestations and feeling the greatness and mercy, sometimes their longing for the meeting, and their feeling the

---

[173] *Mustadarak al-Wasa'il*, "Book of *as-Salat*," sec. on "The Acts of the *Salat*," ch. 2, *hadith* 17.

[174] *Ibid.*, *hadith*s 5 and 14.

[175] Sayyid Ibn Tawus (may his soul be sanctified) has stated this point in his *Falah as-Sa'il*, quoting *al-Lu'lu'iyyat*, concerning the conditions of Imam Hasan ibn Ali (a).

[176] *Bihar al-Anwar*, vol. 77, "Book of Purification," sec. on "*Wudu*"," ch. 34, *hadith* 34, p. 346, quoting *Falah as-Sa'il*.

[177] *Mustadarak al-Wasa'il*, "Book of *as-Salat*," sec. on "The Acts of the *Salat*," ch. 2, *hadith* 35.

mercy and beauty excite them to display pleasure and cheerfulness, and they hail: "Relieve us, O Bilal!"[178] And sometimes (divine) manifestations of Greatness, Power and Sovereignty, drive them to ecstasy, trembling and shivering.

In short, O you helpless! The cordial disciplines of the times are in preparing yourself for entering into the Presence of the Master of this world and the Hereafter, for conversing with Allah, the Almighty and Most High. So, cast a glance at your weakness, helplessness, humility and indigence, and at the Greatness, Glory and Majesty of the Sanctified Essence, Glorified be His Majesty, in Whose Court of Greatness the prophetic Messengers and the favorite angels go into rapture, and confess their incapability, humility and wretchedness. Having so looked, and taught your heart, it would feel afraid and you regard yourself and your worship trivial and worthless. Then, contemplate the extent of the mercy, complete kindness and all-embracing affection of His Sacred Essence, to realize that such a helpless servant, with all his impurities and wretchedness, is invited to His Sacred Court, received by the ceremonies of sending down of angels, heavenly Books and Prophets and Messengers (*a*), who call him to the meeting of intimacy, without this helpless possible servant having any previous aptitude, or there being imaginable, in this invitation to His Presence, any benefit for Him—we take refuge in Allah—or for the angels of Allah and the Prophets (*a*). It is natural, however, that the heart is pleased with this contemplation, and it is filled with hope and expectancy. Therefore, with steps of fear and hope, desire and dread, prepare yourself for the Presence and have ready the required provisions for the Attendance, the most important of which is to attend the Meeting [*mahdar*] with a shy and fearing heart, feeling broken, humiliated, weak and helpless, and believing yourself unworthy to worship and servitude and to be admitted into the Presence, and regarding that giving you permission to enter into worship and servitude was only because of the general mercy and the all-inclusive kindness of the One, the Almighty and Glorified. If you put your humility before your eyes, and humbly and heartily submitted

---

[178] *Al-Mahajjat al-Bayda"fi Tahdhib al-Ahya*, vol. 1, p. 377. Bilal was the Prophet's *muadhdhin*, or the caller for the *salat*. Mawlawi, in a couplet, says:
"The soul is perfect and perfect is its call,
The Chosen One said: "Relieve us, O Bilal!"

to the Sacred Essence of Allah, and if you considered yourself and your worship worthless and trivial, Allah, the Exalted, would be kind to you, raise you and bestow His graces upon you.

OBJECTIVE FIVE

On Some Disciplines Concerning Orientation

Discussed in Two Chapters

ON THE GENERAL SECRET OF ORIENTATION
Chapter One

The appearance of orientation consists of two aspects:

One is (turning to) the forefront, which is turning the face from all dispersed sides.

The other is psychological, and it is the orientation of the face towards the *Kabah*, which is the *umm ul-qura* (the Mother of the Towns) and the center of the extension of the earth.

This appearance has an inside, and the inside has a secret, or rather, secrets. The people of the invisible secrets distract the interior or the spirit from dispersed directions [*jihat*] of the multiplicities of the invisible and visible, and direct the secret of the spirit towards being attached to the One. They regard all the multiplicities as vanished in the secret of the "Collective Oneness" [*ahadiyyat-i jam*]. When this spiritual secret settles in the heart, the *Haqq* (Allah) appears in the heart as the Greatest Name, which is the state of "the Union of the Names" [*jam-i asmai*], and the multiplicities of the Names are vanished and disappear in the Greatest Name, and the heart is directed, in this instance, to the Greatest Name. And when it comes out from inside the heart to the outer visibility, the plan for annihilating [*ifna*] (all) other (than Allah) is to turn away from the east and west of the visible world, and the plan of the orientation towards the Union [*hadrat-i jam*] is the orientation towards the center of the extended earth, which is Allah's hand in the earth.

As regards the traveler to Allah, who travels from the outside to the inside, and advances from the overt to the covert, he is to use this formal orientation towards the center of the earthly blessings, and discarding other diverse orientations, as a means for the cordial moods, and never to be satisfied with the meaningless appearance. He is to divert the heart—which is the focus of Allah's attention—from the different and diverse directions, which are real idols, directing it towards the *qiblah* of the truth, which is the origin of the origins of the blessings of the heavens and the earth, and doing away with the custom of other [*ghayr*] and otherness [*ghayriyyat*] so as to get the secret of **"I have turned my face toward Him Who originated the heavens and the earth"**[179] to some extent, and to have in his heart an example of the manifestations and gleams of the invisible world of the (Divine) Names, so that the diverse directions and the different multiplicities may be burnt away by the divine gleam. Allah, the Exalted, would help him, and the small and big idols in the inmost corner of the heart may be destroyed by the hand of (His) guardianship. However, this is an endless story, so let me drop it and go by.

---

[179] *Surah al-Anam* 6:79

ON SOME OF THE CORDIAL DISCIPLINES OF ORIENTATION
Chapter Two

O you traveler to Allah, know that by turning the outer side of your appearance away from the dispersed points of the world of nature, and turning it to a single point, you have claimed two of the inborn divine dispositions, which the hand of the Invisible has hidden in your essential nature [*khamira-i dhat*], and Allah, with the hand of Beauty and Majesty, has mixed your nature [*tinat*] with them, and you have shown these two inborn states in mundane and visible displays. And, in order not to be deprived of the light of these two divine dispositions, you have proven that you have apparently turned away from all directions, and you solely faced the *qiblah*, which is the place of the appearance of Allah's hand and power. The two divine dispositions are, first, repugnance to imperfection and the imperfect, and, second, loving perfection and the perfect. These two, of which one is original and autogenic, and the other is subordinate and a shadow, are of the dispositions, which are mixed with the nature of the family of mankind without exception. They are in the whole human species disregarding their differences in beliefs, characters, habits, temperaments, places, traditions, and whether nomads or urbans, uncivilized or civilized, learned or ignorant, godly or naturalists. In all of these the two innate dispositions are concocted, even if they themselves do not recognize them in themselves, and differ in distinguishing perfection and imperfection, and the perfect and the imperfect. One who is brutal, bloodthirsty and murderer takes perfection in his victory in assaulting the lives and the honors of the people. He thinks blood-shedding and homicide are perfection, and he spends his life on that, while the ambitious who is in quest of rank, position and wealth in this world thinks that in these he will find perfection, and so, he adores them.

In short, everybody with an objective thinks that objective to be perfection, and the one who attains his objective is the perfect; so he loves it and is repugnant to any other thing. The prophets (*a*), the knowers of Allah, and the people of knowledge have come in order to take the people out of the veil and to save the light of their inborn dispositions from the darkness of ignorance, and to teach them the meaning of perfect and perfection. And, after distinguishing the perfect and perfection, there would remain no need to invite them to attend to that and neglect the others, for the light of the inborn disposition is, in itself, the greatest of the divine guidances, present in all the human species.

In this divine mixture [*majun*], that is, the *salat*, which is the ascension to the Proximity of Allah, facing the *qiblah* and the central point, and giving up and turning away from other diverse directions, denote the wakefulness of the innate disposition, and the emission of the light of the disposition out of the veils. This is a reality for the perfect ones and the people of knowledge. As to us, the people of the veil, the relevant discipline is to tell the heart that in the entire House of Realization [*dar-i tahaqquq*] there is no perfection nor perfect except His Sanctified Essence, the Absolute Perfect, for that Sanctified Essence is a Perfection with no imperfection, a Beauty with no defect, an Actuality with no blemish of potentiality, a Goodness mixed with no evil and a Light with no blemish of darkness. In the entire House of Realization whatever there are of perfection, beauty, goodness, dignity, greatness, illumination, actuality, and happiness, are emissions of the Light of the Beauty of that Sacred Essence, and nobody has any share of personal perfection of that Sacred Essence, and no being has beauty, perfection, light, and magnificence except through His Beauty, Perfection, Light and Magnificence. In short, the splendor of the light of His Sacred Beauty illuminates the world, bestowing upon it life, knowledge and power, as otherwise, the whole House of Realization would have been in complete darkness of non-being, in the latency of non-existence and in the inside of nullity. The one whose heart is lighted with the light of knowledge, sees everything, other than the light of the Beauty of the Beautiful, as void, worthless and non-existing, eternally and forever. It is narrated that when the Messenger of Allah (*s*) heard this poem of Labid,

"Oh, indeed, everything, save Allah, is *batil*
And every pleasure [*naim*] is, inevitably, transient!"

he said: "This is the truest piece of poetry recited by the Arabs."[180]

Having informed your heart about the falsity of all that is in the House of Realization, and about the perfection of the Sacred Essence, there would be no need for the heart to premeditate for turning to the real *qiblah* and loving the Beauty of the Absolute Beautiful, and detesting the entire House of Realization, except the manifestation of the Sacred Essence, as in fact, the very divine disposition in man naturally invites to that, and **"I have turned my face toward Him Who originated the heavens and the earth"**[181] becomes the motto of man"s soul, heart and situation, and **"I do not love the setting ones"**[182] becomes his natural motto.

Thus, O poor, know that the world, excepting Allah, is transient, perishing, vanishing, and *batil*. None of the beings has anything by itself, and none of them in itself has any beauty, glory, light, or splendor. Beauty and splendor exclusively belong to the Essence of Allah. As the Sacred Essence is unique in Divinity and in being Necessary Existent, He is also unique in Beauty, Glory, Perfection, and particularly He is unique in existence, while the humility of essential non-existence [*adam-i dhati*] and nullity are engraved on the foreheads of the others. So, turn the heart, which is the center of the light on the divine innate disposition, away from the different aspects of falsities, nullities and shortcomings, and direct it toward the Center of Beauty and Perfection, and in your pure conscience let the motto of your disposition be what the gnositc of Shiraz says:

Our conscience accommodates none but the Beloved,
Give up both worlds to the foe, suffices us to have the Beloved.

Connection:

Imam as-Sadiq (*a*) is quoted to have said: "When you face the *qiblah*, despair of the world and of what is in it, and of the creatures and of what they are busy with. Empty your heart of whatever takes your attention from Allah, the Exalted. Discern with your heart the Greatness of Allah, the Glorified. Remember your standing before Him on the day when **"Every soul shall become acquainted with**

---

[180] *Ilm al-Yaqin*, vol. 1, p. 106.
[181] *Surah al-Anam* 6:79.
[182] *Ibid.*, 6:76.

what it sent before, and they shall be brought back to Allah, their true Guardian"[183] and stand on the foot of fear and hope."[184]

These noble instructions are for the like of us, the veiled, who are unable to keep the states of our hearts constant, join between Oneness and multiplicity and attend to both Allah and creation. Such being the case, we should despair of the world and what is in it when we turn to Allah and face the *qiblah*. We should also sever our expectancy from the creatures and empty our heart and spirit of whatever takes our attention from Allah, so as to be worthy of His Presence and let a manifestation of majesty appear in the secret of our spirit. And when we gain the light of majesty according to our capacity, we are to remember our return to Allah and our standing in His Sacred Presence on the day when **"Every soul shall be acquainted with what it sent before and they shall be brought back to Allah, their true Guardian"** (*Surah Yunus* 10:30), and they shall cross out all the whims of the soul and the false deities.

Thus, in the Presence of such a Great One, of whose manifestations of Act is this House of Realization, someone like you and a poor man like me, must walk and stand on the foot of hesitation, fear and hope. When we see our weakness, laziness, helplessness, poverty and humility, and discern Allah's Greatness, Haughtiness, Majesty and Might, we are to feel fear and awe from the danger of eminence; and when we understand His unlimited mercy, kindness, leniency, and boundless generosities, we are to be hopeful.

---

[183] *Surah Yunus* 10:30.

[184] *Misbah ash-Shariah*, ch. 13, on "Opening the *Salat*"; *Mustadrak al-Wasa'il*, "Book of *as-Salat*," sec. on "The Acts of the *Salat*," ch. 2, *hadith* 9.

DISCOURSE THREE

THE AFFINITIES [*MUQARINAT*] OF THE *SALAT*

Discussed in Eight Sections

SECTION ONE

On Some Disciplines of the *Adhan* and *Iqamah*

Discussed in Five Chapters

GENERAL SECRET AND DISCIPLINES OF THE *ADHAN* AND *IQAMAH*
Chapter One

Know that the *salik* to Allah has to announce attending the Meeting [*mahdar*], in the *adhan*, to the heart, which is the sultan of the covert and overt powers, and to other soldiers scattered throughout the visible and invisible realms. As the time of the presence and meeting has drawn near, he is to prepare them, so that, if he is of the eager lovers, he may not lose control at the sudden appearance of a manifestation; and if he is of the veiled, he may not enter the Sacred Presence [*mahdar*] without making ready the means and the disciplines for the occasion. Thus, the general secret of the *adhan* is the announcement to the overt and covert powers and the divine armies to attend the Meeting. Its general discipline is to be aware of the greatness of the position, its significance and the majesty of the Presence and the Present, and it is the servility, helplessness, poverty, incapability, and shortcoming of the "possible" (existent) in carrying out orders and deserving to attend the Meeting [*mahdar*], unless the kindness and mercy of Allah, the Most High, extend the helping hand to make up for the shortcomings.

The *iqamah* is to set up the visible and invisible powers in the Presence, and to make them present in the Meeting; and its discipline is fear, awe, shyness, shame, and a firm hope in the boundless mercy. The *salik*, during all the chapters of the *adhan* and the *iqamah*, is to continually inform the heart about the greatness of the Meeting, Presence and the Present, and to continually think of his own humility, inability and shortcoming, in order to bring about (in the heart) fear and awe, while, on the other hand, he is to show to his heart Allah's vast mercy and generous kindness, in order to bring about (in it) hope and eagerness.

So, eagerness and attraction will conquer the loving hearts, and with the steps of love and affection they (the *salik*s) will proceed to the Presence of Intimacy, and their hearts, by means of that invisible attraction, will, till the end of the *salat* and through their love of the Presence and the Present, practice mutual embracing and fondling with remembering Allah and thinking of Him.

Imam Ali ibn Abu Talib (*a*) is quoted to have said: "The best of the people is the one who adores worship, embraces it, wholeheartedly loves it, touches it with his body and disengages himself for it. He would not care whether he gains his share of this world with difficulty or with ease."[185]

And the fearing hearts will be overpowered by the manifestation of the Greatness, and overwhelmed by the attraction of the Omnipotence, so that they (the *salik*s) will be led to ecstasy, their hearts will melt with fear and awe, and their personal shortcomings and their feeling of humility and inability will hold them back from everything.

In a *hadith* Musa ibn Jafar (*a*) is quoted to have said: "Amir al-Muminin (Ali) (*a*) said: "Allah has servants whose hearts are broken by fearing Him, causing them to keep silent." "[186]

Sometimes Allah, the Exalted, manifests Himself to His perfect friends in a kind manifestation, and the attraction of love becomes their guide, as the *hadith* says that the Messenger of Allah (*s*) used to be waiting for the time of the *salat*, his longing ever increasing, until at last he would say to Bilal (the Messenger"s *muadhdhin*): "Relieve us, O Bilal."[187] Sometimes He would manifest Himself through greatness and sovereignty, such that they feel they are filled with fear and awe. Such states are related from the Messenger of Allah (*s*) and the Imams of guidance (*a*). Sometimes He manifests Himself in "the Collective Oneness" [*jami-i ahadi*] according to the endurance of the hearts and the capacities of their vessels. We, the veiled, the busy with the world, the imprisoned in the prison of nature and in the chains of desires and hopes, and the deprived of the divine intellectual happiness, who,

---

[185] *Wasa'il ash-Shiah*, vol. 1, "Book of Purity," sec. on "Preliminaries to Worships," ch. 19, *hadith* 2, p. 61, quoted from the Messenger of Allah (*s*).

[186] *Bihar al-Anwar*, vol. 75, "Book of *ar-Rawdah*," ch. 25, *hadith* 1, p. 309, as cited from *Tuhaf al-Uqul*.

[187] Refer to footnote 178.

because of being drunken with nature, will not come back to sobriety nor get up from the deep sleep till the dawn of eternity, are out of the calculations of these divisions, and excluded from this declaration. Thus, the disciplines of the Presence, which suit us are different, and the performance of the cordial duties has a different form. But what should be the first and foremost, before all else, is to drive out of the heart the despair of Allah"'s mercy, and prevent it from losing hope for His generosity, for these are of *Iblis"* dangerous soldiers and of the inspirations of the human and jinn Satans. We should not imagine that those stations have been cut to suit particular persons, such that our hand of hope is too short to attain them, or man"'s treadings cannot reach them. Hence, we should not mistake hand for foot, and with coldness and weakness, remain sticking to the land of nature forever. No, it is not like what has been imagined! But I still say that the special station of the perfect people of Allah is not possibly attainable by everybody. Yet, the spiritual stations and divine knowledge have unlimited degrees and many ranks. Many of those stations, sciences, states and stages are available to the (human) species, if only their coldness and weakness let them, and if only the obstinacy and fanaticism of the people of ignorance and obstinacy take their hands off the hearts of the servants of Allah, and they turn not to be Satans on the road of their travel to Allah.

So, the discipline of the Presence for us is that at the beginning, as we have not yet passed through the stage of sensation and the appearance, and think of nothing except the mundane greatness and splendor, while knowing nothing of the Divine Invisible Greatnesses, we have to look at Allah"'s Presence [*mahdar*] as we look at a great sultan"'s presence whose greatness has been realized by the heart, informing it that all kinds of greatness, majesty and glory are but manifestations of the greatness of the heavenly world which have descended to this world, and the heavenly world [*alam-i malakut*] is of little importance compared with the invisible worlds. Thus, we are to inform the heart that the world is the Sacred Presence of Allah, the Exalted, since He, the Glorified, is Present at all places and spaces, especially the *salat* which is a special permission for attending the Presence, and a special date for meeting and intimacy with Allah, the Exalted. Now, having incited the heart to feel the Greatness and the Presence, even if at the beginning it was not so easy to do so, the heart gradually becomes familiar with it, and the imagery becomes real. So, by observing the formal disciplines of dealing with the King of the kings and the Sultan of the sultans, and applying the disciplines of the apparent Presence, the heart will also be affected and will feel the greatness, and will gradually attain man"s desired results. Similarly, inciting love and adoration can be achieved by means of perseverance and austerity.

So, at the beginning, one should exhibit the formal mercies and sensual blessings of Allah, the Exalted, to the heart, and then introduce to it the state of Mercifulness, Compassionateness and Bountifulness, until the heart gradually becomes intimate, and the exterior affects the interior, and the kingdom of the interior is illuminated by the effects of the Beauty, and then the desired results will be achieved. If a man carried out the matter and strove in the way of Allah, the Exalted, He would help him and save him by His invisible hand from the darkness of the world of nature, and would throw the light of His Beauty to the dark earth of his heart, and turn him into a spiritual heaven: "And whoever does a good deed, We add unto its good for him. Surely Allah is Forgiving, Thankful."[188]

---

[188] Surah ash-Shura 42:23.

SOME DISCIPLINES AND SECRETS OF *TAKBIRS* IN THE *ADHAN* AND *IQAMAH*
Chapter Two

Know that, as the *adhan* (call to the *salat*) is the announcement of the presence [*hudur*] of the external and internal powers of the soul in the Presence [*mahdar*] of Allah for the sake of praising His Sacred Essence according to all the Names, Attributes, Affairs and *ayahs*—since the *salat*, as has already been mentioned, is a comprehensive praising of the Sacred Essence according to the manifestation of the Greatest Name, which is the state of "the Collective Oneness of the Names" [*ahadiyyat-i jam-i asma*] in His Unity [*hadrat-i wahidiyyat*], and the state of manifestation through the collectivity [*jam*] differentiation [*tafriq*], overtness [*zuhur*] and covertness [*butun*] in the essences [*ayan*] and essential names [*asma-i ayniyyah*]—the *salik*'s attention is first directed to the Majesty of the Sacred Essence according to this general affair [*shan-i jami*]. So, at first, he introduces the said Greatness and Majesty to the invisible and visible powers of his own kingdom. Then, secondly, to the angels of Allah in charge of the invisible powers spread in the kingdom of the soul.   Thirdly, to the beings of the invisible and visible worlds, and fourthly, to the angels of Allah in charge of the Kingdom of the heavens and the earths (lands = *aradin*). So, through these four *takbir*s (saying: "Allah is Greater") he announces the Majesty of the Grand Name (Greatest Name) to all the dwellers of the invisible and visible worlds of the inward and outward kingdoms. And this, by itself, is an announcement of his being incapable of undertaking the duty of praising the Sacred Essence, and an announcement of his falling short of performing the *salat*. This, in itself, is one of the general affairs of the *suluk* and of the comprehensive disciplines concerning praising and worshipping, which must be before the *salik*'s eyes during the whole period of performing the *salat*. That is why the *takbir* is repeated in the *adhan* and the *iqamah*, as well as in the *salat*. It is also repeated when passing from one stage to another so that the *salik*'s innate inability, and the Greatness and the Glory of the Sacred Essence are confirmed in his heart.

As such, its discipline, as it appears, is that the *salik* should, in each *takbir*, remind himself of his inability and Allah's Majesty. On another supposition, it is possible that each one of these preliminary *takbirs* of the *adhan* points to a state: The first *takbir* means: He is Greater than the attributive Essence; the second means: He is Greater than the attributive Attribute; the third means: He is Greater than the attributive Name; and the fourth means: He is Greater than the attributive Act. Thus, it is as if the *salik* says: *Allahu akbar* [Allah is Greater] than your description of His Essence, or of His Essence-manifestations, and He is Greater than your describing Attributes, His Names and His Acts, or their respective manifestations.

In an elaborated speech quoted from Amir al-Muminin Ali (*a*) it is said: "...The other aspect is that *Allahu akbar* implies negation of His quality, as if he (the *muadhdhin* = the one who speaks out the *adhan*) says: "Allah's attribute, with which He is qualified, is far above being comprehended by the describers," for the describers describe Him according to their own measure, not according to the measure of His Greatness and Majesty. He is far above His quality being understood by the describers..." as the *hadith* goes.[189]

Another important discipline of the *takbirs* is that the *salik* is to strive, and, by cordial austerities, he is to prepare his heart to be the place for the Majesty of Allah, the Glorified, and to regard Greatness, Glory, Sovereignty and Majesty to be exclusively ascribed to the Sacred Essence of Allah, the Most High, and to exclude the others from Majesty. If he feels in his heart even a tiny bit of anyone else''s greatness, without taking it to be the light of that of Allah's, his heart is sick and is controlled by Satan. It is quite possible that Satan's intrusion would cause the sovereignty of the majesty of other than Allah, in the heart, to be more than that of Allah's, and the heart would regard him greater than Allah. In this case, man would be counted among the hypocrites. The symptom of this devastating disease is that man regards the pleasure of the creatures to be preferred to the

---

[189] *Bihar al-Anwar*, vol. 81, p. 131, "Book of the *Salat*," ch. on "The *Adhan* and the *Iqamah*," *hadith* 24.

pleasure of Allah, and in order to obtain the pleasure of the created, he would incur the displeasure of the Creator.

As-Sadiq (*a*) is quoted to have said: "When you say: *Allahu akbar*, slight whatever is there between the high (heaven) and the earth, regarding it below His Majesty, because if Allah looked into the heart of the servant while telling the *takbir*, and saw therein something contradicting his *takbir*, He would say: "O you liar! Are you deceiving Me? By My Might and My Majesty, I will deprive you of (tasting) the sweetness of remembering Me, and I will exclude you from My proximity and from getting pleasure through your supplication."[190]

My dear, the fact that our wretched hearts are deprived of the sweetness of remembering Allah, the Exalted, and that the enjoyment of supplication to the Sacred Essence is not tasted by our spirit, and that we are prevented from reaching the proximity of His Threshold and deprived of the manifestations of His Beauty and Majesty, is because our hearts are sick and faulty, attracted by the world, stuck to it and wrapped in the veils of the darkness of nature. And this fact deprives us of recognizing Allah"s Majesty and of discerning the lights of His Beauty and Glory. As long as our look at the beings is Satanic and independent, we shall never drink of the wine of intimacy, not attain the pleasure of supplication. As long as we believe that in the world of existence there can be glory, might, majesty, greatness and dignity for any created being, and as long as we are wrapped in the veils of the created specifications [*taayyunat*], the dominion [*sultan*] of the Majesty of Allah, the Glorified, will not manifest in our hearts.

So, of the disciplines of *takbir* is that the *salik* should not stop at its outer form, or be satisfied with its wordings and with mere pronunciations of the tongue. First, he is to prove to the heart, with the power of argument and the light of divine knowledge, Allah"s Glory and the confinement of greatness and majesty only to the Sacred Essence of Allah, Most High, informing it of the poverty, humility and helplessness of all the possible dwellers and all the corporeal and spiritual beings. After that, with the power of austerity, frequent intimacy [*murawadah*] and complete familiarity, he is to enliven the heart with this divine grace and grant it spiritual and intellectual life

---

[190] *Misbah ash-Shariah*, ch. 13, on "Finishing the *Salat*"; *al-Mahajjat al-Bayda"*, printed by as-Saduq Library, vol. 1 , p. 385; *Mustadarak al-Wasa'il*, "Book of *as-Salat*, sec. on "The Acts of the *Salat*," ch. 2, *hadith* 9.

and happiness. When the *salik* realizes the poverty and the humility of the possible (the creatures) and Allah's Greatness and Majesty, and puts that before his eyes, while his contemplation and remembrance reach their assigned limit, and the heart attains familiarity and tranquility, he will see with the eye of insight the effects of Allah's Glory and Majesty in all beings, and the diseases and faults of his heart will be cured. Only then will he taste the deliciousness of supplication and the sweetness of remembering Allah, and the heart will affirm Allah's Sovereign Majesty, and the effects of Majesty will appear in the exterior and in the interior of the kingdom, and the heart, the tongue, the outside and the inside will go in harmony. So, all the external and internal powers, visible and invisible, recite *Allahu akbar*, and one of the thick curtains is drawn away, and he gets one stage nearer to the truth of the *salat*.

There is a reference to some of what has been said in a lengthy *hadith* in *Ilal ash-Sharai*, quoting Imam Jafar as-Sadiq (*a*) describing the *miraj*. He said: "Allah, the Glorified and Almighty, sent down to the Prophet a carriage of light comprised of forty sorts of light which were around the *Arsh*. The *Arsh* of Allah, Blessed and Most High, blurs the eyes of the onlookers. One of them was yellow, and it became the cause of the yellowness of the yellow. Another one was red, and it became the cause of the redness of the red..." Then he added: "... He [the Messenger (*s*)] sat in it and it ascended him to the lower heaven. The angels ran to the outskirts of the heaven, and then they fell in prostration, and said: "All-Glorified and All-Holy is our Lord, the Lord of the angels and the Spirit. How this light is like the light of our Lord!" Jibrail (Gabriel) said: "*Allahu akbar! Allahu akbar!*" The angels stopped talking, and the heaven was opened. The angels gathered and came to pay tribute to the Prophet (*s*) group after group..." as the *hadith* goes.[191]

In this noble *hadith* there are great secrets to which the hand of our hopes is too short to reach, and what can be said is now out of our purpose, like the secret of the descension of the carriage of light, the secret of the many lights, the secret of their diversity, the secret of the figure forty, the secret of its being sent down by Allah, the secret of their gathering around the *Arsh*, the truth of the *Arsh* in this respect,

---

[191] *Ilal ash-Shara'i*, vol. 2, p. 312, sec. on "The Causes of the *Wudu*", the *Adhan* and the *Salat*," *hadith* 1, p. 312.

the secret of the yellowness of the yellow and the redness of the red caused by them, the secret of the angels'' running, their bowing, praising and glorifying, and likening his light to Allah''s, and the like. To speak about each of them would be lengthy. Yet, that which suits this occasion and testifies to our subject is that the angels of Allah quieted down as they heard Gabriel''s *takbir*, and gathered around the candle of the meeting of the Absolute Guardian. By that *takbir* the first heaven opened, and one of the curtains, which blocked the way to Allah, was drawn away. It should be noted that the curtains, which are pushed aside by the *adhan* are other than the curtains, which are in the opening *takbir*s. We shall probably refer to this concept later on, *insha Allah* (Allah willing).

Concerning there being only two *takbir*s in the *iqamah*, it is probably because the *salik* has set up his powers in the Presence, and has somewhat advanced from multiplicity toward unity, magnifying the Essence and the Names, or the Names and the Attributes; and it may be that the magnification of the Essence and the Names implies the magnification of the Attributes and the Acts.

SOME DISCIPLINES CONCERNING TESTIFYING DIVINITY AND ITS CONNECTION WITH THE *ADHAN* AND THE *SALAT*
Chapter Three

Know that divinity has many states [*maqamat*], which, according to "collectivity" [*jam*], are explained in two: **First:** Divinity of Essence. **Second:** Divinity of Action. If by testifying that divinity is confined to Allah we mean the Divinity of Essence, its truth, with that of *takbir*, will come close to each other if *ilah* (divinity) is derived from *aliha fi sh-shay*, i.e. "He became perplexed about it," or derived from *laha*, i.e. "He became lofty" or derived from *laha yaluhu*, i.e. "He concealed himself." In this case its connection to the *adhan* and the *salat* becomes known by referring to the chapter of *takbir*, and so does its discipline. But to repeat it again, though not void of some advantage, is contrary to brevity. If we take *aliha* to mean: "He worshipped," and *maluh* to mean: "the worshipped," then the *salik* must make the formal testimony of the confinement of deity to Allah, the Most High, comply with the inner cordial testimony, and he should know that should there be in the heart a deity other than Allah, he would be a hypocrite in his testimony.

So, the *salik* is to convey to his heart, by whatever austerity, his testimony about divinity, and to smash in his heart the big and small idols which have been engraved by the intruding hands of Satan and the evil-commanding soul, and to sweep them away, so that he may become fit to be in the Presence of His Sacred Essence. As long as the idols of loving the world and mundane affairs are still in the *kabah* of the heart, the *salik* will find no way to his goal. So, testifying to divinity is to announce to the worldly and heavenly powers that the false deities and the crooked objectives should be trod upon so as to be able to ascend to Allah"s Proximity.

But if the confinement of divinity is intended for Divinity of Action, which is management and effectiveness, the meaning of the testimony will be: I testify that there is no manager and no effective influence in the world of achievement, and in the visible and the invisible save the Sacred Essence of Allah, the Most High. If the *salik*"s heart cherished dependence on any being among the beings, and trusted any individual among the individuals, his heart would be diseased and his testimony false.

Thus, the *salik* must first strengthen, with judicial proof, the fact that "There is no effecter [*muaththir*] in the (world of) existence except Allah." He must not evade the divine knowledge, which is the objective of sending prophets, and not turn away from remembering Allah and from the affairs of the Essence and Attributes, for the source of all (kinds of) happiness is the remembrance of Allah: **"And whoever turns away from remembering Me, his shall surely be a straitened life."**[192] After attaining the truth of this divine delicacy, which is the source of the divine knowledge and the door of the doors of the hidden facts, by way of thinking and reasoning, he is to make his heart, through remembrance and austerity, familiar with them until it believes in them. This would be the first stage of the truthfulness of his words, and it is marked by complete dependence on Allah, and by taking the eye of greed and hope away from all beings, a fact which results in believing in Allah"s Unity of Action, being one of the great states of the people of knowledge. Having ascribed all effects to Allah, and closed the eye of greed against all beings, save His Sacred Essence, the *salik* becomes worthy attending the Sacred Presence, or rather his heart becomes, by nature, attentive to that Presence. Repeating the testimony may be for confirming it, and by the testimony we mean one of the two testimonies, or it may not be a repetition, but one may refer to the Divinity of Essence and the other to the Divinity of Action. In this instance, its repetition at the end may be to confirm them, and that is why it is not mentioned there with the very words: "I testify."

---

[192] *Surah Ta-Ha* 20:124.

A Gnostic Note

Know that testimony is of many stages, of which we shall be satisfied with referring to a few, as suits these pages.

The first is the verbal testimony [*shahadat-i qawliyyah*], which is already known. If the verbal testimony is not accompanied by cordial testimony, even in a lower stage, it will not be a testimony, but a deception and hypocrisy, as it was mentioned in the *hadith* concerning *takbir*, quoted from Imam as-Sadiq (*a*).[193]

The second is the Practical Testimony [*shahadat-i filiyyah*], which means that man testifies through the practices of his organs. For example, he is, in the type and method of his action, to apply the fact that: "There is no effecter [*muaththir*] in the (world of) existence save Allah," and, as his verbal testimony requires him to think that nobody is effective, he should work out the plan of his acts accordingly. Hence, he should not extend the hand of need to anybody except to the Sacred Presence of Allah, the Most High, nor should he open the eye of expectation at any being. He should show himself rich and in no need, before the weak servants, and keep aloof from weakness, humility and inability.

This is frequently referred to by noble *hadith*s, as is in a narrative stated in the noble *al-Kafi*: "A believer's dignity is to manage without the help of the people."[194] Showing oneself well off and prosperous is one of the religious commendable practices, while demanding things from people is undesirable. In short, one must put to practice the divine grace: "There is no effecter in the (world of) existence except Allah" in his external kingdom.

The third is the Cordial Testimony [*shahadat-i qalbiyyah*], which is the source of the practical and verbal testimonies, as without it, these would not come to actuality. And it is that Allah's Unity of Action manifests in the heart, which realizes, by way of its inner secret, the truth of this grace, and separates itself from other beings. Most of the narratives quoted from the infallible *Ahl al-Bayt* (*a*) concerning abandoning looking with greed at what is in the hands of the people, and despairing of the servants, and trusting and confiding in Allah, the Exalted and Most High, refer to this situation.

---

[193] Refer to footnote 190.
[194] *Usul al-Kafi*, vol. 3, "Book of Faith and Disbelief," ch. on "Doing without the People," *hadith* 1, p. 218.

It is in *al-Kafi*, on the authority of Ali ibn al-Husayn (*a*) that he said: "I found that the entire goodness is gathered in cutting one''s coveting what is in the hands of others, and whoever placed no hope on the people in anything, and entrusted himself to Allah, the Exalted, in all his affairs, Allah would respond to him in all the things."[195] *Hadith*s of this kind are many.

The fourth is the Essence Testimony (Personal Testimony = *shahadat-i dhatiyyah*), i.e. the existential testimony, and it appears in the perfect holy men. To the holy men, this testimony is present in all beings, in one way or another. Perhaps the *ayah*: **"Allah bears witness that there is no god but He, and (so do) the angels and the possessors of knowledge,"**[196] is a hint at the Essence Testimony, for Allah, the Exalted, in the state of "the Collective Oneness" [*ahadiyyat-i dhatiyyah*] gives Personal testimony to His own Unity [*wahdaniyyat*], because mere existence by itself denotes the Essence-Oneness [*ahadiyyat-i dhatiyyah*], and in the rising of the Day of Resurrection it appears in Complete Unity [*wahdaniyyat-i tammah*]. This Oneness [*ahadiyyat*] appears first in the mirror of the Collectivity [*jam*], then in the mirror of distinctness [*tafsil*]. For this reason He said: **"...and the angels and the possessors of knowledge."** In this instance there are many states of knowledge [*maarif*] that are out of the obligation of these pages to explain.

Connection:

In the exegesis of Muhammad ibn Masud al-Ayyashi, quoting Abd as-Samad ibn Bashir, it is said: "The beginning of the *adhan* was mentioned to Abu Abdullah (Imam as-Sadiq) (*a*), and he said: "The Messenger of Allah (*s*) was (once) sleeping in the shadow of the *kabah*, when Gabriel came to him with a bowl of water from Paradise. He woke him up and told him to wash himself with it. Then he (the Prophet) was put in a carriage with a thousand colors of light, and he was taken high up to the doors of the heaven. When the angels saw him, they ran away from the doors of the heaven, exclaiming: "Two gods, a god in the earth and a god in the heaven!" Allah commanded Gabriel to shout: *"Allahu akbar! Allahu akbar!"* So the angels returned to the doors of the heaven. The door was opened, and he

---

[195] *Ibid.*, hadith 3.
[196] *Surah Al-i Imran* 3:18.

proceeded until he reached the second heaven. The angels ran away from the doors of the heaven. There he said: "I testify that there is no god but Allah! I testify that there is no god but Allah!" The angels returned, as they realized that he was a creature. Then the door was opened and he went in..." as the *hadith* goes on.[197]

A similar concept is stated in a narrative in *Ilal ash-Sharai*.[198] These *hadith*s denote that testifying to Allah's Divinity opens the doors of the heaven and penetrates the barriers, and causes the angels of Allah to gather. The veil which is penetrated through by testifying to His Divinity and by confessing it to be exclusively His, is of the thick veils of darkness, and, as long as the *salik* is wrapped in it, he will have no way to attend the Presence, and unless this door opens to him, he will not be admitted. That barrier is the veil of the multiplicity of acts, and to fall in this multiplicating veil results in taking the created beings to be effective and influential, which means regarding them to be independent in their action, which is admitting, the impossible and is a great polytheism, while, on the other hand, the result of testifying to the divinity to be exclusively Allah's, is testifying to the Unity of Action and annihilating the multiplicities in Allah's Act, and denying anyone else to have any effect or effectiveness, and believing that independence belongs to Allah, the Exalted. It was by means of this testimony that the angels of the heaven came out of the veil of the multiplicity of "A god in the earth and a god in the heaven," and returned from fleeing away and dispersing to familiarity and gathering, and then the doors of the heaven opened to them. So, the *salik* must also penetrate through this veil of his darkness by way of this testimony and open the doors of heaven to himself, and step out of the heavy veil of the independence, so that the way of ascension to the *miraj* of His Proximity becomes closer. But this cannot be brought about by mere verbal utterances of remembering Allah, as that is why our acts of worship do not cross the limit of the mundane formality, and, thus, no door will be opened to us and no veil will be pushed off our faces.

---

[197] *Al-Ayyashi*"s Exegesis (on the Quran), vol. 1, p. 157, Commenting on *Surah al-Baqarah*, narrative 530.

[198] *Ilal ash-Shara'i*, vol. 2, p. 312.

SOME DISCIPLINES OF TESTIFYING TO THE (PROPHET"S)MESSENGERSHIP IMPLYING TESTIFYING TO THE GUARDIANSHIP
Chapter Four

Be aware that this spiritual journey and faithful ascension cannot be made with this broken leg, ruptured reins, blind eyes and lightless heart: **"And whomever Allah has not given light, for him there is no light."**[198a] Therefore, in setting off upon this spiritual road and ascending to this gnostic *miraj*, it is a must to adhere to the spiritual state of the guides along the ways of knowledge [*marifat*] and the lights [*anwar*] of the road of guidance, who are the devotees and the attainers to Allah. If anybody tries, depending on his selfishness and without clinging to their guardianship, to tread upon this road, his journey will be to Satan and to the pit (of hell) [*hawiyah*]. Scientifically speaking, to connect between the novel [*hadith*] and the Eternal [*qadim*], the changing and the Unchanging, there should be an intermediate, a connector, with the characteristic of being unchanging and changing, eternal and novel. Without such an intermediate, the Emanation of the Eternal and the Unchanging would not pass to the changing and the novel in the divine law, and the universal and existential connection would not take place. As regards the connector between these two, the scientific opinions of the experts in the evidential knowledge [*ulum-i burhani*] are diverse, as the gnostic taste is different, to give the details of which is out of the scope of these papers. In the gnostic taste, the connector is the Sacred Emanation [*fayd-i muqaddas*], the Expansive Existence [*wujud-i munbasit*], which has the position [*maqam*] of the big isthmus [*barzakhiyyat-i kubra*]

[198a] *Surah Nur* 24:40.

and the great intermediate [*wasaTiyyat-i uzma*], and it is the very position of the spirituality and the guardianship of the Seal of the Prophets, which is united with the position of Ali"s General Guardianship [*wilayat-i muTlaq-i Alawiyyah*]. The relevant details are stated in the *Misbah al-Hidayah* by the writer.[199] Similarly, in the ascending spiritual connection—which is the opposite of the descending existential connection, or in other words, it is "the contraction of existence" [*qabd-i wujud*] and returning to the Beginning—there is need for an intermediate, without which it does not take place, and the connection of the imperfect and the chained hearts, and of the limited descending spirits, with the Complete, Super Complete and the Absolute from all aspects, is not implemented without the spiritual intermediates and the invisible connectors.

If somebody thinks that Allah, the Exalted, is self-subsisting [*qayyum*] with each being and encompassing each of the entities [*akwan*] without the intermediation of the intermediates, as is referred to in the noble *ayah*: **"There is no living creature but He holds it by the forelock,"**[200] he is mixing up the states [*maqamat*] and is making a mistake in the status [*itibarat*], mingling the state of the multiplicity of the stages of existence with the vanishing [*fana*] of the individuations [*taayyunat*]. This discussion, however, is not so much connected to this paper, and, actually, what has already been said was caused by the overflowing of the pen.

In short, adhering to the masters of graces [*awliya-i niam*]—who have themselves found the way of ascension to *maarij* and completed their journey to Allah—is a must for the travelers to Allah, as is frequently mentioned in the noble *hadith*s, such that in *Wasail* (*Wasail ash-Shiah*) there is a chapter concerning the invalidity of

---

[199] *Misbah al-Hidayah* is a book written in the Arabic language by Imam Khomeini (may Allah sanctify his honorable soul), explaining some truths and knowledge concerning the caliphate and guardianship. In the Preface to this honorable book he says: "I like to uncover for you, in this paper, by the help of Allah, the guardian of guidance in the beginning and in the end, an indication of the Muhammadan caliphate, and an exudation of the truth of the Alawian guardianship (upon them be the greeting from the beginning to eternity) and how they spread through the invisible and visible worlds...,or rather it should be named: *Misbah al-Hidayah* to Caliphate and Guardianship. I ask Allah success, as He is the best assistant and company, and I ask His pure guardians their patronage in this world and in the other world..." The writer finished writing the book in the month of Shawwal, 1349 A.H.
[200] *Surah Hud* 11:56.

worship without adhering to the guardianship of the Imams (the 12 Imams) and believing in their Imamate. In *Wasail* it is quoted from the noble *al-Kafi*, on the authority of its writer quoting Muhammad ibn Muslim who said: "I was told by Imam Baqir al-Ulum (the fifth Imam) (*a*) who said: "Know, O Muhammad, that the leaders of despotism and their followers are isolated from Allah's religion. They are misleading and misled. So, their deeds are like the ashes at which a violent wind blows on a windy day and it disperses them."[201]

In another narrative from Imam al-Baqir, he said: "If a man spent his nights performing the *salat*, spent his days fasting, gave out all his wealth in charity, and went to *hajj* every year of his life, yet he did not know the guardianship of Allah's friend to follow him and return to him in all his deeds, he would have no right to ask Allah, the Glorious and Almighty, for any reward, nor would he be of the people of faith."[202]

Shaykh as-Saduq, quoting Abu Hamza ath-Thumali, says that he said: "Imam Ali ibn al-Husayn (*a*) asked us: "Which spot is most preferred?" We said "Allah, His Messenger and the son of His Messenger know better." He said: "The best of spots for us is that which is situated between the *rukn* and the *maqam* (two places in the Kabah). If some one lives as long as the life of Nuh—who lived among his people for a thousand years less fifty—and spends it in fasting in daytime and in worshipping at nights in that spot, and then goes to meet Allah without accepting our guardianship, he will not be benefited by it whatsoever."[203]

The narratives on this topic are too many to be contained in this summary.

The discipline of testifying to the Messengership is to convey to the heart the testimony of the Messenger's being sent by Allah, as well as the greatness of the state of the Messengership, especially that of the Last Messenger, since the whole circle of existence, the

---

[201] *Wasa'il ash-Shiah*, vol. 1, sec. on "Preliminaries to Worship," ch. 29, *hadith* 1, p. 90. *Usul al-Kafi*, vol. 1, "Book of Proof," ch. on "Knowing the Imam and Returning to Him," *hadith* 8, p. 259.
[202] *Usul al-Kafi*, vol. 3, "Book of Faith and Infidelity," ch. on "The Pillars of Islam," *hadith* 5, p. 30.
[203] *Iqab al-Amal*, ch. on "He Who Ignores the Merits of *Ahl al-Bayt*," *hadith* 2; *Wasa'il ash-Shiah*, vol. 1, sec. on "Preliminaries to Worship," ch. 29, *hadith* 12, p. 93.

invisible and visible worlds, from the viewpoints of creation, legislation, existence, and guidance, are living on the crumbs of his table. That great man is the means of Allah"s Emanation and the connection between Allah and the creatures. Had it not been for his spiritual status [*maqam*] and absolute guardianship, no existing being could have been worthy of being benefited by the state of the Invisible Oneness [*ghayb-i ahadi*], and Allah"s grace would not have passed over to any being, and the light of guidance would not have shone onto anyone of the internal and external worlds. He is the light mentioned in the *ayah* of *Nur* (Light): **"Allah is the light of the heavens and the earth."**[204]

When the greatness of the legislator of the religion and of the Messenger of the Lord of the worlds enters a man"s heart, the importance of his precepts and rules enter the heart, too. Then, when the heart has comprehended that greatness, the other visible and invisible powers would submit to it, and the sacred *shariah* would be observed in the entire human kingdom. The sign of the truthfulness of the testimony is that its effects will appear in all the invisible and visible powers, and they will keep adherent to it, as has already been stated.

From what has so far been stated, the reason of testifying to the Messengership in the *adhan*, the *iqamah* and the *salat* has become clear, for the traveler on this spiritual road is in need of adhering to that sacred being, so that he may accompany him and have his helping guidance in performing this spiritual ascension.

Another aspect of this testimony is the announcement to the mundane and heavenly powers that the *salat*, which is the reality of the ascension [*miraj*] of the believers and the source of the knowledge of the people of gnosticism and of faith, is the result of the complete revelation [*kashf*] of Muhammad (*s*), who, with his spiritual journey, divine attractions and the embers of the Beneficent, attained a position **"at the distance of two bows or closer still,"**[205] revealing its truth, following the Essential, Nominal and Attributive manifestations and intimate inspirations in the Invisible Oneness. In fact, this is a souvenir, a gift that he brought from his moral and spiritual journey for his *ummah*, which is the best of the *ummah*s, and by that he favored

---

[204] *Surah an-Nur* 24:35.
[205] *Surah an-Najm* 53:9.

them and overwhelmed them with blessings. When this belief sets inside the heart and is fixed by repetition, the *salik* will, as a matter of course, understand the greatness of the state and the place, and will proceed, with fear and hope, to cover this stage, and it is hoped, *insha Allah* (Allah willing), if he does his best to perform it, that master will assist him and lead him to the state of "the Proximity of the One" [*qurb-i ahadiyy*], which is the original innate objective. In the divine sciences it has been proved that the return of all beings is implemented by means of the Perfect Man: **"As He brought you forth in the beginning, so shall you also return."**[206] "With you Allah started and with you He will end, and the return of the creatures is up to you."[207]

A Gnostic Note

In the honorable hadith in Ilal ash-Sharai, which gives details about the salat of the miraj and describes it, it is said that when the Messenger of Allah (s) mounted on the mount of light, which had been sent down by the Lord of Might, and ascended accompanied by Gabriel, and reached the third heaven, the angels ran away, bowed and glorified Allah. Gabriel said: "I testify that Muhammad is the Messenger of Allah. I testify that Muhammad is the Messenger of Allah." The angels gathered and greeted the Messenger of Allah, and asked him about Amir al-Muminin (Ali). The doors of the heavens opened and the Messenger ascended to the fourth heaven. There, the angels of Allah said nothing. Then the doors of the heaven opened, and the angels gathered, and Gabriel finished reciting the iqamah..."208 etc.

Al-Ayyashi, in his exegesis of the Quran, relates almost the same context.

From this hadith one may gather that the angels of each of the heavens were incapable of enduring to see the Ahmadian Beauty, and they fell bowing at seeing his sacred light, and dispersed, thinking it was the light of Allah. Then, as they heard the chapters of the adhan and the iqamah they came back to his intimacy, the doors of the heavens opened and the veils were lifted.

Hence, the salik is to come out from these veils by means of the said testimonies—by testifying to the Messengership he is to

---

[206] *Surah al-A'raf* 7:29.
[207] *Uyunu Akhbar ar-Rida*, vol. 2, p. 272 (*Al-Jamiah al-Kabirah* invocation).
[208] Refer to footnote 191.

completely come out from the veil of the creational individuality [*taayyun-i khalqi*], because the position of Messengership which He assigned to the most honorable of the creatures, is the position of absolute annihilation [*fana*] and complete dependence, since the final absolute Messengership is the big divine isthmus *khilafah* (vicegerency, succession). It is a vicegerency [*khilafah*] in respect of appearance, manifestation, genesis, and legislation. The vicegerent [*khalifah*] is not to be independent nor to have individuality in any way, as otherwise, the vicegerency becomes the principalship itself, which is not possible for any of the beings.

So, the *salik* is to convey the great state of the Ahmadian *khilafat* to the innermost of his heart and soul, by means of which he is to remove the veil and penetrate the barriers, and to completely come out of the veils of the creational individuation. Then, the doors of all the heavens will open to him and he will attain, unveiled, his objective.

A Juristic Branch and a Gnostic Principal

In some unreliable narratives it is stated that after testifying to the Messengership in the *adhan* one is to say: "I testify that Ali is *waliyullah* (Allah's friend)" twice. In other narratives, one is to say: "I testify that Ali is truly Amir al-Muminin" twice. In some others, one is to say: "Muhammad and his progeny are the best of people." Ash-Shaykh as-Saduq (may Allah have mercy upon him) took these narratives to be invented and he denied them.[209] It is well known among the *ulama* (may Allah be pleased with them) that these narratives are not reliable. Some narrators regard them among the commendables, due to "the negligence of the proofs of the laws". This opinion, however, is not far from being true, although if "absolute proximity" [*qurbat-i mutlaqah*] is intended, reciting it is better and more admired, because after testifying to the Messengership, it is desirable to testify to the guardianship and the leadership of the believers. In the *hadith* of *ihtijaj* (argumentation) it is said that Qasim ibn Muawiyah said: "I said to Imam as-Sadiq that the people of the *Sunnah* relate a *hadith* about the *miraj*, that when the Messenger of Allah was taken on the *miraj*, he saw upon the *Arsh*: "There is no god

---

[209] *Man la Yahduruh al-Faqih*, vol. 1, "Book of the *Salat*," ch. on "The *Adhan*, the *Iqamah* and the Reward of the *Muadhdhin*s (Those who call for the *salat*), comment on narrative 35, p. 188.

but Allah, Muhammad is the Messenger of Allah, and Abu Bakr as-Siddiq." He said: "Glory be to Allah! They changed everything even this!" He said: "Yes". Then he continued: "When Allah, the Exalted, created the *Arsh*, He wrote upon it: "There is no god but Allah, Muhammad is the Messenger of Allah, and Ali is the Commander (Leader) of the Faithful. He ordered these to be written on the water, on the Chair (Throne), on the Tablet, on *Israfil*'s forehead, on the two wings of Gabriel, on the shoulders of the heavens and the earth, on the top of the mountains, on the sun and on the moon." Then the Imam added: "When anyone of you says: "There is no god but Allah, Muhammad is the Messenger of Allah," let him say: "Ali is the Commander (Leader) of the Faithful."[210]

In short, this noble remembrance, after testifying to the Messengership is generally recommendable. In the chapters of the *adhan* especially, it is probably commendable. Nevertheless, as the notable *ulama* have denied those narratives, one may pronounce it by way of precaution and with the general intention of proximity (to Allah), not as a feature of the *adhan*.

As to the gnostic note concerning "writing these words on all the beings, as from the High *Arsh* to the low earth," it is that the truth of the *khilafah* and *wilayah* (successorship and guardianship) is the manifestation of divinity, which is the origin of existence and its perfection. Every being which has a share of existence also has a share of the truth of divinity and its manifestation, which is the truth of the *khilafah* and *wilayah*, and the divine grace is fixed on the foreheads of all beings all over the universe, as from the invisible worlds to the end of the visible world. The said divine grace is the truth of "the Expansive Existence" [*wujud-i munbasit*], "the Breath of the Beneficent" [*nafas ar-rahman*] and "the Created-in Right" [*haqq-i makhluqun bihi*], which are the very inside of the Last Successorship and of Ali's General Guardianship. On this, the gnostic Shaykh Shahabadi (may his spirit be sanctified) used to say that the testimony to Messengership implies the testimony to Guardianship, because Guardianship is the inside of Messengership. The writer says that these two testimonies are both implied in the testimony to His Divinity, and the testimony to Messengership implies the other two testimonies, and

---

[210] *Al-Ihtijaj*, vol. 1, p. 230.

also the testimony to Guardianship implies the other two testimonies. Praise be to Allah at the beginning and at the end.

SOME DISCIPLINES OF THE *HAYYA ALA*(S)
Chapter Five

When the wayfarer to Allah has announced by his *takbir*s that Allah is greater than any description, and by testifying to His Divinity has exclusively confined all attributes and praise, or, actually, every influence and effect, to Allah, and confessed his incapability of managing the *amr*, and by the testimony to the Messengership and Guardianship, he has chosen his comrade and company and adhered to the sacred position of successorship and guardianship—as it is said: "The companion (first) then the journey"[211]— then, with quite an explicit tone, he is to prepare his visible and invisible powers for the *salat*, announcing the presence to them by saying: "*Hayya ala 's-salat*," (come to the *salat*) twice. Its repetition is intended to complete awakening [*tanbih*] and waking up [*iqaz*], or one is for the inner powers of the kingdom, and the other is for the outer powers of the kingdom, since they also accompany the *salik* on his journey, as has already been said, and will follow, too.

In this stage, the discipline of the *salik* is to tell his heart and powers, even the innermost of the heart, that the time of presence is near so as to prepare himself for that, fully observing the formal and the spiritual disciplines. Then he is to announce the general secret and result of the *salat*, by the calling: "*Hayya ala l-falah*" and "*Hayya ala khayr il-amal* (come to the best of deeds) so as to wake up the *fitrat* (disposition = nature), because prosperity and salvation are absolute happiness, and all the human beings love absolute happiness by nature. The innate nature [*fitrat*] is in quest of perfection and comfort. The

---

[211] *Wasa'il ash-Shiah*, vol. 8, "Book of *Hajj*," sec. on "The Manners of Travel," ch. 30, *hadith* 11, p. 299, as quoted from al-Barqi's *Mahasin*, p. 357. Similar concepts are in some other narratives, such as: "Inquire about the company before the journey" as in *Nahj al-Balaghah*, ed. by Fayd al-Islam, p. 936, and "The company (first), then the journey," in *al-Ashathiyyat*, ch. on "Bad Neighboring," p. 164.

truth of happiness is the absolute perfection and absolute comfort, and that is brought about in the *salat*, which is the best of deeds, cordially, formally, outwardly, and inwardly. This is because the *salat*, according to its form and appearance, is a great and comprehensive remembrance and a praise of the Greatest Name, which encompasses all the divine affairs [*shuun*]. For this reason, the *adhan* and the *iqamah* open with the word "Allah" and end with it, and *Allahu akbar* (Allah is Greater) is repeated in all stages of the *salat*, and the three *tawhid*s (professions of the Unity of Allah), which are the delight of eyes of the holy men, are effected in the *salat*, in which the form [*surat*] of absolute annihilation and complete return are mixed. According to the interior and the truth, it is ascension to the proximity of Allah, the truth of reaching the Beauty of the Absolute Beautiful and vanishing in that Sanctified Essence, dearly loved by the inborn nature [*fitrat*]. It is by the *salat* that the complete calmness, absolute comfort and the complete mental happiness are achieved: **"Surely by Allah's remembrance are the hearts set at rest."** [212]

Therefore, the absolute perfection, which is attaining to Allah's Court, joining the Necessary Limitless Sea, discerning the Eternal Beauty, and being immersed in the Sea of Absolute Light, is effected in the *salat*, in which absolute comfort, complete rest and perfect calmness also appear, bringing about the two corners of happiness. So, the *salat* is perfect prosperity, and it is the best of the deeds. The *salik* will have to repeat this divine grace, to remind the heart and to wake up his disposition [*fitrat*], and after having it in his heart, his inner nature would attach importance to it and observe it, since it looks for perfection and happiness. The same point is true in respect of the repetition.

When the *salik* reaches this stage, he announces his presence by saying: "*qad qamati s-salat*" (The *salat* has just started). Then, he is to see himself at the Presence of the Master of the kings of the worlds of existence and the Sultan of the sultans and the Absolute Great, and to inform his heart about the dangers of the Presence, all of which are due to the incapability and the inefficiency of "the possible", and to feel ashamed of not carrying out the *amr*, approaching, with the steps of fear and hope, towards the Generous. He is not to regard himself possessing traveling provisions and company. He is to see his heart

---

[212] *Surah ar-Rad* 13:28.

empty of safety, not to think his deeds good ones; rather, worth not a penny. Should this state become firm in his heart, he would hope to get Allah‛s care: **"Or Who answers the distressed one, when he calls unto Him, and removes the evil?"**[213]

Connection and Completion

Muhammad ibn Yaqub, quoting Abu Abdullah as-Sadiq (*a*), says: "When you recite the *adhan* and the *iqamah*, two rows of angels will perform the *salat* behind you, but if you said the *iqamah* (only), one row of the angels would perform the *salat* behind you."[214] There are many other *hadith*s to the same effect, some of which say that the length of each row is as the distance between the east and the west.[215] Another *hadith* says that when Imam as-Sadiq (*a*) was asked about the length of each row, he said: "The length of the shortest row is as the distance between the east and the west, and the length of the longest is as the distance between the heaven and the earth."[216] In some narratives it is said that if he said the *iqamah* without the *adhan*, an angel would stand at his right side and another at his left side, [217]and other similar narratives. The difference among the narratives may be due to the difference among the knowledge and the sincerity of the *musallin*, as can be inferred from some narratives in this respect, such as the narrative concerning performing the *salat* with the *adhan* and the *iqamah* in the desert or wasteland. [218]

In short, when the *salik* sees himself the leader of the *salat* for the angels of Allah, and his heart as the leader of his visible and invisible powers, and gathers, with the *adhan* and the *iqamah*, his visible and invisible powers, together with the angels of Allah, he is to regard his heart—which is the best of the external and internal powers,

---

[213] *Surah al-Naml* 27:62.
[214] *Furu ul-Kafi*, vol. 3, "Book of the *Salat*," ch. on "Starting the *adhan* and the *iqamah*," *hadith* 8, p. 303.
[215] *Thawab al-Amal*, "The reward of the one who performs the *salat* with the *adhan* and the *iqamah*," *hadith* 2, p. 54.
[216] *Ibid.*
[217] *Wasa'il ash-Shiah*, vol. 4, "Book of the *Salat*," sec. on "The *Adhan* and the *Iqamah*," ch. 4, *hadith* 4, p. 620.
[218] *Ibid.*, *hadith* 9: "O Abu Dharr, your Lord boasts over His angels for three persons: a man in a waste land..."

and the intercessor for the other powers—as an *imam*. And, as the heart is liable for the recitings of the *mamumin* [*musallin*] after its leadership, and as their faults are undertaken by it, the *salik* is to be quite keen and a good observant of its presence, and to completely guard the disciplines of the Sacred Presence, making the most of this Sanctified Meeting, admitting the great importance of the attention and the support of the angels of Allah, taking them to be of the favors of the Real Benefactor, and acknowledging his incapability of giving the due thanks to His Sacred Majesty for these great blessings. Surely He is the Benefactor!

SECTION TWO

Concerning the *Qiyam*
(the Standing Position in the *Salat*)

Discussed in Two Chapters

THE GENERAL SECRET OF THE *QIYAM*
Chapter One

Know that the people of knowledge regard the *qiyam* (the standing position in the *salat*) to be a sign of Unity of Actions. Similarly, they see that the *ruku* (bowing in the *salat*) refers to the Unity of Attributes, and the *sujud* (prostration) refers to the Unity of Essence—these will be explained in their proper places. But *qiyam*''s reference to the Unity of Action is in the very standing position as well as in the wordings recited while standing.

As to the standing position and its reference to the Unity of Action, it is because it denotes the servant''s observation of his duty toward Allah, as well as His position [*maqam*] of Self-Existence, manifested in the Sacred Emanation as a manifestation of Action. In this manifestation the position of Allah''s Activeness [*failiyyat*] is displayed, and all the beings are absorbed in the manifestation of Action and perished under the Manifest Majesty. In this instance, the gnostic discipline of the *salik* is to remind his heart of this divine grace and to give up, as much as he can, his personal individuations [*taayyunat-i nafsiyyah*], and to explain to his heart the truth of the Sacred Emanation, and to bring to the core of his heart the fact concerning Allah''s Self-Existence [*qayyumiyyat*] and that the creatures are dependent upon Him. Hence, after the fixation of this fact in the *salik*''s heart, his recitation will be by the tongue of the *Haqq* (Allah), and the praiser [*dhakir*] and the praised [*madhkur*] will be the *Haqq* (Allah) Himself, and some of the secrets of the Fate will be exposed to the gnostic''s heart, and "You are as You praised Yourself"[219] and "I take refuge in You from You"[220] will be disclosed to him in some degrees, and the heart of the gnostic will receive some of the secrets of

---

[219] Of an invocation from the Messenger of Allah (s) in his prostration. *Furu ul-Kafi*, vol. 3, p. 324; *Misbah ash-Shariah*, ch. 5; *Awaliy 'ul-Laali*, vol. 1, p. 389, *hadith* 21
[220] *Ibid.*; *Misbah al-Mutahajjid wa Silah al-Mutaabbid*, p. 308.

the *salat*, such as looking at the place of prostration, which is of dust, the principal origin (of man), or subjugating the neck and declining the head, as required, implying humility and destitution of "the possible", and the annihilation under the Might and the Sovereignty of (His) Majesty. **"O mankind! It is you who are in need of Allah, and Allah is He Who is the Self-Sufficient, the Praised One."**[221]

As concerning the wordings of the recitation being a reference to the Unity of Action, we shall explain that in details when we come to comment on the blessed *surah* of *al-Hamd, insha Allah* (Allah willing).

---

[221] *Surah al-Fatir* 35:15.

ON THE DISCIPLINES OF THE *QIYAM*
Chapter Two

These [disciplines] are such that the *salik* is to consider himself present in the Presence [*mahdar*] of Allah, and regard the world as His Presence, and himself one of the audience at that gathering, standing before Allah, trying to convey the Greatness of the Present and the Presence to his heart, letting it understand the importance and the significance of supplicating to Allah, the Exalted, and, by thinking and contemplating, before starting the *salat*, to prepare the heart to understand the importance of the situation, obliging it to humbleness, submission, calmness, fear, hope, humility and modesty till the end of the *salat*. He is to stipulate that his heart should be keen on observing these affairs, and think about the great holy men and guides, and about their moods and how their conducts with the Master of the kings were, so as to learn a lesson from the Imams of guidance and imitate them as his models, not being satisfied with just knowing the names of the infallible Imams, the date of their birthday, death day, the length of their honorable lives and similar details, which are of little advantage. Actually, he is to go through their biography and godly conducts, in order to find out the method of their worship and how their journey to Allah was carried out, and how their gnostic stations, which can be inferred from their miraculous speeches, were.

It is much regretted that we are negligent, intoxicated by nature, empty self-conceited and the stooges of the vile Satan in all matters, without there being any sign of our getting up from our deep sleep and endless forgetfulness. We get so little benefit from the positions and the knowledge of the Imams of guidance (a) that it is negligible, satisfying ourselves with the outer appearance of their lives, completely disregarding the objectives for which the prophets have been sent, and, actually, we are covered by the proverb: "To take a swelling for a fleshy."²²² We shall, therefore, relate some of the relevant narratives, so that some of the believing brethren may have a remembrance. Praise be to Allah and thanks to Him!

Muhammad ibn Yaqub, quoting Imam as-Sadiq (a), says: "Whenever Ali ibn al-Husayn (a) used to stand for the *salat*, his face turned pale. Going down for prostration, he would not raise his head until he was wet with perspiration."²²³

On the same authority he says: "My father used to say, when Ali ibn al-Husayn (a) used to stand for the *salat*, he looked like a trunk of a tree, nothing of which would move unless the wind would move it."²²⁴

In *al-Ilal*, Aban ibn Taghlib, quoting Muhammad ibn Ali ibn al-Husayn, says: "I said to Abu Abdullah [as-Sadiq] (a): I noticed that when Ali ibn al-Husayn (a) stood for the *salat*, his color changed." He said to me: By Allah, Ali ibn al-Husayn knew before whom he was standing."²²⁵

In a *hadith* in *Falah as-Sail*, on the authority of as-Sayyid Ali ibn Tawus, it is said: "...then Abu Abdullah (a) said: The *salat* will not be complete except for the one who has a full purity and a mature completeness , and is away from temptation and deviation, and knows [Allah] and [so] stands [before Him], submits [to Him] and persists. He, thus, stands between despair and hope, [between] patience and worry, as if the promises to him have been done, and the threats upon him have happened, lowering his fame [*ird*] and manifesting his aim. He sacrifices for Allah his soul, treads upon the road to Him as his goal, not unwillingly, severs the relations of interest for the sake of the One to Whom he bounds and comes, and from Whom he seeks help. Should he achieve all these, the *salat* would be of the ordered type and of the informed about, and it is the very *salat* which forbids evil and vice."²²⁶

Muhammad ibn Yaqub, quoting our master, Zayn al-Abidin (a), says that he said: "As regards the rights of the *salat*, you are to

---

²²² It means: "To be by the appearance" or "To take an unreal matter for a real one."

²²³ *Furu" ul-Kafi*, vol.3, p. 300. Book of the *Salat*," ch. On "Submission in the *Salat* and Disapproving Toying," *hadith* 5.

²²⁴ *Ibid.,hadith* 4.

²²⁵ *Ilal 'ush-Shara'i* p. 88, as in *Wasa'il ash-Shiah*, vol. 4 p. 685, "Book of the *Salat*" sec. on "The Acts of the *Salat*" ch. 2, *hadith* 4.

²²⁶ *Falah 'us-Sa'il*, ch.2, "On the Description of the *Salat*", p. 23.

know that it is a visit to Allah and that in it you are standing before Him. If you realized that, you would deserve to be, through it, in the position of a slave who is humble, desirous, horrified, frightened, hopeful, distressed, imploring, and glorifying the state of the One in front of Whom he stands with complete stillness, solemnity, submissiveness of the limbs, humility, well supplicating to Him for himself, requesting Him to free his neck, which is encircled by his faults and consumed by his sins; and there is no power except by Allah.[227]

The Prophet (s) is quoted to have said: "Worship your Lord as if you see Him. If you do not see Him, He sees you.[228]

In *Fiqh ur-Rida* it is stated: "When you want to perform the *salat*, do not go to it lazily, sleepily, hurriedly, or unmindfully. You are to approach it calmly, solemnly and slowly. You are also to display submission, imploringly and humbly, to Allah. You are to show awe and sings of fear and hope, with caution and apprehension. Thus, you are to stand before Him, as an escapee and sinful slave stands at attention before his master, on the alert, with joined heels, erected trunk, not looking to right and left, reckoning as if you see Him, and if you do not, He certainly does see you..." as the *hadith* goes.[229]

In *Uddat ud-Dai* it is stated: "It is narrated that the imploring moanings of Ibrahim (a) used to be heard from a mile's distance, such that Allah praised him by saying: **"Ibrahim was mild, imploring, penitent."**[230] When performing his *salat*, a sound of fizz , like that of a boiler, was heard coming from his chest. A similar sound was also heard from the chest of our Prophet (s). Fatimah (a) used to pant in the *salat* because of her fear of Allah."[231] And there are other similar *hadith*s.

There are too many noble narratives on these subjects to be covered in these papers. Contemplating these few narratives suffices

---

[227] *Mustadrak al-Wasa'il*, "Book of the *Salat*," sec. On "The Acts of the *Salat*," ch. 2, *hadith* 3.
[228] *Bihar al-Anwar*, vol. 74, p. 74, Book of Flower Garden," "The Prophet's Preachings," ch. 4, *hadith* 3; *Makarim al-Akhlaq*, p. 59.
[229] *Mustadrak al-Wasa'il*, "Book of the *Salat*," sec. on "The Acts of the *Salat*," ch. 1. *hadith* 7, extracted from *Fiqh ar-Rida*, p. 101, ch. On "The Obligatory *Salat*s."
[230] *Surah Hud* 11:75.
[231] *Mustadrak al-Wasa'il*, "Book of the *Salat*," sec. on "The Acts of the *Salat*," ch. 2, *hadith* 15.

the people of thought and remembrance, in respect of the formal, cordial and spiritual disciplines, as well as concerning the way of standing before Allah.

Think a little of the conditions of Ali ibn al-Husayn, the supplications of that great man and his implorings to Allah, the Exalted as well as his elegant invocations, by which he taught the disciplines of servitude to the servants of Allah. I do not allege that the supplications of those great men were intended to teach how to worship, for it would be an empty and meaningless statement prompted by being ignorant of the state of Lordship and of the knowledge of *Ahl al-Bayt* (a). Their fear and awe were much greater than anybody else"s, and the Greatness and Majesty of Allah were manifested in their hearts more than in anyone else"s heart. I only say that the servants of Allah should learn from them how to worship Allah and how to travel to Him. When you read what they used to say in their supplications and invocations, you should not read them as mere pronunciations of the tongue. They should be pondered upon, and their behavior with Allah, their displaying humility, inefficiency and destitution, are also to be noted.

By the Beloved! Ali ibn al-Husayn was one of the greatest blessings which Allah, the Most High, had bestowed upon His servants as a grace, bringing him down from the sacred world of Proximity, for the sake of teaching the ways of servitude to His servants: **"Then, on that Day, you shall most certainly be questioned about the bliss."**[232] If we are asked: "Why did you not appreciate the value of that bliss and did not get benefit from that great man?," we shall have no reply but to droop down our heads for being ashamed, and to be burnt with the fire of remorse and regret, when no regret would avail.

A Piece of Good Advice

My dear, now that the chance is available, and you are still in the prime of life, the way of journeying to Allah is open, the doors of His mercy are not closed, the soundness of the organs and powers is obtained and the land of planting [*dar az-zar*] in the material world is still there, strive to realize the value of these divine favors in order to be benefited by them. Try to acquire the spiritual perfections and the eternal happiness. Take advantage of all these branches of knowledge

---

[232] *Surah at-Takathur* 102:8.

which the honorable divine Quran and the infallible *Ahl al-Bayt* (a) have spread in the land of the dark nature, and illuminated the world with their divine bright light. Enlighten the land of your dark nature, as well as your eyes, ears, tongue and your other external and internal powers, with the light of Allah, the Exalted, and change this dark earth to another one, luminous, or rather to an intellectual heaven: **"On the day when the earth shall be changed to a different earth,"**[233] **"And the earth shall beam with the light of its Lord."**[234] On that day, if your earth is not changed to a different one, and if it is not lighted with the light of the Lord, you will encounter darkness, difficulty, horror, pressure, humility and torture.

At present, our external and internal powers are darkened with satanic darkness. Should we remain so, our material earth with its inborn light will gradually change into a dark dungeon, empty of the inborn light and veiled from the rules of the divine disposition. This is misfortune entailing no happiness, a darkness which comes to no luminosity, a horror which does not see the face of tranquility, and a torment which has no comfort with it: **"...And to whomsoever Allah does not give light, he has no light."**[235] I take refuge in Allah, the Exalted, from the satanic conceitedness and from the evil-commanding soul.

The principal objective of the great prophets, in legislating the laws, in establishing the rules and in the coming down of the heavenly books—especially the all-embracing Holy Quran, the projector of whose pure light is the Seal of the Messengers (*s*)—is spreading monotheism and divine knowledge, and uprooting infidelity, atheism, hypocrisy and dualism, for the secret of monotheism and abstraction is flowing in all the cordial and formal worships. The Shaykh, the gnostic and perfect, Shahabadi, (may my soul be his ransom), used to say: "Worship is the operation of *tawhid* [monotheism] in the kingdom of the body from the inside of the heart."

In short, the sought-for result of worship is acquiring knowledge, confirming monotheism and other knowledge in the heart. This objective cannot be attained except when the *salik* vindicates his cordial shares of worship, and passes from the shape and form to the

---

[233] *Surah Ibrahim* 14:48.
[234] *Surah az-Zumar* 39:69.
[235] *Surah an-Nur* 24:40.

core and the truth, without lingering in this world and the surface, for loitering in such affairs is a hindrance [thorn] in the way of mankind. Those who call for the mere external appearance [*surat*], preventing the people from the internal disciplines, alleging that religion has no meaning and no reality other than its appearance and surface, are but the satans on the road to Allah, and the thorns in the way of humanity. To be saved from their evil, one has to take refuge in Allah, the Exalted, for they extinguish the divine inborn light, which is the light of [divine] knowledge, *tawhid*, guardianship and other kinds of knowledge, and draw the covers of imitation, ignorance, tradition [*adat*] and fancies [*awham*] on it, deter the servants of Allah, the Exalted, from advancing to His threshold, and from reaching to His Beautiful Beauty, and block the way of knowledge. They direct the pure and sincere hearts of Allah's servants—in which He, with His hand of Beauty and Majesty, hid the seeds of knowledge in their disposition, and sent the great prophets and heavenly Books to breed and bring them up—to the world, to its ornaments, to its materialities and corporalities, and to its falsities, and divert them from spiritualities and intellectual happiness, confining the invisible world and the promised paradises exclusively to food, drink, sex and other animal desires.

They think that Allah, the Exalted, has laid out His table-cloth of mercy, sent down, with so much ceremony, His Books, employed His noble angels and assigned great prophets, just for the sake of satisfying hunger and sex. The most they know is: Take care of your stomach and sex drive so that you may satisfy your desire in the other world. The importance which they attach to a sexual intercourse lasting for five hundred years [in Paradise according to a narrative] they do not attach to *tawhid* and prophethood, and they take knowledge to be a preliminary to satiate their libido and gluttony. If a godly philosopher, or a divine gnostic, wanted to open a door of mercy to the servants of Allah, or to read a paper of divine wisdom to them, they would spare no abuse, curse and forged accusations without throwing them at him. They are so indulged in mundane affairs, and so concerned about sex and stomach, unknowingly, that they do not desire any other happiness in this world except satisfying their animal lust, despite the fact that the intellectual happiness, should they care for it, would not injure their lust for sex and food.

Like ourselves, since we have not yet crossed the limit of animality, we think of nothing but food and sex, to which we may attain by the grace of Allah, the Exalted. We are not, however, to believe that happiness is confined to that, and that the paradise of Allah, the Exalted, is restricted only to this paradise of animals. As a matter of fact, Allah, the Exalted, has such worlds that no eye has ever seen, no ear has ever heard of, and never occurred to any heart. Yet, the people of divine love and knowledge pay attention to none of those paradises, and are interested in neither of the invisible and visible worlds. To them, paradise is meeting Allah.

If we want to relate the relevant Quranic *ayah*s and the *hadith*s quoted from the infallible *Ahl al-Bayt*, it would not be within the scope of these papers. Actually, even what has been said was out of the overflowing of the pen. Our major objective is to direct the attention of the hearts of the servants of Allah to what they have been created for, that is, to know Allah, which is superior to all sorts of happiness, and everything else is but a preliminary to it. By referring to "the thorns on the road of the *suluk*", we did not mean the great *ulama* of Islam, nor the honorable *faqih*s of the Jafari school (may Allah's contentment be upon them), but we do mean some of the people of ignorance and those who pretend to be of the people of knowledge by means of insufficiency [*qusur*] and ignorance [*jahl*], not by means of negligence [*taqsir*] and abstinacy [*inad*],and who became highway robbers of the servants of Allah. I take refuge in Allah from the evil of an overflowing pen, bad intention and false objective. Praise be to Allah at the beginning and the end, externally and internally.

SECTION THREE

On the Secret of the *Niyyah* [Intention]

Discussed in Five Chapters

THE TRUTH OF THE *NIYYAH* IN WORSHIP
Chapter One

Know that the *niyyah* [intention] is to decide or to determine to do something. It is the soul''s decision on performing some acts after conceiving it and then acknowledging its advantage and judging its necessity. It is a psychological and conscientious condition, which appears after the said procedures. It is, then, expressed as a decision, a determination, a want, a will, an objective and the like. It appears in all voluntary actions, as there can be no voluntary act without undergoing the said process, and it is there in the entire action, in reality, not allegorically. It does not need, however, that the details should be in the mind from the very beginning or even during the process, nor should one necessarily imagine the objective and the decision in detail. It sometimes happens that man does the act according to a decision, and yet he is completely unaware of the detailed picture of the act and the decision, while the fact is there, and it takes place in the outside, motivated by that fact. This is quite consciously obvious in the voluntary acts.

In sum, this decision and determination, which is the *niyyah* in the terminology of the *faqih*s (may Allah be pleased with them), is, inevitably in every act, such that if one wanted to do a voluntary act without it, it would not be possible. Nevertheless, the whisperings of the wicked Satan and the sportings of fancy overrule reason and disguise the necessities in the eyes of the helpless man, and man, instead of spending his precious life in improving and purifying his deeds, and in freeing them from internal evils, and instead of spending it in acquiring monotheistic knowledge, Godliness and being in quest of Allah, the vile Satan whispers in his ears and induces him to spend only half of his life in quest of a necessary and obligatory matter. Satan''s snares and artifices are too many—one may be induced by him to give up the act altogether, while the other whom he despairs of inducing to drop the act, induces him to commit other follies, such as self-conceitedness and hypocrisy. If Satan could not succeed in this, he would try to falsify one's worship by way of causing him to pretend holiness: by slighting the worships of the people in his eyes, and by causing him to regard the people indifferent [heedless]. Then he induces him to spend all his life on matters such as the *niyyah*, which is inseparable from the act, or the *takbir* or the recitation, which are common and ordinary acts. At any rate, Satan would not leave man alone before nullifying his worship by one way or another.

Satanic whisperings come through diverse ways, which we cannot discuss for the time being, nor scrutinize them all. But the whispering in the *niyyah*, from among them, may be the most ridiculous and the strangest, because if someone tried, with all his powers, to do a voluntary act in all his life, without a *niyyah* [an intention], it would be impossible for him to do it. Nevertheless, you may find some wretched, sick and feeble-minded person who spends a considerable time at every *salat* just to have a firm intention. Such a person is more like the one who thinks a long time whether he is to decide to go shopping or to go for a lunch. This helpless man, to whom the *salat* should be his ascension to His proximity, and the key to his happiness, and, by applying its cordial disciplines and realizing the secrets of this divine grace he should perfect his essence [*dhat*] and secure his growth [*nashah*] of life, he, on the contrary, neglects all these matters, or, much worse, besides regarding them unnecessary, he takes them all to be false, and uses his dear and valuable capital to serve Satan and to obey his slinking whispers, placing the God-given reason [*aql*], which is the light of guidance, under the rule of *Iblis*.

Abdullah ibn Sinan says: "I mentioned before Imam as-Sadiq (a) [a case concerning] a man who was afflicted with frequently performing the *wudu* and the *salat*, and described him to be a man of reason. The Imam said: "What reason has he in obeying Satan?" I asked him: "How is it that he is obeying Satan?" He said: "If you ask him wherefrom his hesitation comes to him, he will tell you it is of the work of Satan."[236]

In short, man should uproot this by whatever means of austerity and strife, for it deprives him of all happiness and good. It may be that forty years of a man's worship are not correctly performed

---

[236] *Usul al-Kafi*, vol. 1, "Book of Reason and Ignorance," *hadith* 10, p. 13.

even in the outer appearance or according to the juristic formal details, let alone the internal religious disciplines. More ridiculous is that some such fastidious persons think that the worships of all people are invalid and take them to be negligent in respect of religion, whereas their religious authorities—whose instructions they follow—are also among the ordinary people. If he is a learned man, let him refer to the Prophet"'s tradition to see that the Messenger of Allah (s) and the Imams of guidance (a) were also like the ordinary people in these matters. From among all the people only this group of fastidious persons, act contrary to the Messenger of Allah (s), the infallible Imams (a), the jurists of religion and the scholars of the *ummah*, regarding the acts of worship of all of them worthless, believing their own to be done according to precaution and that they take good care of religion. Take, for example, the case of the *wudu*. The narratives about the *wudu* of the Messenger of Allah (s) are many and successively transmitted. It seems that the Messenger of Allah (s) used a single handful [of water] to wash his face, another for his right hand and a third for his left hand.[237] The Imami *faqih*s are unanimous on definitely regarding this *wudu* to be the correct one. The Book of Allah, too, apparently confirms it. As to the second washing, or the second handful, it is objected by some, while there is no harm in the second handful, or the second washing, although its recommendation is questionable. But the third washing is undoubtedly an innovation and renders the *wudu* invalid, according to both the narration and the *fatwa*. Now, look at the acts of this helpless fastidious person who is not satisfied with twenty handfuls [of water], each one of which is enough to fully wash the hand and to consider it a "complete wash". In this case his *wudu* is undoubtedly invalid. But this wretched, feeble-minded person, who performs this act in obedience to Satan"'s orders and whispers, thinks that what he does is correct and according to precaution; then, by contrast, he takes the acts of all others to be incorrect and invalid. Here the noble *hadith* proves true in respect of calling this man insane. The one who thinks correct an act, which is contrary to the act of the Messenger of Allah (s), and regards an act, which is in conformity with the Prophet"'s to be incorrect, is either a renegade or an insane. But as this desperate person is not a renegade,

---

[237] *Furu ul-Kafi,* vol. 3, "Book of Purity," ch. on the "Description of the *Wudu",* p. 24.

he must be insane, obedient to Satan and disobedient to the Beneficent [*ar-rahman*].

There is no remedy for this acute disease except through contemplation and reflection on the aforementioned matters, making a comparison between his act and that of the pious, the scholars and the *faqih*s (may Allah be pleased with them). If he sees that his act differs from theirs, he is to push Satan's nose into the dust and to completely ignore that evil creature. Then, after that if Satan tries and whispers in his ears several times: "Your act is invalid," let him reply: "If the acts of all the *faqih*s of the *ummah* are invalid, mine is invalid, too." It is hoped that after some time spent contradicting Satan, taking refuge in Allah, the Exalted, with invocations and imploring, from his evils, this disease will be cured and Satan's greedy eye will be lifted from him. The same instructions are also recommended in the noble *hadith*s to remedy excessive doubt, which is also of the satanic inspirations.

In the noble *al-Kafi*, on the authority of Imam al-Baqir (a), it is stated that he has said: "When doubts in the *salat* become too frequent, do not give heed to them, and regard the *salat* to be correct. It is hoped that this state would leave you, as it is not caused but by Satan."[238]

In another narrative, Imam al-Baqir (a), or Imam as-Sadiq (a), is quoted to have said: "Do not make it Satan's habit to frequent you by breaking your *salat*, as this will stir his greed against you. Satan is evil and gets accustomed to what he is habituated to."

Zurarah says that the Imam added: "That malignant wants to be obeyed. So, if he is disobeyed he will not come back to you."[239]

This is an important cure for all cases of Satan's intrusions and of the jestings of devilish fancies. In some *hadith*s invocations are also recommended. You may, in this respect, refer to *Wasail ash-Shiah*, *Mustadrak al-Wasail* at the end of the book *al-Khalal*.

---

[238] *Ibid.*, "Book of the *Salat*," ch. on "The One who Doubts in His *Salat*, *hadith* 8, p. 359.
[239] *Ibid.*, *hadith* 2.

SINCERITY
Chapter Two

One of the important disciplines of the *niyyah*, which is of the important parts of all worships and of the general and comprehensive instructions, is "sincerity". Its nature is purging the act of worship from the impurity of doing it for other than Allah, and clearing the heart from discerning anything other than Allah, the Exalted, in all formal, intellectual, external, and internal acts. It achieves its perfection by absolutely neglecting the other [than Allah], and decisively pounding upon I-ness, selfishness, the other and the otherness. Allah, the Exalted, says: **"Surely Allah's is the pure religion."**[240] So, if the religion was mixed with any selfish and Satanic desires, it would not be pure; and that which is not pure is not acceptable to Allah, and that which has a blemish of otherness and selfishness is outside the limits of Allah's religion.

Allah, the Exalted, says: **"And they were not enjoined except that they should worship Allah, making the religion His sincerely."**[241]

And He also says: **"...And whoever desires the tillage of this world, We give him thereof, but in the Hereafter he will have no portion."**[242]

It has been narrated that the Messenger of Allah (*s*) said: "Every person gets according to his intention. So, the one whose intention is to migrate to Allah and His Messenger, his migration will be to Allah and His Messenger; and the one whose intention of

---

[240] *Surah az-Zumar* 39:3.
[241] *Surah al-Bayyinah* 98:5.
[242] *Surah ash-Shura* 42:20.

migration is to attain to this world [to get something of it] or to marry a woman, his migration is to what he has intended."[243]

Allah, the Exalted, says: **"And whoever leaves his house migrating to Allah and His Messenger, and then death overtakes him, his reward is, indeed, with Allah."**[244] Maybe this noble *ayah* covers all degrees of sincerity: One is the formal migration of the body. If this migration was not purely for the sake of Allah and His Messenger, but was for the sake of personal desires, then it would not be a migration to Allah and His Messenger. This is the formal juristic degree of sincerity.

Another one is the spiritual migration, and internal journey, which starts from the dark house of the self, with its goal being Allah and His Messenger. It, after all, returns to Allah Himself, because the Messenger, as a messenger, has no independence of his own; rather, he is an *ayah*, a mirror and a representative. So, to migrate to him means migrating to Allah: "The love of Allah's close friends is loving Allah."

So, the gist of the meaning of the noble *ayah*, based on this possibility, is that the one who leaves the house of the self, and gets out of the mansion of selfishness, on a spiritual migration and a gnostic cordial journey to Allah, disregarding his self, dignity and prestige, his reward will be with Allah. But if the *salik* to Allah demands, in his *suluk* to Allah, a personal desire, such as attaining stations, or even attaining Allah's proximity for himself, this *suluk* will not be to Allah. Actually, the *salik* has not even got out of his self; that is, his journey is inside his own house, roaming from side to side and from corner to corner.

Therefore, if the journey is within the limits of the self [*nafs*] for the sake of attaining self-perfections, it will not be a journey to Allah, it is, in fact a journey from self to self. Nevertheless, the *salik* in his journey to Allah, will, inevitably, experience this kind of travel. No one, except the perfect *walis* [friends of Allah] (a) can commence his divine journey without a journey within himself, as that exclusively belongs to the perfect ones (a). Perhaps the noble *ayah*: **"Peace it is till the break of the dawn,"**[235] is a hint at this safety from the Satanic

---

[243] *Mustadrak al-Wasa'il*, sec. on "Preliminaries to the Acts of Worship," ch. 5, *hadith* 5.
[244] *Surah an-Nisa"* 4:100.
[235] *Surah al-Qadr* 97:5.

and selfish conducts during all the stages of the journey in the dark nights of nature, which is the night of *Qadr* in respect of the perfect ones, till the dawn of the Resurrection Day, which means, to the perfect ones, seeing the Beauty of the One. But the others would not be safe in all the stages of the journey. As a matter of fact, no *salik* would be free from Satan''s intrusions in the early stages.

So, it has become clear that this degree of sincerity—whose first stage in the journey to Allah is safety, till its last, which is the attainment of real death, or rather till after the second real life, which is the "sobriety [*sahw*] after the self-effacement [*mahw*]"—would not happen to the people of *suluk* and the common people of gnosticism and of austerity. The sign of this kind of sincerity is that Satan''s temptation will have no way into those possessing it, and Satan''s covetous eye will turn in complete despair away from them, as is said by Satan in the Quran: **"By Your Might I will tempt them all, except Your sincere servants from among them."**[246] Here, sincerity is ascribed to the servant himself, not to his act, which is a state loftier than sincerity in act. Perhaps the well-known noble *hadith* of the Prophet (*s*) who said: "The one who keeps being sincere to Allah for forty mornings, fountains of wisdom will flow from his heart to his tongue,"[247] refers to all the degrees of sincerity, i.e. sincerity of act, of attribute and of essence, and probably it appears in sincerity of essence, for which the other degrees of sincerity are requisites.

To explain this noble *hadith*, and to state what is meant by "fountains of wisdom", the way they flow from the heart to the tongue, the effect of sincerity in this flowing and the significance of "forty mornings", are out of the scope of this thesis, as they need a separate book. The thesis titled *Tuhfat ul-Muluk fi s-Sayri was-Suluk*, ascribed to the knower of Allah, the late Bahr al-Ulum, is mostly concerned with the explanation of this noble *hadith*. It is a nice thesis, though somewhat arguable. For this reason some say that it was not written by the said great personality, which is quite possible.

---

[246] *Surah Sad* 38:82, 83.
[247] *Bihar al-Anwar*, vol. 67, "Book of Faith and Disbelief," ch. on "Sincerity", *hadith* 10, p. 242, quoting *Uyunu Akhbar ar-Rida*, vol. 2, p. 69, with a slight difference. The same content is stated in the latter source, *hadith* 25, p. 249.

A BRIEF ACCOUNT ON SOME STAGES OF
SINCERITY TO FIT WITHIN THESE PAPERS
Chapter Three

One of these stages is to purge the act, whether cordial or formal, from the blemish of acquiring the creatures" pleasure and attracting their hearts for the sake of a praise, and advantage or anything else. And the counterfeit of it is the act performed hypocritically, which is a juristic hypocrisy and is the meanest of all degrees of hypocrisies, and such a hypocrite is the lowest and meanest of all hypocrites.

The second stage is to purge the act from wanting the fulfillment of mundane objectives and transient desires, although these acts may be fulfilled in order to attain Allah"s grace, such as performing night *salat*s [*nafilah*] for improving one"s sustenance, or performing the *salat* of the first day of the month, for example, in order to be safe from the plights of the month, or giving out alms to ward off diseases, and other worldly objectives. Some jurisprudents (may Allah"s mercy be upon them) regard this degree of sincerity to be necessary for the correctness of the acts of worship, in case the objective of performing the act is to attain it. But this is contrary to investigation according to the juristic rules. Yet, this *salat* has no value, whatsoever, in the eyes of the people of knowledge, and it is like all other lawful gains, or maybe even lower.

The third stage is to purge the act from trying to attain corporeal paradises, houris, luxurious abodes and the likes of the corporeal pleasures. Its counterfeit is the worship of the traders, as is described in the noble *hadith*s. This, too, is, to the people of Allah, similar to other gains, though the wage of the acts of this trader is more and higher, in case he carries them out and rids them from the formal viles.

The fourth stage is to purify the act from being afraid of the threatened bodily punishment and torture. The counterfeit of this is the worship of the slaves, as is mentioned in the narratives.[248] To the people of the heart, this kind of worship is also of no value and far from being a service to Allah, while, to the people of knowledge, it makes no difference if a man performs an act out of fearing the penalties and punishments of this world or the tortures of the Hereafter, or for the purpose of possessing worldly women, or for obtaining the paradisiac women, none of them will be for Allah, and they [only] show the intention [reason=*dai*] for the performance of an act, which, according to juristic rules, takes the act out of formal invalidity. But in the market of the people of knowledge this stuff is of no value.

The fifth stage is to purge the act from trying to attain intellectual happiness and everlasting spiritual pleasures, and to join the cherubim, the group of the sacred intellects and the favorite angels. Its counterfeit is acting for this purpose. Although this stage is great and an important goal, and the wise men and researchers attach great importance to this stage of happiness and regard it very valuable, yet, in the ways of the people of Allah, this stage has also its shortcomings in *suluk*, and its *salik* is also regarded as a trader or a worker, though his trade and business are different, in many ways, from those of others.

As regards this stage, I mean the sixth one; it is to purge the act from being afraid of not attaining those pleasures and of being deprived of this happiness. Its counterfeit is to act for this stage out of fear. Although this is a lofty stage and is beyond the desire of one like the writer, yet, to the people of Allah, this is also the worship of the slaves, for it has causes.

The seventh stage is to purge it from attaining the delights of the Divine Beauty and enjoying the pleasures of the lights of limitless glories, which are the Paradise of Meeting [the Lord]. This stage, I mean the stage of Meeting Allah, is one of the most important goals of the people of knowledge and those of heart, and the hands of the hopes of the common people are too short to reach it. Only a few of the

---

[248] See, for example, *Wasa'il ash-Shiah*, vol. 1, sec. on "The Preliminaries to the Acts of Worship," the narratives of chapter 9, p. 45; *Usul al-Kafi*, vol. 3, "Book of Faith and Disbelief," ch. on "Worship", narrative 5, p. 131.

people of knowledge are favored with the happiness of this honor. And the people of love and attraction are of the perfect ones among the people of Allah and His chosen ones. Yet, this perfection is not the most perfect degree of the people of Allah. It is one of their many common states. What we read in some invocations, such as the *Shabaniyyah* supplication, that Imam Ali (a) and his pure progeny demand the said state, or allude to their being in that state, does not mean that their states are limited to this one, since the eighth stage, which is on the same level as this one, and which is purging the act from the fear of separation, is also not of the perfect states of the perfect ones. Imam Ali"s saying: "How could I forbear separating from You?"[249] is just a reference to a brim-full common state of him and of one like him.

Generally speaking, purging the act from these two stages is also a must to the people of Allah, for to act with them will be endued with causes and not free from selfish wants. It is, thus, perfect sincerity. Next, there are other stages that are out of the limits of sincerity, and fall under the criterion of monotheism, abstraction and guardianship, all of which do not fit here.

---

[249] *Misbah al-Mutahajjid*, p. 778 (Supplication of Kumayl).

REFUTING A GROUP OF IGNORANTS
Chapter Four

Now as you have got acquainted with the stages of sincerity and states of the acts of worship to some extent, get ready to acquire them, since to have knowledge without putting it to practice is worthless, and knowledge is a stronger evidence against the claimant and he is more exposed to argument. Alas! It is regretted that we are completely deprived of the divine knowledge, the spiritual states of the people of Allah and the lofty positions of the men of heart. A group of us completely deny all the states and regard their people to be erroneous, and their acts *batil* [false] and worthless. They even take those who mention them with admiration, or invite to their states, to be forgers and their invitation to be a paradox. There is no hope in drawing the attention of such groups to their own faults and shortcomings, and in waking them up: **"Surely you cannot guide everyone whom you love;"**[250] **"...You cannot make those in the graves hear."**[251]

Yes, those who, like the helpless writer, know nothing at all, and whose hearts are not living up to the life of knowledge and divine love, are but dead ones, for whom the bodily covers are their rotten graves. This dust of the body and dark narrowness of the skeleton have shut them off from all the worlds of light and light upon light: **"...And he for whom Allah has not assigned light, for him there is no light."**[252] Much as you try to recite of *hadith*s and of the Quran to these groups concerning divine affection and love and concerning longing for meeting [Him], and exclusively being attached to Him, they still try to interpret, justify and explain them according to their own opinions. All those *ayah*s about meeting Allah and divine love

---

[250] *Surah al-Qasas* 28:56.
[251] *Surah Fatir* 35:22.
[252] *Surah an-Nur* 24:40.

they interpret to be a meeting with the trees of Paradise and the beautiful women. I wonder what these groups would do with the texts of the *Shabaniyyah* Supplication, which says: "O Allah! Grant me to be completely devoted to you, and lighten the eyes of our hearts with the light of looking at You until the eyes of the hearts penetrate the barriers of light to reach the Source of Greatness, and our souls hang to the Might of Your Sanctity. O Allah! Make me one of those whom You called and he responded, and when You looked at him, he was stunned because of Your Majesty."[252a]

So, what do "barriers of light" mean? Does "looking at Allah" mean looking at the palaces of Paradise? Does "the Source of Greatness" mean heavenly palaces? Does "the hanging of the souls to the Might of Sanctity" mean hanging to the skirts of the houris for sensual desires? This "being stunned because of His Majesty", does it mean being spellbound at the beauties of the women of Paradise? Those ecstasies and faintings which used to befall the Messenger of Allah (s) during his ascending *salat*, and those lights of grandeur, and the things loftier than them, which he used to discern, in that meeting in which the Archangel Gabriel (a) was not admitted and he dared not to advance even for an inch farther, were those ecstasies for one of the very good women? Or did he discern lights like those of the sun and the moon or much brighter? That sound heart, which was referred to by the infallible [*masum*] (a) in explaining the verse: **"Except him who comes to Allah with a sound heart,"**[253] by saying: "A sound heart is the one which meets Allah while there is nothing in it save Him,"[254] does it mean that "there is nothing in it save Allah" denotes "nothing save the generosity of Allah," which is to mean an allusion to "nothing save [say] pearls and apricots"?

Woe to me for letting the rein of the pen be loose and engage in ecstatic phrases. But, by the life of the beloved, no particular aim was intended by those words, except that there might be, for my brothers in faith, especially the learned, a sort of warning, so that they might not, at least, deny the states of the people of Allah, for such a denial would be the origin of every wretchedness and misfortune. We did not intend

---

252a Refer to footnote 5.
253 *Surah ash-Shuara"*26:89
254 *Usul al-Kafi*, vol. 3, "Book of Faith and Disbelief," ch. on "Sincerity," *hadith* 5, p. 26.

to say who *Ahlullah* [the people of Allah] are. Actually, our intention was that their states should not be denied. As to who the owners of those states are, Allah alone knows them, since it is a matter of which no one is informed: "The one who got an information did not come back."[255]

There is another group who do not deny the states of the people of knowledge and are not against the people of Allah. But their indulgence in worldly matters, trying to obtain them, and their taking to the transient pleasures, have prevented them from acquiring knowledge, practice, intellectual intuition [*dhawq*] and ecstasy [*hal*]. They are like those sick people who do know they are sick, but their stomach would not let them be cautious and accept taking bitter medicine, while the former group are like the patients who would never believe in the existence of such patients and such a disease in actuality, and despite the fact that they themselves are afflicted with this disease, they deny its existence.

Another group took to acquiring knowledge and engaged in learning theories, but as regards the truths of knowledge and the states of the people of Allah, they satisfied themselves with terms and vocabularies, and with the gaudiness of phrases and expressions. They tied themselves and other wretched ones in the chains of words and terms, and out of all "states," they satisfied themselves with mere talk. Among them there are a few who do know themselves, but, in order to preside over some other unfortunate persons, they use these meaningless terms as a means of winning a living, and, with their deceitful expressions and attractive talks, they capture the pure hearts of the servants of Allah. These are the human Satans whose harm is no less than that of the accursed *Iblis* himself against the servants of Allah. These unfortunate ones do not know that the hearts of the servants of Allah are the abode of Allah, and no one has the right to occupy them. They are usurpers of Allah's abode and destroyers of the real *kabah*. They carve out idols and place them in the hearts of the servants of Allah, which are the *kabah*, or rather *al-Bayt al-Mamur* [Allah's Populous House]. They are the sick people who pretend to be

---

[255] "Those who claim to be in quest of it are uninformed,
The one who got an information did not come back."
—Sadi

211

physicians, and involve the servants of Allah in diverse deadly diseases.

The members of this group are distinguished for being more interested in guiding the wealthy people and the notable personalities than in guiding the poor and the indigent, and their followers are more of the well-off and notable people. Even they themselves appear in the apparel of the wealthy people. They play on such deceptive talks that while they are polluted with a thousand kinds of mundane impurities, they can show themselves as purifiers and of the people of Allah. The wretched fools and their followers close their eyes against all their tangible faults, and flatter themselves with empty terms and utterances.

Now as we have reached this stage of our speech, it is worthwhile to relate one or two *hadith*s narrated in this respect, although it would be out of the content of our discourse. However, getting the blessings of the *hadith*s of *Ahl al-Bayt* (a) is a good thing:

Shaykh as-Saduq (may Allah have mercy upon him) in his book *Al-Khisal*, quoting Abu Abdullah [as-Sadiq] (a), says: "There are among the scholars those who like to compile their knowledge, and do not like to be quoted. These are at the first step of the Fire. Other scholars are proud when they admonish, but they disdain being admonished. These are at the second step of Fire. Some scholars prefer to put their knowledge at the disposal of the noble and the wealthy, excluding the poor from it. These are at the third step of the Fire. Other scholars behave like the tyrants and the monarchs in their knowledge, and if they were redressed or neglected in some of their affairs, they would become angry. These are at the fourth step of the Fire. Some scholars look for the *hadith*s of the Jews and the Christians in order to support their own knowledge and increase their own *hadith*s. These are at the fifth step of the Fire. Other scholars appoint themselves to give out religious decrees, telling the people: "Ask me," whereas they may not be right even in a single letter, and Allah does not like the pretentious. These are at the sixth step of the Fire. There are among the scholars those who take knowledge to be a sense of honor and intellect. These are at the seventh step of the Fire."[256]

Al-Kulayni (may Allah have mercy upon him), in his comprehensive [book] *al-Kafi*, quoting Imam al-Baqir (a), says: "The one who seeks knowledge in order to vie with the scholars, or to argue

---

[256] *Al-Khisal* , vol. 2, ch. 7, *hadith* 33, p. 352.

with the fool, or to attract the people to himself, let him have his seat in the Fire—Presidency does not befit except its deserver."[257]

Also quoting Imam as-Sadiq (a) he says: "Whenever you see a scholar loving this world accuse him of being against your religion, as the lover of a thing seeks to get what he loves." And he said: "Allah, the Exalted, revealed to David (a): „Do not place between Me and yourself a scholar who is infatuated with this world, as he would prevent you from the way of My love, for those are the robbers of My loving servants. The least I would do to them is to extract the sweetness of supplication to Me from their hearts."[258]

Those from among this group, who are not impostors or fraudulent, and are themselves *saliks* on the road to the Hereafter, striving to acquire knowledge and high states, it sometimes happens that they are fooled by Satan, the highway robber, and get conceited, thinking that the states and knowledge [*maarif*] are really nothing but the very scholarly terms and expressions which they themselves or others, have coined. They spend the prime of their years and the best of their lives, in multiplicating those terms and composing books and papers, such as a group of versed *mufassir*s (exegetes of the Quran) who think that the advantage of the Quran is confined to recording a collection of different ways of its recitation, the meanings of its vocabularies and conjugation of its verbs, its verbal and moral beauties, aspects of its miraculous inimitability, its conventional meaning, and its different impressions on different persons, but they are completely ignorant of the Quran's message, its spiritual dimensions and divine knowledge [*maarif*]. They are more like a sick man who has gone to a physician and received his prescription, and thinks that he will be treated by way of recording and preserving the recipe and by the mode of its ingredients. This disease will kill such people, for knowing the recipe and going to the doctor come to no avail at all.

O dear! All sciences are practical. Even the science of *tawhid* (monotheism) also consists of cordial and formal acts. *Tawhid*, grammatically, denotes turning plurality into singleness—a spiritual and cordial act. Unless you recognize the real and the true cause in the

---

[257] *Usul al-Kafi*, vol. 1, "Book of the Merit of Knowledge," ch. on "The One who Gains His Living from His Knowledge," *hadith* 6, p. 59.
[258] *Ibid.*, *hadith* 4.

multiplicity of acts, unless you have a truth-finding eye to discern Allah in nature, unless you regard the natural and non-natural multiplicities as perished [*fani*] in Allah and His acts, and unless the authority of Allah"s Unity of Acts has not spread its banner in your heart, you will be far away from purity, sincerity, clearness and purification, as well as from *tawhid*. All of the hypocrisy of acts and most of the cordial hypocrisies are caused by the incompleteness of the unity of acts. The one who regards the weak and unfortunate people to be effective in this world, and occupying the domain of Allah, how can he regard himself in no need of attracting their hearts, and purge and purify his act from Satan"s polytheism? You will have to make the spring clean so that clear water may come out of it, as otherwise, from a muddy spring you may not expect to get clear water. If you regard the hearts of Allah"s servants to be at the disposal of Allah, and make your heart taste the meaning of: "O You Who change the hearts," and let your heart hear it, you, with all your weakness and helplessness, will not try to capture the hearts. If you make your heart understand the truth of "...**In His Hand is the dominion of everything,**"[259] "**His is the (whole) dominion,**"[260] and "**In His Hand is the dominion,**"[261] you will need not attract any hearts, nor think that you are in need of the weak hearts and the weak people, and you will attain a state of cordial satisfaction. You felt yourself being in need of something, and took the people to be undoers of knotty problems, and thus you thought you needed to attract the hearts of the people, thinking that by pretending holiness, you would have at your disposal the hearts of the people. Hence, you needed to be a hypocrite. Had you taken Allah to be the solver of all difficulties, and that you do not have the universe at your disposal, you would not have needed those acts of polytheism.

O you, the polytheist who claim to be a monotheist! O you, an *Iblis* [a devil] appearing in the shape of a human being! You have inherited this legacy from the accursed Satan, who, thinking himself effective, calls out: "**I will lead them astray**".[262] That wretched, miserable being is wrapped in veils of polytheism and self-conceit. Those who believe themselves and the world to be independent and

---

[259] *Surah Ya-Sin* 36:83.
[260] *Surah Fatir* 35:13.
[261] *Surah al-Mulk* 67:1.
[262] *Surah Sad* 38:82.

not under management, neither controlled nor owned, have inherited that from *Iblis*" mischief. So, wake up from [your] deep sleep and convey to your heart the noble *ayah*s of the Divine Book, the Lord"s Luminous Page. These great *ayah*s have been sent down for me and you to wake up, yet, we confine all our shares to reciting it in formal artistic intonation, disregarding its informative knowledge, until Satan overcomes and rules us such that we become under his control.

For the time being, we end the discourse here, leaving it for a later time. We shall, *insha Allah*, talk about the disciplines of recitation, opening the way for ourselves and for the servants of Allah to be benefited by the Glorious Quran, with Allah"s permission and His good help. *Was-salam* [And that is an end to the matter].

SOME OTHER STAGES OF SINCERITY
Chapter Five

Now as the string of the speech has reached this point, I have but to state some other stages of sincerity befitting this state.

One of the stages of sincerity is to purge the act from thinking of deserving a reward. The counterfeit of it is the act blemished with demanding the expected reward. This is not free from a degree of admiring the act, and the *salik* is to rid himself of it. The assumption of deserving reward is caused by the deficiency in one"s knowledge of his condition and of the right of Allah, the Exalted. This is also a fruit of the satanic evil tree stemming from being proud of oneself, one"s act, I-ness and selfishness. How hopeless man is! As long as he is wrapped in the veils of being proud of his acts, believing them to be of his own, and regarding himself the manager of the affairs, he will not be cured from this disease, and will not be able to purge his act and purify his intention. Therefore, the *salik* is to strive to inform his heart, through cordial austerity and mental and gnostic conduct, that all acts are of Allah"s blessings and gifts which He carries out by the hand of His servant. Should the Unity of Acts get fixed in the heart of the *salik*, he would not regard his acts as to be of himself, therefore he would not demand any reward, and, actually, he would regard the reward to be a favor and the blessings to be new beginnings.

This divine delicacy is frequently stated in the words of the pure Imams (a), especially in *as-Sahifah as-Sajjadiyyah* (a book of invocations and supplications by Imam Ali ibn-Husayn as-Sajjad), a divine and luminous book, which has descended from the gnostic heaven of the knower of Allah, the luminous intellect, Sayyid as-Sajidin [the Master of the Prostrating Worshippers], for the sake of salvation of the servants of Allah from the prison of nature, demonstrating the discipline of servitude and of being at the service of the Lord. In the thirty-second invocation he says: "...so praise be to

You for Your beginning with great favors, and for Your inspiring gratitude for [Your] benevolence."[263]

He also says on another occasion: "...since all Your benevolence is favor and every one of Your blessings is a new beginning."[264]

In *Misbah ash-Shariah* it is said: "The least limit of sincerity is the servant"s doing all his best, then he should not attach to his act [of worship] any value with Allah, by which he would impose on his Lord [to give him] a reward for his act."[265]

Another stage of sincerity is to purge the act from demanding much and being pleased with it and depending on it. This is also one of the important tasks of the *salik*, lest he should be retained back from joining the caravan of the travelers to Allah, confining himself to the dark dungeon of nature. This is a situation stemming from the vile satanic tree, and from the selfishness inherited from the legacy of Satan who has said: **"You created me of fire and created him of clay."**[266] This is but man"s ignorance of his own state [*maqam*] and of the state [*maqam*] of Allah, the Glorified.

If this wretched "possible (existent)" could only recognize his own state of deficiency, incapability, weakness and helplessness, and realize Allah"s state of greatness, grandeur and perfection, he would never boast of his act and of performing an act. Wretched! His act [of worship], which would be worth only a few pence for a whole year, should it prove to be complete and correct, he would ask, for only two of its *rakat*s, unlimited expectations. It is this expectation and much demanding that originate many immoralities and other acts of mischief, which cannot be mentioned here for fear of becoming lengthy.

The noble *hadith*s frequently refer to this subject, as is in the noble *al-Kafi*, quoting Imam Musa ibn Jafar (a) to have said to some of his sons: "My son, you are to be diligent, never to clear yourself from falling short of fully worshipping and obeying Allah, the Most High, for He can never be worshipped as He deserves."[267]

---

[263] *As-Sahifah as-Sajjadiyyah,* invocation 32.

[264] *Ibid.*, invocation 12.

[265] *Misbah ash-Shariah*, ch. 76, on "Sincerity."

[266] *Surah al-Araf* 7:12; *Surah Sad* 38:76.

[267] *Usul al-Kafi*, vol. 3, "Book of Faith and Disbelief," ch. on "Admitting Shortcomings," *hadith* 1, p. 116.

In another *hadith*, he (a) said: "Any act you do for Allah, take yourself as falling short of it, since all the people, in their acts, between themselves and Allah, are derelict [*muqassir*], except the one whom Allah, the Exalted, protects against that."[268]

He (a) is also quoted to have said: "Do not consider plenty the plenty good deeds."[269]

The complete *Sahifah*, describing the angels, says: "Those who, looking at Hell breathe out to the people of disobedience, say "Glory to you, O Allah, we have not worshipped You as You deserve to be worshipped." "[270]

O you helpless! When the Messenger of Allah (s), who was the most knowledgeable among Allah's creatures, and whose act [of worship] was the most luminous and the greatest of all others", admitted his shortcoming and inability, and who says: "We have not known You as You ought to be, and we have not worshipped You as You deserve it,"[271] and when the infallible Imams (a), in the Presence of His Sanctity, display their shortcomings and deficiencies, what can a tiny gnat do?[272] Yes, their status and knowledge urged them to admit the incapability of "the possible existent" and the Greatness and Glory of the "Necessary Existent", Allah, the Exalted, whereas we, the helpless, because of ignorance and diverse veils, arrogantly show off our ostentation and pride in our acts. Glory be to Allah! How right Amir al-Muminin Ali (a) was when he said: "Man's self-admiration is one of the enviers of his intellect."[273] Is it not irrational that Satan should make obscure for us a necessary matter, and we should not try to intellectually reason it? We ourselves, know, of necessity, that our acts [of worship] and the acts of mankind as a whole, as well as the acts of the angels of Allah, and the spiritual people, cannot be compared with the acts of the Messenger of Allah (s) and the Imams of guidance (a), as ours can have no value whatsoever, and cannot be of

---

[268] *Ibid.*, *hadith* 4.
[269] *Ibid.*, vol. 3, "Book of Faith and Disbelief", ch. on "Slighting the Sin," *hadith* 2, p. 394; also vol. 4, ch. on "Reckoning the Deeds," *hadith* 17, p. 196.
[270] *As-Sahifah as-Sajjadiyyah*, invocation 3.
[271] *Mirat 'ul-Uqul* vol. 8, "Book of Faith and Disbelief," ch. on "Thanks-Giving," p. 146.
[272] "Where a falcon drops its feathers, what can a tiny gnat do?" *Amthal* and *Hikam*, by Dehkhuda, vol. 2, p. 579. The poet's name is not mentioned.
[273] *Nahj al-Balaghah*, ed. by Fayd al-Islam, maxim 203, p. 1172.

any regard at all. Yet, those great ones confess their shortcomings and do not conceal their incapability of performing the worship due to Allah, the Exalted, according to so many successive *hadith*s. These two necessary cases make us to conclude that we should not be pleased with any of our acts. Or even if we spend as long as the life of the world in worshipping and in acts of obedience, we should still be ashamed, abashed and disgraced. Nevertheless, Satan has so deeply established himself in our hearts, and so strongly has his control over our minds and senses, that the states [*ahwal*] of our hearts have been changed to the contrary, let alone our failure in deriving the necessary conclusions from those preliminaries.

The great man (Ali ibn Abi Talib), whose strike on the Day of the Trench was more merited than the worship of all *jinn* and *ins* (mankind), according to the confirmation of the Messenger of Allah (*s*)[274]—and Ali ibn al-Husayn, with all his worships and austerities, though known to be the greatest worshipper of all Allah''s creatures, shows his inability to attain his state of worshipping[274a]—declares his shortcoming in this respect more than we do. The Messenger of Allah (*s*)—at whose threshold Ali al-Murtada and all, other than Allah, are servants and live on the crumblings of his blessed table of knowledge and are the students of his teachings—after receiving the cloak of honor of the Final Prophethood, the complete circulation of perfection and the last brick of knowledge and *tawhid*, continued, for ten years, to stand on his feet in Hira cave, performing his worshippings in obedience to Allah, until his feet swelled such that Allah revealed: **"Ta-Ha, We have not sent down the Quran upon you that you should be distressed,"**[275] i.e.: "O "pure" and "guide"! We did not reveal the Quran to you to cause you difficulty. You are pure and you guide the people, and if they disobey you, it is because of their own shortcoming and misfortune, not because of any shortcoming in your conduct or guidance." Nevertheless, he still announces his inability and falling short.

Sayyid ibn Tawus (may his soul be sanctified) quotes from Ali ibn al-Husayn (a) a *hadith* which we shall relate to honor our thesis and, although it is a bit lengthy, since it is an explanation of the

---

[274] *Bihar al-Anwar*, vol. 39, *"Tarikh-i Amir al-Mu'minin,"* p. 2.
[274a] *Ibid.*, vol. 46, *"Tarikh-i Ali ibn al-Husayn"* ch. 5, *hadith* 65, p. 75.
[275] *Surah Ta-Ha* 20:1, 2.

position of that master, yet the smelling sense of the souls will be scented by it and the palate of the hearts will take a delight in it.

He (may his soul be sanctified), quoting az-Zahri, in *Fath al-Abwab*, says: "I, together with Ali ibn al-Husayn (a), called upon Abdul Malik ibn Marwan. Abdul Malik, regarding it as magnificent to see the mark of prostration between the two eyes of Ali ibn al-Husayn (a), said: "O Abu Muhammad, perseverance is obvious on your face, and Allah has already been beneficent to you, as you are a part of the Messenger of Allah (s), a close relative with a firm relation to him, and you have a great favor upon your family and your contemporaries. You have been given such merits, knowledge, godliness and piety that have been given to no one like you or before you, except your past ancestors." He continued praising and extolling him. Ali ibn al-Husayn (a) said: "All that which you have described is of Allah''s favor, support and grace. But how is [my] thanking Him on what He has favored [me], O Amir al-Mu''minin? The Messenger of Allah (s) used to stand in his *salat* on his feet till they got swollen, and he remained thirsty during his fasting such that his mouth would dry up. He was asked: "O Messenger of Allah! Did not Allah forgive what has passed and what is to come of your sins?" He replied: "Am I not to be a thankful servant?" Praise be to Allah for what He has favored us with and for His testing us, and praise be to Him in the Hereafter and in this world. By Allah, even if my limbs were cut to pieces and my eyeballs ran down my chest just to pay tribute to Allah, the Most Glorified, for just a tenth of one tenth of a single one of all His favors, which no reckoner can reckon, nor the praise of the praisers can pay the tribute due to a single one of them, I could not pay the due tribute to Him. Never, by Allah, unless He grants me that nothing should keep me from praising and remembering Him all days and nights, secretly and publicly. Had I not been under obligations to my family and to other people, in particular and in general, who have rights from me, and which I cannot but fulfill to them as it is possible and as is in my capacity, I would have turned my eye to the heaven, and my heart to Allah, and then I would have never taken them back till He would take my breath—He is the best of judges." Then he (a) wept, and so did Abdul Malik..." as the *hadith* goes.[276]

---

[276] *Bihar al-Anwar*, vol. 46, "Fath al-Abwab," p. 57.

We forgo mentioning other stages of sincerity, which do not suit the position of these papers, lest it should be lengthy and boring.

SECTION FOUR

Some Disciplines of Recitation and Its Secrets

This section includes *tafsir* [exegesis] of the blessed *surah* of *al-Hamd*, and a part of *tafsir* of the blessed *surah*s of *at-Tawhid* and *al-Qadr*. It is the most favored section of this thesis.

Discussed in Two Torches

TORCH ONE

General Disciplines of Reciting the Glorious Quran

Discussed in Six Chapters

THE DISCIPLINE OF REVERENCE
Chapter One

One of the important disciplines of reciting the Divine Book, shared by the gnostic and the common man, and which brings about good results causing luminosity for the heart and the interior life, is to regard it with "reverence", which depends on realizing its greatness and majesty. This, however, is actually out of the scope of explanation and beyond the human capacity, because understanding the greatness of a thing depends on understanding its truth, while the truth of the Divine Holy Quran, before being sent down to the stages [*manazil*] of creation and before undergoing practical modes [*atwar*], is of the affairs [*shuun*] of His Essence and of the facts of Knowledge in His Unity [*hadrat-i wahidiyyat*]. It is the truth of a "Self-Speech" [*kalam-i nafs*], which is the "Essential Argument" [*muqariat-i dhatiyyah*] in His Names. This truth appears to no one, neither by means of formal sciences or cordial knowledge nor by unseen disclosure, except through complete divine revelation to the blessed person of the Final Prophet (*s*), in the intimacy of *qaba qawsayn* [at the distance of two bows" length], or even in the secret privacy of *aw adna* [or nearer]. The hand of hope of the human species is short of that, except, that of the sincere of Allah"s friends who, according to the spiritual lights and the divine facts, share in the spirituality of the Prophet"s sacred essence and, through their complete subordination, they vanished in him. They receive the disclosing knowledge by inheriting it from him, and the truth of the Quran may be reflected in their hearts, with the same luminosity and perfection with which it appeared in the heart of that great personality, without its descending to [mundane] stations and taking [mundane] forms. That Quran is without change and alteration, and it is of the book of divine revelation. The one capable of carrying this Quran is the noble person of the absolute friend of Allah, Ali ibn Abi Talib (a). Others cannot take this fact in, unless it descends from the station of *ghayb* [the invisible] to the station of visibility and takes the seen form, wearing the apparel of mundane words and letters. This is one of the meanings of "changing" [*tahrif*] or alteration which has occurred in all Divine Scriptures as well as the Quran, changing all the noble *ayah*s, which, with a change, or rather many changes, according to the stations and stages which continue from His "Names" to the last of the worlds of vision and visibility, are placed within the reach of man. The number of the stages of the change corresponds to the number of the stages of the *butun* of the Quran exactly. The meaning of the change [*tahrif*] here is the descent from absolute *ghayb* to absolute visibility, in accordance with the degrees of the worlds, whereas the *butun* is the return from absolute visibility to absolute *ghayb*. So, the beginning of the change, and the beginning of the *butun* are opposed. Whenever a *salik* attains a stage of the *butun,* he gets rid of a degree of the change. When he arrives at the absolute *butun,* which is the seventh, according to the general classification, he absolutely gets rid of the change [*tahrif*]. So, perhaps the Quran appears to some to be full of different changes. To another, it may appear with few changes, while to a third it appears with no change at all. It may also appear to somebody changed in some instances and unchanged in some others, or with some sorts of changes in a third instance.

As you know, understanding the greatness of the Quran is beyond the capacity of the intellect. Yet, a general hint at the greatness of this Divine Book, which is within the reach of everybody, is of many advantages.

Do know, dear, that the greatness of a speech or a book is derived from the greatness of the speaker and the writer, from the greatness of its contents and objectives, from the greatness of its results and fruits, from the greatness of its intermediate conveyer, from the greatness of its receiver and its carrier, from the greatness of its keeper and protector, from the greatness of its commentator and explainer or from the greatness of the time of its being sent down and how it was sent. Some of these, however, are by nature the causes of greatness, others are indirectly so, and some are proofs of the greatness. All the said matters are contained in this luminous Book in their very best and satisfaction, or, actually they are its distinguished characteristics. No other book shares them with it, or covers all of them comprehensively.

As regards the greatness of the speaker, the composer and its owner, He is the Absolute Great, for all kinds of greatness that can be imagined on the earth and in the heavens, and all powers descending in the visible and the invisible, are but seepage of the manifestations of the greatness of the act of His Sacred Essence. Allah, the Exalted, would not show Himself to anybody through manifesting His Greatness from behind thousands of veils and curtains, as a *hadith* says: "Allah has seventy-thousand veils [of light and darkness; if removed away, the lights of His Face would burn everything other than Him.]."[277] To the people of knowledge, this noble Book has been issued from Allah, the Exalted, the Origin of all affairs of the Essence, Attributes and Acts, and of all manifestations of Beauty and Majesty. The other divine Books do not enjoy a similar status and position.

As regards the greatness of the contents, objectives and subjects, it requires a separate chapter, or, say, separate chapters, sections, a thesis or a book, so that one may relate only a part of that. We shall, nevertheless, generally refer, in a separate chapter, to its universal principles. In the said chapter we shall point out, *insha Allah*, its greatness in respect of its results and outcome.

As regards the greatness of the messenger and the conveyer of its revelation, he is the Faithful Gabriel, the Great Spirit. After that the noble Messenger of Allah (*s*) had quitted the apparel of the nature of the flesh and directed the heart towards His Majesty, he got in touch with that Great Spirit. He is one of the four pillars of the House of Realization, or rather he is the greatest of its pillars and the most honorable of them, since that noble and luminous Archangel is the guardian of knowledge and wisdom, and the conveyer of the spiritual provisions and moral nourishments. From the Book of Allah and the noble *hadith*s one realizes the greatness of Gabriel and his preference to other angels.[278]

As regards the greatness of its receiver and carrier, it is the pure and pious, Ahmadian single [*ahmadi-yi ahadi*], Muhammadan collective [*jami-yi muhammadi*] heart, to which Allah, the Exalted,

---

[277] *Bihar al-Anwar*, vol. 55, p. 45. This *hadith* is (also) related by the Sunni sources.
[278] See *Surah*s *ash-Shuara"* 26:193, *an-Najm* 53:5-9 and *at-Takwir* 81:19-24. See also *Bihar al-Anwar*, vol. 56, "Book of the Heaven and the World," sec. on "The Angels" and "Another Chapter on Describing the Favorable Angels," *hadith*s 23-24, p. 258.

appeared in all affairs [*shuun*] of the Essence, Attributes, Names and Acts. He [the Prophet] is the Seal of prophethood and the absolute guardian, the most generous of all creation, the best of the human beings, the gist [*khulasah*] of the universe, the essence [*jawharah*] of existence, the substance [*usarah*] of the House of Realization, the last brick and the owner of the big isthmus and great vicegerency [*khilafat*].

As regards the greatness of its keeper and guardian, He is the Sacred Essence of Allah, the Exalted as He says in the noble *ayah*: **"It is We Who have sent down the Reminder [the Quran], and verily We are its keeper."**[279]

As regards its commentators and explainers, they are the pure infallible ones—beginning with the Messenger of Allah and ending with "the Proof of the Time" [*hujjat-i asr*], may Allah enhance his advent—who are the keys of existence, the repositories of dignity, the sources of wisdom and inspiration, the origins of knowledge and learning, and the possessors of the state of collectivity [*jam*] and distinctness [*tafsil*].

As regards the time of revelation, it is *Laylat al-Qadr* [The Night of Majesty], which is the greatest of nights and **"better than a thousand months"**. It is the most luminous of times. In fact, it is the time of the attainment [*wusul*] of the General Guardian [*wali-yi mutlaq*] and the Seal of the Prophets (*s*).

As regards how it was revealed and its relevant ceremonies, they are beyond the limits of the capacity of these few papers. They require a special chapter, which, owing to its elaboration, will have to be omitted.

---

[279] *Surah al-Hijr* 15:9.

BRIEF HINTS AT THE OBJECTIVES, SUBJECTS AND CONTENTS OF THE GLORIOUS DIVINE BOOK
Chapter Two

Know that the Glorious (Divine) Book, as it declares itself, is a book of guidance, showing the way to human conduct, to educate the souls, to cure the spiritual sicknesses and to throw light on the road to Allah.

Generally speaking, Allah, due to His All-Embracing mercy upon His servants, sent this Glorious Book from His Sacred state of proximity, down, in proportion to the descending worlds until it reached this world of darkness and prison of nature and was put in the dress of words and letters in order to release those imprisoned in this world"s dark dungeon and to unite those chained by the fetters of hopes and desires, lifting them from the lowest level of shortcomings, weakness and animality to the peak of perfection, strength and humanity, taking them away from Satan"s neighborhood to the company of heavenly people, and to lead them to the state of "proximity" so as to let them attain the stage of meeting Allah, which is the highest objective and the want of the people of Allah. So, this is the Book of inviting to Allah and happiness, and explaining how to attain that stage. Its contents, generally, concern this same journey to Allah, or help the *salik* and traveler to Allah. In short, one of its important objectives is to invite [mankind] to know Allah, and [another is] to explain divine knowledge concerning the affairs of the Essence, Names, Attributes and Acts. At the top of this is the Unity of Essence, Names and Acts, some of which are explicitly mentioned and some others are only hinted at.

It should be noted that this comprehensive Divine Book deals with the above-mentioned information, from knowing the Essence to knowing the Acts, in such a way that each class of the people comprehends of it according to its capacity. The noble *ayah*s on *tawhid*, and on the Unity of Acts in particular, are explained by the literalist scholars, the traditionalists and the *faqih*s (may Allah be pleased with them) in such a way that their explanations are entirely contrary to the explanations of the people of knowledge and the scholars of the latent meaning of the Quran. The writer believes that each of these explanations is correct in its own place, since the Quran cures the internal pains, and treats each patient in a certain way. See different noble *ayah*s, such as: **"He is the First and the Last, and the Manifest and the Hidden,"**[280] **"Allah is the light of the heavens and the earth,"**[281] **"And He it is Who in the heaven and in the earth is God,"**[282] **"And He is with you,"**[283] **"Wherever you turn there is Allah"s Face,"**[284] and many others on the Unity of Essence, and the last *ayah*s of the *Surah* of *al-Hashr* and other ones on the Unity of Attributes, and the *ayah*s: **"And you threw not when you did throw, but Allah threw,"**[285] **"All praise is for Allah, the Lord of the worlds,"**[286] and **"All that is in the heavens and all that is in the earth glorify Allah,"**[287] concerning the Unity of Acts. Some of them strictly, and some others more strictly, have gnostic indications. For each class of the external and the internal scholars each of them is the remedy, in a way, for an illness. As, although it is said in the noble *al-Kafi* that the first *ayah*s of *Surah al-Hadid* and the blessed *Surah* of *Ikhlas* [*Tawhid*] were intended for the deep thinkers of the End of the Time,"[288] yet the people of literalism are also benefited by them all right—a fact which proves the miraculousness and the comprehensiveness of this noble Book.

Of its other objectives and topics is its call for purifying the souls and purging the insides from the impurities of nature, and attaining happiness. Generally, it shows how to travel to Allah. This noble subject is divided into two important branches: One is *taqwa* in

---

[280] *Surah al-Hadid* 57:3.
[281] *Surah an-Nur* 24:35.
[282] *Surah az-Zukhruf* 43:84.
[283] *Surah al-Hadid* 57:4.
[284] *Surah al-Baqarah* 2:115.
[285] *Surah al-Anfal* 8: 17.
[286] *Surah al-Fatihah* 1:2.
[287] *Surah al-Jumuah* 62:1; *Surah at-Taghabun* 64:1.
[288] *Usul al-Kafi*, vol. 1, "Book of *at-Tawhid*," ch. on "Lineage," *hadith* 3, p. 123.

all its stages, including bewaring of other than Allah, and complete negligence of all other than Him. The other is faith in all its stages and affairs, including devotion to Allah, and return and repentance to His Sacred Essence. These are of the important objectives of this noble Book as most of its subjects, directly or indirectly, connote them.

Another subject of this Divine Book is to relate the stories of the prophets, Allah's friends and the wise men, and how He educated them, and how they educated the people. These stories are of great advantages and cover many instructions. They include so many pieces of divine information, teachings and divine educational instructions, either openly or allegorically that perplex the mind. Glorious is Allah and praise and gratitude are for Him. Just take the story of the creation of Adam (a), the angels' being ordered to bow down to him, the teaching of the names and the cases of *Iblis* and Adam (a) which are repeatedly narrated in the Book of Allah. They offer so many teachings, educational instructions, knowledge and information for **"him who has a heart or lends ear and he is a witness"**[289] that bewilder man. The stories of the Quran, such as the stories of Adam, Moses, Abraham and other prophets (a) are repeatedly stated in order to show that this Book is neither a book of stories nor of history, but a book of journeying to Allah, a book of *tawhid*, knowledge, admonitions and aphorisms. In such matters repetition is required so as to fix them in the hard-hearted souls and to have effects as an admonition to them. In other words, whoever wants to educate, teach, warn and bring good tidings, has to express his intentions in different styles and diverse ways, such as narrations and tales, or historical stories, and sometimes in quite an explicit way, and sometimes by way of allusion and indirect hints, symbols and examples, so that different souls and scattered hearts can each be benefited by them.

As this noble Book is intended for the happiness of all classes and the human race, and as the human species differ in the condition of their hearts, in their customs, behaviors, time and place, they cannot be attracted in the same way. Many of them may not be prepared to accept the instructions and the original matter in a direct, clear and explicit language, or to be affected by it. They are to be approached in accordance with the construction of their brains in order to make them comprehend what is intended. Some others are not interested in stories,

---

[289] *Surah Qaf* 50:37.

tales and histories, as they are in quest of the cores of the matters and the real aims. They cannot be taken on the same basis with the former ones. Many hearts are fit for being frightened and warned; other hearts are attracted by promises and hopes. Consequently, this noble Book uses different methods, styles and ways for its invitation of the people. Thus, such Book has inevitably to resort to repetition. Attracting and admonishing, without repetition, would be far from eloquence. The expected effect in the souls cannot be obtained without repetition.

Nevertheless, in this noble Book, the topics are so sweetly related that their repetition never bores the hearers. Furthermore, each repetition of a subject brings fresh details and features that have not formerly been mentioned, or rather in each repetition there is an additional important gnostic or ethical point around which the case revolves. In order to expand upon this, one has to carefully study the stories of the Quran, which cannot be contained within the summaries of these papers. This weak person [the writer] has a fixed hope to write, with Allah''s help, a book about the stories of the Quran, deciphering their puzzles and explaining their teachings and educational qualities, as much as possible, though carrying out this task by somebody like the writer is but a raw desire, or a false fancy.

At any rate, relating the stories of the prophets (a), describing their conducts and behaviors, how they educated the people, and remembering their advices, admonitions and good arguments are of the largest chapters of knowledge and philosophies, and of the loftiest passages to happiness and instructions which Allah, the Exalted and Most Glorified, opened to His servants. Although the people of knowledge, *suluk* and austerity have their share plentifully, other people also have their boundless portion, as is stated in the noble *ayah*: **"When the night over-shadowed him, he saw a star. He said: "This is my Lord." But when it set, he said: "I do not love the setting (ones)." "**[290] The people of knowledge understand well the spiritual *suluk* and the conduct of Abraham (a). They also learn how to travel to Allah, and perceive the truth of the self's spiritual journey from the farthest (deepest) darkness of nature, expressed in **"the night over-shadowed him,"** till absolutely casting down the egoism and egotism, leaving I-ness and self-worship, attaining the state of sanctity and joining the meeting of intimacy, which is expressed in: **"I have turned**

---

[290] *Surah al-Anam* 6:76.

234

my face toward Him Who created the heavens and the earth...”[291] Others learn from it the outer journey and how *Khalil ar-Rahman* (the intimate friend of the Beneficent) educated his people. Likewise, there are other stories and tales, such as the stories of Adam, Ibrahim (Abraham), Moses, Yusuf (Joseph), Isa (Jesus) and the meeting between al-Khidr (Elias) and Moses, by which the people of knowledge, austerity and hardship, and others are benefited differently. In this part included, or in a separate objective, are the aphorisms and the admonitions of His Sacred Essence, Who, on every suitable occasion, has invited the people, with His tongue of Power, to divine knowledge, *tawhid* and glorification, such as the blessed *Surah* of *Ikhlas*, the last *ayah*s of the *Surah* of *al-Hashr* and the early *ayah*s of the *Surah* of *al-Hadid* and other instances in the noble divine Book. The people of heart and of good past enjoy a good share of it. For example, when the people of knowledge recite: **“And whoever leaves his house migrating to Allah and His Messenger, then death overtakes him, his reward is, indeed, with Allah...”**[292] they understand from it the proximity of the *nafilah* [supererogatory act] and *faridah* [obligatory act], while, at the same time, others understand from it a bodily migration, say, to Mecca or to Medina, or they understand it to be an invitation to purifying the soul and internal austerity, as in the noble *ayah*: **“He will, indeed, be successful who purifies it, and he will, indeed, be unsuccessful who seduces it,”**[293] and the like; or it is a call to good deed, as it is obvious; or it is a warning against anyone of these things. This part also includes the aphorisms of Luqman and of other notables and believers that are sporadically mentioned in this divine Book, such as the case of the “Companions of the Cave.”

Another subject of this luminous Book concerns the states of the disbelievers, the deniers and the opposers of the truth and reality, and those who act obstinately towards the prophets and the Imams (a). It explains their fates and how they were annihilated, such as the episodes of Pharaoh, Korah, Nimrod, Shaddad, the Companions of the Elephant, and other disbelievers and sinners, in all of which there are admonitions, aphorisms and even knowledge for those who deserve

---

[291] *Ibid.*: 79.
[292] *Surah an-Nisa"* 4:100.
[293] *Surah ash-Shams* 91:9-10.

them. This part includes the cases of the accursed *Iblis*, as well as the expeditions of the Messenger of Allah (*s*), (or in a separate part) from which noble subjects are also learnt, such as how the Companions of the Messenger of Allah (*s*) used to fight in order to awaken the Muslims from the sleep of negligence, and to incite them to fight for the sake of Allah to uplift the word of truth and to abolish the *batil* (falsehood).

Another subject dealt with in the Glorious Quran is explaining the pure laws of the literal meaning of the *shariah* and the disciplines and divine rules, which are stated in this luminous Book, in a general way, the most important of which is introducing the principal subjects and disciplines, such as the chapters of the *salat, zakat, khums, hajj, sawm, jihad*, marriage, inheritance, penalties, punishments, trading, and the like. This section, which is the science of the appearance of the *shariah*, is a public concern and is for all the classes, and it is intended to build up this world and the Hereafter. All the classes of people can benefit from it according to their individual capacities. This is frequently invited to in the Book of Allah, as well as in the *hadith*s and narratives, which freely expand upon the characteristics and details. The works and writings of the religious scholars on this section are more and higher than on other sections.

Another topic dealt with in the Glorious Quran is the conditions of the *maad* [Resurrection], arguments proving it, its torments, punishments and rewards, and the details of Paradise, Hell, punishing, and of putting in a state of comfort and ease. This section handles matters such as the conditions of the people of happiness and their ranks, like the people of knowledge, the favorites, the people of austerity, the travelers to Allah, the devotees, and the ascetics, as well as the conditions and degrees of the people of wretchedness, such as the infidels, the veiled, the hypocrites, the deniers, the disobedient and the sinners. But that which has more advantages to the conditions of the common people is more expanded upon and is in a more explicit language, whereas that which is more advantageous to a particular class of people is referred to by way of allegories and allusions, such as: **"And an approval from Allah is far greater"**[294], and other *ayah*s about meeting Allah, and such as: **"Nay, surely they shall on that**

---

[294] *Surah at-Tawbah* 9:72.

day be veiled from their Lord,"[295] in respect to another group. In this section, i.e. the section concerning details about the Resurrection and the Return to Allah, countless information and difficult secrets are stated, such that, without a demonstrative conduct [*suluk*] or a gnostic light, their nature cannot be comprehended.

Another subject of this divine Book is the proofs and evidences which Allah, the Exalted, Himself presents to prove the truthful matters and divine knowledge, like the argument proving [the existence of] Allah and His Oneness, His transcendence, His Knowledge, His Power and His other attributes of perfection. In this section one can sometimes find very refined proofs from which the people of knowledge derive complete benefit, such as: **"Allah bears witness that there is no god but He."**[296] One also finds proofs which are used by the scholars and philosophers in one way, and by the people of formalism and the common people in another way, such as the *ayah*: **"Had there been in them any gods other than Allah, they both would have been corrupted,"**[297] and the *ayah*: **"...otherwise each god would have certainly taken away what he had created,"**[298] and like the first *ayah*s of the *Surah* of *al-Hadid* and the blessed *Surah* of *at-Tawhid* and other *ayah*s. Also there are arguments proving the Resurrection and the return of the spirits and originating another creation, and the arguments proving the existence of Allah's angels and the great prophets, stated in many occasions in this Glorious Book. These were the arguments of the Sacred Essence Himself, and there are the arguments and proofs of the prophets and wise men quoted by Allah to prove the divine knowledge, such as the arguments of Ibrahim, the intimate Friend of Allah (a), and other arguments.

These were the important subjects of this Book, though there are many other different subjects, which require considerable time to count.

---

[295] *Surah al-Mutaffifin* 83:15.
[296] *Surah Al-i Imran* 3:18.
[297] *Surah al-Anbiya"*21:22.
[298] *Surah al-Mu'minun* 23:91.

HOW TO BE BENEFITED BY THE QURaN
Chapter Three

Now that you have got acquainted with the subjects and the objectives of the Divine Book (the Quran), you will have to take into consideration an important point, as by doing so the door of being benefited by it will be opened to you, and the passage to knowledge and wisdom will be wide open to your heart. This point is to look at this Glorious Book as an educational one, a teaching book by which you should be benefited, regarding it your duty to learn from it. By learning, teaching, benefiting and being benefited we do not mean its different literary, syntactical and morphological aspects, nor its eloquence and rhetoric and other stylistic points, nor being interested in its stories, tales and episodes from the historical point of view in order to get information about the past nations. None of these is included in the objectives of the Quran, and they are, in fact, far away from the main objective of this divine Book.

The fact that our advantage from this great Book is quite small is because we usually do not take it to be a book of teaching and education. We recite the Quran just for its reward. So, we pay attention only to our intonation when reciting it. We want our recitation to be perfect and correct so as to obtain its reward, and then we stop at that and feel satisfied with it. Thus, we spend some forty years reciting the Quran without being benefited by it, except the reward for reciting it. If we do look at its teaching and educational side, we concern ourselves with its eloquence and syntax and its miraculous aspects, or even somewhat higher, we engage ourselves with its history, the occasions of the revelation of the *ayah*s, the times of their revelation, which *surah* or *ayah* was revealed in Mecca and which in Medina, the differences in recitations and in the exegeses of the Sunnis and the Shiah and other secondary affairs which are outside the main objective and they themselves cause us to be barred from the Quran and to neglect remembering Allah. Even our great commentators of the Quran are very much concerned about one or another of the said affairs, without opening the door of learning to the people.

The writer believes that so far no *tafsir* [exegesis] has yet been written to the Book of Allah. Generally, to write a *tafsir* for a book means to explain the objectives of the book and to draw the attentions to what its author wants to say. This noble Book, which Allah, the Exalted, testifies to be a book of guidance and teaching, and the light of the road of man"s journey, its exegete should find in each one of its stories, or even in each *ayah*, a directive guiding to the invisible world, so as to show to the learner the road to happiness, to knowledge and to humanity. A *mufassir* (commentator or exegete) is the one who tells us what was the "objective" of the revelation, not the "occasion" of the revelation as is explained in the exegeses. In the very story of Adam and Eve and their affairs with *Iblis*, from the very moment of their creation till their descent to the earth, story of which is repeated by Allah several times in the Quran, there are so many overt and covert teachings [*maarif*] and admonitions, and it reminds us of so many of spiritual faults and Satanic characters, as well as many perfections of the soul and human knowledge which it introduces to us, whereas we still disregard them.

In short, the Book of Allah is a book of knowledge and ethics, and an invitation to happiness and perfection. So, its exegesis should also be a book of gnosticism and ethics, explaining the gnostic and ethical points of view, and other aspects of inviting to its happiness [*saadat*]. The commentator who neglects these points, disregards them or attaches no importance to them, is actually neglecting the objective of the Quran and the main aim of revealing the (divine) books and sending the messengers. This is a grave mistake that has prevented the *ummah* for many centuries from being benefited by the Glorious Quran, and it has blocked the road of guidance in their faces. We have to learn the objective of the revelation of the Quran—disregarding the intellectual and argumentative aspects, which show us the goal by themselves—from the Quran itself. The author of a book knows better his own objective. So, let us have a glance at what the author of this Book Himself says concerning the affairs of the Quran. He says: **"This is the Book, wherein is no doubt, a guide for the *muttaqin* (those** who fear Allah).”[299] He describes His Book as being a book of guidance. In a short *surah* He repeats saying: **"We have made the Quran easy for remembrance, but is there any one who will mind?"**[300] He says: **"...We have revealed to you the Reminder that you may explain to mankind what has been sent down to them and that haply they will reflect,"**[301] and **"A Book We have revealed to you, blessed, that they may ponder over its *ayah*s and that men of understanding may remember,"**[302] and many other noble *ayah*s, to restate which would be lengthy.

This opinion of ours is not intended to criticize the *tafsir*s, as every one of their authors has taken great pains and striven hard in order to write a noble book, so, may Allah bless them and grant them good reward. We intend just to say that the door must be open before the people to be benefited by this Book, which is the only one leading to Allah and the only one for educating the souls with the divine disciplines and laws, the greatest means of connection between the created and Creator, the strong handle and the firm cord of adhering to the Might of Divinity. Let the scholars and commentators write Persian and Arabic exegeses with the aim of explaining the gnostic and ethical teachings and instructions, showing the way of connecting the created to the Creator, and expounding the migration from *Dar al-Ghurur* (the House of Conceit = this world) to the *Dar as-Surur wal-Khulud* (the House of Pleasure and Eternity)], according to what has been deposited in this noble Book. The author of this Book is not as-Sakkaki or the Shaykh, whose objectives were eloquence and rhetoric, nor is He Sibawayh or al-Khalil, whose objectives were grammar and syntax, nor is He al-Masudi or Ibn Khillakan, whose objectives revolved around the history of the world. This Book is not like the stick of Moses or his White Hand, nor is it like the breath of Christ who could raise the dead (by Allah's permission), to have been sent down only as a miracle to prove the true prophethood of the Holy Prophet. This divine Book is, as a matter of fact, a book of enlivening the hearts with the everlasting life of divine knowledge. It is Allah's Book that invites to divine affairs. So, the commentator has to teach

---

[299] *Surah al-Baqarah* 2:2.
[300] *Surah al-Qamar* 54:17.
[301] *Surah an-Nahl* 16:44.
[302] *Surah Sad* 38:29.

these divine affairs to the people, and the people have to refer to his commentary to learn those affairs, so that they may attain its advantage: **"And We reveal of the Quran that which is a healing and a mercy to the believers, and it adds only to the perdition of the wrongdoers."**[303] Which perdition is graver than that we keep reciting the Divine Book for thirty or forty years and refer to the exegeses, and yet we do not get its real objectives? **"Our Lord! We have wronged ourselves. If You do not forgive us and have mercy upon us, we shall certainly be of the losers."**[304]

---

[303] *Surah al-Isra"* 17:82.
[304] *Surah al-Araf* 7:23.

THE OBSTACLES AND BARRIERS PREVENTING BEING BENEFITED BY THE QURAN
Chapter Four

Now that the greatness of the Book of Allah has been understood by considering all the required aspects of greatness, and the way of being benefited by it has been opened, it will be necessary for the learner of, and the benefit-deriver [*mustafid*] from, the Book of Allah to apply a further important discipline in order to get [the best] advantage. It is removing the causes which prevent the advantage, and which we call "the veils" between the benefit-deriver and the Quran. These veils are many, to some of which we shall refer presently.

One of these thick veils is self-conceit, through which the learner sees himself, because of this veil, in no need of getting any benefit from the Quran. This is one of Satan's important masterpieces, by which he always tries to inspire man with imaginary perfections, telling him to be contented with what he has, and to disregard everything other than that which he already has. For example, he makes the people of *tajwid* [reciting the Quran with intonation] contented with this small knowledge which they have, making it quite big in their eyes, slighting other knowledge to them, and making them compare the carriers of the Quran with themselves, causing them to be deprived of understanding the luminous divine Book and of getting any advantage from it. Similarly, he causes the men of letters to be contented with the meaningless from making them believe that all the Quranic affairs are only those that they have. He engages the exegetes, as usual, with the ways of recitation, the different opinions of the linguistics, the times of revelation, the occasions of revelation, whether the *ayah* was revealed in Mecca or in Medina, the number of the *ayah*s, their letters and the like. The scholars are also kept indulged in only learning the different aspects of indications, the diverse ways of arguments and the like. Even the philosopher, the wise man and the gnostic are imprisoned by Satan behind the thick veil of terminology, concepts and so on. The benefit-deriver [*mustafid*] must tear open these veils in order to look at the Quran from behind them, taking care not to stay at any one of these veils, so as not to be left behind the caravan of the travelers to Allah, nor be deprived of the sweet divine invitations. The Glorious Quran itself instructs that one should not remain still and should not be satisfied with a certain limit. This is frequently referred to in the stories of the Quran. Moses (a), a great prophet as he was, was not contented with that position, nor was he satisfied with his high position of knowledge. He no sooner met that perfect man, al-Khidr, than he addressed him, quite humbly and modestly, saying: **"May I follow you that you may teach me right knowledge of what you have been taught?"**[305] He kept following him and acquired the knowledge he wanted to learn. Prophet Abraham (a) also was not satisfied with the great state of faith and the special knowledge of the prophets (a). He asked the Lord: **"My Lord! Show me how You give life to the dead."**[306] He wanted to proceed from the state of cordial faith up to the state of tangible confidence. Higher even than that is when Allah, the Exalted, told the Seal of the Prophets, the most learned person of all Allah's creatures, to say: **"...Say: O my Lord! Increase me in knowledge."**[307] Such instructions of the divine Book and relating the stories of the prophets, are but for us to learn from them, and to bring us to conscience and wake us from our negligent sleep.

Another one of the veils is that of the false ideas, and the *batil* ways, which are sometimes caused by the inabilities of the person himself, and they are mostly the outcome of subordination and imitation. This veil particularly conceals from us the Quranic knowledge. For example, if, by listening to our fathers, mothers, or some ignorant preacher, we got a false idea fixed in our hearts, it would be a veil, a barrier between us and the noble divine *ayah*s [of the Quran]. Thus, even if there were thousands of *ayah*s and *hadith*s defying that idea, we would either dismiss them on the basis of their exoteric meanings, or we would not consider them with the aim of

---

[305] *Surah al-Kahf* 18:66.
[306] *Surah al-Baqarah* 2:260.
[307] *Surah Ta-Ha* 20:114.

understanding. Regarding beliefs and knowledge there are numerous examples, but I shall abstain from counting them, as I do know that this veil cannot be torn by the sayings of someone, like me. Nevertheless, just to present a sample, I will refer to one of them, which is somewhat easier to understand: Despite all the *ayah*s which have been revealed in respect of meeting Allah and knowing Him, all the narratives that were related to the same subject and all the indications and allusions, open and hidden, in the invocations and the supplications of the Imams (a), some uninformed and vulgar persons have spread the belief that the way to knowing Allah was completely closed. The door of knowing Allah and discerning the Beauty [of Him] is interpreted to be the same as meditating upon the very Essence of Allah, which is prohibited, or rather impossible. They may even refrain from entering this field and prefer not to acquaint themselves with such knowledge, which is the delight of the eyes of the prophets and holy men [*awliya*]. It is much to be regretted by the people of Allah to see a chapter of knowledge, which can very aptly be described as the goal of sending the prophets and the most cherished demand of the holy men, should be so prohibited to the people that a simple mentioning it would be regarded complete disbelief and mere heresy. These people take the knowledge [*maarif*] of the prophets and the holy men [*awliya*] to be the same as the knowledge [*maarif*] of the common people and [unlettered old] women about Allah's Essence, Names and Attributes. Sometimes they say even more than that: "So-and-so has good, vulgar beliefs. We wish we kept to the same vulgar belief." This is quite correct, because when this wretched person utters these words, he has already lost his vulgar beliefs, and, at the same time, regards other beliefs, which are the beliefs of the elite and the people of Allah, to be false. This wish is quite similar to the wish of the disbelievers who, as in the noble *ayah*, say: **"...and the disbeliever shall say: O would that I were dust!"**[308]

Should we want to relate in detail the *ayah*s and the narratives concerning the meeting with Allah, in order to expose this corrupt belief caused by ignorance and Satanic conceit, we would need to write a separate book. Especially, if we wanted to explain the knowledge which has been neglected due to this thick Satanic veil, it would be clear that this negligence is one of the stages of neglecting

---

[308] *Surah an-Naba"* 78:40.

and discarding the Quran, and it is probably the most regretful stage, as is described in the Quran: **"And the Messenger said: O my Lord! My people have treated this Quran as a forsaken [thing]."**[309] Forsaking the Quran has many stages and countless degrees, and we may possess a good number of them.

If we bound this divine Book in a nice and valuable cover, and we kissed it and put it on our eyes whenever we wanted to recite it or to take an *istikharah* (consulting the Quran to do or not to do something) with it, would it mean that we did not forsake it?

If we spent most of our lives perfecting our intonation when reciting the Quran, and improving our linguistic and rhetorical knowledge of it, would it mean that we brought the Quran out of being forsaken?

If we learnt the different ways of reciting the Quran and other relevant subjects, would we be declared not guilty of deserting it?

If we took in all the aspects of the miraculousness and the artistic beauties of the Quran, would we be excluded from the complaint of the Messenger of Allah? Never! None of these is intended by the Quran and its Great Revealer! The Quran is a divine Book, and it contains divine affairs. The Quran is the string connecting the creatures to their Creator, and through its instructions there should be a spiritual and invisible tie between the servants of Allah and their Lord. From the Quran there should emerge divine sciences and intuitive knowledge. The Messenger of Allah, according to a narrative in the noble *al-Kafi*, said: "Knowledge is of three kinds: a clear *ayah*, a fair obligation and a current tradition."[310]

The Glorious Quran is the bearer of these sciences. If we could take them in, we would not be deserting the Quran. If we accepted the calls of the Quran, and learnt from the stories of the prophets (a) which are full of admonishments, information and philosophies, and if we absorbed the admonitions of Allah, the Exalted, of the prophets and of the wise men, as stated in the Quran, we would not be deserting it, as indulging in the formal picture of the Quran is also keeping to the earth, and is of Satan's whisperings, from which one must seek refuge with Allah.

---

[309] *Surah al-Furqan* 25:30.
[310] *Usul al-Kafi*, vol. 1, "Book of the Merits of Knowledge," ch. on "The Description of Knowledge and its Merits," *hadith* 1, p. 37.

Another veil that prevents us from being benefited by this luminous Book is to believe that except what the exegetes have written or understood, no one has the right to make use of the noble Quran. Contemplating and thinking about the noble *ayah*s are mistakenly regarded to be interpretation, as interpretation according to one"s own opinion is not allowed, and thus, because of this false belief and invalid opinion, the Glorious Quran was deprived from being utilized in any way and, consequently, it was completely deserted, despite the fact that to utilize it morally, faithfully and gnostically has nothing to do with exegesis, be it according to opinion or else. For example, suppose someone could get out some lessons from the dialogue between the prophets Moses and al-Khidr (a), how they talked to one another, how severely Moses, great a prophet as he was, traveled in order to acquire the knowledge which he lacked, and he implored al-Khidr (a) in the way stated in the noble *ayah*: **"May I follow you that you may teach me right knowledge of what you have been taught?"**[311] then al-Khidr"s reply, the excuses of Moses (a), the greatness of the station of knowledge, and how a student should behave toward his tutor, in which there may be twenty disciplines. What connection all these have with exegesis, or exegesis according to opinion? Many advantages of the Quran are of this kind. Take, for example, someone, who, in respect of Islamic teachings, understands from Allah"s saying: **"All praise is for Allah, the Lord of the worlds"** that all praise and extolment are exclusively Allah"s. He learns from it His Unity of Actions, and says that from the noble *ayah* he deduces that every perfection, beauty, might and majesty which are in the world—and which the eye of the squint-eyed and the heart of the veiled ascribe to the beings—are Allah"s and no being has itself any share of them. Therefore, praise and extolment are solely Allah"s, and nobody shares them with Him. But has this anything to do with exegesis, be it according to opinion or not? There are so many other affairs from which many usages can be obtained, though having no connection with exegesis whatsoever. Besides, to exegete according to opinion is still arguable, as probably it does not concern the *ayah*s about knowledge and the speculative sciences, which conform with the criteria of intellectual proofs, nor the ethical *ayah*s which have to do with intellect, since such exegeses coincide with the strong intellectual

---

[311] *Surah al-Kahf* 18:66.

proofs or with explicit rational indications, such that if an exterior does not conform with them, they are to be turned away from that exterior. For example, the noble *ayah*s: **"And your Lord comes, and the angels rank on rank,"**[312] or **"The Beneficent has settled on the Throne,"**[313] in which the conventional [*urf*] understanding contradicts the proof, to refute the exterior and to explain them by proof is not explaining according to opinion, and can never be prohibited.

Therefore, it is possible, or believed, that exegesis according to opinion concerns the *ayah*s of precepts, of which the hand of opinion and intellect is short, and they must be devotionally and obediently taken from the treasurers of revelation and the descending places of the angels of Allah, as most of the noble *hadith*s in this respect defy the Sunni jurisprudents who wanted to comprehend Allah's religion by way of their own intellects and by comparisons. Some noble narrative says: "Nothing is farther away from the intellects of men than the exegesis of the Quran."[314] Another noble narrative says: "Allah's religion cannot be conceived well by intellects."[315] Such narratives prove that by "Allah's religion" they mean devotional obedience to the religious precepts, or else, proving the Maker, *tawhid*, Glorification, the Resurrection Day and Prophethood, or rather all sorts of knowledge are within the intellect's lawful right and field of specialty. That which is in the expressions of some notable narrators who said that proving monotheism depends on traditional proof is strange, or, more aptly, it is one of the disasters from which we must take refuge with Allah. This speech does not need to be condemned and disgraced, but our complaint is to Allah.

Another veil that prevents understanding this heavenly Book and being benefited by its knowledge and admonitions is the veil of disobediences [*maasi*] and the opacity caused by rebellion against the sanctity of the Lord of the worlds. By this veil the heart is prevented from understanding the truths. It must be noted that just as there is a corresponding image for each of the good and bad deeds in the heavenly world, there is a similar one inside the soul, through which

---

[312] *Surah al-Fajr* 89:22.

[313] *Surah Ta-Ha* 20:5.

[314] *Bihar al-Anwar*, vol. 89, "The Book of the Quran," ch. 8, *hadith* 48, p. 95; Ayyashi's *Exegesis*, vol. 1, p. 12.

[315] *Bihar al-Anwar*, vol. 2, "Book of Knowledge," *hadith* 41, p. 303, as quoted from *Ikmal ad-Din* [Completing the Religion].

the innermost part of the soul gets either luminous and likewise the heart gets purified and luminous, in which case the soul becomes clear and polished like a mirror, prepared to receive the invisible manifestation and the appearance of the truths and knowledge, or the soul gets dark and devilish, in which case the heart becomes like a rusty and tarnished mirror, unable to reflect any divine knowledge and invisible truths. A heart in such a condition will gradually fall under the authority of Satan, and *Iblis* becomes the possessor of the kingdom of the spirit, and the hearing and seeing, and the other senses and powers, too, become at the disposal of that evil creature. The hearing becomes completely blocked against the divine teachings, and the eyes do not see the splendid divine signs and they become blind to Allah's truth, signs and *ayah*s. The heart does not become learned in religion, and is deprived of meditating on the clear signs of Allah, His Names and His Attributes, as Allah, the Exalted says: **"They have hearts with which they do not understand, and they have eyes with which they do not see, and they have ears with which they do not hear. They are as cattle—nay, they are even worse..."**[316] Their look at the world is like the look of the cattle and the animals at it, void of value and deliberation. Their hearts, like the hearts of the animals, lack meditation and remembrance, or rather, the more they think of the *ayah*s and hear admonitions and instructions, the more their negligence and haughtiness increase. Thus, they are even lower than the beasts and graver in going astray.

Another one of the thick veils, which is a heavy curtain between us and the teachings and admonitions of the Quran, is the veil of loving this world, which causes the heart to be completely devoted to it, and the inclination of the heart entirely turns towards mundane matters, neglecting remembering Allah and turning away from both remembrance and the One to be remembered. The more the love for this world and its affairs, the thicker the veil and the curtain on the heart. Sometimes this love so overwhelms the heart, and the power [*sultan*] of endearing post and position becomes so influential that the light of the divine nature [*fitrat ullah*] in the heart is put off, and the doors of happiness are closed to man's face. It is, however, possible that the locks of the hearts mentioned in the noble *ayah*: **"Will they, then, not meditate on the Quran, or are there locks on the**

---

[316] *Surah al-Anam* 6:179.

hearts?"[317] are those locks of mundane attachments. The one who wants to be benefited by the Quranic knowledge and to make use of the divine admonitions will have to purge the heart from such impurities, and drive away the pollution of cordial sins, which are being engaged with other than Him, because the non-purified [heart] is no place for these secrets. Allah, the Exalted, says: **"It is surely a noble Quran, in a protected Book; none shall touch it save the purified ones."**[318] Just as the touching of the external body of this Book is not allowed for the one whose external body is not purified, by both legislation and obligation, similarly its knowledge, admonitions and secrets are prohibited to the one whose heart is smeared with the filths of the mundane longings. Allah, the Exalted, says: **"This is the Book, wherein is no doubt, a guide for those who fear Allah."**[319] The one who does not fear Allah and is faithless—according to the God-fearing and faith of the common people—is deprived from the formal lights of the admonitions of the Quran and of its true beliefs, while the one who does not fear Allah and is faithless—according to other degrees of fearing Allah, which are the fearing of the elite, of the upper elite and of the uppermost elite—is deprived from the other degrees of the Quran. However, going into the details and relating other *ayah*s to the same effect would lengthen the subject. Nevertheless, we are going to end this chapter with an honored *ayah*, which will be sufficient for the wakeful people, provided that it is well pondered upon.

Allah, the Exalted, says: **"...Indeed there has come to you from Allah a light, and a clear Book, with which Allah guides him who seeks His pleasure unto the ways of safety, and brings them out of darkness into the light by His permission, and guides them unto a straight path."**[320]

There are many specific points in this noble *ayah*, and to explain them we would need to write a separate thesis, for which there is no opportunity now.

---

[317] *Surah Muhammad* 47:24.
[318] *Surah al-Waqiah* 56:77-79.
[319] *Surah al-Baqarah* 2:2.
[320] *Surah al-Ma'idah* 5:15-16.

MEDITATION
Chapter Five

One of the disciplines of reciting the Quran is the presence of heart, to which we have already referred in this book, when we discussed the general disciplines of the acts of worship; so, there is no need to repeat it.

Another one of its disciplines is meditation, by which we mean that the reciter of the noble *ayah*s should look for the destination and the objective. Now as the objective of the Quran, as the very luminous Book says, is guiding the people to the ways of safety, bringing them out of the stages of darkness into the world of light, and leading them to the straight path, one must, by way of meditating on the noble *ayah*s, attain the stages of safety, from its lowest stage, which belongs to worldly dominion, up to its final stage, which is the realization of a sound heart [*qalb-i salim*], according to the explanation received from *Ahl al-Bayt* (a) saying that a sound heart meets Allah when it is occupied by none other than Him.[321] The soundness of the worldly and heavenly powers should be the quest of the reciter of the Quran, as he will certainly find it in this heavenly Book if he meditates on it. When the human powers become safe from Satan"s intrusion, and when the way to safety is found and followed, man, in each stage of safety, will be saved from a degree of darkness, and the bright light of Allah will inevitably shine in him. If he gets rid of all sorts of darkness, the first of which is the darkness of the world of nature, with all its affairs, and the last of which is the darkness of being inclined to multiplicity with all its affairs, the absolute light will shine in his heart, leading him to the straight path of humanity, which is, in this instance, the path of the Lord: **"Surely my Lord is on a straight path."**[322]

---

[321] *Usul al-Kafi*, vol. 3, p.26, "The Book of Faith and Disbelief", ch. on "Sincerity," *hadith* 5.
[322] *Surah Hud* 11:56.

Contemplation is very much invited to, praised and applauded in the Glorious Quran. Allah, the Exalted, says: **"And We have revealed to you the Remembrance that you may explain to mankind what has been sent down to them and that haply they may reflect."**[323] In this noble *ayah* reflection is strongly applauded, because the aim of sending down this great heavenly Book, the great luminous paper, is that **"haply they may reflect."** This is quite significant that the mere possibility of reflection causes the revelation of this great generosity [*karamat*]. In another *ayah* He says: **"Therefore, narrate the narratives [*qasas*] that they may reflect."**[324] There are so many *ayah*s of this like or almost the like, as well as narratives [*riwayat*] which invite to reflection. The Messenger of Allah (s) is quoted to have said, on the revelation of the *ayah* **"Surely in the creation of the heavens and the earth and the alternation of the night and the day there are signs for men of understanding"**[325]: "Woe to the one who reads it and does not reflect upon it."[326] An important point in this respect is that one should know what the commended reflection is, as there is no doubt in the fact that it is praiseworthy to think about the Quran and the *hadith*s. The best expression for it is that of the Khajah Abdullah al-Ansari (may Allah sanctify his soul). He says: "Do know that reflection is the insight"s attempt to understand the purpose."[327] That is, reflection is a seeking by the "insight" [*basirat*], which is the eye of the heart, wanting to attain the aim and the result, which are the utmost perfection. It is quite clear that the destination [*maqsad*] and the aim [*maqsud*] are the absolute happiness, attainable through theoretical and practical perfection.

Therefore, it is man"s duty to obtain the humane objective and result, being happiness, from the noble *ayah*s of the divine Book and from its stories and tales. And, since happiness is to attain absolute safety, the world of light and the straight path, man should find through the honored Quran the ways to safety, the source of the absolute light and the straight path, as was stated in the previously

---

[323] *Surah an-Nahl* 16:44.

[324] *Surah al-Araf* 7:176.

[325] *Surah Al-i Imran* 3:190.

[326] *Nur ath-Thaqalayn*, vol. 1, p. 350 (with a slight literal difference).

[327] *Manazil as-Sa'irin*, section "The Beginnings," ch. on "Reflection."

mentioned noble *ayah*. When the reciter gets the aim, he becomes clear-sighted in getting to it, and the door of being benefited by the Quran opens to him, and with it the doors of the mercy of Allah open, too. He, then, would not spend his dear and short years and his capital for obtaining happiness on matters which are not intended by the Message, preventing himself from indulging in useless discussion and talk about such an important subject.

Having directed his heart"s eye for some time to this purpose, neglecting other matters, the eye of the heart gets sharp in observing, and meditating on the Quran becomes common to him, and the ways of utilization open to him, and there open to him such doors that had not already been open to him, and he obtains from the Quran such matters and knowledge that he had never obtained before. At that time he can understand the meaning of the Quran being a cure for the spiritual ailment, as is confirmed by the noble *ayah*: **"And We reveal from the Quran that which is a healing and a mercy to the believers, and it adds only to the perdition of the wrongdoers,"**[328] and the meaning of the saying of Imam Ali (a): "Learn the Quran, for it is the spring [*rabi*] of the hearts; and seek cure with its light, since it is the cure for the hearts."[329] He does not seek from the Quran the cure of only the physical ailments, but regards the main aim to be the cure of the spiritual ailments, which is the very objective of the Quran. The Quran has not been sent down to cure the physical ailments, although such ailments do get cured by it. The prophets (a), too, did not come to cure physical ailments, although they did cure them. As a matter of fact, they were the doctors for the souls, and the curers of the hearts and the spirits.

---

[328] *Surah al-Isra"*17:82.
[329] *Nahj al-Balaghah*, sermon 109 (with some change in the wording).

APPLICATION TO ONE'S OWN CONDITION
Chapter Six

One of the important disciplines of reciting the Quran that causes one to get so many good results and advantages is "application" [*tatbiq*]; that is, each *ayah* which he recites and thinks about, he is to apply its concept to his own condition, to make up for his shortcomings by resorting to it, and to cure his ailments with it. Take, for example, the honored story of Adam (a). See what caused Satan to be expelled from the Sacred Threshold of Allah, despite his countless acts of worship and long devoted bowings, so that you may purge yourself of it, because the state of Allah's proximity belongs to the pure ones, and with Satanic conducts and character no one can be admitted to that Sacred Presence. From the noble *ayah*s one can learn that the reason behind *Iblis*' refusing to bow down was self-conceit and self-admiration: **"I am better than he. You have created me of fire while him You have created of clay."**[330] This self-conceit led him to selfishness and ostentation, which is arrogance. This led him to obstinacy, which is independence and disobedience, and hence he was expelled from the Sacred Court. We, from the beginning of the life, call Satan as the accursed and the discarded, and yet we ourselves possess his very vile characteristics. It has not occurred to us that anyone possessing the same reasons, which caused the dismissal of Satan, will be dismissed, too. Satan has no particular specialty; whatever reason expelled him from the threshold of Allah's proximity would never let us into that proximity. I am afraid that the curses, which we send to *Iblis*, are to be shared by us, too.

We may further think of the same noble story, and what caused the superiority of Adam (a) over Allah's angels, so that we ourselves may acquire them, too, as much as possible. The cause was "teaching

---

[330] *Surah al-Araf* 7:12.

the names," as the Quran says: **"And He taught Adam all the names."**[331] The high degree of teaching the names is realizing [*tahaqquq*] the state of Allah''s Names, such as the high degree of counting the Names as in the noble *hadith*: "Allah has ninety-nine names; whoever reckons them enters Paradise"[332] which means realizing [*tahaqquq*] their truth, by which man obtains the Paradise of the Names.

Man, by way of cordial austerities, can be the manifestation [*mazhar*] of Allah''s Names and the great divine sign, and his existence becomes a divine one, and the hand of the divine Beauty and Majesty manages his kingdom. In another *hadith* it is also said: "The connection of a believer''s soul to Allah, the Exalted, is stronger than the connection of the sun''s ray to it or to its light."[333]

In another authentic *hadith* it is said: "When the servant approaches Me through his supererogatory acts, I love him, and when I love him I become his ears with which he hears, and I become his eyes with which he sees, and I become his tongue with which he speaks, and I become his hand with which he takes."[334]

In a *hadith* it is said: "Ali is Allah''s eye and hand"[335] and similar ones, as in a *hadith*: "We are His Most Beautiful Names."[336] In this respect, rational and traditional proofs are plenty.

Generally speaking, whoever wants to get a good share and advantage from the Quran have to apply each of the noble *ayah*s to his own condition so that he may get its complete benefit. For example, the noble *ayah* of the *Surah al-Anfal* says: **"The believers are those whose hearts feel fear when Allah is mentioned, and when His *ayah*s are recited to them they increase them in faith, and in their Lord do they put their confidence."**[337] A *salik* must see whether he

---

[331] *Surah al-Baqarah* 2:31.

[332] *Bihar al-Anwar*, vol. 4, pp. 186-7.

[333] *Usul al-Kafi*, vol. 3, "The Book of Faith and Disbelief" ch. on "The Believers'' Brotherhood to One Another," *hadith* 4, p. 242.

[334] *Usul al-Kafi*, vol. 4, "The Book of Faith and Disbelief", ch. on "The One Who Hurts the Muslims and Slights Them," *hadith* 7, p.53.

[335] In a sermon by Imam Ali (a), it is said: "I am Allah''s eye and His truthful tongue and His hand." *Maaniy 'ul-Akhbar*, *hadith* 14, p. 17; *At-Tawhid*, ch. 22, *hadith* 2, p. 65.

[336] *Usul al-Kafi*, vol. 1, "The Book of *at-Tawhid*", ch. on "Wonders," *hadith* 4, p. 196.

[337] *Surah al-Anfal* 7:2.

falls in line with these three attributes or not: Does mentioning Allah make his heart collapse and fear fall upon him? When the noble divine *ayah*s are recited to him, will the light of faith increase in his heart? Are his confidence and trust in Allah, the Exalted? Or is he void of any one of these stages and devoid of these attributes? If he wants to know whether he fears Allah and that his heart falls down because of that, let him look at his deeds. The one who fears Allah, would not dare to do an act of pertness, or to violate any divine law in the Presence of His Sacred Majesty. If his faith increases by the divine *ayah*s, the light of faith flows to his external kingdom, too. It is impossible for the heart to be luminous while the tongue, the speech, the eye, the sight, the ear and the hearing remain in the dark. A luminous person is the one whose entire worldly and heavenly powers are radiant, diffusing light, and, besides guiding him to happiness and the straight path, they throw light on the road for others and guide them along the road to humanity. Likewise is the one who depends upon Allah and puts his trust in Him, in which case he cuts his eye of covetousness off others, and puts down his burden of need and poverty at the threshold of the Absolute Self-Sufficient, and regards others as poor and helpless as himself.

So, the duty of the traveler to Allah is to expose himself to the Glorious Quran, and, as the criterion to tell a true and valid *hadith* from a false and invalid one is to expose it to the Book of Allah, and the one which is not in harmony with it is to be judged as false and nonsense, similarly, the criterion for telling straightness from crookedness, and happiness from wretchedness, is that it is to turn out in the Book of Allah to be straight and correct. And, as the character of the Messenger of Allah is the Quran, he [the *salik*] should make his character coincide with the Quran, so that it corresponds to that of the perfect friend of Allah. The character which is contrary to the Book of Allah is nonsense and false. Likewise, he is to conform all his [other] knowledge, [*maarif*], condition of heart, internal and external deeds with the Book of Allah, so as to be in harmony with it, and the Quran becomes the image of his inside:

You are the clear Book that
By its letters the hidden is exposed.[338]

---

[338] This is a line of a poem which begins with:
You think you are a small matter

There are other disciplines in this field, some of which have already been mentioned early in this book under the title "the general discipline of worship," and some others are mentioned here. Going on explaining further disciplines will lengthen our discourse; therefore, we relinquish them, and Allah is the Knowing.

Conclusion

Hereunder the translation of some noble narratives are related to complete the advantage and to have the blessings of the sayings of the [Prophet"s] pure progeny:

The noble *al-Kafi* on the authority of Sad, quotes Imam al-Baqir (a) to have said: "O Sad, learn the Quran, for it comes on the Resurrection Day in the best of forms," then he added to the same effect, saying that it would pass through each rank of the masses of the believers, the martyrs, the prophets and the ranks of the angels, and all of them say: "This is brighter than us," until the Messenger of Allah (s) introduces it... as the *hadith* goes.[339]

Imam as-Sadiq (a) is quoted to have said: "When Allah, the Exalted, gathers all the first and the last peoples, they suddenly see a person proceeding, having an image the better of which has never been seen before."[340]

There are many other *hadith*s of similar content that prove the sayings of the people of knowledge to the effect that for each being in this world there is a matching image in the Hereafter.

From the *hadith*s of this chapter it is deduced that the deeds also have their images in that world. The noble *al-Kafi*, on the authority of Imam al-Baqir (a), says: "The Messenger of Allah (s) said: "I, the Book of Allah and my progeny will be the first to come to the Almighty, the Omnipotent, then my *ummah* will come after us. Then I ask: What did you do with the Book of Allah and my *Ahl al-Bayt*?"[341]

In another *hadith*, the Almighty, the Glorified, says to the Quran: "By My Omnipotence and Majesty, and by My High State, I

While in you is contained the biggest world.
The poem is ascribed to Imam Ali (a).
[339] *Usul al-Kafi* ,vol. 4,p. 394, "Book of the Merits of the Quran," ch. 1, *hadith* 1.
[340] *Ibid.*
[341] *Usul al-Kafi*, vol. 4, p. 400, "Book of the Merits of the Quran," ch. 1, *hadith* 4.

will surely honor him who has honored you, and I will disdain him who has disdained you."³⁴²

We must know that if we did not revive the precepts and the teachings of the Quran by putting them to practice and understanding their truth, we would not be able to reply the question of Allah's Messenger on that day. Which disdain is worse than discarding its objectives and neglecting its calls? Honoring the Quran and its people, who are the infallible *Ahl al-Bayt*, is not done only by kissing its cover or their holy shrines. This is a weak sign of honoring and respecting, which will only be acceptable if done according to its instructions and their teachings. Otherwise they would be more like scorning and sporting. Noble *hadith*s strongly warn those who recite the Quran and then do not practically follow its teachings. In *Iqab al-Amal*, by Shaykh as-Saduq (may Allah be pleased with him), quoting the Messenger of Allah (s), it is stated that he said in a *hadith*: "The one who teaches the Quran and does not act according to it, and loves this world and prefers worldly pleasures to it, is worthy of Allah's wrath and is placed on the same level with the Jews and the Christians who threw the Book of Allah behind their backs. The one who recites the Quran with the intention of obtaining reputation [*sumah*] and mundane gains will meet Allah with a bony, fleshless face, and the Quran will slap his nape to push him into the fire and let him join those before him. And the one who recites the Quran without following its instructions, will be raised blind on the Resurrection Day. He will ask: „O my Lord, why have You raised me blind whereas I was a seeing one?" He will reply: „It is so because Our signs came to you but you forgot them, and so you are forgotten this day"³⁴³ Then he is ordered to be thrown into the Fire. But the one who recites the Quran for the pleasure of Allah and for learning the features of the religion, his will be a reward, the equal of the reward given to all the angels and the prophets and Messengers (a).

"The one who learns the Quran to show off, seeking reputation by way of arguing with the fools, to take pride in his knowledge against the scholars and to seek with it mundane matters, Allah, on the Resurrection Day, will separate all his bones from one another, and there will be no torture in the Fire severer than his, and there will be no

---

³⁴² *Ibid., hadith* 14.
³⁴³ *Surah Ta-Ha* 20:125-6.

sort of torment unless he is subjected to it, owing to Allah‛s strong anger and displeasure.

"If the one who learns the Quran is humble with his knowledge, teaches the servants of Allah and asks Allah for whatever reward there is with Him, there will be in Paradise no one whose reward is more than his, and there will be in Paradise no high rank and lofty state unless his share of it is higher and his state is loftier."[344]

Concerning meditating on the meaning of the Quran, learning lessons from it and being affected by it there are many narratives, such as the *hadith* in the noble *al-Kafi*, on the authority of Imam as-Sadiq (a), that he said: "It is in this Quran the stand of the guiding light and the torches for the dark nights. So, let the scrutinizer roam with his wide open eyes to see clearly, because thinking is the life of the discerning heart, like the enlightened one who walks with light in the dark."[345] The Imam means that as man needs common light to see his way in the dark so as not to fall over in a precipice, with the Quran, which is the light that guides and the torch which lights the road of gnosticism and faith, he is to advance on the dark road to the Hereafter and to Allah so as not to tumble down into devastating precipices.

In *Maaniy ul-Akhbar* there is a *hadith* from Imam Ali (a) saying: "The true jurisprudent is the one who would not leave the Quran reluctantly and turn to something else. Beware that there is no good in a knowledge without understanding; there is no good in the reciting without contemplation; and there is no good in a worship without deep knowledge of it."[346]

In *al-Khisal* and *Maaniy ul-Akhbar*, the Messenger of Allah (s) is quoted to have said: "The bearers of the Quran are the informed ones [urafa] among the people of Paradise."[347] It is obvious what is meant by "the bearers" of the Quran. It means the bearers of the Quranic knowledge and teachings, the result of which in the Hereafter is to regard them among the learned and the people of heart. To merely bear the external form of the Quran, without getting its lessons and being benefited by its teachings, and to convey its knowledge and

---

[344] *Iqab al-Amal*, pp. 332, 337 and 366.

[345] *Usul al-Kafi*, vol. 4, p.400, "Book on the Merits of the Quran," ch. 1, *hadith* 5.

[346] *Maaniy 'ul-Akhbar*, p. 226, ch. on "The Meaning of the True Jurisprudent," *hadith* 1.

[347] *Maaniy 'ul-Akhbar*, p. 323, ch. on "The Meaning of the Informed Ones of the People of Paradise," *hadith* 1; *Al-Khisal*, vol.1, p. 28, ch. on "The One," *hadith* 100.

admonitions, without putting its precepts and laws into application, would be like that which is said by Allah, the Exalted: **"The likeness of those who are entrusted with the Torah, yet they apply it not, is as the likeness of the ass carrying books."**[348]

Noble *hadith*s on the Glorious Quran, its affairs and disciplines are too many to be contained in this small book. Peace be upon Muhammad and his progeny.

---

[348] *Surah al-Jumuah* 62:5.

TORCH TWO

On Some Disciplines of Recitation in the *Salat*

Discussed in Seven Chapters

DEGREES OF RECITATION AND
THE GROUPS OF RECITERS
Chapter One

Know that for the recitation during this spiritual journey and divine ascension there are degrees and stages, and here we shall suffice ourselves with some of them.

First, the reciter is one who pays no attention to other than improving the recitation and bettering the expression. His only care is for the good utterance of these words and correct pronunciation of the letters from their correct outlets so that a duty can be performed and an order be fulfilled. It is well known that the task for such persons is heavy and difficult; their hearts are unwilling and their insides are deviated. These have no share of worship, though they are not punished with the punishment of the deserter [of the *salat*], unless from the invisible treasure a grace appears and the said chattering receives a beneficence and a favor. It sometimes happens that this group, while their tongues are busy remembering Allah, their hearts are completely away from that, engaged in the mundane multiplicity and worldly matters. As a matter of fact, the people in this group are outwardly in the *salat*, while inwardly and actually they are busy with this world and worldly desires and whims. Sometimes it also happens that their hearts busy themselves thinking about correcting the formal shape of the *salat*. In this case they are busy, by both the tongue and the heart, with the form of the *salat*, and it is acceptable and agreeable from them.

The second group is those who would not be contented with that limit and take the *salat* to be a means of remembering Allah, and the reciting to be praising and glorifying Him. This group is of many ranks and degrees, the mentioning of which would be lengthy. Probably it is this group to which the following Divine *Hadith* refers:

"I have divided the *salat* between Me and My servant, half of it for Me and half of it for My servant. When he says: „In the name of Allah, the Beneficent, the Merciful,'' Allah will say: „My servant has remembered Me,'' and when he says: „All praise is for Allah,'' Allah says: „My servant has praised and glorified Me,'' and this is the meaning of „Allah hears from the one who praises Him.'' And when he says: „The Beneficent, the Merciful,'' Allah says: „My servant aggrandized Me. And when he says: „Master of the Day of Judgment,'' Allah says: „My servant glorified Me.'' [In another version: „My servant has entrusted himself to Me']. And when he says: „You do we worship and You do we seek help from,'' Allah says: „This is between Me and My servant.'' And when he says: „Guide us to the straight path,'' Allah says: „My servant has this right, and it is granted to him.''[349]

Now as the *salat*, according to this noble *hadith*, is divided between Allah and the servant, the servant has to completely pay what is due to Him, according to the discipline of servitude stated in this noble *hadith*, so that Allah, the Exalted, may treat him as is becoming of His Lordly graces, since He says: **"And fulfill My covenant; I shall fulfill your covenant."**[350]

Allah, the Exalted, confined the disciplines of servitude in recitation to four pillars:

The first one is "remembrance" [*tadhakkur*] which is to happen by "In the Name of Allah, the Beneficent, the Merciful," and the *salik* servant should look at the entire "House of Realization" [*dar-i tahaqquq*] as a name perished in the Named [*musamma*]. He should teach his heart to be seeking the *Haqq* and wanting the *Haqq* in every particle of "the possibles" [*mumkinat*], and bring the natural disposition of learning the names—which is fixed in the nature of his essence according to the requirement of the universality of the growth [*nashah*] and its being the manifestation of the Great Name of Allah, to which Allah refers by saying: **"And He taught Adam all the names,"**[351]—to the state of actuality and manifestation. Such a state is the result of having privacy with Allah and of deep remembrance and

---

[349] *Al-Mahajjat al-Bayda'*, vol. 1, p. 388; *Bihar al-Anwar*, vol. 92, p. 226. *Sahih Muslim*, vol. 2, p. 92, with differences in expression.

[350] *Surah al-Baqarah* 2:40.

[351] *Ibid.*, 31.

contemplating the divine affairs [*shuun*], to the extent that the heart becomes a complete divine servant such that there can be found in every nook of it no name except that of Allah, the Exalted.

This is a stage of perishing in divinity that (even) the relapsed and hard hearts of the deniers cannot deny what we have just said, unless their denial be satanic, for such hearts feel repulsion, by nature, on hearing Allah"s name or His remembrance, may God save us from that! If a word of divine knowledge or one of Allah's Names was mentioned, they would feel distressed. They would not open the eyes of their hearts except at the desires of the appetites of the stomach and sex. There are among these people those who admit for the prophets and holy men [*awliya*] (a) nothing other than corporeal states and bodily Paradise, i.e. satisfying the animal desire. They take the greatness of the states of the other world to be similar to the greatness of this world, with vast orchards, running rivers and a multitude of houris and youths and palaces. When there is a talk about love, affection and divine attraction, they assault the speaker with vulgar language and ugly words, as if they themselves have been insulted and they were retaliating. These people block the way of humanity and they are the thorns of the road to knowing Allah, and the satans who deceive men, hindering groups upon groups of the servants of Allah from Allah, His names, His attributes, His remembrance and remembering, and directing their attentions to the animal stomach and sexual desires. They are satanic agents who sit in ambush on the straight path of Allah according to the *ayah*: **"I shall surely lurk in ambush for them on Your straight path,"**[352] in order to prevent the servants of Allah from getting familiar with their Lord and from ridding themselves of the darkness of animal desires, including inclination towards houris and palaces. These people may resort to evidences from the invocations of the prophets and the infallible *Ahl al-Bayt* (a) in which they also demand houris and palaces. But this is due to the shortcomings of this group who recognize no difference between loving Allah's grace, which is loved because it is the gift of the Beloved, in itself being a sign of affection and care, and merely loving the houris and palaces independently, which is within the nature of the animal desire. Loving Allah's gifts is Loving Allah, which consequently covers the favors of Allah and His graces:

---

[352] *Surah al-Araf* 7:16.

I love the whole world, for the whole world is of Him.[353]
The love of the abode did not infatuate me,
But the love of the one who resides therein.[354]

Otherwise, what would, Ali ibn Abi Talib (a) do with houris and palaces? How could that great man be associated with the appetites of the self and the animal desires? The one whose worship is that of a free man, his reward cannot be that of traders. The rein of the pen snapped and I wandered away from the main subject.

In general, the one who is accustomed to reciting divine *ayah*s and names from the Book of divine genesis and record, his heart will gradually take the form of remembrance and of an *ayah*, and the interior of his essence will turn out to be Allah's remembrance, His name and His *ayah*, as they interpret "remembrance" to be the noble Prophet and Ali ibn Abi Talib (a), and "The Beautiful Names" to be the Imams of guidance (a). Ayatullah is also interpreted to be those great men and it is conformed to them. They are the divine *ayah*s, the Beautiful Names of Allah and the great remembrance of Allah. The state of "remembrance" is such a high one that it is beyond the patience of explanation and the limits of writing and recording. It suffices for the people of knowledge and divine attraction, and the people of affection and love, as in the *ayah*: **"Therefore remember Me; I shall remember you."**[355]

Allah, the Exalted, tells Moses (a): **"I am the companion of whoever remembers Me."**[356] A narrative in *al-Kafi* says that the Messenger of Allah (s) said: "Whoever remembers Allah frequently, He will like him."[357]

In *Wasail ash-Shiah*, Imam Jafar as-Sadiq is quoted to have said that Allah, the Exalted, said: "O son of Adam, remember Me in yourself; I will remember you in Myself. O son of Adam, remember

---

[353] This is the second hemistich of a line from Sadi's poetry, as below:
By the world I am cheerful as the world is cheerful by Him,
I love the whole world as the whole world is of Him.
[354] A line from the poetry of Majnun Amiri (Qays ibn al-Mulawwah al-Amiri). *Jami ash-Shawahid*, p. 220, ch. "The W with the M."
[355] *Surah al-Baqarah* 2:152.
[356] *Usul al-Kafi*, vol. 4, p. 255, "Book of Invocation," ch. on "That Which is Obligatory of Remembering Allah," *hadith* 4.
[357] *Ibid., hadith* 3.

Me in privacy, I will remember you in privacy. O son of Adam, remember Me in public, I will remember you in a public better than yours." He also said: "No servant remembers Allah in the presence of the people unless Allah remembers him in the presence of the angels."[358]

The second pillar is "praising" Allah [*tahmid*], as is the *musalli*'s saying: "All praise is for Allah, the Lord of the Worlds."

Know that when the *musalli* attains the state of "remembrance", and regards all the particles of the beings, and the high and low creatures, to be divine names, and when he dismisses from his heart the idea of being self-sufficient, and looks at the beings of the visible and invisible worlds with the eye of dependence, he will be in the stage of "praising," and his heart will confess that all kinds of praising exclusively belong to the Divine Essence, and the others have no share of it, because they have no personal perfection requiring any sort of praising and glorifying. We shall explain in detail this divine grace, in our interpretation of this blessed *surah, inshaallah* (Allah willing).

The third pillar is "magnifying" [*tazim*], which is established by "The Beneficent, the Merciful." When the servant traveling to Allah has, under the pillar of "praising", confined all praise to Allah, excluding the existential multiplicities from perfection and praise, he will get nearer to the horizon of Oneness, his eye of plurality will gradually get blind to multiplicity, and the form of Beneficence [*rahmaniyyat*]—which is the expansion of the existence—and the form of Mercifulness [*rahimiyyat*]—which is the expansion of the perfection of the existence—will be manifested to his heart, and he will call Allah by the two names, which are all-embracing and comprehensive, and in which multiplicities are vanished. So, the manifestation of perfection causes the heart to feel awe from the Beauty, and thus, Allah's greatness is implanted in his heart.

As this condition is fixed, he will move to the fourth pillar, which is the state of "sanctifying" [*taqdis*], and it is actually "glorifying" [*tamhid*]. In other words, it is entrusting the affairs to Allah, that is, discerning the position of Ownership and Omnipotence of Allah, and the falling down of the dust of plurality [*kathrat*] and the

---

[358] *Wasa'il ash-Shiah*, vol. 4, "Book of the *Salat*", sec. on "Remembrance," ch. 7, *hadith* 4, p. 1185.

breaking of the idols of the heart and the appearance of the owner of the house of the heart, and possessing it with no Satanic intruding. In this condition he reaches the stage of privacy, and there will be no veil between the servant and Allah, and **"You do we worship and You do we seek help from,"** takes place in that particular privacy and the meeting of familiarity. For this reason He said: "This is between Me and My servant." And when the everlasting favor encompasses him and awakens him, he will demand consistency of this stage and establishment [*tamkin*] of His Presence, by requesting: **"Guide us to the straight path,"** in which, **"Guide us"** is interpreted to mean: "Make us firm, consistent and steady." This is for those who have slipped out of the veil and attained "the Eternally Wanted" [*matlub-i azal*]. As to us, the people of the veil, we will have to ask Allah, the Exalted, for guidance with its ordinary concept. This may further be explained in the exegesis of the blessed *surah* of *al-Hamd, inshaallah* (Allah willing).

Completion:

From the noble Divine *Hadith*[359] [*hadith-i qudsi*] it appears that the *salat* is completely divided between Allah and the servant, and only the *surah* of *al-Hamd* was given as an example. So, we may add, for example, that the *takbir*s of the *salat*, whether the opening *takbir*s or the other ones which are said during changing states in the *salat*, are the share of Divinity, the portion of the Sacred Essence. If the servant traveling to Allah performed this duty of servitude and carried out what was due to Divinity as his capacity was capable of, Allah, the Exalted, with His everlasting special favors, would also grant His servant his due share, which is the opening of the door of intimacy and revelation, as is referred to in the noble *hadith* in *Misbah ash-Shariah*: "As you utter the *takbir*, regard small all creatures in relation to the greatness of Allah," and it adds: "Examine your heart during the *salat*. If you tasted the sweetness of the *salat*, and if in your soul you felt pleased and gay by it, and your heart enjoyed the supplication to Allah and conversing with Him, know that Allah has approved your *takbir*s. Otherwise, without feeling pleasure in supplication, and being

---

[359] Refer to footnote 349.

270

deprived of tasting the sweetness of worship, you should know that Allah has denied you and dismissed you from His Threshold."[360]

Consequently, in each one of the acts and states of the *salat*, there is a share for Allah, and the servant is to perform it, being the disciplines of servitude at that stage. The servant also has his share, which, after performing what the discipline of servitude requires, Allah, out of His covert grace and overt mercy, will bestow upon him His favor. If in these divine times he found himself deprived of His special favors, he must know that he did not act according to the disciplines of servitude. The relevant sign for the common people is that the heart does not taste the sweetness of supplication and the delicacy of worship, and he is deprived of the cheerfulness, pleasure and devotion to Allah. The worship that is void of delight and pleasure is spiritless, and it will not be useful for the heart.

So, dear, make your heart familiar with the disciplines of servitude, and let your soul [*ruh*] taste the sweetness of remembering Allah. This divine grace, at the beginning, takes place through intense remembrance and intimacy. During remembrance the heart must not be dead or overcome by negligence. Having taught your heart to be familiar with remembrance, the divine favors will gradually be bestowed upon you, and the heavenly doors will be opened to you, and this is marked by repulsion from this world, by inclination towards the world of eternity, and by preparedness for death before its arrival.

O Allah! Grant us to have a share of tasting the pleasure of supplicating to you and the sweetness of conversing with you. Place us among the remembering group and in the circle of those who are devoted to Your Glorified Sanctity, and bestow upon our dead hearts an everlasting life, and make us break off the others and make us inclined to be devoted to You, surely You are the Giver of favor and grace.

---

[360] *Misbah ash-Shariah*, ch. 13, "At Ending the *Salat*"; *Al-Mahajjat al-Bayda*," printed by as-Saduq Library, vol. 1, p. 385; *Mustadrak al-Wasa'il*, "The Book of *as-Salat*," sec. on "The Acts of the *Salat*," ch.2, *hadith* 9.

SOME DISCIPLINES OF *ISTIADHAH*
Chapter Two

Allah, the Exalted, says: **"And when you recite the Quran take refuge in Allah from the outcast Satan. He has no authority over those who believe and on their Lord rely. His authority is only over those who befriend him and those who associate partner with Him."**[361] Among the important disciplines of recitation, especially the recitation in the *salat*, which is a spiritual journey to Allah, the real ascension and the ladder to reach the people of Allah, is the *istiadhah*, seeking refuge in Allah, from the outcast Satan, who is the thorn of the road to knowledge, and the one who blocks the way of the *salik*"s travel to Allah, as Allah, the Exalted, says through him, in the blessed *surah* of *al-Araf*: **"He said: „As You have led me astray, I shall lurk in ambush for them on Your straight path."**[362] He has sworn to lurk for the sons of Adam on the straight path to prevent them from entering it. So, the *salat*, which is the straight path of humanity and the ascension for reaching Allah, cannot take place without *istiadhah* from this brigand, and without taking refuge in the fortified fort of Divinity from his evil, there can be no security. This *istiadhah*, this taking refuge, cannot be implemented with empty utterances, a lifeless form or a world with no Hereafter. It is observed that there were people who did utter these words for forty or fifty years, yet they were not saved from the evil of this bandit, and, actually, in their conducts and acts, and even in their beliefs they followed Satan and imitated him. Had we really taken refuge from the evils of this wicked one, the Sacred Essence of Allah, the Exalted, Who is the Absolute Gracious, the Omnipotent, the All-Merciful, the All-Knowing and Generous, would have granted us His protection, and our faith, moralities and deeds would have been amended. So, we must know

---

[361] *Surah an-Nahl* 16:98-100.
[362] *Surah al-Araf* 7:16.

that our being left behind the travelers on the road to Allah is due to Satan's temptations and because we have fallen under his control owing to our own shortcomings and inefficiency in applying the spiritual disciplines and acquiring the required conditions of the heart. So, it is because of this that we get nothing of the spiritual results and the external and internal effects of our invocations, supplications and worships. From the noble *ayah*s of the Quran and the noble *hadith*s of the infallible Imams (*s*) many disciplines can be discovered. But to count them all would need a complete scrutinizing research, which prolongs the discussion. It suffices us to mention only a few of them.

One of the important disciplines of *istiadhah* is "sincerity," as Allah the Exalted, quotes Satan to have said: **"By your Might I will tempt them all, except Your sincere servants from among them."**[363] This "sincerity," as is clear from this noble *ayah*, is something higher than the practical sincerity, whether by the heart or by the limbs, because, it is in the objective case [in its Arabic form = *mukhlasin*]. Had it been for sincerity in action, it should have been in the nominative case. Therefore, this sincerity is intended to denote the purification of the human personality with all the visible and invisible affairs, of whose emissions is the practical sincerity, although, at the beginning of the *suluk*, this fact and divine grace would not easily take place except by difficult practical austerities, especially the cordial ones, which are its origin, as is referred to in the well-known *hadith*: "The one who keeps being sincere to Allah for forty mornings, fountains of wisdom will flow from his heart to his tongue."[364] So, whoever could sincerely devote himself to Allah for forty mornings— which is the period of fermenting [*takhmir*] the clay [*tinat*] of which Adam was created, and the connection between these two is well-known to the people of knowledge and of heart—and dedicate his cordial and formal acts sincerely to Allah, his heart will become godly, and the godly heart produces nothing other than fountains of wisdom. Then, his tongue, which is the greatest interpreter of the heart, will speak wisdom. So, at the beginning, sincerity of the act leads to the

---

[363] *Surah Sad* 38:82-83.
[364] *Bihar al-Anwar*, vol. 67, p. 242, "Book of Faith and Disbelief," ch. on "Sincerity," *hadith* 10, quoted from *Uyunu Akhbar ar-Rida*, vol. 2, p. 69 (with a slight difference). The same subject is referred to in the latter book, *hadith* 25, p. 249.

purification of the heart, and when the heart becomes purified, the lights of Majesty and Beauty—which are deposited by divine fermentation [*takhmir*] in the human clay—are reflected in the mirror of the heart and become manifest there, and from the innermost of the heart they appear on the external body.

In short, the sincerity, which frees one from the satanic authority, is devoting the identity of the soul [*ruh*] and the innermost of the heart to Allah, the Exalted. It is a reference to this that Imam Ali (a), in his *Shabaniyyah Supplication,* says: "O Allah, grant me complete devotion to you."[365] When the heart reaches this stage of sincerity and it is cut off other than Allah, and in the kingdom of his existence there is no admission to other than Allah, Satan—who approaches man by other than Allah"s way—will have no power over him, and Allah will admit him into His shelter, and he will be placed in the fortified fortress of divinity, as He says: "The expression „there is no god but Allah" is My fort, so whoever enters My fort is safe from My torture."[366] Entering the fort of „there is no god but Allah" is of several degrees. Likewise, being safe from the torture is also of several degrees. So, the one who, externally, internally, cordially and formally, is admitted to Allah"s fortress and under His protection, will be safe from all degrees of torture, including being veiled off Allah"s Beauty and being separated from meeting the Beloved, the Most High and Almighty—which veiledness and separation are at the top of the tortures. Imam Ali (a), in the Kumayl Invocation, says: "Suppose that I can patiently bear Your torment, how can I patiently bear separation from You?" Our hand is short of that. The one who could reach that stage would be a real servant of Allah, under the vaults [domes] of divinity, and Allah, the Exalted, would manage his kingdom, getting him out of the *Taghut*"s patronage. This is the dearest state for the men of Allah and the most special degree for the pure, and the others have no share of it. It is most likely that the owners of hard hearts among the deniers and of stiff souls among the obstinate, who are far away from such a state, deny it altogether and regard any talk about it to be false and in vain. Or they rather take such affairs, which are the delight of the holy men [*awliya*], and which are frequently mentioned by the Book and the *Sunnah*, to be—God forbid!—of the fabrications of the

---

[365] *Bihar al-Anwar*, vol. 91, p. 99.
[366] *At-Tawhid*, p. 25; *Bihar al-Anwar*, vol. 3, p.13 and vol. 90, p. 192.

sufis and false rumors of the literalists. We, by referring to these states, which are, in fact, the states of the perfect ones, do not claim to have a share of them or look at them covetously, but we do so because to deny them is not agreeable to us, and we believe that mentioning the holy men [*awliya*] and their positions is effective in purging, saving and reforming the hearts, because good mention of the people of guardianship and knowledge causes affection, familiarity and close connection. Such connection leads to mutual attraction [*tajadhub*], which, in its turn leads to co-intercession [*tashafu*], whose outward is getting out of the darkness of ignorance to the lights of guidance and knowledge, and its inward is the intercession in the Hereafter, because the intercession of the intercessors would not happen without close connection and inward co-attraction [*tajadhub*], since it would not be based on guess and *batil* [falsehood].

However, despite the fact that this stage is not but for the perfect ones among the holy men [*awliya*] and the chosen ones [*asfiya*] (a), and that the perfect state of this stage is, in the origin [*bil-isalah*], exclusively for the Seal of the Prophets (s), the luminous and pure Ahmadian single [*ahadi-yi ahmadi*], Muhammadan collective [*jami-i muhammadi*] heart, and subordinately [*bi t-tabaiyyah*], it is for the perfect and pure ones of the *Ahl al-Bayt,* yet the believers and the sincere ones are not to give up hoping for some of its degrees, and to be satisfied with formal and practical sincerity, and the external and juristic purity, because stopping in the stations is one of the masterpieces of *Iblis* who is sitting at the entrance of the path of man and humanity, trying every possible means to prevent him from ascending to perfections and reaching higher stages. So, one has to double his vigilance and strengthen his will, so that this divine light and grace may move from the outside to the inside, and from the visible to the invisible. The more stages of sincerity one passes, the better he will be stationed under Allah's protection, and the truth of *istiadhah* will be implemented, and the hands of the devilish Satan will be short of reaching him.

Hence, if you devoted the visible human form exclusively to Allah, and if you placed the external mundane armies of the soul, which are the powers dispersed in the kingdom of the body, under the shelter of Allah, and if you purified the seven earthly realms, which are the eye, the ear, the tongue, the stomach, the sexual organ, the hand, and the leg, from the impurities of disobedience and placed them at the disposal of Allah"'s angels, who are the divine armies, these realms would gradually become divine and under the command of Allah, until they also become Allah"'s angels, or get like Allah"'s angels **"who do not disobey Allah in what He commands them, and do as they are commanded."**[367] Hence, the first degree of *istiadhah* takes place, and Satan and his soldiers leave the external kingdom and turn to the inside, assaulting the invisible powers of the soul. Thus, the *salik*'s task becomes harder and his *suluk* stricter. So, his steps should be stronger, and his watchfulness more perfect. He is to take refuge in Allah, the Exalted, from the spiritual destructions, such as self-conceit, hypocrisy, arrogance, pride and the like, and to gradually start purifying his inside from the moral opacities and internal impurities.

In this stage, or rather in all stages, he is to be attentive to Allah"'s Unity of Acts, and to remind his heart of this divine grace and heavenly table [*maidah*], which are of the important matters of *suluk* and of the pillars of *uruj*. He is also to make his heart taste the fact that Allah, the Exalted, is the owner of the heavens, the earth, the inside, the outside, the visible, and the invisible, so that the heart may get accustomed to His Unity in deity and deny any association in management [*tasarruf*] and be divinely concocted and theistically educated. In this state the heart will find no asylum, refuge, sanctuary and help except with Allah alone, and, consequently and actually, he will seek refuge with Allah, the Sanctified State of Divinity. Unless he cuts off his heart from the others" management, and closes his eye of greed on other creatures, he cannot truthfully turn to get his refuge with Allah, and his claim will be a false one, and according to the method of he people of knowledge he will be regarded among the hypocrites, and ascribed to deceit and treason.

In this fearful valley [*wadiyy*] and dangerous deep ocean, if one takes advantage of the sayings of a godly wise man or a luminous gnostic, whose string of knowledge is connected to the perfect friends of Allah, concerning the Three Unities, it will be a good help to the inner heart. But the condition for taking that advantage is that he should do it regarding it as an *ayah*, a sign and *suluk* to Allah, for otherwise it would become a thorn on the road and a veil covering the face of the Beloved. The Messenger of Allah (*s*), as it is stated in the

---

[367] *Surah at-Tahrim* 66:6.

noble *al-Kafi*, calls this knowledge an "indisputable *ayah*" [*ayat-i muhkam*].[368]

Generally speaking, when the root of Allah's Unity of Acts is strongly implanted in the heart, and irrigated with the water of knowledge accompanied with nice deeds, which knock at the heart's door, its fruit will be remembering the state of divinity, and the heart will gradually become pure and ready for receiving actual manifestation. When the house is free from the traitor, and the nest from the alien, the Owner of the house controls it and Allah's guarding hand brings the invisible and visible powers of the kingdom of the inside and the heart and of the outside kingdom of the body under its rule and authority, and the Satans are completely expelled from this stage, too, and the internal kingdom returns to its independence, which is being under Allah's shelter. This is the second degree of the divine grace, the *istiadhah*. After this stage come other stages, such as, the *istiadhah* of the spirit and the *istiadhah* of the secret, which are out of the scope of these pages. Even what was said was of the overflowing of this servant's pen, or it was written at the command of the pen of the Lord, Most High and Almighty, and to Him is the refuge.

Another discipline and condition of *istiadhah* is that which is referred to in the *ayah* stated at the beginning of this chapter, i.e. "faith" [*iman*], which is other than knowledge, even though it is proved by means of philosophic proofs: "The legs of the argumentatives are of wood."[369]

Faith is a matter of the heart, and happens through intense remembrance, contemplation, intimacy and privacy with Allah. Despite the fact that Satan had knowledge about the Beginning and the Return, as the Quran says, he is counted with the disbelievers. If faith was this argumentative knowledge, those who possess this knowledge must be away from the intrusion of Satan, and the light of guidance of the Quran would illuminate their inside, whereas we notice that despite such marks, there is no sign of faith. So, if we want to be out of Satan's control, and be under the protection of Allah, the Exalted, we

---

[368] "Knowledge is of three kinds: an indisputable *ayah*, a fair obligation and a current tradition." *Usul al-Kafi*, vol. 1, p. 37, "Book of the Merit of Knowledge," ch. on "The Description of Knowledge and its Merits," *hadith* 1.

[369] The legs of the argumentatives are of wood,
Wooden legs are quite shaky.

Mawlawi

must, by intense cordial austerity and continual, or frequent, proximity and privacy, bring the facts of faith to the heart in order to let it be divine. Then, having been so, it will be free from Satan''s control, as Allah, the Exalted, says: **"Allah is the Guardian of those who believe. He brings them out of darkness into the light."**[370] So, the believers, whom Allah, the Exalted is the manager, the guardian of their inside and outside, their secret and their publicity, are free from Satan''s control and enter into the Beneficent''s kingdom. He brings them out of all degrees of darkness to the absolute light—from the darkness of disobedience and insolence, the darkness of the dirty moral impurities, the darkness of ignorance, disbelief, polytheism, self-deceit, selfishness, and self-admiration, to the light of obedience and worship, the light of virtuous characters, the light of knowledge, perfection, faith, monotheism, godliness, piety, and friendship with Allah.

Another one of its disciplines is "reliance" [*tawakkul*] on Allah, which is also part of faith and of the real lights of the grace of faith. It means entrusting the affairs to Allah, which results from the heart''s belief in the Unity of Acts, whose details are out of the capacity of this book.

When the *salik* servant finds no refuge and no shelter other than Allah, and believes that the management of the affairs is exclusively confined to His Sacred Essence, a certain condition of devotion, refuge and trust shows up in his heart, and his *istiadhah* becomes real. So, as he truthfully takes refuge in the strong fortress of the Lordship and divinity, He shall certainly protect him with His most spacious and generous mercy, for He is the possessor of great favor!

Completion and Conclusion

We noted in this chapter that the truth of the *istiadhah* is a mood or state of mind that is created by a complete evident knowledge of Allah''s Unity of Acts, and by believing in that Unity. That is, after he understood, by way of explicit and strong intellectual proofs and traditional evidences, quoted from the Quranic texts, and through the signs and the wonders of the Divine Book and noble *hadith*s, that the Power of Creation and independence of effectiveness, or rather, the very origin of effect, is exclusively confined to the Sacred Divine

---

[370] *Surah al-Baqarah* 2:257.

Essence, and other beings have no share of it, as is proved in its stance, he should convince his heart of it, and, with the pen of intellect, he should write on the page of his heart the truth of "There is no god but Allah, and there is no effecter [*muaththir*] in the [world of] existence except Allah." When the heart takes in this grace of faith and proved fact, there appears in it a state of devotion and exclusivity [to Allah]. Believing that Satan is the highway robber of humanity and its staunch enemy, there appears in his heart an apprehensiveness, which is the reality of the *istiadhah*. And, as the tongue is the spokesman of the heart, it translates that state of apprehensiveness, with complete need and necessity in words: **"I take refuge in Allah from the accursed Satan,"** which it utters truthfully. If there were no effects of these facts in the heart, and it was under the control of Satan, as well as the other parts of one"s existing kingdom, the *istiadhah* also takes place, but with the management of Satan, and verbally he does say: **"I take refuge in Allah from the accursed Satan,"** but in fact, as it is an act of Satan himself, it is actually taking refuge in Satan from Allah, and the *istiadhah* performs its counter function, and Satan mocks at the one who utters the *istiadhah*—a mockery whose result is known only after removing the cover and pushing aside the curtain of nature. Such a person, whose *istiadhah* is merely verbal, is like the one who wants to take refuge from an endless hostile army in a strong fortress, but instead, he heads to the enemy turning away from the fortress, while he continues saying: "I take refuge in this fortress from the evil of the enemy." Such a person, besides being inflicted with the evil of the enemy, becomes subject to the enemy"s mockery, too.

ON THE FOUR PILLARS OF *ISTIADHAH*
Chapter Three

One: *al-mustaidh* [the one who seeks refuge]
Two: *al-mustaadhu minhu* [that from which refuge is sought]
Three: *al-mustaadhu bihi* [the one with whom refuge is sought]
Four: *al-mustaadhu lahu* [that for which refuge is sought]

Do know that there are so much detailed explanations for these pillars that are out of our intention. Yet, we are satisfied to mention a summary of them:

The first pillar is concerning *al-mustaidh*. It is a humanistic truth from the very first stage of the *suluk* to Allah till the final end of self-annihilation [*fana-i dhati*]. "When the absolute annihilation was complete, Satan would perish and the *istiadhah* would take place."

To expand on this summary we may say that as long as man is dwelling in the abode of the self and nature, and has not yet started his spiritual journey and *suluk* to Allah, and is still under Satan"s control in all degrees and affairs, he has not yet understood the truth of *istiadhah*, and the mere utterances of his tongue are useless, or rather they fix and strengthen the Satanic authority, unless Allah, the Exalted, grants him His favor. When he gets engaged in his journey and *suluk* to Allah and starts his spiritual travel, what hinders him on the road and thorns his way, as long as he is continuing his journey and *suluk*, is his own Satan, whether of the Satanic spiritual forces, or of the *jinn* or *ins*, for when the *jinn* and *ins* become thorns of the road, they will, actually, be the assistants of Satan and act on his command. Allah, the Exalted, refers to this in the blessed *surah* of *an-Nas*: "**... from the evil of the slinking whisperer, who whispers in the breasts of men, from among the jinn and men.**" If the Satan is from the *jinn*, it is understood from the noble *ayah* that the slinking whisperer, i.e. Satan, is originally [*bi l-isalah*] a *jinn* and subordinately [*bi t-tabaiyyah*] an *ins.* But if Satan is another reality resembling the *jinn*, it appears from the noble *ayah* that these two species, i.e. the *jinn* and the *ins*, are also Satanic similitudes [*tamaththulat*] and his manifestations. In another *ayah* it is said: **"...the Satans of *ins* and *jinn*."**[371] In this blessed *Surah* the pillars of *istiadhah* are mentioned, as we stated before and as it is clear.

In a word, before starting the journey to Allah, man is not a *mustaidh*. When the gnostic [*arif*] comes to the end of the journey, and there remains no trace, at all, of the remnants of servitude, and he reaches the stage of the absolute personal annihilation [*fana-i dhati*], there will remain no trace of the *istiadhah, mustaadhu minhu* and *mustaidh*, and in his heart there will be nothing except Allah and His Divine Sovereignty, and he will be unaware of himself and his heart, and "I take refuge in You from You"[372] is also out of this state. When there is a state of wakefulness [*sahw*], intimacy and return, there still is a trace of *istiadhah*, but not the *istiadhah* of a *salik*. For this reason, the Final Messenger of Allah (*s*) is also ordered to do the *istiadhah*, as Allah, the Exalted, says:

"Say: I take refuge in the Lord of daybreak,"[373]
"Say: I take refuge in the Lord of men,"[374] and
"Say: My Lord! I take refuge in You from the evil suggestions of the Satans, and I take refuge in You, O my Lord, from their presence."[375]

So, man in two states is not *mustaidh*: One is before starting the *suluk*, which is the state of being completely veiled, at the Satan's disposal and under his control. The other is when the *suluk* comes to the end, which is the absolute annihilation, in which there is no trace of the *mustaidh, mustaadhu minhu, mustaadhu lahu* or *istiadhah*.

In two states he is a *mustaidh*: One is in his *suluk* to Allah, in which he takes refuge from the thorns of the road of attainment [*wusul*] that are sitting on the straight path, as Satan says in the Quran: **"As You have led me astray, I shall lurk in ambush for them on**

---

[371] *Surah al-Anam* 6:112.
[372] An extract from an invocation of the Prophet (*s*) during his *Salat.* See *Furu al-Kafi*, vol. 3, p. 324. *Misbah al-Mutahajjid wa Silah al-Mutaabbid*, p. 308.
[373] *Surah al-Falaq* 113:1.
[374] *Surah an-Nas* 114:1.
[375] *Surah al-Mu'minun* 23:97-98.

Your straight path."[376] The other is when he is wakeful and returning from the absolute annihilation, in which he does the *istiadhah* [taking refuge] from the coloring seclusions [*ihtijabat*] and others.

The second pillar is concerning *al-mustaadhu minhu*, which is the accursed *Iblis*, the outcast Satan, who prevents man from attaining his goal and implementing his objective, by means of his diverse snares. Some great men of the people of knowledge say that Satan, in his reality, is the entire world in its aspect of being other than Allah. The writer does not agree with this, because this aspect of being other than Allah, which is a fancied form that has no truth and is void of any sort of realization [*tahaqquq*] and reality, is but one of *Iblis'* snares in which he gets man engaged. It may be a reference to the point that is said in the *ayah*: **"Rivalry in worldly increase distracts you, until you come to the graves."**[377] Or else, *Iblis* himself is a reality with an abstract ideal, and the reality of universal *Iblis*, the head of all *Iblises*, is the universal fancy [*wahm al-kull*], as the universal abstract intellectual fact, the first man [Adam], is the universal intellect [*aql al-kull*]. The individual worldly fancies are of the affairs [*shuun*] and manifestations [*mazahir*] of the universal *Iblis*, as the individual intellects are of the affairs [*shuun*] and manifestations [*mazahir*] of the universal intellect [*aql-i kull*]. A detailed explanation of this subject is out of the capacity of this thesis.

In a word, what becomes a hindrance and a thorn on the road of the divine *suluk* to Allah is Satan or his manifestations, whose acts are also of Satan"s. And what, of the states of the invisible and visible worlds and of the happenings [*awarid*] that happen to the soul, and of its different states, becomes a veil on the face of the Beloved [*janan*], whether of the mundane terrestrial worlds, such as poverty, and richness, soundness and illness, ability and disability, knowledge and ignorance, plagues and defects, etc., or of the invisible, abstract and ideal worlds, such as paradise and hell, and relevant knowledge, even the argumentative intellectual sciences which belong to *tawhid* and glorifying Allah..., all of them are of *Iblis'* snares by which he diverts man from Allah and from having intimacy and privacy with Him. Even diversion through moral [*manawi*] states and standing [*wuquf*] in spiritual stages, whose outside is to stand at the path of humanity, and

---

[376] *Surah al-Araf* 7:16.
[377] *Surah at-Takathur* 102:1-2.

whose inside is to stand at the path of Allah—which is the spiritual bridge of the hell of separation and parting, and which ends in the paradise of meeting, the bridge which is exclusive to a small group of the people of knowledge and of heart—are also of the big snares of the chief *Iblis*, from which one must seek refuge in the Sacred Essence of Allah, the Exalted.

In short, whatever diverts you from Allah and secludes you from the Beautiful Beauty of the Beloved, the Glorified, is your Satan, be it in the form of an *ins* or a *jinn*. And whatever is used to prevent you from that goal is of Satan''s snares, be it of the kinds of positions and ranks or of the types of sciences and perfections, or professions and industries, or luxury and comfort, or hardship and humility, or anything else. These are of the dispraised worldly matters. In other words, when the heart loves something other than Allah, that will be its world, and that is disapproved. It is a satanic snare from which one should take refuge in Allah. It is quite likely the point to which the Messenger of Allah (*s*) referred by his invocation: "I take refuge in Allah''s generous countenance, and with His words, which no pious or impious can pass, from the evil of what descends from the heaven and ascends to it, from the evil of what enters into the earth and what comes out of it, from the evil of the troubles of the night and the day, and from the evil of the knockers at the night and day, except the knocker who brings good."[378]

Taking refuge in Allah''s countenance face and Allah''s words means being drowned in the sea of Beauty and Majesty, and whatever keeps man off it is of the evils and belongs to the world of Satan and his tricks, from which one must take refuge in Allah''s countenance, be it of the perfect heavenly truths or of the earthly imperfect ones, unless it is the knocker that brings good—the divine knocker who invites to Absolute Good, that is, Allah, the Exalted.

The third pillar is concerning *al-mustaadhu bihi*. Know that the truth of *istiadhah* is implemented in the *salik* to Allah, and attained through the travel and *suluk* to Allah. That is, *istiadhah* belongs to the *salik* during the stages of the *suluk*. Therefore, the truths of *istiadhah*, *mustaidh*, *mustaadhu minhu* and *mustaadhu bihi* differ according to the degrees and the stages of the travelers to Allah. A reference to this is probably in the noble *surah* of *an-Nas*: **"Say: I seek refuge in the**

---

[378] *Bihar al-Anwar*, vol. 91, p. 215.

Lord of men, the King of men, the God of men." From the beginning of the *suluk* till the limits of the state of the heart, the *salik* takes refuge with the state of the Lordship: It is possible that this Lordship is the Lordship of Act, so as to conform to "I take refuge with the complete words of Allah."³⁷⁹ And when the journey of the *salik* ends in the state of the heart, the state of the divine sovereignty appears in the heart, in which case he takes refuge in the state of "The King of men" from the evils of *Iblis*" cordial intrusion and his despotic inner authority, as he took refuge, in the first state, from the evils of Satan"s breast intrusion, as it is said: **"... who whispers in the breasts of men"** although the "whispering" in the hearts and the spirits is also by the "slinking" Satan. Perhaps this is because it is in the instance of a general introduction and on the basis of an apparent attribute that suits everybody. When the *salik* passes the state of the heart to the state of the spirit, which is of the divine "blowing," and whose connection to Allah is closer than that of the sunlight to the sun, in this stage anxiety, passion, attraction, ardent love, and eagerness, begin to appear, and in it he takes refuge in the **"God of men."** And when he advances higher than this stage and has before his eyes the Essence without a mirror for the affairs [*shuun*], in other words, when he reaches the state of the secret, he will be suited to say: "I take refuge from You in You."³⁸⁰ There are, in this respect, other details that do not suit this essay.

However, you may know that to take refuge in Allah"s Name suits all stages because of its comprehensiveness, as, in fact, it is an absolute *istiadhah*, while other *istiadhah*s are limited ones.

The fourth pillar is concerning *al-mustaadhu lahu*, i.e. the aim of the *istiadhah*. You may know that what is required essentially [*bi dh-dhat*] by the *mustaidh* person is of the kinds of perfection, happiness and good, which differ in accordance with the degrees and ranks of the *salik*s. As long as the *salik* is still within the frame of the soul and the veil of nature, the aim of his journey is to attain self-perfections and the low natural kinds of happiness. This belongs to the early stages of the *suluk*. Getting out of the soul"s confinement, and

---

³⁷⁹ *Iqbal al-Amal*, p. 640, the invocation recited on the first day of the month of Rajab.
³⁸⁰ Extracted from an invocation by the Prophet (*s*) during his *Salat*. See *Furu al-Kafi*, vol. 3, p. 324; *Misbah al-Mutahajjid wa Silah al-Mutaabbid*, p. 308.

having acquired a taste of spiritual states and abstract perfections, his goal will be higher and his aim more perfect, neglecting all personal positions, and his objective will be attaining cordial perfections and internal happiness. Then, turning the rein of the travel away from this state, and reaching at the door of the house of the spiritual secret, the beginnings of the divine manifestations start appearing in his inside, and the tongue of his inside, at the beginning says: "I direct my face towards Allah's face," and later on, "I direct my face towards Allah's Names or towards Allah," and after that: "I direct my face to Him." Perhaps **"I direct my face to the One Who created the heavens and the earth"**[381] is related to the first stage because of the creatorship [*fatiriyyat*].

In a word, whichever the *salik*'s stage, his real objective is to attain essential perfection and happiness. But as with happiness and perfection, in any given stage, there is a Satan with a snare of his snares to prevent him from reaching his objective, the *salik* will have to take refuge in Allah from that Satan and his evils and tricks in order to get his original aim and essential objective. So, the *salik*'s objective of the *istiadhah* is, in fact, obtaining the looked-for perfection and wanted happiness. The aim of the aims, and the final want, is Allah, the Glorified, the Almighty. In this stage, or after it, everything vanishes except Allah, the Exalted, and the *istiadhah* [taking refuge] from Satan will be a consequent and done in full wakefulness. Praise is Allah's at the beginning and at the end.

---

[381] *Surah al-Anam* 6:79.

ON SOME DISCIPLINES OF NAMING
[*TASMIYAH*]
Chapter Four

In *At-Tawhid*, quoting Imam ar-Rida (a), it is stated that when he was asked to explain the *bismillah*, he said: "When one says "*bismillah*" (in the name of Allah), he means: I put on myself a *simah* (mark) of Allah''s *simahs*, which is worship." Asked: "What is *simah?*" He said: "It is the mark."[382]

Do know—may Allah make you and me of those who bear Allah''s marks—that to enter in the stage of *tasmiyah* (naming or marking) is not easy for the *salik* before entering first the stage of *istadhah* and completing the steps of this stage. As long as man is under the control of Satan and his authority, he is marked with satanic marks. If man''s inside and outside were completely overcome by Satan, he would in all his stages be a sign or a mark of Satan. If, in this instance, man uttered the *tasmiyah*, he would be uttering it by Satan''s will, power and tongue, and from his *tasmiyah* and *istiadhah* there would be no result except confirming the Satanic authority. If, with Allah''s help, he woke up from his negligence, and came to conscience, and understood the necessity of continuing the journey to Allah within the station [*manzil*] of wakefulness through the divine disposition and the lights of the Quranic teachings and the traditions of the guides along the road of *tawhid*, and his heart recognized the obstacles on the road, there would appear in him a state [*hal*] of *istiadhah*, and then, with the support of Allah, he would enter the station [*manzil*] of *istiadhah*. When he got purified from the satanic filths, the divine lights would be manifested in the mirror of the *salik* in proportion to the extent of his purifying his inside and outside. At first, the lights would be mixed with darkness, or the darkness would be

---

[382] *At-Tawhid*, ch. 31, hadith 1, p. 229; *Maaniy ul-Akhbar*, p. 3.

overwhelming: "**... they have mingled a good deed and an evil one...**"[383] As the *suluk* gets steadier, the light overcomes the darkness, and the marks of the Lord appear in the *salik,* and his *tasmiyah* appears somewhat real, and gradually the Satanic marks—which, outwardly, contradict the Virtuous City [*madinat-i fadilah*], and, inwardly, are conceit, arrogance and the like, and in the inmost part of the inward, are egotism, selfishness and the like—leave the kingdom of the inside and the outside, and, in their place come the marks of Allah—which, outwardly, observe the regime [*nizam*] of the Virtuous City, and inwardly, are servitude and humility of the soul, and in the inmost part of the inside, wanting Allah and regarding for Him.

Then when the kingdom becomes godly and gets rid of the Satans of *jinn* and *ins,* and the divine marks appear in it, the *salik* gets to the state of *ismiyyat* (nameness, nomination, naming).

So, first, *salik*'s *tasmiyah* (naming) is to be distinguished by the divine marks and signs, then he is promoted and attains the state of *ismiyah,* which is a state in the beginnings of the proximity of the *nafilah* (supererogation), and when this proximity of *nafilah* takes place, he will enjoy full state of *ismiyah,* and there remains nothing of servant and servitude. The one who reaches this stage, his complete *salat* will be uttered by Allah's tongue, a state that can happen only to a few of Allah's friends.

As regards the common people and the imperfect ones like us, the discipline is to brand our heart with the mark of servitude during uttering the *tasmiyah,* and to inform the heart about Allah's marks, signs and *ayah*s, not satisfying ourselves with unintentional wordings, haply we may be covered by the eternal favor and make up for the past, and there opens before our hearts a door of learning the Names and of attaining the objective.

It is further possible to say that in the said noble *hadith,* by a *simah* of "the *simah*s of Allah," it is meant the mark or sign of the mercy of the "Beneficent" and the mercy of the "Merciful." These two noble Names are of the all-embracing ones, under whose blessing shadow the entire world of realization has reached, and does reach, the existence itself and its perfection, and the mercies of the Beneficence [*rahmaniyyah*] and Mercifulness [*rahimiyyah*] cover the whole house of existence [*dar-i wujud*]. Even the mercy of Mercifulness, of whose

---

[383] *Surah at-Tawbah* 9:102.

manifestations is the guidance of all guides on the road of *tawhid*, covers all, except those who were diverted from the disposition of rectitude, and, owing to their own ill-selection, prevented themselves from being benefited by it, not that the Mercifulness did not cover them. Even in the Hereafter world, which is the day of harvesting the bad and good cultivations, those who have bad cultivations are inevitably short of being benefited by the mercy of the Merciful.

To be short, the *salik* who wants his *tasmiyah* to be implemented, will have to convey Allah''s mercies to his heart to have it believe in the favors of the Beneficent and the Merciful, which is marked out on the heart by his looking with kindness and leniency at the servants of Allah, desiring goodness and righteousness to all of them. This look is that of the great prophets and the perfect holy men [*awliya*] (a), although they had two looks: one for welfare and the happiness of the community, the system of the family and the regime of the Virtuous City, and the second for the happiness of the individual. They were very much concerned about the happiness of these two. The divine laws, which are established, disclosed, enforced and carried out by them, take complete care of the happiness of those two. Even in carrying out penalties and punishments and the like, which seem to have been coined in conformity with the laws of the Virtuous City, the happiness of both are taken into consideration, because these affairs are mostly for educating the soul and bringing it to happiness. Even those who had no light of faith and happiness, and were killed by the fighters in *jihad* and the like, such as the Jews of Banu Qurayzah, this killing (being killed) was for their goodness and reformation. It can be said that killing them was of the complete mercy of the Seal of the Prophets (*s*), because by their survival in this world they would prepare every day diverse punishments for themselves, while the whole life in this world cannot be compared with the tortures and the hardships of a single day in the Hereafter. This is quite obvious to those who have knowledge about the extent of the tortures and punishments in the Hereafter and their reasons and causes. So, the sword that was put to the necks of the Jews of Banu Qurayzah and their like was nearer to the horizon of mercy than to the horizon of anger and wrath.

The chapter of *al-amru bi l-marufi wa n-nahyi an il-munkar* (Bidding unto honor and forbidding dishonor) belongs to the mercy of the Merciful. So, the one who bids unto honor and forbids dishonor

289

must make his heart taste the mercy of the Merciful, and his aim of bidding and forbidding should not be showing off, ostentation, and imposition of the bidding and forbidding. Should one have such aims in his mind, the objective of bidding unto honor and forbidding dishonor—which is the happiness of the people and the enacting of Allah"s precepts in the land—would not be implemented. Sometimes it may happen that the result of an ignorant"s bidding unto honor turns out to be contrary to what was intended, and many bad things happen because of a single ignorant bidding and forbidding, prompted by a selfish desire and Satanic conduct. But if the sense of mercy, pity and the right of manhood and brotherhood drive man to guide the ignorant and awaken the negligent, the quality of the explanation and guidance, which is the symptom of a kind heart, appears in such a way that its effect in the deserving materials will be quite obvious and will soften the hard-hearted and bring them down from their arrogance and denial. It is much to be regretted that we do not learn from the Quran. We do not look with an eye of contemplation and learning at this Divine Book, and our benefit from this Wise Reminder is almost nothing. Contemplating the honored *ayah*: **"Go, both of you, to Pharaoh, for he has become insolent, and speak to him in a gentle speech, haply he may remember or fear,"**[384] would open ways of knowledge and doors of hope and expectation to man"s heart.

Pharaoh, whose insolence reached the extent of saying: **"I am your Most High Lord,"**[385] and his haughtiness and corruption were so much that he began to **"slaughter their sons and let their women live"**[386] after his dream, which the soothsayers and the magicians interpreted to be about the appearance of Moses the son of Imran (a), he immediately separated the women from the men, ordered the innocent boys to be killed and did so much mischief [*fasad*]. Allah, the Beneficent, through His Mercifulness, cast His look at the entire earth and chose the humblest and most perfect person, i.e., the great prophet, the highly generous messenger, Moses the son of Imran (peace be upon our Prophet and his progeny and upon him), and educated and taught him with his educating hand, as He says: **"And when he attained his maturity and became full-grown, We granted him**

---

[384] *Surah Ta-Ha* 20: 43-44.
[385] *Surah an-Naziat* 79:24.
[386] *Surah al-Qasas* 28:4.

wisdom and knowledge; and thus do We reward the good-doers,"[387] and backed him by his honorable brother, Aaron (a). These two honorable, who were the prime of humanity, had been chosen by Allah, as He said: "And I have chosen you"[388] or "... and that you might be formed (brought up) before My eye (in My sight),"[389] or "... and I have brought you up for Myself. Go you and your brother with My signs and do not slacken in remembering Me,"[390] and other noble *ayah*s which refer to this subject and we do not need to relate them, and the heart of the gnostic enjoys them in such a way that it cannot be talked about, especially the two honorable phrases: "and that you might be formed [brought up] before My eye" (in My sight)" and "I have brought you up for Myself." You, too, if you open the eye of your heart, you will hear such a nice spiritual melody that all the hearings of your heart and corners of your being will become full of the secret of *tawhid*.

To be short, Allah, the Exalted, with a lot of ceremonies and preparations, educated Moses, His interlocutor, by spiritual education, as He says: "and We tried you with many trials."[391] He sent him to the old man, Shuayb [Jethro], to accompany for years that sage man of guidance and the elect of the world of humanity. He, the Exalted, says: "Then you stayed for years among the people of Madyan, then you came hither as ordained, O Moses."[392] Afterwards, for higher (heavier) trying and examining, He sent him into the desert on the road to ash-Sham (Syria), where He caused him to lose his way, put him under heavy rains in the deep darkness, and caused his wife to start having a hard labor. Thus, all the doors of nature were closed to him. Then, as his noble heart ached of multiplicity, and, through the pure natural disposition, he submitted himself to Allah, and as his divine and spiritual journey in that boundless desert came to an end, "He perceived on the side of the mountain a fire... and when he came to it, he was called from the right side of the valley in the blessed field, from the tree: O Moses! Verily I am Allah, the Lord of the

---

[387] *Ibid.*: 14.
[388] *Surah Ta-Ha* 20:13.
[389] *Ibid.*: 39.
[390] *Ibid.*: 41-42.
[391] *Ibid.*: 40.
[392] *Ibid.*

worlds.[393] After all those examinations and spiritual education, what for did Allah prepare him? It was in order to invite, guide, preach and save a single disobedient slave [Pharaoh] who used to shout: "I am your Most High Lord," causing so much mischief in the land. Allah could have burned him down with the flash of a lightning of His anger, but the mercy of His Mercifulness sent him two great prophets and still advised them to talk to him with kindness and leniency, such that he might remember Allah and be afraid of his own deeds and their aftermath. This is the instruction for how to conduct *al-amru bi l-marufi wa n-nahyi an il-munkar.* It is the way of how to guide someone like Pharaoh, the *taghut* (the tyrant). Now, as you, too, want to bid unto honor and forbid dishonor, and to guide the creatures of Allah, remember these noble and divine *ayah*s and learn from them, since they have been revealed for remembrance and learning. Face the servants of Allah with a heart full of affection and love, cherishing in the bottom of your heart their good. Having found your heart beneficent and merciful, you may then bid unto honor and forbid dishonor, and guide the people, so that the hard hearts may become soft with the flash of your emotional heart, and the iron of the hearts turn supple with the admonitions warm with the fire of your love.

This valley, however, is other than the valley of Hate on Allah's behalf, and love on Allah's behalf," which means that one should bear enmity for the enemies of the religion, as is stated in the noble *hadith*s and the Glorious Quran. That is true in its relevant place, and this is also true in its relevant place, for which there is no space to explain now.

---

[393] *Surah al-Qasas* 28:29-30.

A BRIEF EXEGESIS OF
THE BLESSED *SURAH* OF *AL-HAMD* AND
SOME DISCIPLINES OF PRAISING
AND RECITATION
Chapter Five

Scholars differ about the relation of *"ba"* [ب] in the *Bismillah ir-Rahman ir-Rahim*. Each one of them says something about it according to his way of thinking, knowledge and gnosticism. For example, men of letters relate it to the entry "beginning" [*ibtida*] or "seeking help" [*istianat*]. As to some narratives to the effect that *Bismillah* means: "I seek help [from Allah]," it is either in accordance with the common taste, as is very much current in the *hadith*s, and the difference of many *hadith*s is ascribed to this predicate, and it is thus that Imam ar-Rida (a) explained *Bismillah* to mean: "I put on myself a *simah* (mark) of Allah's,"[394] or "seeking help" denotes too delicate a meaning to be understood by the common people, as it includes the secret of *tawhid* in a subtler way.

Some people of knowledge say that it refers to "appeared" [*zahara*], that is: "Existence appeared by *Bismillah*."[395] This is in accordance with the people of knowledge, *suluk* and gnosticism, who say that all beings, the atoms of existence and the invisible and visible worlds are the manifestations of the all-embracing Name of Allah, i.e. "The Greatest Name." Consequently, "name," which means a sign, a mark, or height and elevation, is Allah's effusive and actual manifestation, which is called "Effusive Emanation" [*fayd-i munbasit*] and "luminous annexation" [*idafa-i ishraqi*], because, according to this conduct, the whole of the House of Realization, as from the abstract

---

[394] Refer to footnote 382.
[395] This aspect of the meaning of the *Bismillah* is stated by Muhyiddin ibn al-Arabi in his *al-Futuhat al-Makkiyyah*, vol. 1, p. 102.

intellects down to the lowest degrees of existence, are the phenomenalizations [*taayyunat*] of this emanation [*fayd*] and the descents [*tanazzulat*] of this grace [*latifah*]. This conduct is supportable by many noble divine *ayah*s and honorable *hadith*s of the infallible and purified Ahl al-Bayt (a), such as the noble *hadith* in al-*Kafi* which says: "Allah created the Will [*mashiyyat*] through the Will itself, then He created all the things through Will."[396] This honorable *hadith* is interpreted according to the opinion of each interpreter's creed. The most obvious one is that which is in conformity with the creed saying that "Will" means, here, the Will in Action, which is the "Effusive Emanation," and the "things" are the stages of existence, and which are the phenomena [*taayyunat*] and the descents [*tanazzulat*] of this grace. So, the *hadith* will thus mean that Allah, the Exalted, has created the Will of Act—which is the shadow [*zill*] of the Old Essential Will—through the Will itself, without intermediation, and the other creatures of the invisible and visible worlds have been created in the wake of that. Yet, Sayyid Muhaqqiq Damad (may his grave be sanctified), a great scholar and strict researcher as he was, interpreted this noble *hadith*[397] in a strange way. Similarly, the explanation of the late Fayd (may Allah have mercy upon him) is also far from being correct.[398]

However, "Name" is the very manifestation of Act, with which this House of Realization is realized (actualized). The term "Name," referring to real things, is frequently noticed to be used by Allah, His Messenger and the infallible Ahl al-Bayt, who said: "We are the Beautiful Names."[399]

In the noble invocations one frequently recites: "By Your Name in which You manifested to so and so."[400]

It is possible that the *Bismillah* at the opening of each *surah* belongs to the same *surah*. For example, the *Bismillah* of the blessed *surah* of al-Hamd belongs to the *surah* itself. This opinion coincides

---

[396] *Usul al-Kafi*, vol. 1, p. 149, "Book of *at-Tawhid*," ch. on "The Will is Among the Attributes of Action...," *hadith* 4; *Bihar al-Anwar*, vol. 4, p. 145.

[397] *Mirat al-Uqul*, vol. 2, p. 19; *Al-Wafi*, vol. 1, p. 100.

[398] *Al-Wafi*, vol. 1, sec. on "Knowing His Attributes and Names, the Glorified," ch. on "The Attributes of the Act," explanation of *hadith* 4, p. 100.

[399] *Usul al-Kafi*, vol. 1, "Book of *at-Tawhid*," ch. "Rarities," *hadith* 4, p. 196.

[400] From the noble invocation called *Dua as-Simat*. See *Misbah al-Mutahajjid*, p. 376.

with the gnostic taste and the way of the people of knowledge, as it is to say that the praise of the praisers and the eulogy of the eulogists point to the self-subsistence of the Name "Allah." Therefore, the *tasmiyah* comes as a preliminary to all words and acts—which is an act of religious supererogation—and it is to remind that whatever word or act done by man is by the self-subsistence of the divine Name, since all the particles of existence are the phenomena of "Allah's Name," and, in a way, they themselves are "Allah's Names." On this basis, the meaning of the *Basmalah*, according to the majority, is different in each *surah*, each word and each act. The jurisprudents say that the *Bismillah* must be defined for each *surah*, that is, if for a *surah* a *Bismillah* was recited, the next *surah* cannot be commenced with that same *Bismillah*. From the juristic point of view, this is not without reason, as, actually, it is reasonable within the scope of this research. But, considering the vanishing of multiplicities in the Greatest Name of Allah, all *Bismillah*s have a single meaning.

These two opinions are also applied to the stages of existence and the stations of invisibility and visibility. In the view of multiplicity and seeing the phenomena, all the multiplied beings, the stages of existence and the phenomena of the world are the different names of the Beneficent, the Merciful, the Powerful and the Gracious. In the view of the vanishing of multiplicities and the effacement of the lights of existence in the eternal light of the Sacred Emanation [*fayd-i muqaddas*], there is nothing except the Sacred Emanation [*fayd-i muqaddas*] and the All-Embracing Name of Allah. Both of these two opinions are also present in the Divine Names and Attributes. According to the first opinion, the state of Unity [*wahidiyyat*] is the state of multiple Names and Attributes, as all multiplicities are from Him. According to the second opinion, there is no name and form [*ism wa rasm*] except the Greatest Name of Allah. These two opinions are wise and thought upon. But if the view became gnostic through opening the doors of the heart, and through the steps of conduct and cordial austerity, Allah, the Exalted, will appear in the hearts of its possessors through His manifestations in Act, Name and Essence, sometimes in the Attribute of multiplicity and sometimes in the Attribute of Unity. The Glorious Quran refers to these manifestations, both overtly, as in His saying: **"And when his Lord manifested (His light) to the mountain, He made it crumble to dust, and Moses fell**

down senseless,"[401] and covertly, as in the scenes witnessed by Ibrahim (a) and the Messenger of Allah (*s*), which are referred to in the *surah*s *al-Anam* and *an-Najm* as well as in the narratives and the invocations of the infallibles (a) which frequently refer to the same topic, especially in the great *dua* [invocation] called *"as-Simat,"* whose authenticity and text cannot be denied by the deniers, and it is accepted by both the *Sunni*s and the *Shiah*s, and by both gnostics and common people. In this noble invocation there are many high meanings and teachings smelling which raptures the gnostic"s heart, and its breeze blows divine breath into the *salik*"s spirit. It says: "By the light of Your Face with which You appeared to the mountain and made it crumble to dust, and Moses fell down senseless; by Your Glory which appeared at the mount of Tur of *Sina*, with which You talked to Your servant and messenger, Moses the son of Imran (a); and by Your rise in *Sair* and Your appearance on the mount *Faran*..."[402]

In short, the *salik* to Allah has to inform his heart, when reciting the *Bismillah*, that all the outward and inward beings and all the visible and invisible worlds, are under the education of the Names of Allah, or rather, they are manifest by the manifestation of the Names of Allah, and all his motions and stillness, and all the world"s, are based on the self-existence of the Greatest Name of Allah. So, his praises are for Allah, and his worship, obedience, monotheism, and sincerity are all because of the self-existence of the Name of Allah. It is by intense remembrance, which is the aim of worship, that this state, this divine grace, is established and fixed in his heart, as Allah, the Exalted, in His intimate meeting and sacred assembly, with His interlocutor, said: **"Verily I am Allah; there is no god but I; so worship Me and perform the *salat* for My remembrance."**[403]

The objective of performing the *salat* is, He said, to remember Him. After intense remembrance, another way of knowledge will be opened to the heart of the gnostic and he will be attracted to the world of Unity until the tongue of his heart recites: **"Praise is for Allah by**

---

[401] *Surah al-Araf* 7:143.
[402] Extracted from the *dua* of *as-Simat*, *Misbah al-Mutahajjid*, p. 376.
[403] *Surah Ta-Ha* 20:14.

Allah," and "You are as You praised Yourself,"[403a] **and "I take refuge in You from You."**[403b] That was a summary of the relation of the "B" [*ba*] in *Bismillah*, and some information obtained from it. As to the secrets of the "B" [*ba*], and the dot under the "B" [*ba*] of *Bismillah*, which, in its innermost, refers to the Alawian position of guardianship, and the state of the Quranic Collective Union [*jam ul-jam*], they need a wider scope to explain.

As regards the truth of the Name, it has an invisible station, an invisible of the invisible, and it has a secret, a secret of the secret, a state of manifestation and a manifestation of the manifestation. The Name is the mark [*alamat*] of Allah and is vanished in His Sacred Essence. So, any name which is nearer to the horizon of the Unity, and farther from the world of multiplicity, is more complete in nomination [nameness = *ismiyyat*]; and the most complete name is that which is innocent from multiplicities, even the multiplicity of knowledge, and that is the invisible manifestation of "Ahmadian Oneness" [*ahadi-yi ahmadi*] in the Essence [*hadrati-yi dhat*] by the state of the "Holiest Emanation" [*fayd-i aqdas*], which may be what was referred to by the noble *ayah*: **"... or closer still".**[404] Then there is the manifestation by the Greatest Name of Allah in the Unity [*hadrat-i wahidiyyat*]; then there is the manifestation by the "Holy Emanation" [*fayd-i muqaddas*]; then there are the manifestations by the attributes of multiplicity in the essences [*hadarat-i ayan*], etc. till the last stage of the House of Realization. The writer has already explained this brief in *Misbah al-Hidayah*[405] and in the exegesis of *Dua us-Sahar*.[406]

"Allah" is the state [*maqam*] of appearance in the "Holy Emanation" if by "Name" the existential individuations [*taayyunat-i wujudiyyah*] are meant, in which case applying "Allah" to it as a union between the manifest and the manifestation, and the vanishing of the

---

[403a] Refer to footnote 219.
[403b] Refer to footnote 220.
[404] **"So he was at the measure of two bows or closer still."** *Surah an-Najm* 53:9.
[405] Refer to footnote 199.
[406] The exegesis of *Dua"us-Sahar* is of the exudations of the pen of Imam Khomeini (may Allah be pleased with him) in Arabic. The aim of writing it, as the exegete himself says, was to explain some aspects of the noble invocation called *"mubahilah."* (The invocation of *Sahar* has been narrated from the pure Imams [*a*]). The writing of this noble book was completed in 1349, L.H.

Name in the Named, is not objectionable. Perhaps, the *ayahs* "**Allah is the light of the heavens and the earth,**[407] and "**And He it is Who in the heaven and in the earth is God,**"[408] are a reference to this state, and an evidence proving the said application. It is the state of Unity [*wahidiyyat*] and the Union [*jam*] of the Names. In other words, it is the state of the Greatest Name if by "Name" the state of manifestation by the "Holy Emanation" is intended. This is probably more obvious than the other possibilities. Or it is the state of the Essence or the state of the "Holiest Emanation" if by "Name" the "Greatest Name" is intended. Consequently, the states of "Beneficent" [*rahman*] and "Merciful" [*rahim*] are different, according to these possibilities, as is clear.

It is possible that "Beneficent" and "Merciful" are adjectives for "Name," or they may by adjectives for "Allah," but they are more suitable to be adjectives for "Name," because in praising they are adjectives for "Allah," and thus, it will be immune from repetition, although their being adjectives for "Allah" is also justifiable. In repetition there is, however, a point of eloquence. If we take them to be adjectives for "Name," it supports the idea that by "Name" the Essential Names [*asma-i ayniyyah*] are intended, because only the Essential Names can bear the adjectives of "Beneficent" and "Merciful." So, if by "Name" the Essential Name and the manifestation in the state of Collectivity are intended, "Beneficent" and "Merciful" will be attributes of the Essence, which, in the manifestations by the state of Unity, are confirmed for "the Name of Allah," and the mercy of the Beneficent and the Merciful in Act is of their demotions [*tanazzulat*] and appearances. And if by the "Name" the collective manifestation in Act [*tajalli-yi jami-yi fili*] is intended, which is the state of Will, the "Beneficence" and "Mercifulness" are attributes of Act. So, the mercy of the "Beneficence" [*rahmaniyyat*] is the expanse of the origin of the existence, which is general and for all beings, but it is of the particular attributes of Allah, because in expanding the origin of the existence, Allah, the Exalted, has no partner, and the hands of other beings are short of having the mercy of creating: "There is no effecter in the [world of] existence except Allah, and there is no God in the House of Realization but Allah."

---

[407] *Surah an-Nur* 24:35.
[408] *Surah az-Zukhruf* 43:84.

Regarding the mercy of "Mercifulness" [*rahimiyyat*], of whose exudations [*rashahat*] is the guidance of the guides on the road, it is especially for the fortunate and the high dispositions, but it is of the general attributes, of which other beings have their share, too, as it has already been explained that the mercy of Mercifulness is of the general mercies, and that the wicked [*ashqiya*] have no share of it because of their own evils, not because of any limitation. Therefore, guidance and invitation are for the entire human family, as is confirmed by the Glorious Quran. However, another opinion says that the mercy of the "Mercifulness" belongs only to Allah, and no one else has any share of it. The noble narratives, taking into consideration the different opinions and estimations, also differ in explaining the mercy of Mercifulness. Sometimes it is said: "The „Beneficent" is a particular Name for a general Attribute, and the „Merciful" is a general Name for a particular Attribute."[409] In another instance it is said: "(He is) Beneficent to all His creatures, and Merciful to the believers in particular."[410] It is also said: "O Beneficent of this world, and Merciful of the Hereafter,"[411] or "O Beneficent and Merciful of this world and the Hereafter."

A Gnostic Research

Men of letters say that *Rahman* (Beneficent) and *Rahim* (Merciful) are derived from *rahmah* (mercy) and that both denote hyperbole, but in *Rahman* the exaggeration is more than it is *Rahim*. Analogy requires that *Rahim* should have preceded *Rahman,* but since *Rahman* is as a personal proper name and cannot be ascribed to other beings, it thus came first. Some say that both have the same meaning, and the repetition is for mere confirmation. The gnostic taste— according to the highest levels of which the Quran has been revealed—requires that *Rahman* should precede *Rahim*, because the Quran, according to the people of heart, is the descendant of the divine manifestations, and the written form bearing the divine Beautiful Names, and, as *ar-Rahman* is the most all-embracing of the divine

---

[409] *Majma ul-Bayan*, vol. 1, p. 21, quoting Imam Jafar as-Sadiq (a), with a slight difference.
[410] *Maaniy ul-Akhbar*, p. 3; *Bihar al-Anwar*, vol. 89, p. 229.
[411] *Usul al-Kafi*, vol. 4, p. 340, "the Book of the Invocation," ch. on "Invoking on Calamities," *hadith* 6; *As-Sahifah as-Sajjadiyyah*, Invocation 54.

Names next to the Greatest Name, and as the people of knowledge are certain that the manifestations by the embracing Names [*asma-i muhitah*] are prior to the manifestations by the embraced Names [*asma-i muhatah*], and as every Name that is more embracing, its manifestation is prior, too, therefore, the first manifestation in the Unity [*hadrat-i wahidiyyat*] is the manifestation in the Greatest Name of Allah. Then comes the manifestation in the state of the Beneficence and after that comes the manifestation in the state of Mercifulness [*rahimiyyat*]. Similarly, in the manifestation of the appearance in Act, it is the manifestation in the state of "Will," which is the Greatest Name in this scene [*mashhad*] and the appearance of the Greatest Name of the Essence that has priority over all manifestations. The manifestation in the state of Beneficence—which embraces all the beings of the invisible and visible worlds, and to which the *ayah*: "My **mercy encompasses all things**"[412] refers—is to precede other manifestations, as the saying, "His mercy precedes His anger"[413] refers to that in some aspects.

Generally speaking, as the *Bismillah,* according to the inside and the spirit, is the form of the manifestations in Act, and according to the secret and the secret of the secret, it is the form of the manifestations of Names, or rather of Essence, and these manifestations appear first in the state of "Allah," then in the state of the "Beneficent," and then in the state of the "Merciful," the pronounced and written forms should also be like that so as to be in conformity with the divine system. Regarding the "Beneficent" and the "Merciful" in the noble *Surah* of *al-Hamd,* which come later than "The Lord of the worlds," it may be because in the *Bismillah* the attention is directed to the appearance of the existence from the hidden and invisible places of existence. In the noble *surah* the attention is paid to the return and the inside. However, in this possibility there is a problem. Maybe it refers to the comprehensiveness of the mercy of "Beneficence" and "Mercifulness," or there may be another point. In any case, the said point concerning the *Bismillah* deserves to be believed in, and probably this is out of the blessings of the Mercy of the Mercifulness bestowed upon the heart of this humble person. Praise be to Him for what He has favored.

---

[412] *Surah al-Araf* 7:156.
[413] *Ilm al-Yaqin,* vol.1, p. 57.

A Discussion and an Acquisition

The formalist scholars say that *ar-Rahman* and *ar-Rahim* are derived from *ar-rahmah*, implying compassion and kindness. Ibn Abbas (may Allah be pleased with him) is quoted to have said: "They are two compassionate words, one of which is more compassionate than the other: *ar-Rahman*, the compassionate, and *ar-Rahim*, the kind to His servants providing them with livelihood and favors."[414] As kindness and compassion require an emotion [*infial*], certain interpretation is given for ascribing them to the Sacred Essence, and thus that is regarded allegorical [*majazi*].

Some others, concerning such attributes in general, say: "Take the results and leave the preliminaries."[415] Regarding ascribing them to Allah, the Exalted, it is based on the effects and acts, not on the beginnings and attributes. So, the meaning of *ar-Rahim* and *ar-Rahman* as ascribed to Allah is the One Who treats His servants mercifully. The Schismatics [*mutazilah*] regard all Allah''s attributes as said above, or something like it, and, consequently, attributing them to Allah is also allegorical. But it is, however, unlikely to be allegorical, especially in respect of *ar-Rahman*, which, if admitted to be allegorical, would entail accepting something quite strange. That is, this word is coined for a meaning which is not allowed to be used allegorically and could not be. In fact, it will be an allegory with no reality. Think of it. People of research, in reply to such objections, say that words are coined for general meanings and absolute facts. So, to be confined to compassion and kindness is not included in what the word "mercy" was coined for, but the common mind has fabricated this attachment, as otherwise it has nothing to do with the coining [*wad*]. This, as it seems, is far from research, because the one who coined it was obviously one of these common people, and the abstract meanings and the absolute facts have not been considered. Yes, if the coiner [*wadi*] was Allah, the Exalted, or the prophets, according to divine revelation and inspiration, it would be a justification. This, however, is not confirmed, and the external form of this speech is questionable, yet, it is not clear whether this external form was what the men of research intended. It is even possible to say that although

---

[414] Jalaluddin as-Suyuti, *Ad-Durr al-Manthur fi Tafsiri bil-Ma'lhur*, vol. 1, p. 9, quoted from *al-Asma"was-Sifat* by al-Bayhaqi.
[415] A current proverb. *Asrar al-Hikam*, by Sabzewari, p.52.

the coiner [*wadi*] of the words may not have considered, during the coining, the general abstract meanings, yet what had actually been intended for the words were the very general abstract meanings. For example, the coiner of the word "light" had naturally in mind all kinds of accidental [*aradiyyah*] and sensible lights, as he knew nothing about what is behind these lights. But that which the word "light" denotes is the luminosity, not the mixture of light and darkness. If he was informed that those accidental and limited lights are not pure, but mixed with darkness and torpidity, and if he was asked whether he had intended the word to denote the luminosity or the mixture of light and darkness, he would certainly say that he had intended its luminosity, and the darkness never occurred to him in this respect. We likewise know that the person who coined the word "fire" he thought of nothing other than the worldly fires, and that what made it to occur to him was those fires of this world, and he knew nothing about **"The fire kindled by Allah which rises above the hearts,"**[416] more so if the coiner did not believe in the other world. Nevertheless, this occurrence cannot be a means of limiting the fact, as "fire" refers to the quality of the fire, not that the coiner tried to abstract the meanings, such that it appears strange and far-fetched. But, actually, we say that the words denote the meanings for which they were coined, without any particular limit. Therefore, there is no exception in the case, and the freer the meaning from the aliens and strangers, the nearer it will be to the truth, and farther from the shortcomings of allegory. Take, for example, the word "light" which was coined for being manifest by itself and for manifesting the other, despite the fact that using it for the accidental and mundane lights is not far from the truth, because by using it for them, the limits and the mixing with darkness are not intended, only the self-manifestation and the manifestativeness are intended. But using it for the heavenly lights—whose appearances are more perfect, nearer to the horizon of the intrinsicness [*dhatiyyah*] and stronger in manifestativeness in quantity and quality, and whose mixing with darkness and blemishes is less—is nearer to the truth; and using it for the Lights of Majesty [*anwar-i jabarutiyyah*] is, for the said reason, closer to the truth; and also using it for the Sacred Essence of Allah, the Most High, Who is the Light of the Lights and free from all aspects of darkness, and is mere Pure Light, is the very pure and absolute

---

[416] *Surah al-Humazah* 104:6-7.

truth. It can even be said that if "Light" has been coined for "the apparent by itself and manifesting the other," using it for other than Allah, the Exalted, is a reality to the partial intellects, but to the intellects supported (by Allah), and to the people of knowledge, it is allegorical, and it is real only when used for Allah, the Exalted. Likewise are the words that are coined for concepts of perfection, such as meanings like existence and perfection.

Consequently, we say that in "Beneficent," "Merciful," "Compassionate," "Kind" and the like, there is an aspect of perfection and completeness, and an aspect of emotion and shortcoming, and these words have been devised for that aspect of perfection, which is the origin of that truth. As regards the emotional aspects, which are of the requisites of the growth [*nashah*] and of the strange and alien things of the truth, which, after the descent of these truths in the places of possibility and the low mundane worlds, are concomitant and tangled with them—like the darkness which mingles with the light in the descending growth [*nashah*]— have nothing to do with the meaning of the object. So, using it for a Being Who possesses the Absolute Perfection, and Who is innocent of all aspects of emotion and shortcoming, is the mere pure truth. This explanation, in addition to its being close to the taste of the people of knowledge, suits the conscience of the people of literalism, too.

Hence, it has become clear that such attributes of perfection, which have by descending in some growths [*nashaat*], been mixed and interrelated with another matter—of which the Sacred Essence of Allah is innocent—are not allegorical when ascribed to Allah, the Exalted, in their absolute concept. And Allah is the Guide.

* * * * * * * * *

When He says: "*Alhamdu lillah*" (All praise is for Allah), it means that all forms of praise are exclusively for the Divine Sacred Essence. So, do know, dear, that under this noble word is the secret of the particular *tawhid*, or rather the most particular one. The fact that all forms of praise, that the praisers offer, exclusively belong to Allah, the Exalted, is quite obvious, by evidence, to the people of wisdom and the well-versed in high philosophy, because it is proved that the entire House of Realization is the Expanded Shadow [*zill-i munbasit*] of Allah and His Flowing Emanation [*fayd-i mabsul*], and that all the apparent and hidden favors, whoever the donor may be, as it appears and as the common people think, are Allah's, and no being participates with Him. Even the preparatory participation in this respect is the opinion of the people of the common philosophy, not the high philosophy. So, as praise is offered for favors, gifts and beneficence, and as there is no benefactor in the House of Realization except Allah, all praises belong to Him. And also as there are no Beauty and no Beautiful save His Beauty and Him, all praises return to Him.

In other words, every praise and extolment by any praiser or extoller is because of a favor and perfection on the other side. As to the place and the occasion of the favor and the perfection that diminish and limit these, they have no participation in the praise and extolment, rather they are incompatible and contradictory. So, all praises and extolments return to the part [*hazz*] of Divinity, which is perfection and beauty, not to that of the creature, which is deficiency and limitation.

In other words still, eulogizing the Perfect and thanking and praising the Benefactor [*munim*] are of the God-given dispositions, which are in the innermost of all beings. Among other divine dispositions is the feeling of disgust with the shortcomings, imperfections and what decreases the favor. The absolute favor which is free from all fault, and the complete Beauty and Perfection which are innocent of all kinds of deficiency, exclusively belong to Allah, while the other beings decrease the absolute favors and the absolute beauty and limit them, not that they increase and support them. Thus, all peoples are disposed to thank and praise the Sacred Essence of Allah, and disregard the other beings, except those beings who, according to their journey through the kingdoms of perfection and the towns of love, have been annihilated in the Glorious Essence of Allah, since loving them and praising them are the very loving of Allah and praising Him. "Loving Allah's favorites is loving Allah."

Up to here we have been explaining the positions of the ordinary people who are still within the veils of multiplicity and have not yet got rid of all sorts of hidden, and deeply hidden, polytheism, nor have they reached the perfect degree of sincerity and purity.

But, according to the knowledge [*irfan*] of those whose hearts have been annihilated in certain states, all the favors and all perfection, beauty and majesty are the form of the manifestation of the Essence, and all praises and thanks belong to the Sacred Essence of Allah, or rather praise and thanks are from Himself to Himself,[417] as is referred to by the connection of *Bismillah* (In the Name of Allah) to *al-hamdu lillah* (all praise is for Allah).

Know that the *salik* to Allah, the striver in the way of Allah, should not be satisfied with the scientific limit of this knowledge [*maarif*], spending his whole life on induction [*istidlal*], which is veil, or rather the greatest veil, for to cover this distance with "wooden legs,"[418] or even by the "bird of Solomon,"[419] is not possible. It is the valley of the holy men and the stage of the humble [*warastegan*]. Without **"taking off the shoes"**[420] of loving rank, honor, women, children, and, unless he gives up dependence and inclination towards other than Allah, he will not be able to step into the sacred valley, which is the place of the sincere ones and the godly men. If the *salik* set his foot in this valley with the truths of sincerity, kicking off multiplicity and this world—which are fancy upon fancy—should there be in him any remnants of selfishness, a hand from the invisible world would assist him, and his mountain of I-ness would be shattered by the divine manifestation, and he would undergo a state of "senselessness" and "annihilation." These states in the hard hearts—which have no share and no information except concerning this world, and which know nothing but the Satanic conceit—seem irregular and abnormal, and they ascribe them to fantasies, despite the fact that the annihilation which we now have in nature and in this world is stranger and more wondrous than the annihilation which the people of gnosticism and *suluk* claim. We are negligent of all the invisible worlds, which, from all aspects, are more apparent than this world, or rather of the Essence and Attributes of the Sacred Essence to Whom appearance exclusively belongs, while to prove those worlds and the

---

[417] In the Name of Allah. It must be noted that confining all praisings or the quality [*jins*] of praising to the two possibilities in the "*a*" [*alif*] and "*l*" [*lam*] is contrary to the philosophic causality, even if the causality is taken by its strict meaning, and it cannot be justified except by the tongue of the Quran and the gnosticism of the holy men [*awliya'*] (a).

[418] This is a reference to a line of poetry by Mawlawi, which has previously been explained.

[419] This refers to a line of poetry by Hafiz, in which he says: "I did not reach the faraway palace of the phoenix (of truth) by myself; I could cover it only by the help of Solomon's bird (the hoopoe, i.e. the guide of wisdom)".

[420] A reference to *ayah* 12 of the *Surah Ta-Ha*: **"...put off your shoes, you are in the sacred valley..."**

Sacred Essence of Allah, the Most High, we cling to evidences and induction.

Bewilderment upon bewilderment comes from this story,
The swoon of the elite is the meanest (or the most special).[421]

If the word *akhass* is written with the letter *sad* (ص) there can be not so much bewilderment, because the annihilation of the imperfect in the perfect is natural and is in accordance with the divine law. But the bewilderment is when the word *akhass* is written with the letter *sin* (س), as this swoon and the annihilation are happening to us all. Our ears and eyes are so absorbed and annihilated in nature that we are completely unaware of the uproars of the invisible world.

A Tradition and a Research

Be informed that men of letters and the formalists say that "praising" [*hamd*] is thanking [*thana*] by the tongue for a voluntary favor [*jamil*], and, as they are unaware of all tongues except this fleshy tongue, they regard all praising and glorifying Allah, or rather all the talks of the Sacred Essence, to be a sort of figurative speech. They likewise take the talking, the praising and glorifying Allah by all beings to be allegorical. So, they regard Allah's talking to be creating talking, while in the other beings they regard praising and glorifying to be genetic [*takwini*] and intrinsic [*dhati*]. They think that speaking is, in fact, exclusively confined to their own species, thinking that the Sacred Essence of Allah, the Most High, and other beings, are unable to speak, or rather they are—God forbid!—dumb. They take this to be declaring the innocence of the Sacred Essence, whereas this is a limitation [*tahdid*], or even a disruption [*tatil*], and Allah is innocent of such innocence, as most of the glorifications of the common people are limitation and assimilation [*tashbih*]. We have already explained how the words were coined for the general and absolute meanings. Now we add: We are not, however, very keen on confirming that the divine facts should necessarily come true under linguistic terminological facts, as it is the correctness of the application [*itlaq*] and the

---

[421] In some copies we find the word *akhass* (whose English equivalent is "most special"). In some other copies it is *akhass* (which means "the meanest"). The line is by Mawlawi.

intellectual truth that are the criterion in such discussions, even if the linguistic fact is also proved, according to the former discussion. Therefore, we say that language, speaking, speech, writing, book, praising, and thanking are of diverse degrees in proportion to the existential growths [*nashaat-i wujudiyyah*], as each one corresponds to its own growth [*nashah*] and degree. And praising [*hamd*], in each instance, is for a favor [*jamil*] and glorifying [*madh*] is for a beauty and a perfection. So, when Allah, the Most High, according to His Self-Knowledge [*ilm-i dhati*], saw, in the Invisible Ipseity [*huwiyyat*], His Beautiful Beauty, in the most complete degree of knowing and seeing, He was delighted [*mubtahij*] at His Beautiful Essence at the highest degree of delight [*ibtihaj*]. So, He manifested in the eternal manifestation and at the highest degree of manifestation in the Essence [*hadrat-i dhat*] for the Essence. This manifestation and disclosing the hidden secret and the "Self-Argument" [*muqariat-i dhatiyyah*] is a "Self-Speech" [*kalam-i dhati*], which takes place with the tongue of the Essence in the Unseen [*hadrat-i ghayb*]. Witnessing this spoken manifestation is hearing the Essence. This praising of the Essence for the Essence of Allah, is Allah's praise which the other beings are incapable of understanding, such that the sacred person of the Sealing Prophet, the most honorable and the nearest to Allah, confesses his incapability and says: "I cannot count the praises for You, You are as You have praised Yourself."[422] It is known that counting the praises is a branch of knowing the Perfection and Beauty, but as the complete knowledge of the absolute Beauty is not possible, similarly the real praise cannot be performed. The utmost knowledge [*marifat*] of the people of knowledge and gnosticism is to confess incapability.

The people of knowledge say that Allah, the Exalted, praises and glorifies Himself with five tongues, which are the tongue of the Essence as such, the tongue of the Unseen Oneness [*ahadiyyat-i ghayb*], the tongue of the Collective Unity [*wahidiyyat-i jamiyyah*], the tongue of the Distinct Names [*asma-i tafsiliyyah*], and the tongue of the entities [*ayan*]. These are other than the tongue of manifestness, the first of which is the tongue of Volition [*mashiyyat*], down to the end of the ranks of the individuations, which are the tongue of the existential multiplicities.

---

[422] *Misbah ash-Shariah*, ch. 5; *Awaliy al-Laali*, vol. 1, p. 389.

Know that all the beings have a share, or even shares, of the invisible world, which is mere life running throughout the entire House of Existence. This subject is proved to the people of high philosophy by proofs, and to the people of heart and knowledge by witnessing and eyeing. The noble divine *ayah*s and the *hadith*s of the guardians of the revelation (a) refer to it quite explicitly. The veiled people of the common philosophy and literalism, who could not recognize the speech of the beings, resort to interpretation and justification. It is quite strange that the people of literalism, who invalidate the people of philosophy for interpreting the Book of Allah according to their own understanding, they themselves resort, in this respect, to interpreting so many of the plain *ayah*s and the outright correct *hadith*s, just because they could not recognize the talking of the beings, even without having a proof at their disposal. So, they interpret the Quran without any proof and only because of improbability [*istibad*]. At any rate, the House of Existence is the origin of life and the truth of understanding and consciousness. The glorification of the beings is pronunciational, conscious and volitional, not genetic, innate, as the veiled claim. All beings are acquainted with the state [*maqam*] of Allah, the Most High, in proportion to their share of being. Now, as there is no being busier with nature and more indulgent in multiplicity than man, he, thus, is more wrapped in veils than other beings, unless he takes off his garment of being a human, and pierces the veils of multiplicity and otherness, so as to be able to witness, unveiled, the Beauty of the Beautiful, in which case, his praise and glorification would be more comprehensive than all praises and glorifications, and he would be worshipping Allah with all His divine affairs and all His Names and Attributes.

Completion

Know that the noble saying [*kalimah*]: **"All praise is for Allah,"** according to what had already been said, is of the all-inclusive sayings [*kalimat*], and, if with its delicacies and truths one praises Allah, he will be performing the most that is in the capacity of a human being to perform. Hence the noble *hadith*s refer to it. It is narrated that Imam al-Baqir (a) once came out of a house and found that his mount had gone. He said: "If I find the mount, I will praise Allah as praising deserves." When his mount was found, he mounted, tidied his clothes and said: "All praise is for Allah."⁴²³ The Messenger of Allah (*s*) is quoted to have said: " ,,There is no god but Allah" is half of a scale, and ,,All praise is for Allah" fills the other half of the scale."⁴²⁴ This is because of what we have said that "All praise is for Allah" includes monotheism, too.

The Messenger of Allah (*s*) is also quoted to have said: "The servant"s saying, ,,All praise is for Allah" is heavier, in His scales, than seven heavens and seven earths."⁴²⁵ He (*s*) is also quoted to have said: "If Allah gave to one of His servants the entire world, and then that servant said: ,,All praise is for Allah,; that saying would be better than what he had been given."⁴²⁶ Further quotation from him (*s*) says: "Nothing is more loved by Allah than one"s saying: ,,All praise is for Allah," as Allah Himself has so praised Himself.⁴²⁷ There are many similar *hadith*s.

* * * * * * * * *

Allah, the Exalted, said: "*Rabbi l-alamin*" (the Lord of the worlds). If "*rabb*" means: "the Most High" [*mutaali*], "the Constant" [*thabit*] and "the Master" [*sayyid*], then it is of the Names of the Essence. If it means: "the Possessor" [*malik*], "the Owner" [*sahib*], "the Victorious" [*ghalib*] and "the Omnipotent" [*qahir*], then it is of the attributive Names. If it means: "the Educator" [*murabbi*], "the Benefactor" [*munim*], and "the Completer" [*mutammim*], then it is of the Names of Acts.

"*Al-Alamin*" (the worlds), if it means: "Everything other than Allah," which covers all the stages of existence and the stations [*manazil*] of the invisible and visible, then we have to take "*rabb*" to be of the Names of Attributes. If "world" is "the visible world" [*alam-i mulk*], which gradually takes place and reaches its perfection, then "*rabb*" means a Name of Act. At any rate, here it does not mean a

---

⁴²³ *Usul al-Kafi*, vol. 3, p. 152, "Book of Faith and Disbelief," ch. on "Thanking," *hadith* 18.

⁴²⁴ *Bihar al-Anwar*, vol. 90, p. 210, quoted from Shaykh at-Tusi, *al-Amali*, vol. 1, p. 18.

⁴²⁵ *Mustadrak al-Wasa'il*, printed by the *Ahl al-Bayt* Foundation, vol. 5, p. 314.

⁴²⁶ *Makarim al-Akhlaq*, p. 307, section 10, ch. 3 on praising Allah (with a slight difference).

⁴²⁷ Reference untraceable.

Name of Essence. Maybe, in a way, *"Alamin"* refers to the visible worlds, which attain their suitable perfection under the divine education [*tarbiyat*] and management [instruction = *tamshiyat*]. In this case the word *"rabb"* means educator, being one of the Names of Acts.

Do know that in this paper we refrain from explaining the linguistic, literary and structural aspects of the *ayah*s, because others have mostly handled them. Certain points that have not been handled at all, or inaccurately handled, we shall properly deal with them.

It must be noted that the Names of Essence, Attributes and Acts, which have been referred to, are according to the terms of the people of knowledge. A learned man of the people of knowledge, in *Insha ad-Dawair* has divided the Names into the Names of Essence, the Names of Attributes, and the Names of Acts. He has said:

"The Names of Essence are: *Allah, ar-Rabb* (the Lord), *al-Malik* (the King), *al-Quddus* (the Holy), *as-Salam* (the Peace), *al-Mumin* (the Faithful), *al-Muhaymin* (the Protector), *al-Aziz* (the Almighty), *al-Jabbar* (the Omnipotent), *al-Mutakabbir* (the Haughty), *al-Ali* (the Exalted), *al-Azim* (the Tremendous), *az-Zahir* (the Outward), *al-Batin* (the Inward), *al-Awwal* (the First), *al-Akhir* (the Last), *al-Kabir* (the Great), *al-Jalil* (the Majestic), *al-Majid* (The Glorious), *al-Haqq* (the Truth), *al-Mubin* (the Manifest), *al-Wajid* (the Finder), *al-Majid* (the Noble), *as-Samad* (the Everlasting Refuge), *al-Mutaali* (the Most High), *al-Ghani* (the Independent), *an-Nur* (the Light), *al-Warith* (the Inheritor), *Dhu l-Jalal* (the Owner of Majesty), and *ar-Raqib* (the Watcher).

The Names of Attributes are: *al-Hayy* (the Living), *ash-Shakur* (the Grateful), *al-Qahhar* (the Conqueror), *al-Qahir* (the Subduer), *al-Muqtadir* (the All-Powerful), *al-Qawiyy* (the Strong), *al-Qadir* (the Able), *ar-Rahman* (the Beneficent), *ar-Rahim* (the Merciful), *al-Karim* (the Generous), *al-Ghaffar* (the Forgiver), *al-Ghafur* (the Forgiving), *al-Wadud* (the Affectionate), *ar-Rauf* (the Compassionate), *al-Halim* (the Clement), *as-Sabur* (the Patient), *al-Barr* (the Righteous), *al-Alim* (the Omniscient), *al-Khabir* (the Aware), *al-Muhsi* (the Counter), *al-Hakim* (the Wise), *ash-Shahid* (the Witness), *as-Sami* (the Hearer) and *al-Basir* (the Seer).

The Names of Acts are: *al-Mubdi* (the Beginner), *al-Wakil* (the Guardian), *al-Baith* (the Resurrector), *al-Mujib* (the Responsive), *al-Wasi* (the Expansive), *al-Hasib* (the Reckoner), *al-Muqit* (the Nourisher), *al-Hafiz* (the Protector), *al-Khaliq* (the Creator), *al-Bari* (the Maker), *al-Musawwir* (the Shaper), *al-Wahhab* (the Giver), *ar-Razzaq* (the Provider), *al-Fattah* (the Opener), *al-Qabid* (the Restrainer), *al-Basit* (the Spreader), *al-Khafid* (the Abaser), *ar-Rafi* (the Exalter), *al-Muizz* (the Honorer), *al-Mudhill* (the Humiliator), *al-Hakim* (the Wise), *al-Adil* (the Just), *al-Latif* (the Subtle), *al-Muid* (the Restorer), *al-Muhyi* (the Life-Giver), *al-Mumit* (the Death-Giver), *al-Wali* (the Patron), *at-Tawwab* (the Relenting, the Accepter of Repentance), *al-Muntaqim* (the Avenger), *al-Muqsit* (the Equitable), *al-Jami* (the Comprehensive), *al-Mughni* (the Enricher), *al-Mani* (the Deterrent), *ad-Darr* (the Harmful), *an-Nafi* (the Beneficial), *al-Hadi* (the Guide), *al-Badi* (the Magnificent), and *ar-Rashid* (the Prudent).[428]

Concerning these divisions it is said that although they are all Names of Essence, yet considering the appearance of the Essence, they are called the Names of Essence, and, considering the appearance of the Attributes or the Acts they are called the Names of Attributes or of Acts. That is, whichever of these is more apparent, they are named after it. Consequently, sometimes in a Name two or three aspects appear at the same time, in which case it is regarded as a Name of Essence, Attribute and Acts, or of two of these three, like "*ar-Rabb*," as has been said. But this question does not come to suit the writer''s taste, nor does it suit the gnostic taste. What is apparent in this sorting is that the criterion for these Names is that when the *salik* with the steps of knowledge reaches the stage of complete annihilation in Acts, Allah, the Exalted, appears to his heart through the manifestations of Names of Acts. After the annihilation in Attributes, the manifestations will be in the Names of Attributes, and after the annihilation in Essence, the manifestations will be in the Names of Essence. Should his heart have the ability of preservation after coming to sobriety, whatever he tells of his seeings of Acts would be Names of Acts. Similarly, whatever he tells of his seeing of Attributes would be Names of Attributes, and likewise the Names of Essence. There are, in this connection, details that do not suit these pages. That which is stated in the *Insha ad-Dawair* is not correct according to its own criterion, as is obvious on having a look at the Names.

It can be said that these divisions of "the three Names" are referred to in the Glorious Quran, in the last noble *ayah*s of the *surah* of "*al-Hashr*." Allah, the Exalted, says: "**He is Allah, other than**

---

[428] *Insha"ad-Dawa'ir*, p. 28.

Whom there is no god, the Knower of the invisible and the visible. He is the Beneficent, the Merciful,"[429] up to the end of the noble *ayah*s.

Perhaps the first of these noble *ayah*s refers to the Names of Essence, the second refers to the Names of Attributes and the third refers to the Names of Acts. Giving precedence to the Names of Essence over those of Attributes, and these over those of Acts, is according to the order of the facts of existence and of the divine manifestations, not according to the witnessings [*mushahadat*] of the people of witnessing [*ashab-i mushahadah*] and the manifestations in the hearts of the people of heart. It should be realized that the noble *ayah*s have other secrets, but to mention them does not suit the situation. That the second *ayah* is the Names of Attributes, and the third is the Names of Actions, is quite clear. That **"the Knower of the invisible and the visible," "the Beneficent" and "the Merciful"** are of the Names of Essence, is based on the fact that "the invisible" and "visible" are of the internal and external Names, and "Beneficence" [*rahmaniyyat*] and "Mercifulness" [*rahimiyyat*] are of the manifestations of "the Most Holy Emanation" [*fayd-i aqdas*], not of "the Holy Emanation" [*fayd-i muqaddas*]. Confining these Names to the remembrance of Allah, whereas "Living" [*hayy*], "Constant" [*thabit*] and "Lord" [*rabb*] seem nearer to the Names of Essence, is probably because of their comprehensiveness, as they are of the mothers of Names. And Allah knows better.

A Remark

There is a great controversy about the word, the derivation and meaning of *"al-alamin,"* (the worlds). Some say that *"al-alamin"* is plural, covering all kinds of creation, material and abstract, and each kind is a world in itself. It is a plural that has no singular of its root. This is a well-known opinion.

Some others say that *"alam"* is passive participle and *"Alim"* is active participle. So, *"alamin"* means *"malumin"* (the known). But, not only that this opinion has no proving evidence and is unlikely, it is also quite silly and irrelevant to say *"rabb ul-malumin"* (the Lord of the known).

---

[429] *Surah al-Hashr* 59:22.

Some say that *"alamin"* is derived from *"alamah"* (sign) which covers all beings, since everything is a sign and an *ayah* of the Sacred Essence. The letters *"waw"* (و) and *"nun"* (ن) refer to the rational beings, giving them priority to the other beings.

Others say that it is derived from *"ilm"* (knowledge). At any rate, regarding it to embrace all creation is correct, as it is justified to take it to cover the rational beings. But *"alam"* is used for everything other than Allah, and is also used for every individual or category. If the one who uses it for every individual and category is of the people of tradition and language, he considers every thing to be a sign of the Creator: "In every thing He has a sign..."[430] And if he is a divine gnostic, he considers every being to be the appearance of the all-embracing Name covering all the truths, by way of the appearance of the Collective Oneness [*ahadiyyat-i jam*] and the Secret of the Existence. According to this consideration, the entire world and every part of it, can be regarded as the Greatest Name in the state of the Collective Oneness. "The Names are all in all, and such are the signs."

Consequently, the objection of the great philosopher, *Sadr ul-Millat-i wad-Din* [*Sadr ul-Mutaallihin*] (may his soul be sanctified), to those like *al-Baydawi* is applicable, because they have not tasted of this drink [school = *mashrab*]. But to the ways of the people of gnosticism it is inapplicable. However, as the argument of *al-Baydawi* and that of the philosopher, on this topic are too lengthy, we refrain from mentioning them. The interested readers may refer to the exegesis of the said late philosopher on *Surah al-Fatihah*.

If *"ar-rabb"* is of the Names of Attributes, meaning "Master" or "Owner" and the like, the meaning of *"al-alamin"* may be "everything other than Allah," whether the owned were the beings of the kingdom of the world, or the abstract invisible beings. If it is of the Names of Acts—as it apparently is—the meaning of *"al-alamin"* will only be the kingdom of the visible world, as, in which case, *"ar-rabb"* will mean "the Educator"—a meaning which is of gradual effectiveness, while the abstract worlds are innocent of gradualness, though, to the writer, the spirit of "graduation" in the world of *"dahr"* (eternity, perpetual duration) is, in a way, certain; and, in the same way, we have also proved the temporal contingency [*huduth-i zamani*],

---

[430] "In every thing He has a sign proving that He is One." *Kashf al-Asrar*, by Maybudi, vol. 1, p. 436. Some ascribe this verse to the Arab poet, Abu 'l-Atahiyah.

meaning the spirit of time and the eternity of graduation [*dahriyyat-i tadrij*] in the abstract worlds. In the gnostic way, the temporal contingency is also proved for all worlds, but not in the same way as referred to by the theologians and the people of *hadith*.

Another Remark

Do know that "praising" [*hamd*] is for a "favor" [*jamil*]. From the noble *ayah* it is deduced that praising and extolment are confirmed for the state of the Greatest Name as the all-embracing Name [*ism-i jami*], which has the state of being the Lord of the worlds, **"the Beneficent," "the Merciful"** and **"the Master of the Day of Judgment."** So, these noble Names, i.e. *"Rabb," "Rahman," "Rahim"* and *"Malik"* should have an effective role in the praising. Later on, we shall explain in details Allah's saying: *"Maliki yawm id-din"* (The Master of the Day of Judgment). Now, we shall talk about the proportionality of the state of Divinity to "praising." It is so from two aspects:

The first is that as the very praiser is a part of the "worlds," or he may even be "a world" by himself, and from the point of view of the people of knowledge, each one of the beings is a world by itself, he praises Allah, for He, with the hand of divine education, has taken him out of weakness, deficiency, fear and the darkness of the mass of non-existence to strength, perfection, security and the luminous world of humanity. He has also taken him past the corporeal, elemental, mineral, vegetable, and animal stations, under a system arranged according to self-and-substantial movements, and the dispositional and natural inclinations, to the station of humanity, which is the most honorable station of beings. Furthermore, He continues to educate him until he becomes what you can never imagine in your fancy.

"Then I become non-existent—
Such non-existence that the organ
Says to me: "Our return is to Him.""[431]

The second is that educating [rearing = *tarbiyat*] the system of the kingdom of the world, such as the celestial spheres, elements, substances and accidentals, is preliminary to the existence of the perfect man, who is, in fact, the product of the juice [*usarah*] of the world of realization and the ultimate end of the beings of the world,

---

[431] Poetry by Mawlawi.

314

and he is, as such, the last product. And, since the visible world moves according to the substantial self-movement, and this is a self-completing movement, wherever it ends, it would be the objective of creation and the end of the journey. If we look in a universal way at the universal body, [*jism-i kull*], universal nature, universal vegetable, universal animal and universal man [*insan-i kull*], we notice that man is the last product who has been created after the substantial self-movements of the world and they have ended in him. So, the educating (rearing) hand of Allah, the Exalted, has been educating (rearing) man in all the world of realization, and man is the first and the last.

That which has been said was about the minor Acts and according to the stages of existence, as otherwise, if taken according to the absolute Act, the Act of Allah, the Exalted, can have no objective except His own Sacred Essence, as is proved in its relevant instances. Should we look at the minor Acts, we would realize that the objective of creating Man is the absolute invisible world, as is stated in the Divine Sayings [*qudsiyyat*]: "O son of Adam! I created all things for you, and I created you for Myself."[432] Allah in the Glorious Quran, addressing Moses, son of Imran (peace be upon him and upon our Prophet and his progeny), says: **"I have made you for Myself."**[433] He also says: **"And I chose you."**[434] So, man is created for Allah and made for His Sacred Essence. From among all the beings man is the chosen and the elect. The destination of his journey is attaining the door of Allah, annihilation in the Essence of Allah, and sticking to the Court of Allah. His return [*maad*] is to Allah, from Allah, in Allah and by Allah. In the Quran He says: **"Surely to Us is their return."**[435] Other creatures return to Allah through Man, or rather their return is to Man, as it is stated in the *Jamiah* invocation, in which some aspects of the states of guardianship are explained. It says: "The return of the creatures is to you and their reckoning is upon you." It also says: "With you Allah opened and with you He closes,"[436] and also in the noble *ayah*: **"Surely to Us is their return, and surely upon Us is their reckoning."**[437] In the said invocation: "The return of the

---

[432] *Ilm al-Yaqin*, vol. 1, p. 381.
[433] *Surah Ta-Ha* 20:41.
[434] *Ibid* 20:13.
[435] *Surah al-Ghashiyah* 88:25.
[436] *Uyunu Akhbar ar-Rida*, vol. 2; *al-Jamiah al-Kabirah* invocation, p. 272.
[437] *Surah al-Ghashiyah* 88:25-26.

creatures is to you and their reckoning is upon you," is one of *tawhid*'s secrets, referring to the fact that to return to the Perfect Man is to return to Allah, as the Perfect Man is absolutely annihilated and lasts by Allah's everlasting, having no individuality, I-ness and selfishness of his own, rather he is of the Beautiful Names and the Greatest Name, to which the Quran and the *hadith*s frequently refer.

The Quran contains such delicate points, facts, secrets, and subtleties about *tawhid* that the minds of the people of knowledge are bewildered, and this is the great inimitability of this heavenly and luminous Book, besides its excellent syntax, graceful expression, wonderful elegance, miraculous style, the way of inviting and foretelling the unseen, perfecting the precepts, controlling and managing the family and the like, each one of which is independently extraordinary and beyond man's power. It can even be said that the Glorious Quran's being distinguished for its eloquence as one of its inimitabilities well-known all over the world was because the early Arabs were famous for their eloquence, and, thus, they could understand only that aspect of the Quran's inimitability. The Arabs of that time could not comprehend its other more important dimensions, which needed a higher degree of understanding. Nowadays, too, those who have a similar level of thinking can comprehend nothing of this divine grace, except its literal elegance, beautiful rhetoric and eloquent expressions. As regards those who are well versed in the secrets of knowledge and the graces of *tawhid* and abstraction, know that what attracts them, and what is the goal of their hopes, in this divine Book and heavenly revelation is only its knowledge [*maarif*], and they are not so much interested in its other aspects. Whoever casts a glance at the Quran's gnosticism, and at the gnostics of Islam who acquired their knowledge from it, and then makes a comparison between them and the scholars of other religions, concerning their works and knowledge, will very well recognize the higher standard of the knowledge of Islam and the Quran, which is the base of the foundation of religion and faith, and the final objective of sending the Messengers and revealing the Books. To believe that this Book is a divine revelation and that its knowledge is divine does not cost him any difficulty.

A Faithful Awakening

Do know that the Sovereignty [*rububiyyat*] of Allah, the Exalted, over the worlds is of two kinds:

The first is the "General Sovereignty," which covers all the beings of the world, and it is the genetic upbringing (education), which takes every being out of the limits of its shortcomings to its suitable perfection, under the control of the Divine Sovereignty. All the natural and substantial developments and the essential and accidental movements and improvements are under the control of the Lord. In short, from the stage of the primary matter till the stage of animality and the gaining of the corporeal and spiritual powers of animality, and the genetic evolution, each one of them testifies that "My Lord is Allah, Glory and Majesty to Him."

The second is the "Legislative Sovereignty," which exclusively belongs to the human species, and the other beings have no share of it. This education is guiding to the roads of salvation, showing the ways to happiness and humanity, and warning against what contradicts them, as explained by the prophets (a). If somebody voluntarily placed himself at the disposal and education of the Lord of the worlds, and was brought up by Him, such that the actions of his organs and powers, external and internal, would not be prompted by his self, but to be divine, in that case he would attain the human perfection, which exclusively belongs to the human species.

Up to the stage of animality, man goes side by side with the other animals. To step out of this stage he will have to choose, on his own free will, one of the only two ways before him: One is the way to the stage (abode) of happiness, which is the Straight Path of the Lord of the worlds: **"My Lord is on the Straight Path."**[438] The other is the way of wretchedness, which is the crooked path of the accursed Satan. Therefore, if he puts the powers and organs of his kingdom at the disposal of the Lord of the worlds to be educated by Him, his heart, which is the sultan of this kingdom, would gradually submit to Him. When the heart becomes a subject to the Lord of the worlds, other soldiers [*junud*] would follow it, and the whole kingdom would be under His education. Then his invisible tongue, which is the shadow [*zill*] of the heart, would be able to say: "My Lord is Allah. Glory and Majesty to Him," in reply to the angels of the world of the grave, who ask him: "Who is your Lord?" And, as such a man has obeyed the

---

[438] *Surah Hud* 11:56.

Messenger of Allah, imitated the Imams of guidance and acted according to the Divine Book, his tongue would be expressive in saying: "Muhammad (*s*) is my Prophet, Ali and his infallible sons are my Imams and the Quran is my Book." But if he did not turn his heart to divinity, and the image of *La ilaha illallah, Muhammadun rasulullah, Aliyyun waliyullah* (There is no god except Allah, Muhammad is the Messenger of Allah and Ali is the friend of Allah) was not engraved on the page of his heart such that to become the portrait of the inside of the soul, and if there was no reciprocal spiritual and moral connection between him and the Quran as to act according to it, thinking about it, remembering and contemplating on it, all his knowledge [*maarif*] would be effaced from his memory when suffering from the agonies of death, the death-sickness, and in the death itself—that monstrous calamity.

My dear! Man, under a typhoid fever and the deterioration of his mental faculties, forgets all his knowledge, except things that have become a second part of his constitution, owing to continual remembrance and close intimacy with them. Should he be inflicted with a serious incident or a dreadful accident, he would be neglecting a lot of his affairs, and the line of forgetfulness would underline his acquired information. So, how about the agonies, sufferings and difficulties of death? What would happen to him then? If the hearing and the heart were not opened, if the heart was not hearing, to instruct him with the necessary beliefs at the time of dying and after it would be of no avail. *Talqin* (reminding the dead of his beliefs) can be useful only to those whose hearts have acquired the true beliefs and whose hearts" ears are usually open, but at the very moments of death agonies they may undergo a fit of forgetfulness, and thus, the *talqin* will be a means for the angels of Allah to convey it to their ears. But if man is deaf, with no hearing ears suitable for the worlds of *barzakh* and the grave, he can never hear the *talqin* and it can benefit him naught. There is a hint at some of these in the noble *hadith*s.

* * * * * * * * * *

Ar-Rahman ir-Rahim (The Beneficent, the Merciful):

Do know that for all the Names and Attributes of Allah, the Most High, there are generally two states [*maqam*] and two ranks [*martabah*]:

One is the state of the Names and Attributes of Essence, which are constant in His Unity [*hadrat-i wahidiyyat*], such as the Essential Knowledge, which is of the Essential affairs and manifestations, and the Essential Power and Will, and other Essential affairs [*shuun-i dhatiyyah*].

The other is the state of the Names and Attributes of Acts, which are confirmed for Allah through the manifestation by the Holy Emanation, such as the "Active Knowledge" [*ilm-i fili*], which the Illuminists regard as confirmed, and on it depends the "Detailed Knowledge" [*ilm-i tafsili*]. The most merited of the wise men, Khajah Nasiruddin (may Allah make his face bright), has proved this, following the opinion of the Illuminists who say that the criterion for the "Detailed Knowledge" is the "Active Knowledge."[439] However, although this subject is contrary to research—because the "Detailed Knowledge" is confirmed for the Essence, and that the exposure and the details of the Essential Knowledge are higher than the "Active Knowledge" and more extensive, as is proved and confirmed, in its relevant place, by a luminous proof—yet, the original question, that the system of the existence is within Allah's Active and Detailed Knowledge, is proved and confirmed according to the tradition of proving and the method of gnosticism, despite the fact that the higher method and the sweeter gnostic taste have, beside such ways, another way: "The lover's religion is other than that of the others."[440]

Generally speaking, for the mercy of "Beneficence" and "Mercifulness," there are two ranks and two manifestations: one is in the appearance of the Essence in His Unity [*hadrat-i wahidiyyat*] through the manifestation of the Holiest Emanation. The other is in the appearance of the cosmic entities [*ayan-i kawniyyah*] through the Holy Emanation. If the *ar-Rahman* and *ar-Rahim*, in the blessed *Surah*, are of the Essential Attributes—as is more obvious—it will be possible to regard them, in *Bismillah ir-Rahman ir-Rahim*, to be related to *"ism"* (Name), rather than Attributes of Act. Consequently, there is no repetition at all that one may claim them to be confirmatory repetition, or exaggeration. Based on this, the meaning of the noble *ayah* will be: With His Beneficent and Merciful will, praise be to His Beneficent and

---

[439] *Masariul- Masari*, by Khajah Nasiruddin, edited by Muizzi, p. 141.
[440] The lover's religion is other than that of the others,
The lovers" religion and creed is Allah. (Mawlawi)

Merciful Essence—Allah knows better. And, as the state of Divine Will is the manifestation of the Sacred Essence, the state of "Beneficence" and "Mercifulness," which is of the determinations [*taayyunat*] of the state of Divine Will, is the display [*jilwah*] of the Essential Beneficence and Mercifulness. There are, however, other possibilities, which we have left out, as the said one is more obvious.

* * * * * * * * * *

Maliki yawm id-din (The Master of the Day of Judgment):
Many of the reciters have read: *maliki,* and there are many literary justifications for both versions, such that even a great scholar (may Allah have mercy upon him) has written a thesis on preferring *malik* to *malik.* But the arguments of both parties are not quite convincing.

That which comes to the writer"s notion is that *malik* is preferable, or rather, particularly assigned, because this blessed *surah* and the blessed *surah* of *at-Tawhid,* are unlike the other *surah*s of the Quran, since these two *surah*s are recited by the people in their obligatory and non-obligatory *salat*s, and in every era hundreds of millions of the Muslims have heard them from hundreds of millions of other Muslims, and these from former hundreds of millions, and so on, by hearing these two noble *surah*s from one another, recited, exactly the same, with no letter advanced and no letter retarded, no letter increased and no letter decreased, by the Imams of guidance and the Messenger of Allah (*s*). Although most of the reciters read it *malik,* and many of the scholars prefer *malik,* yet none of those things damaged this certain, necessary and successively proved fact, and no body imitated them. And although the scholars allowed imitating anyone of the reciters, no one—except the abnormal [*shadhdh*] whose opinion is negligible—necessarily recited *malik* in his *salat*s, or if somebody did recite *malik,* it was as a precaution [*ihtiyat*], besides saying *malik,* too, such as my learned teacher of the traditional science, Haj Shaykh Abd ul-Karim Yazdi (may his grave be sanctified), who used, at the request of some of his contemporary scholars, to recite *malik,* too. Nevertheless, this is too weak a precaution, or, as the writer believes, it is out of question.

The weakness of the said question becomes clear under the saying that in *Kufi* penmanship *malik* and *malik* are mistaken for each other. This claim can be uttered in respect of the *surah*s which are not frequently recited, though still with difficulty, but not in respect of this *surah* which has been confirmed through hearing and reciting, as is quite clear. Such a claim is an empty and incredible one.

This very argument is also true in respect of *kufuwan*, as its recitation with "*w*" [*maftuhah*] and "*f*" [*madmumah*]—which is Asim"s recitation alone—is also confirmed by way of hearing and rehearing, and other recitations do not necessarily contradict that, though some think that they practice precaution by reciting the version of the majority with "*hamzah*" instead of the "*w*"—an irrelevant precaution.

If there can be any argument in respect of the narratives in which we are ordered to recite like the people recite[441]—which actually deserves arguing, as it is believed that these narratives wanted to say: recite as the people, in general, do, not that you are free to choose any one of the "seven recitations," for example—in that case, to recite "*malik*" and "*kufuwan*" other than the way commonly recited by the Muslims and written in the Quran, is incorrect. At any rate, the precaution is their recitation as current among the people and written in the Quran, because that way of recitation is correct to every creed. Allah knows better.[442]

A Philosophic Research

Do know that Allah"s ownership is not the same as the ownership of the servants, nor is it like the kings" ownership of their kingdom, as these are conventional annexations, while annexing the creatures to Allah is not of that kind, although to the jurisprudents this sort of ownership of Allah is longitudinally [*tulan*] confirmed. This, however, does not contradict what has been observed in this respect. Nor does it resemble man"s owning his own organs and limbs, nor his internal and external powers, although this latter ownership is nearer to Allah"s ownership than the aforementioned ones. It is also not like the soul's owning its own self-action, which is of the soul"s affairs, such as creating mental images, whose contractions and expansions arc

---

[441]Such as: "Recite as the people recite" or "Recite as you have learnt." *Wasa'il ash-Shiah*, vol. 4, "The Book of *as-Salat*," ch. on "Recitation in the *Salat*" ch. 74, *hadith*s 1-3, p. 821.

[442] Apparently, recitation according to any one of the ways of the recitations is unanimously agreed upon.

somewhat under the control of the soul"s will, nor is it like the ownership, of the intellectual worlds, of what is of lower ranks, even if they were effective in those worlds through annihilating [*idam*] and creating [*ijad*], for all the beings of the world of possible realization, on whose foreheads the humility of poverty is marked, are bound by limits and restricted by measures, even to the extent of the essence. And whatsoever is bound by a limit is isolated from its act, in proportion to its limitedness, and it enjoys not a true existential inclusiveness [*ihata-i qayyumi*]. Therefore, all things, according to the degree of their own essence, oppose and contradict their passive elements [*munfailat*], and because of this they do not enjoy self-existential inclusiveness [*ihata-i dhatiyya-i qayyumiyyah*].

But concerning the ownership of Allah, the Exalted, which is by illuminative annexation and self-existential inclusiveness, it is the true real self-ownership [*malikiyyat-i dhatiyyah*], in which there is not the least of any defective contradicting isolation in His Essence and Attributes with any one of the beings. The ownership of the Sacred Essence of all the worlds is the same, without treating the beings with discrimination at all, or being nearer to, and more inclusive of, the abstracts and the invisible worlds, than of the other worlds, as otherwise it would require limitation and isolating disunity, accompanied by need and potentiality; High Exalted is Allah, the Great, above all that! A reference to this is perhaps in the saying of Allah, the Exalted: **"And We are nearer to him than you,"**[443] **"And We are nearer to him than his jugular vein,"**[444] **"Allah is the light of the heavens and the earth,"**[445] **"And He it is Who is God in the heaven and God in the earth,"**[446] and **"Allah"s is the kingdom of the heavens and the earth."**[447] The Messenger of Allah (*s*) is quoted to have said: **"If you are lowered down with a rope to the lowest of the earth, you will come down onto Allah."**[448] Imam as-Sadiq (a) is also quoted to have said, as in *al-Kafi*: "No space can confine Him and no space can accommodate Him, and He is no nearer to a place than to

---

[443] *Surah al-Waqiah* 56:85.
[444] *Surah Qaf* 50:16.
[445] *Surah an-Nur* 24:35.
[446] *Surah az-Zukhruf* 43:84.
[447] *Surah al-Baqarah* 2:107.
[448] *Ilm al-Yaqin*, vol. 1, p. 54.

another."[448a] Imam Ali an-Naqi is quoted to have said: "You must know that when Allah is in the lowest heaven He is, at the same time, on the Throne. All things are equally known, controlled, owned and encompassed by Him."[449]

Nevertheless, although the ownership of His Sacred Essence covers all things and all worlds equally, the noble *ayah* says: "**The Owner of the Day of Judgment.**" This specification is probably because the Day of Judgment is the day of gathering. So, the Owner of "The Day of Judgment," which is the day of gathering, is (also) the Owner of the other days which are dispersed, and "the dispersed in the visible world are gathered (collected) in the invisible world."

Or maybe it is because of the appearance of the Ownership and Omnipotence of Allah, Glorified be His Majesty, on the "Day of Gathering," which is the day of the return of the possibles to the threshold of Allah, and the ascension of the beings to the Court of Allah.

Expanding on this brief so as to suit this paper is that as long as the light of existence and the sun of the truth is descending down from the hidden places of invisibility towards the world of visibility, it tends to occultation and being veiled. In other words, in every descent there is a specification [*taayyun*], and in every specification and limitation there is a veil. And as man is the composite [*majma*] of all specifications and limitations, he is veiled with all the seven dark veils and the seven veils of light, which are the seven earths and seven heavens, according to interpretations. Perhaps returning to the "lowest of the low" means being wrapped in all kinds of veils. This occultation of the sun of existence, and the mere light in the horizon of specifications [*taayyunat*] can be described as the "night" and "The Night of the *Qadr*." And as long as man is wrapped in these veils, he is deprived of seeing the Beauty of the Eternity and of eyeing the prime light. When all beings, in their ascending march from the low stations of the world of nature, with the natural movements—which are deposited in their innate constitution from the light of the attraction of the divine disposition, according to the determination [*taqdir*] of the Holiest Emanation in His Knowledge—return to the original homeland

---

[448a] *Usul al-Kafi*, vol., p. 170, "Book of *at-Tawhid*," ch. on "Movement and Mobility," *hadith* 3.
[449] *Ibid.*, *hadith* 4.

and the real place of promise [*miad*]—as is frequently referred to by the noble *ayahs*—they once again get rid of the luminous and dark veils, and the ownership and the sovereignty of Allah, the Exalted, are manifested, and He appears in Unity and Sovereignty. Here, where the Last returns to the First, and the Outside connects to the Inside, and where the rule of the appearance falls and the government of the inside is manifested, the absolute owner addresses—and there is no addressed except His Sacred Essence—**"Whose is the Sovereignty this Day?,** and as there is no answer, He says: **(It is) Allah"s, the One, the Almighty."**[450]

This absolute day, the day when the sun of the truth rises from behind the veil of the horizon of the individuations, is "the Day of Judgment" in a way, since every being, under the shadow [*zill*] of its suitable name, vanishes in Allah. When the Trumpet is blown, it appears from that name and accompanies the followers of that name: **"A group in Paradise and a group in Flaming Fire."**[451]

The perfect man in this world gets out of these veils according to his journey to Allah and migration to Him, and the regulations of the Resurrection, the Hour and the Day of Judgment appear before him and are proved to him. So, Allah, with His Sovereignty, appears to his heart through this *salat* ascension, and his tongue becomes the interpreter of his heart, and his appearance becomes the tongue of his internal seeings. This is one of the secrets of confining the Ownership [*malikiyyat*] to the Day of Judgment.

An Inspiration Concerning the *Arsh*

Do know that concerning the *Arsh* and its carriers there are different opinions. Similarly the noble narratives outwardly differ, too, although inwardly there is no difference, since, according to the gnostic view and demonstrative way, the *Arsh* covers so many meanings.

One of its meanings—which I did not see in the language of "the people" [*qawm*]—is the Unity [*hadrat-i wahidiyyat*], which is on the level of the "Holiest Emanation," and its carriers are four names, of the Great Names: The First, the Last, the Outward and the Inward.

---

[450] *Surah Ghafir* 40:16.
[451] *Surah ash-Shura* 42:7.

324

Another—which also I did not see in the language of "the people" [*qawm*]—is the "Holy Emanation," which is on the level of the Greatest Name, and its carriers are: *ar-Rahman, ar-Rahim, ar-Rabb* and *al-Malik*.

Another one of its concepts is the phrase "all that is other than Allah" [*ma siwallah*] and its carriers are the four angels: Seraphiel, Gabriel, Michael and Izrael.

Another is the "Universal Body" [*jism-i kull*], which is carried by four angels who are the images of the Archetypes [*arbab-i anwa*], as is referred to in *al-Kafi*.[452]

Sometimes it is regarded to be the "Knowledge," which may be Allah's Active Knowledge [*ilm-i fili*] which is the state of the great guardianship [*wilayat-i kubra*] and its carriers are four of Allah's perfect friends from the ancient nations: Noah, Abraham, Moses and Jesus (peace be upon our Prophet, his progeny and upon them), and four persons of the perfect ones of this nation: the Seal of the Prophets, Amir al-Muminin Ali, al-Hasan and al-Husayn (a).

Now, as this introduction has been understood, do know that in the noble *surah* of *al-Hamd* (the Opening), after the name "Allah" that refers to His Essence, the four noble names: *ar-Rabb, ar-Rahman, ar-Rahim,* and *Malik,* are particularly mentioned, maybe because these four noble names are the carriers of the *Arsh* of His Unity [*wahdaniyyat*] in respect of the inside, while their outer appearances are Allah's four favorite angels who are the carriers of the *Arsh* of "Realization" [*tahaqquq*]. So, the blessed name of *ar-Rabb* is the inside [*batin*] of Michael, who, as *ar-Rabb*'s manifestation, is in charge of the provisions and the education in the world of existence. The noble name of *ar-Rahman* is the inside [*batin*] of Seraphiel, who is the caretaker [*munshi*] of the spirits, the blower of the Trumpet and the spreader [*basit*] of the spirits and the images, as the spread [*bast*] of existence is also in the name of *ar-Rahman*. The noble name of *ar-Rahim* is the inside of Gabriel, who is in charge of teaching and perfecting the beings. The noble name of *Malik* is the inside of Izrael, who is in charge of taking [*qabd*] the spirits and images, and of returning the outside [*zahir*] to the inside [*batin*]. So, the blessed *surah*, up to "**The Owner of the Day of Judgment,**" includes the *Arsh* of Unity and the *Arsh* of Realization, with reference to its

---

[452] *Usul al-Kafi*, vol. 1, pp. 131 and 132.

carriers. Thus, the entire circle of existence and the manifestations of the invisible and the visible, which are translated by the Glorious Quran, are mentioned up to this part of the *surah*. This very concept is also entirely covered by the *Bismillah*, which is the Greatest Name. It is also in the "*ba*" [ـب], which is in the position of causality, and in the dot of *bism*, which is the secret of the causality. And, as Ali (a) is the secret of guardianship [*wilayat*] and causality, therefore, it is he who is the dot under the "*ba*" [ـب].[453] That is, the dot under the "*ba*" [ـب] is the translator of the secret of guardianship. Contemplate. The reason for contemplation is the difficulty that is in the *hadith*. And Allah knows better!

A Gnostic Notice

Perhaps giving priority to *ar-Rabb* before stating *ar-Rahman* and *ar-Rahim* and then *Malik* at the end, is a delicate reference to the way of man's journey [*suluk*] from the material mundane creation up to the complete annihilation, or up to the state of the presence before the Master of the kings. So, as the *salik* is still at the beginning of the journey, he is gradually being brought up by *Rabb al-Alamin* (the Lord of the worlds), for he is of the world and his conduct [*suluk*] is under the control of time and graduation. After leaving the transitory world of nature by the steps of his conduct, the stage of the inclusive names, which do not belong only to the world—in which the aspect of "differentiation" is predominant—is established in his heart. And, as the noble name of *ar-Rahman* is more particular than the other inclusive names, it is stated then, and, as it is the manifestation of mercy and the stage of absolute spreading, it precedes *ar-Rahim*, which is nearer to the horizon of the interiority. Hence, in the gnostic conduct, the external names appear first, then after that, the internal names, because the *salik*'s march is from multiplicity [*kathrat*] to singleness [*wahdat*], until he ends up in the purely internal names, including the name of *Malik*. Thus, with the manifestation of Ownership, the multiplicity of the invisible and visible worlds will vanish, and the complete annihilation and Absolute Presence will take place. As he frees himself from the veils of multiplicity with the appearance of unity and Divine Sovereignty, and attains the visual

---

[453] *Al-Asfar al-Arbaah*, vol. 7, p. 32; *Asrar al-Hikam*, p. 559.

witnessing, he converses in presence (with Allah) and says: "**You do we worship.**"

Hence, the whole circle of the travelers'' journey is also contained in the noble *surah*, from the last veils of the world of nature up to the removing of all the dark and luminous veils and attaining the Absolute Presence. This Presence is the *salik*'s great resurrection and the rising of his Hour. In the noble *ayah*: "**...and all who are in the heavens and the earth swoon away, except him whom Allah wills...,**"[454] the exception may be this group of the people of *suluk* who would swoon away and be annihilated before the Trumpet is blown. By saying: "I and the Hour are like these two"[454a] when joining his two forefingers, the Messenger of Allah (*s*) may have referred to this concept.

A Literary Notice

In the current exegeses that we have seen, or which are quoted from, the word "*din*" is said to mean judgment and reckoning. The lexicons give these meanings, too. The Arab poets have also used it so, such as the poet who says: "Beware that you will be judged as you judge," and there is a saying ascribed to Sahl ibn Rabiah stating: "There remained but hostility. We so judged them as they did."[455] It is said that "*dayyan*," which is one of the Divine Names, denotes this very meaning. Perhaps by "*din*" the true religion is intended. And as on the Day of Resurrection the results of the religion appear and the religious facts come out from behind the curtain, for this reason it is called *yawm ud-din* (the Day of Judgment), the same as "today" is called *yawm ud-dunya* (the day of this world or the mundane day) on which appear the results of this world, while the true image of the religion is not apparent. This bears a similar concept of Allah''s saying: "**...and remind them of the days of Allah,**"[456] which are the days in which Allah treats a nation with force and sovereignty.

---

[454] *Surah az-Zumar* 39:68.
[454a] *Al-Ashathiyyat*, p. 212, ch. on "What Necessitates Patience;" *Bihar al-Anwar*, vol. 2, p. 39, "Book of Knowledge," *hadith* 72. From *Majalis* of Shaykh Mufid.
[455] "When evil appeared, in the morning and in the evening, naked,
    And there remained but hostility,
    We so judged them as they did."
Poetry by Sahl ibn Shayban, *Jamiush-Shawahid*, ch. on "F and L," p.185.
[456] *Surah Ibrahim* 14:5.

The Day of Resurrection is a "day of Allah" as well as the "day of religion," since it is the day of the appearance of the Divine Sovereignty and the day of the emergence of the truth of Allah's religion.

* * * * * * * * * *

Iyyaka nabudu wa iyyaka nastain (**You do we worship and You do we seek help from**): Do know, dear, that when the servant, the *salik* on the road of knowledge, understood that all thanks and praises exclusively belong to Allah's Sacred Essence, and attributed to Him contraction [*qabd*] and expansion [*bast*] of the existence, and regarded the reigns of the affairs, at first and at last, the beginning and the end, to be in the grasp of His Ownership, and the Unity of Essence and of Acts manifested in his heart, he would exclusively confine worship and seeking help to Allah, regard the entire world of realization submitting, willingly or unwillingly, to the Sacred Essence, and recognize no able one, in the world of realization, so as to ascribe to him any help. What is claimed by some of the people of formalism that to confine worship [to Allah] is real, but to confine seeking help only to Him is not real—by arguing that the help of other than Allah can also be sought, and it is in the Glorious Quran: **"and help one another in goodness and piety,"**[457] and also: **"and seek help through patience and *salat*,"**[458] and it is known that the conduct of the noble Prophet, the Imams of guidance (a), their companions and the Muslims was based on seeking help from other than Allah in lawful matters, such as getting the help of the beast of mount, the servant, the wife, the friend, the messenger, the worker and the like—is but a talk suitable to the formalists. But the one who has knowledge about the Unity of Acts of Allah, the Exalted, and regards the system of the existence to be a form of the activity of Allah, the Exalted, seeing, either plainly or by rational proof, that there is no effecter in the [world of] existence save Allah, regards, with the eye of insight and luminous heart, confining "seeking help" to be a real confinement, and takes the help of the other beings to be a form of Allah's help. According to what these people say, there is no reason for confining the praises to Allah, the Exalted, since, according to this opinion, other beings also have their behaviors,

---

[457] *Surah al-Ma'idah* 5:2.
[458] *Surah al-Baqarah* 2:45.

328

options, beauty and perfection which deserve praising and thanking. They even say that giving life and death, and providing and creating are some other affairs which are common between Allah and the creatures. The people of Allah regard such matters to be polytheism, and in the narratives they are regarded hidden polytheism, as it is said that [resorting to] turning the ring in the finger to remember something is regarded as a hidden polytheism.[459]

In short, **"You do we worship and You do we seek help from"** is a part of praising Allah, and it is a reference to real monotheism. The one in whose heart the truth of monotheism has not yet appeared, and he has not purged it from polytheism absolutely, his saying **"You do we worship"** would not be real, and he cannot confine his worship and seeking help to Allah, and he would not be a godly man and a theist. When monotheism manifests in his heart, he will, in proportion to the degree of this manifestation, give up all beings and cling to the Might of the Sanctity of Allah to the extent he sees that **"You do we worship and You do we seek help from"** takes place by the name of Allah; and some facts of **"You are as You praised Yourself"**[459a] manifest in his heart.

An Illuminative Notice

The point of changing from the 3rd person to the 2nd has become clear from the statements of this thesis. Although in itself it is one of the ornaments of speech and the characteristics of rhetorics, frequently seen in the speeches of the eloquent orators, and is a decoration to the speeches, and, at the same time, by changing from one mood to another, one removes the addressee's boredom and gives a fresh vividity to his spirit, yet, as the *salat* is the ascension for reaching the presence of Holiness, and the ladder to the state of intimacy, this noble *surah* gives the order to start the spiritual ascension and the gnostic journey. The servant, at the beginning of the travel to Allah, is imprisoned and wrapped in the dark veils of the world of nature and in the luminous ones of the invisible world, while

---

[459] Abu Abdullah as-Sadiq (a) said: "The (hidden) polytheism is stealthier than the crawling of the ants." He also said: "... of it is (resorting to) turning the ring to remember a thing, and the like." *Maaniy ul-Akhbar*, p. 379, ch. on "Rare Meanings," *hadith* 1; *Bihar al-Anwar*, vol. 69, p. 96.
[459a] Refer to footnote 219.

the travel to Allah is getting out of these veils by the steps of spiritual conduct. Actually, migration to Allah is turning away from the house of self and from the house of creation to Allah, leaving multiplicities, rejecting the dust of otherness and attaining the Unities [*tawhidat*]. It is absence from creation and presence before the Lord. When in the noble *ayah* **"Owner of the Day of Judgment"** he finds that multiplicity disappears under the shining light of the Ownership and Omnipotence, he experiences a state of effacement from multiplicity and being present before Allah, the Exalted, and, by personally conversing and witnessing the Beauty and Majesty, he offers himself to servitude, and presents his quest for Allah and his piety to the Sacred Presence and the meeting of intimacy.

The fact that the pronoun *iyyaka* is used for this purpose is because this pronoun returns to the Essence in which multiplicity is vanished. So, the *salik* in this situation may have a mood of Unity of Essence, turning away from the multiplicity of names and attributes, and the heart turns towards the Essence that is free from the veils of multiplicity. This is the perfect monotheism which was referred to by the Imam of the monotheists, the head of the gnostics, the leader of the lovers, the pioneer of the attracted and the beloved, Amir al-Muminin [Ali], may Allah bless him and his infallible offspring, who said: "The perfect monotheism is the negation of ascribing attribute to Him,"[460] as an attribute denotes otherness [*ghayriyyat*] and plurality [*kathrat*], while this inclination, though to the plurality of Names, is far from the secrets of monotheism and the facts of abstraction. Thus, probably, the secret of Adam''s sin was inclination towards the plurality of Names, which was the spirit of the forbidden tree.

A Gnostic Inquiry

Be informed that the literalists show some opinions in respect of "*nabudu*" (we worship) and "*nastain*" (we seek help), concerning their being in the first person plural number, whereas the speaker is actually a single person.

They say that, in this connection, a lawful trick has occurred to the worshipper in order to have his worship accepted by Allah, the Exalted. By using a plural pronoun he places his worship among the

---

[460] *Usul al-Kafi*, vol. 1, p. 191, "Book of Monotheism," ch. on "General *Hadiths* on Monotheism," *hadith* 6.

worshipping of other creatures, among whom, of course, are the perfect ones of Allah's friends whose worship is accepted by Allah, the Exalted, and presents it to the threshold of Holiness and the Court of Mercy, making sure that his worship will, implicitly, be accepted, since it is not of the custom of the Generous to discriminate in the deal.

They also say that as the *salat* was imposed first in congregation, so it came in the plural.

Talking about the general secret of the *adhan* and the *iqamah* we stated a point from which this secret can be recognized to some extent. That is, the *adhan* is proclaiming that the visible and invisible powers of the *salik* are ready to be present in His Presence, and the *iqamah* is to have them stand upright before Him. When the *salik* prepared his visible and invisible powers to be present in the Presence, and the heart, which is their leader, stood upright as their Imam, then the *salat* has been started and "The believer alone is a congregation."[461] So, "*nabudu, nastain* and *ihdina*" ("We worship," "we seek help" and "guide us"), all would be performed by this congregation in the Holy Presence. In the narrations and the invocations of the pure infallible *Ahl al-Bayt* (a) who are the source of gnosticism and divine vision, there is a reference to this concept.

Another opinion which occurs to the writer is that the *salik* regards all the praises and thanks from every praiser and thanker, in the visible and invisible worlds, to be exclusively confined to the Holy Essence of Allah. It is also clearly proved in the proofs of the Imams of proofs, and in the hearts of the gnostics that all the beings in the circle of the existence—worldly and heavenly, big and small—have the life of sensibility and understanding of animality, or rather of humanity, and they praise and glorify Allah, the Exalted, rationally and consciously. It is fixed in the nature [*fitrat*] of all beings, the human species in particular, to submit to the Holy Presence of the Perfect and the Absolute Beautiful, and their foreheads are on the dust of His Holy Threshold, as is stated in the Glorious Quran: "**...and there is not a single thing but glorifies Him, but you do not understand their glorification.**"[462] Other noble *ayah*s, and narratives

---

[461] *Wasa'il ash-Shiah*, vol. 5, p. 379, "Book of *as-Salat*," sec. on "Congregational *Salat*," ch. 4, *hadith*s 2 and 5.
[462] *Surah al-Isra"* 17:44.

x

of the infallibles, which are full of this divine grace, support this fixed judging proof. So, if the traveler to Allah could find this truth through argumentative reasoning, faithful taste or gnostic vision, he would realize, whatever position he is in, that all the particles of the existence and the dwellers of the invisible and visible worlds, worship the Absolute Worshipped and seek their Creator. Thus, the plural form [of the pronoun] is used because all beings, in all their movements and stillness, worship the Sacred Essence of Allah, the Exalted, and seek His help.

A Notice and a Point

Know that the reason for giving priority to *iyyaka nabudu* over *iyyaka nastain*—despite the usual custom that seeking help for worship comes before worship—is that "worship" is prior to "seeking help," not to "helping." Sometimes "helping" happens without "seeking help." Also they say that, as these two are related to each other, advancing or retarding can make no difference, as it is said: "You did observe my due, so, you did me good." or "You did me good, so you did observe my due." Furthermore, seeking help is for future worship, not for present worship. The dullness of these opinions is not concealed from the people of taste [*ahl-i dhawq*].

Maybe the point is that confining "seeking help" to Allah, the Exalted, comes, according to the state of the travel to Allah, later than confining "worship" to Him. It is quite obvious that a good number of the monotheists in worship, who confine "worship" to Allah, are polytheists in "seeking help" and do not confine it to Allah, as we have already quoted some exegetes who believe that confining "seeking help" to Allah is not real. So, confining "worship" to Allah, in its conventional concept, is of the first states of the monotheists, and confining "seeking help" is an absolute rejection of other than Allah.

It should not be hidden, however, that "seeking help" does not mean to "seek help" only in worshipping, but in all affairs, and this is after rejecting the means and neglecting multiplicities, and completely turning to Allah. In other words, confining "worship" is seeking Allah, wanting Him and giving up turning to other than Him. And confining "seeking help" is seeing Him, and giving up seeing other than Him. This "giving up seeing other than Him" comes, according to the stations of the gnostics and the stages of the *salik*s, later than "giving up seeking other than Him."

A Gnostic Advantage

O traveling servant, know that confining "worship" and "seeking help" to Allah is also not of the states of the monotheists and perfect stages of the *salik*s, because it implies a claim contrary to monotheism and abstraction. They even believe that seeing worship, worshipper, worshipped, help-seeker, and the one whose help is sought, and seeking help are contrary to monotheism. In the real monotheism, which appears in the heart of the *salik*, such multiplicities vanish, and seeing such affairs is effaced. Yes, those who have come to themselves from the invisible attraction and have attained sobriety, multiplicity does not form a veil for them, because people are of many groups:

A group consists of the veiled, such as we, the helpless, who are wrapped in the dark veils of nature.

Another group consists of the *salik*s, the travelers to Allah, the emigrants to the Court of Holiness.

A third group consists of the united [*wasilan*], who have come out of the veils of multiplicity and have been engaged with Allah, neglecting all creatures and veiled against them, as they have undergone a complete swoon and an absolute annihilation.

Another group consists of those who have come back to the creatures, and who have the post of completers and guides, such as the great prophets and their successors (a). Although they are among multiplicity and in charge of guiding the people, multiplicity does not veil them, but it forms an isthmus-like state for them.

Consequently, "*iyyaka nabudu wa iyyaka nastain*" has different implications in respect of the different groups mentioned above. To us, the veiled, it is a mere allegation and an image. But if we become aware of our veil and recognize our shortcoming, our worship becomes more luminous in proportion to the degree of our awareness of our shortcoming, and becomes, accordingly, accepted by Allah, the Exalted. To the *salik*s, it is nearer to the truth in proportion to the traveling step. To the united [*wasilan*], in respect of seeing Allah, it is the truth, and, in respect of seeing multiplicity, it is a mere image and a customary act. To the perfect ones, it is mere truth, and so, they have veil neither against Allah nor against the creatures.

A Faithful Awakening

Do know, dear, that as long as we are in this heavy veil of the world of nature, spending our life on colonizing the world and its pleasures, and being negligent of Allah, the Exalted, of remembering Him and of thinking about Him, all our worshippings, invocations and recitations will contain no truth—neither in *al-hamdu lillah* (praise is for Allah) we can confine praises to Allah, nor in *iyyaka nabudu wa iyyaka nastain* can we find a way to the truth. With these empty claims in the presence of Allah, the Exalted, the favorite angels, the messenger prophets and the infallible guardians, we will be disgraced and humiliated. The one whose tongue of state and speech never stops praising the people of this world, how can he say, "**All praise is for Allah?**" The one whose heart is inclined to nature, and is empty of any divine scent, and whose dependence is on the people, with which tongue can he utter: "**You do we worship and You do we seek help from.**" So, if you are the man for this field, then tuck up the skirt of determination, and, with intense remembrance and contemplation of Allah"s Greatness, and of the creatures" humiliation, inability and poverty, try first to convey the facts and the delicate matters mentioned in this thesis, to your heart, and enliven your heart by remembering Allah, the Exalted, so as to bring to your heart"s sense of smell a scent of monotheism, and, with the help of the Unseen, to find a passage to the *salat* of the people of knowledge. If you are not the man for this field, at least you are to continually remember your faults, pay attention to your humility and inability, perform your duties out of shame and disgrace, and avoid claiming servitude. And these noble *ayah*s, with whose graces you are not acquainted, recite them either through the tongues of the perfect ones, or consider yourself merely reciting the form of the Quran, so that, at least, you may not claim a false allegation.

A Juristic Branch

Some jurisprudents see that it is not allowed to intend composition [*insha*] in sentences like *iyyaka nabudu wa iyyaka nastain*, thinking that it would be a contradiction to the Quran and reciting it, since recitation is relating the words of someone else. This talk has no justification, because as one can praise someone with his own words, he can use somebody else"s words for the purpose. For example, if we praised somebody using Hafiz"s poetry , it would be true that we have praised the intended person, and it would also be true that we have recited Hafiz"s poetry. So, if we, by saying **"All praise is for Allah, the Lord of the worlds,"** actually compose all the praises for Allah, and by saying **"You do we worship"** we compose the confinement of worship to Allah, it will come true that with Allah's words we have praised Him, and with Allah's words we have confined worship to Him. But if somebody emptied the words from their compositional meaning, he would be acting contrary to precaution, if not to say his reciting would be *batil* (invalid). However, if someone did not know it, it would not be necessary for him to learn it, as the formal reciting with its own meaning would do.

Some of the noble narratives refer to the fact that the reciter composes, as is in the *Hadith Qudsi*: "When he [the servant] says in his *salat*: **"In the Name of Allah, the Beneficent, the Merciful,"** Allah says: "My servant remembered Me", and when he says: **"All praise is for Allah,"** Allah says: "My servant praised Me"...etc.[463] If the *"bismillah"* and "praising" were not composed by the servant, "remembered Me" and "praised Me" would have no meaning. In the *hadiths* of *Miraj* it is said: "Now that you have arrived, recite My Name"[464] [i.e. say the *bismillah*]. From the moods of the Imams of guidance (a) on reciting "The Owner of the Day of Judgment," and "You do we worship," and from their repeating these *ayahs*, it is clear that they were composing, not merely reciting, like: Ismail testifies that there is no god but Allah.[465]

One of the important differences of the ranks of the *salat* of godly people is due to this very difference in their recitation, as we have already referred to some of it. This, however, would not come about unless the reciter was intending the composition in his recitations and remembrances. Evidences proving this are much more than this. In short, composing these concepts by the divine words is not objectionable.

---

[463] *Bihar al-Anwar,* vol. 92, p. 226. Muslim's *Sahih,* vol 2, p. 92, with a slight difference in words.

[464] *Ilal ush-Shara'i,* p. 315, of the *hadith* "The *Salat* of *al-Miraj.*"

[465] This is a sentence which, according to narration, Imam as-Sadiq (a) wrote on the shroud of his deceased son. It is said that a group of the Muslims, called the *Akhbaris,* who used to literally apply the texts of the *akhbar* [*hadiths*], used to write this very sentence on the shrouds of their deceased. *Wasa'il ash-Shiah,* "Book of Purity," sec. on "Shrouding," ch. 29, *hadith* 2.

An Advantage

The linguists say that "worship" means utmost submission and humbleness. They also say that since worshipping is the highest degree of submission, it does not befit except the one who is at the highest degree of existence and perfection, and the greatest of the degrees of grace and benevolence, and as such, worshipping other than Allah is polytheism. Probably, "worshipping"—which in the Persian language means "adoration" and "servitude"—actually implies more than that which has been said, i.e. it is submission to the Creator and the Lord. It follows that such a submission is inseparable from taking the worshipped to be the Diety and Lord, or for example, His semblance and manifestation. Consequently, worshipping other than Allah is polytheism and disbelief. However, absolute submission, without this belief or deciding this meaning, even reluctantly, and even if it reached the utmost submission, would not be a reason for disbelief and polytheism, although some kinds of it are regarded to be *haram* such as placing the forehead on the dust by way of submission; though this is not worshipping, but it is apparently religiously prohibited. Therefore, the homage paid by the followers of a religion to their religious leaders, believing that they, too, are servants in need of Allah, the Exalted, for everything—for the existence itself and for its perfection—and that they are good servants who, although can have no advantage, harm, life and death for themselves, are, through their servitude, in the proximity of the Court of Allah, the Exalted, and subject to His care, and a means of His grants, cannot be mixed with any blemish of polytheism and disbelief. To respect the favorites of Allah is to respect Him, and "To love Allah's elects is to Love Allah."

Among the groups of "I call Allah to witness, and Allah is sufficient as a witness," the group that is—by the blessing of *Ahl al-Bayt* of revelation and infallibility, the resources of knowledge and wisdom—more excellent in unifying, glorifying and exalting Allah, the Most High, than all other groups of humanity, is the group of the 12-Imam *Shiah*s. Their books of the principles of belief—such as the honorable book of *al-Kafi*, and the honorable book of *at-Tawhid* by ash-Shaykh as-Saduq (may Allah be pleased with him)—and speeches and invocations of their infallible Imams, which, in unifying and glorifying Allah, the Most High, are the issues of the said resources of revelation and inspiration, testify that such sciences were unprecedented among humanity, and that no one has glorified and exalted Allah, the Most High, like them, after the holy revelation of the Divine Sacred Book, the Glorious Quran, which is written by the hand of the Omnipotent.

Despite the fact that the *Shiah*s, in all countries and times have been following those infallible, pure and monotheist Imams of guidance, and through their explicit reasoning and proofs they have known Allah, and glorified and unified Him, yet, some groups, whose heresy is quite clear in their beliefs and books, opened the door of contestation and abuse against them, and, owing to the inner hostility which they had, accused the followers of the infallible *Ahl al-Bayt* of polytheism and disbelief. Although, in the market of knowledge and philosophy, this is worthless, yet its corrupting effect is that the incomplete people and the ignorant and the common, may be driven away from the sources of knowledge towards ignorance and wretchedness. This is a grave crime against humanity which is never retrievable. Concerning this subject, and according to rational and religious criteria, the responsibility of the crime and the sin of this defective, ignorant and helpless group is to be upon the conscience of the unfair who, for their imagined transitory interests prevented the spread of the divine knowledge and precepts, and were the cause of the wretchedness and the adversity of the human species, and rendered all the painful efforts of "the best of men" [*khayr al-bashar*] lost and nill, closing the door of the House of Revelation and the Quran in the face of the people. "O Allah, curse them an intense cursing and torture them a painful torment."

"Guide us to the straight path," etc.

Do know, dear, that there is a reference in the noble *surah* of *al-Hamd* (the Opening) to the conduct of the people of knowledge and austerity, and up to **"You do we worship"** it covers the complete journey from creation up to Allah. When the *salik* proceeds from the Manifestations of Acts to the Manifestations of Attributes, and thence to the Manifestations of Essence, and comes out from the luminous and dark veils, and attains the state of presence and witnessing, there happens complete annihilation and full consumption [*istihlak-i kulli*]. When the journey to Allah ends by the setting of the horizon of servitude and the rise of the sovereignty of ownership in the **"Owner of the Day of Judgment,"** at the end of this *suluk* there takes place a state of establishment and stability, and the *salik* comes to himself, and becomes sober and attentive to his own state, but as a result of being attentive to Allah. This is contrary to the state of returning [*ruju*] to Allah, for attending to Allah was a result of attending to the creatures. In other words, during the journey to Allah he used to see Allah in the veil of creation, and after returning from the state of complete annihilation, which takes place in the **"Owner of the Day of Judgment,"** he sees the creation in the light of Allah, and thus, he says: **"You do we worship"** giving priority to the object, the addressee, over himself and his worship. And, as in this position there may be no stability, and slipping can be imagined, he demands his stability and firmness from Allah, the Exalted, and says: **"Guide us"** which means: make us firm, as was explained.

It must be noted that the said position and the said explanation are for the perfect ones of the people of knowledge. Their first state is that in the state of returning from the journey to Allah, He, the Exalted, becomes their veil against the creation. And their state of perfection is the state of great *barzakh* (isthmus), in which neither the creation becomes the veil against Allah, such as we, the veiled, nor Allah becomes the veil against creation, such as the eager united, and the attracted annihilated. So, their **"Straight path"** is this isthmus situation, in the middle between the two creations (worlds) [*nashatayn*], and it is the path of Allah. Therefore, **"those upon whom You have bestowed favors"** are the ones whose aptitude [*istidad*] has been established by Allah, the Exalted, through the manifestation of the "Holiest Emanation" in His knowledge [*hadrat-i ilmiyyah*], and, after complete annihilation, He has returned them to their kingdom. **"Those inflicted by wrath,"** according to this exegesis, are those who are veiled before the union [*wusul*], and **"Those who have gone astray"** are those who have vanished in the Presence [*hadrat*].

As regards the imperfect ones, if they have not yet started their *suluk*, these matters will not come true in their respect, and their "path" is the apparent religious form. For this reason **"the straight path"** is interpreted to mean "religion," "Islam" and the like. If they are of the people of *suluk*, by "guidance" they mean "showing the way," and by **"the straight path"** they mean the shortest way of reaching Allah, which is the way of the Messenger of Allah (*s*) and *Ahl al-Bayt* (a), as the exegetes say that it means the Messenger of Allah, the Imams of guidance and Amir al-Muminin [Ali] (a). In a *hadith* it is said that the Messenger of Allah (*s*) once drew a straight line in the middle and other lines at its sides and said: "This middle straight line is from me."[466] The expression "a middle nation" in the noble *ayah* **"We have made you a middle nation,"**[467] probably means an absolute middle covering all meanings, including the middle in knowledge and spiritual perfections, which is an isthmus big position and a great middle. For this reason this station belongs to the perfect ones of Allah''s friends. That is why it is in the narrative that by this the Imams of guidance (a) are intended, as Imam al-Baqir (a) says to Yazid ibn Muawiyah al-Ijli: "We are the middle nation and we are the witnesses of Allah over mankind."[468] In another narrative, he also says: "To us returns the extravagant [*ghali*] and to us refers the negligent [*muqassir*],"[469] in which *hadith* there is a reference to what has been said.

An Illuminative Notice and A Gnostic Illumination

Do know, you who are in quest of Allah and truth, that when Allah, the Exalted, created the system of the existence and the demonstrations [*mazahir*] of the invisible and the visible, owing to His Essential love to be known in the Names and Attributes, according to the noble *hadith*: "I was a Hidden Treasure, then I liked to be known, so I created the creatures to become known,"[469a] He devised a natural love and innovated an inborn longing in the dispositions of all beings, so that by that divine attraction and godly fire of love they may be driven to go in quest of the Absolute Perfection and to long for the Absolute Beautiful. For each one of them He assigned a divine inborn light with which they may find the way to the destination and the objective. These fire and light, the one is the *rafraf* of arrival [*wusul*], and the other the *buraq* of ascension—both were the heavenly mounts of the Messenger of Allah (*s*). Perhaps the "*buraq*" and the "*rafraf*" of the Messenger of Allah (*s*) were the means [*raqiqah*] of this grace [*latifah*] and the corresponding worldly image [*surat-i mutamaththila-i mulkiyyah*] of this truth, and that is why they were sent down from Paradise, which is the *batin* (interior, core) of this world.

---

[466] A nearly similar narrative is related in *Ilm al-Yaqin*, vol. 2, p. 967.

[467] *Surah al-Baqarah* 2:143.

[468] *Usul al-Kafi*, vol. 1, p. 270, "The Book of Divine Proof", ch. "The Imams are the Witnesses of Allah over His Creatures," *hadith* 2.

[469] *Al-Ayyashi's Exegesis*, vol. 1, p. 63, *hadith* 111.

[469a] *Asrar al-Hikam*, p. 20.

As the beings have descended in ranks of individuations and have been veiled from the Beautiful Beauty of the Beloved, Glorified His Greatness, Allah, the Exalted, takes them out of the dark veils of individuations and the luminous I-nesses, by the said fire and light and by the blessed name of "the Guide," which is the reality of these means [*raqayiq*], so that they may reach the proximity of their Beloved, their Real Objective, through the shortest way. Thus, that light is "the guidance" of Allah, the Exalted, and that fire is the divine "assistance" and the journey is on the shortest path which is the **"straight path,"** since Allah, the Exalted, is on that **"straight path."** It is probably a reference to this guidance, journey and destination that the *ayah* says: **"There is no living creature but He holds it by its forelock, surely my Lord is on the straight path,"**[470] as it is clear to the people of knowledge.

It must be noted that every being has its own path, light and guidance: "The ways to Allah are as many as the breaths of the creatures."[471] And, as in every individuation [*taayyun*] there is a veil of darkness, and in every being and I-ness there is a luminous veil, and as Man is the meeting place [*majma*] of the phenomena [*taayyunat*] and the collector of entities [*jami-i wujudat*], he is the most veiled of the beings from Allah, the Exalted. The noble *ayah*: **"Then We reduced him to the lowest of the low"**[472] is probably a reference to this point. For this reason, the path of mankind is the longest and darkest of all paths. And, as Man''s "Lord" is the Greatest Name of Allah, to Whom the external, the internal, the first, the last, mercy, might, and generally, the counter names, all are the same, Man, himself, has to go through the big isthmus stage at the end of his journey, and this is the reason why his "path" is the most delicate of all paths.

A Faithful Notice

As has been said and is known, there are stages and degrees for guidance in respect of the kinds of the journeys of the travelers to Allah and the stages of the *suluk*s of the *salik*s. We shall briefly refer

---

[470] *Surah Hud* 11:56.
[471] A *hadith* ascribed to the Messenger of Allah (*s*). Sayyid HaydarAmuli, *Jami ul-Asrar wa Manba ul-Anwar*, pp. 8, 95 and 121; Lahiji's *Commentary on Gulshan-i Raz*, p. 153; *Naqd an-Nusus*, p. 185; *Minhaj ut-Talibin*, p. 221; *Al-Usul al-Asharah*, p. 31.
[472] *Surah at-Tin* 95:5.

to some of those stages, so that, meanwhile, the **"straight path,"** the "path of the immoderates" [*sirat-i mufritin*] and the "path of the extravagants" [*sirat-i mufarritin*], who are those who have been "inflicted by wrath" and those who have "gone astray," can be distinguished according to each one of the stages.

First is that the light of guidance is inherent, as has already been said in the former "notice." In this stage of guidance, the **"straight path"** is the *suluk* to Allah without there being any visible or invisible veil, or it is the *suluk* to Allah without being veiled with body or heart sins, or it is the *suluk* to Allah without extravagance [*ghuluww*] or negligence [*taqsir*], or it is the *suluk* to Allah without being veiled with luminous or dark veils, or it is the *suluk* to Allah without the veils of unity or multiplicity. Probably the *ayah*: **"He causes whom He wills to go astray, and guides whom He wills"**[473] is a hint at this stage of guidance and veilings ordained in the Fate [*hadrat-i qadar*], which, to us, is the stage of Unity [*wahidiyyat*] manifested in the immutable essences [*hadarat-i ayan-i thabitah*]. Yet, to expand upon this subject is out of the scope of this paper, or it is even beyond the limits of writing it down: "It is one of Allah"s secrets and one of Allah"s covers."[474]

Second is guidance by the light of the Quran, and on its counter side is extravagance or negligence in knowing it, or stopping at its exterior or its interior, as some of the formalists believe that the Quranic Sciences are the very conventional and common meanings and the vulgar and positive concepts, and, on the basis of this belief, they do not meditate upon the Quran or contemplate it. Their advantage from this luminous Book—which undertakes man"s spiritual, bodily, heart and formal happinesses—is confined only to its formal and external instructions. They disregard all those *ayah*s which enjoin, or recommend, contemplating and remembering the Quran and making use of the light of it, by which many doors of knowledge can be opened. It seems as if the Quran has been revealed only to invite to the worldly pleasures and animal needs, and just to confirm the station of bestial desires.

---

[473] *Surah an-Nahl* 16:23 and *Surah al-Fatir* 35:8.
[474] Ascribed to Amir al-Mu'minin [Ali] (a). *At-Tawhid*, p. 383, ch. on "Fatalism," *hadith* 32.

Some of the Esoterics [*ahl-i batin*] think that they should turn away from the external meaning of the Quran and its formal calls—which are the instructions of observing the disciplines of being in the divine presence and how to travel to Allah, of which they are unaware. They deviate from the exterior of the Quran, deceived by the tricks of the accursed *Iblis* and the evil-commanding soul, believing themselves to be adherent to its internal sciences, despite the fact that the way to the internal passes through observing the disciplines of the external.

These two groups are, at any rate, out of moderation and are deprived of the light of guidance to the Quranic straight path, and are ascribed to extremism on both sides. The researching scholars and the learned scrutinizers should consider both the exterior and the interior and observe the formal and the spiritual disciplines, lighting the external with the light of the Quran, and the internal with the lights of knowledge, monotheism and abstraction.

Let the people of literalism [*ahl-i zahir*] know that to confine the Quran to the disciplines of the external forms and a handful of practical moral instructions and common beliefs about *tawhid,* Names and Attributes, is unobserving the Quran"s due respect, and regarding the *Shariah* of the Seal of the Prophets (*s*) as imperfect, whereas no *Shariah* should be thought to be more perfect than that, as otherwise being the "Seal" would be impossible according to the criterion of justice. So, as the Islamic Law is the Seal of the divine Laws, and as the Quran is the Seal of the revealed Books, and the last connection between the Creator and the creatures, the facts of *tawhid*, abstraction and divine knowledge, which are the original objective and the essential aim of the divine religions, laws and the revealed Books, should represent the last of the stages and the utmost peak of perfection, or else, there must necessarily be a shortcoming in the Law, in which case, it would be contrary to the divine justness and the Lord"s kindness, which, in itself, is a dishonorable impossibility and an ugly disgrace, which cannot be washed off the true religions by the seven seas—we take refuge in Allah from that!

Let the Esoterics [*ahl-i batin*] know that to reach the original objective, the real end, is nothing but purifying the outside and the inside, and without holding to the outer form and the outside one cannot get to the inside. Without wearing the apparel of the outer form of the *Shariah*, the way to the inside cannot be found. So, neglecting the outside means invalidating both the outside and the inside of the divine Law. This is one of the tricks of the Satans of the *Jinn* and *Ins*. We have explained some aspects of this point in our book *"Explanations of Forty Hadiths,"* as said before.

Third is guidance by the light of the *Shariah*.
Fourth is guidance by the light of Islam.
Fifth is guidance by the light of faith.
Sixth is guidance by the light of certainty.
Seventh is guidance by the light of knowledge [*irfan*].
Eighth is guidance by the light of love [*muhabbat*].
Ninth is guidance by the light of guardianship.
Tenth is guidance by the light of abstraction and monotheism.

Each one of these has the extremes of excessiveness [*ifrat*] and shortcomings [*tafrit*], exaggeration [*ghuluww*] and negligence [*taqsir*]. To go into details would make it lengthy. The noble *hadith* in *al-Kafi* may be a hint at a part, or all, of it. It says: "...We, the offspring of Muhammad, are the moderate type. The extremist [*ghali*] would not perceive us, and the follower [*tali*] would not outstrip us."[475] In a *hadith* from the Prophet (s), it is said: The best of this *Ummah* is the moderate type, with whom the followers catch up, and to whom the extremists return.[476]

A Gnostic Notice

Know that for every being of the invisible and visible worlds, and of this world and the Hereafter, there is a beginning [*mabda*] and a destination [*maad*]. Although the divine Ipseity [*huwiyyat*] is the beginning and the destination [*marja*] of all [beings], the Holy Essence of Allah, the Most High, as He is, would not manifest to the high and low beings without the veil of Names. According to this state, which is a no-state [*lamaqami*] that has no name and no form, and is not qualified with the Names of Essence, of Attributes and of Acts, no creature has any relation with Him, nor any connection and mixing: "How can there be any comparison between dust and the Lord of the Lords!"[476a]—the details of this have been mentioned in our *Misbah al-*

[475] *Usul al-Kafi*, vol. 1, p. 136, "Book of Monotheism," ch. on "Forbidding any Attribute...," *hadith 3*.
[476] *Lisan al-Arab*, entry *"namat"*, vol. 7, p. 417, quoting Imam Ali (a).
[476a] Afif Usayran, the editor of the book, "Preliminaries" of *Ayn al-Qudat*, on page 276 of that book, has put it as a *hadith. Asrar al-Hikam* by Sabzewari, p. 23.

Hidayah. So, the firstness [*mabdaiyyat*] and the originality [*masdariyyat*] of His Sacred Essence are in the veils of Names, and as the Name is the very Named itself, it is, at the same time, its veil, too. Therefore, manifestation in the invisible and visible worlds is according to the Names and is veiled by them. For this reason, His Sacred Essence has, in the display [*jilwah*] of the Names and Attributes, manifestations in His Knowledge [*hadrat-i ilmiyyah*], whose individuals the people of knowledge call "the fixed entities" (figures emblematic of the Names of Allah = *ayan-i thabitah*]. Consequently, each nominal manifestation [*tajalli*] in His Knowledge requires a fixed entity, and each Name has, by the determination [*taayyun*] of His Knowledge, in the outer world, an appearance [*mazhar*] whose origin and end are the same Name which is suitable for it; and the return of every being from the world of multiplicity to the invisibility of the Name which is its origin and beginning, is its "straight path." So, every one [of the beings] has a special journey and a special path, as well as a predestined beginning and end, in His Knowledge, willingly or unwillingly. The difference of the appearances [*mazahir*] and paths is due to the difference of the apparent [*zahir*] and the Names.

It must be noted that man's "stature" [*taqwim*] in the highest of the high [*ala illiyyin*] is the collection of Names [*jam-i asmai*]. For this reason he is reduced to the lowest of the low [*asfal-i safilin*], and his "path" starts from the lowest of the low and ends up in the highest of the high. It is the path of those who are favored by Allah with an absolute favor [*nimat*], the favor of the perfect collection of the Names, which is the highest of the divine favors. Other paths, whether the paths of the happy [*suada*] and the "favored ones" [*munamun alayhim*], or the paths of the wretched [*ashqiya*], stand at either end of extravagance or negligence [*tafrit*], in proportion to how much they lack of the emanation of the Absolute Favor. So, the path of the perfect man alone is that of those who have been absolutely favored. This path originally is assigned to the holy person of the Seal of the Prophets (*s*), and, concomitantly [*bittaba iyyah*], it is confirmed for other holy men [*awliya*] and prophets. To understand this talk, and [its connection with] the fact that the generous Prophet is the Last Prophet, one needs the understanding of the "Names" and the "Entities" [*ayan*], explained in the book *Misbah al-Hidayah.* Allah is the guide to the way of uprightness.

Quotings for Further Information

The dignified Shaykh Bahai (may Allah sanctify his soul), in his *al-Urwat al-Wuthqa*, says: "Although the favors of Allah are too numerous to be numbered by counting, as Allah says: **"And if you count Allah"s favors, you will not be able to number them,"**[477] yet, they are of two kinds: the mundane favors and the favors of the Hereafter. Each one of them is either natural or acquired, and each one of them is either spiritual or corporeal. So, they are, all in all, eight kinds:

First: mundane, natural and spiritual, such as the blowing of the spirit and the emanation of the intellect and comprehension.

Second: mundane, natural and corporeal, such as the creation of the organs and their powers.

Third: mundane, acquired and spiritual, such as emptying the self from low affairs, and adorning it with pure morals and high faculties.

Fourth: mundane, acquired and corporeal, such as decorating [the body] with laudable forms and good ornaments.

Fifth: of the Hereafter, natural and spiritual, such as His forgiving the sins of us, and His being pleased with those of us who have already repented. This is the exact text of the Shaykh in this example. It seems that it is a mistake on the part of the copier. Probably he meant to say that Allah, the Exalted, may forgive us without first repenting. Refer to it.

Sixth: of the Hereafter, natural and corporeal, such as rivers of milk and honey.

Seventh: of the Hereafter, acquired and spiritual, such as forgiveness and pleasure [of Allah] preceded by repentance, and as the spiritual pleasure which is concomitant to acts of worship.

Eighth: of the Hereafter, acquired and corporeal, such as the bodily pleasures which are obtained by the acts of worship.

The intended favor here is the last four kinds, and the things that are the means of attaining to these kinds from the first four kinds.[478] (The end of the Shaykh"s talk, may Allah sanctify his soul).

---

[477] *Surah Ibrahim* 14:34; *Surah an-Nahl* 16:18
[478] *Al-Urwat al-Wuthqa*, p. 38.

Nice as these divisions of the Shaykh are, the most important one of the divine favors, the greatest objective of the noble divine Book, has slipped off the Shaykh"s pen. He has satisfied himself with the favors of the imperfect or the medium class. Although in his talk he refers to "spiritual pleasure," yet the spiritual pleasure of the Hereafter which is obtained by the acts of worship is the share of the middle class, if not the share of the imperfect.

Generally, apart from what the Shaykh has said concerning the animal pleasures and the shares of the soul, there are other favors of which three are important:

One is the favor of knowing the Essence and the Unity of Essence, whose principle is the *suluk* to Allah, and its result is the paradise of meeting [Allah]. But if the *salik*"s attention is directed to the result, there can be a default in his *suluk* because this is the state of abandoning oneself and its pleasures, whereas caring for the result is caring for oneself, and this is worshipping oneself, not Allah. It is multiplication [*takthir*], not unification [*tawhid*]. It is a [Satanic] disguise, not abstraction.

Another one is the favor of knowing the Names—a favor which is ramified in as many branches as the multiplicity of the Names. If its items are individually counted, they will amount to a thousand, and if it is taken in its two-name or multi-name compounds, it will be uncountable. **"And if you count Allah"s favors, you will not be able to number them."**[479] The unification of Names, in this state, is the favor of knowing the Greatest Name, which is the state of the "Collective Oneness of the Names" [*ahadiyyat-i jam-i asma*]. The result of knowing the Names is the paradise of Names, [for] each person in proportion to knowing a single Name or many Names, individually or collectively.

The third is the favor of knowing the Acts, which also has infinitely many branches. The state of *tawhid* in this stage is the Collective Oneness of the manifestation of Acts, which is the state of the "Holy Emanation" and the state of the "Absolute Guardianship." And its result is the paradise of the Acts, which is the manifestations of Allah"s Acts in the heart of the *salik*. The manifestation that happened to Moses, the son of Imran, when he said: **"I see a fire,"**[480] was

---

[479] *Surah Ibrahim* 14:34.
[480] *Surah Ta-Ha* 20:10; *Surah an-Naml* 27:7; *Surah al-Qasas* 28:29.

probably a Manifestation of Acts, and the saying of Allah, the Exalted: **"And when his Lord manifested His glory to the mountain, He made it crumble to dust, and Moses fell down in a swoon,"**[481] was a Manifestation of Names or of Essence.

Therefore, the path of those "upon whom favor is bestowed," is, in the first place, "the path" of the journey to the Essence of Allah, and the "favor" in that instance is the Manifestation of the Essence. And, in the second place, "the path" is the *suluk* to the Names of Allah, and the "favor" in that instance is the Manifestation of the Names. And in the third place, the journey is to the Act of Allah, and its "favor" is the Manifestation of the Acts. The people of these states do not seek the common paradises and pleasures, whether spiritual or corporeal. These states, according to some narratives, are confirmed for some believers.[482]

Conclusion

Know that the blessed *Surah* of *al-Fatihah* (the Opening), as it contains all the stages of existence, also contains all the stages of *suluk* and, further, it contains, by way of allusion [*isharah*], all the objectives of the Quran. Delving deep into these matters, though it needs a complete expansion and a logic other than this one, yet to refer to each one of them is not profitless, or rather it has many advantages for the people of knowledge and certitude.

So, in the first place we say that it is possible that **"In the Name of Allah, the Beneficent, the Merciful"** is a hint at the entire circle of existence and at the two bows of descension and ascension. So, **"Name of Allah"** is the state of the Oneness of "contraction and expansion" [*qabd wa bast*]. **"The Beneficent"** is the state of "expansion and appearance," which is the bow of descension, and **"The Merciful"** is the state of "contraction and covertness," which is the bow of ascension. **"All praise is for Allah"** is possibly a reference to the world of Might [*alam-i jabarut*] and the Higher kingdom, whose realities are the absolute praisings. **"The Lord of the worlds"** that concerns "education" and "worlds," which is the state of differentiation [*sawaiyyat*], is probably a reference to the worlds of nature, which, by the substance of essence, are moving, passing, and

---

[481] *Surah al-Araf* 7:143.
[482] *Bihar al-Anwar*, vol. 77, p. 23.

under education. **"The Owner of the Day of Judgment"** refers to the state of Unity, Omnipotence [*qahhariyyat*] and the return of the circle of existence. Up to here the entire circle of existence, descending and ascending, has been covered.

In the second place we say that the *istiadhah*, which is an act of supererogation, can be a reference to forsaking other than Allah, and running away from the Satanic domain. And, as this is a preliminary [stage] to the other states, not a part of them—since abandoning is the preliminary to be adorned [with virtues], and in itself it is not of the states of perfection—therefore, the *istiadhah* is not a part of the *surah*, but a prelude to enter into it. The *tasmiyah* [the *bismillah*] may point to the state of the Unity of Acts and of Essence, and joining both together. **"All praise is for Allah"** up to **"The Lord of the worlds"** may be a reference to the Unity of Acts. Perhaps **"The Owner of the Day of Judgment"** is a hint at complete annihilation and Unity of Essence, and from **"You do we worship"** the state of sobriety and return starts. In other words, *istiadhah* is a journey from the creatures to Allah, a coming out of the house of the soul. *"Tasmiyah"* is a reference to "realizing the love of Allah" [*tahaqquq beh haqqaniyyat*] after taking off creation and multiplicity. **"All praise is for Allah"** up to **"The Lord of the worlds"** is a reference to the journey from Allah, by Allah and in Allah. This journey terminates by **"The Owner of the Day of Judgment."** In **"You do we worship"** the journey from Allah to the creatures begins with the attainment of sobriety and return. This journey ends with **"Guide us to the straight path."**

In the third place we say that this noble *surah* contains the main divine objectives in the Quran, since the principal objectives of the Quran are: the completion of knowing Allah and acquiring the three Unities, the connection between Allah and the creatures, how to travel to Allah, the return of the *raqaiq* (the divine means) to the "Truth of the truths" [*haqiqat al-haqaiq*], introducing the divine manifestations, collectively [*jam-an*] and distinctly [*tafsil-an*], in single [*fard-an*] and in compound [*tarkib-an*], directing the creatures, in *suluk* and in realization [*tahaqquq-an*], and teaching the servants, in knowledge, practice, gnosticism and vision. All these facts are contained in this noble *surah*, much brief and short as it is.

Therefore, this noble *surah* is "The Opening of the Book," "The Mother of the Book" and the general form of the objectives of the Quran. And, as all the objectives of the Divine Book return to a single objective, i.e. the truth of monotheism, which is the goal of all prophethood and the ultimate aim of all the great prophets (a), and the truths and the secrets of monotheism are contained in the noble *ayah* of *bismillah,* so, this noble *ayah* is the greatest of the divine *ayah*s and contains all the objectives of the Divine Book, as is confirmed by the noble *hadith*[483]. As the *"ba"* [ب] is the appearance of *tawhid,* and the dot[484] under it is its secret, the, whole Book, its overt and covert, is in that *"ba"* [ب]. And the perfect man, that is, the blessed person of Ali (a) is the very dot of the secret of *tawhid.*[485] There is no *ayah* in the world greater than that blessed person after the Seal of the Messengers (s), as is stated in the noble *hadith.*[486]

Completion

Some noble narratives related about the merit [*fadl*] of this blessed *Surah*:

The Messenger of Allah (s) has been quoted to have said to Jabir ibn Abdullah al-Ansari (may Allah be pleased with him): "O Jabir, don"t you want me to teach you the most merited *surah* revealed by Allah in His Book?" Jabir said: "O yes, may my father and mother be your ransom, Messenger of Allah, teach me." He, thus, taught him [*surah*] *"al-Hamd,"* the Mother of the Book. Then he said: "O Jabir, don"t you want me to tell you about it?" "Yes, may my father and mother be your ransom, Messenger of Allah, tell me," said Jabir. "It is a cure for every ailment except death," he said.[487]

Ibn Abbas related that the Messenger (s) once said: "For everything there is a foundation. The foundation of the Quran is „the Opening" [*surah*] and the foundation of the „Opening" is *bismillah ir-*

---

[483] *Ibid.,* vol. 92, p. 238. Three *hadith*s are narrated in this respect.

[484] There may be an objection to our saying: the dot under the *"ba"* [ب], that in the *Kufi* penmanship which was common when the Quran was revealed, there were no dots (in the alphabet). To this, one may say that this fact and reality will make no difference, although its role appeared late, which, in fact, had no effect on the facts. Rather, there is not a decisive evidence in support of the said claim. Mere convention is not a proof of absolute non-existence. So, think it over!

[485] "I am the dot under the *"ba"* [ب]," *Asrar al-Hikam,* p. 559.

[486] *As-Safi"s Exegesis,* vol. 2, p. 779, commenting on the noble *ayah:* **"About the great event"** (*Surah an-Naba"* 78:2).

[487] *Al-Ayyashi"s Exegesis,* vol. 1, p. 20, *hadith* 9.

Rahman ir-Rahim (In the Name of Allah, the Beneficent, the Merciful).[488]

He is also quoted to have said: "The Opening [*surah*] of the Book is the cure for every illness."[489]

Imam Jafar as-Sadiq (a) is quoted to have said that if the *surah* of the Opening did not cure a person, nothing else would cure him.[490]

Imam Ali (a) is quoted to have said that the Messenger of Allah (s) said: "Allah, the Exalted, told me: **"O Muhammad, We have given you *sab ul mathani* [another name of the *surah* of the "Opening"] and the great Quran."**[491] I am graced with a separate favor by the Opening of the Book, which is put on the same level as the Quran. Indeed, the Opening of the Book is the most honored thing in the treasures of the *Arsh*, and Allah, the Exalted, has bestowed its honor upon Muhammad (s), sharing no one of the prophets in it, except Solomon, to whom Allah gave the *Bismillah* of the Opening *surah*, i.e. *Bismillah ir-Rahman ir-Rahim,* as Bilqis says: **"An honorable letter has been thrown to me. It is from Solomon, and it is: In the Name of Allah, the Beneficent, the Merciful."**[492] So, whoever recites it, believing in loving Muhammad and his offspring, obeying its command and believing in its outside and inside, Allah, the Exalted, will grant him, for each of its letters a favor, which is, in fact, preferred to the whole world and whatever is in it of different kinds of properties and good things. Whoever listens to it being recited will get one-third of that which is given to its reciter. So, let everyone of you increase his share of this blessing offered to him, as it is a chance that you must not be late in taking it, otherwise your hearts will regret it much.[493]

---

[488] *Majma ul-Bayan*, vol. 1, p. 17.
[489] *Ibid.*
[490] *Al- Ayyashi's Exegesis*, vol. 1, p. 20; *Bihar al-Anwar*, vol. 89, p. 237, *hadith 34.*
[491] *Surah al-Hijr* 15:87.
[492] *Surah an-Naml* 27:29 and 30.
[493] *Uyunu Akhbar ar-Rida*, vol. 1, p. 301, under the title: "Concerning the Different Narratives Quoted from Imam Ali ibn Musa," *hadith* 60. *Bihar al-Anwar*, vol. 89, p. 227, *hadith* 5.

Imam as-Sadiq (a) is quoted to have said: "It is no wonder if [the *surah* of] *al*-Hamd is recited seventy times over a dead and it comes back to life."[494]

The Messenger of Allah (*s*) is quoted to have said: "Whoever recites the *surah* of „the Opening of the Book" will get the reward of reciting two-thirds of the Quran.[495] Another narration says: "It will be like reciting the whole Quran."[496]

Ubay ibn Kab narrated: "I recited to the Messenger of Allah (*s*) the *surah* of the Opening. He said: "By the One in Whose Hand is my soul, Allah did not reveal in the Torah, nor in the Gospel, the Psalms or the Quran a *surah* like "The Opening of the Book." It is *ummul kitab* (The Mother of the Book) and *as-sab ul-mathani* (the repeated seven [*ayahs*]). It is divided between Allah and His servant, and it is for His servant to demand whatever he wants."[497]

Hudhayfah ibn al-Yaman (may Allah be pleased with him) is quoted to have said that the Messenger of Allah (*s*) said: "Allah, the Exalted, may send an inevitable punishment upon a nation. Then one of their children recites: „All praise is for Allah, the Lord of the worlds," in the Book of Allah. On hearing this, Allah, The Most High, postpones torturing them for forty years."[498]

Ibn Abbas said that once they were sitting with the Messenger of Allah (*s*) when an angel came and said: "Good tidings to you for the two lights which have been given to you, and never given to the prophets before you. They are „The Opening of the Book" and the seals of the *surah* of *al-Baqarah* .No one recites a single word of them unless his demand is granted."[499] This narrative is also related in *al-Majma*, with nearly the same content.[500]

---

[494] *Nur ath-Thaqalayn Exegesis*, vol. 1, p. 4, commenting on the *surah* of *al-Hamd*, *hadith* 8.
[495] *Bihar al-Anwar*, vol. 89, p. 259. *Majma ul-Bayan*, vol. 1, p. 17.
[496] *Ibid.*
[497] *Majma ul-Bayan*, vol. 1, p. 17.
[498] *At-Tafsir al-Kabir*, vol. 1, p. 178.
[499] *Mustadrak al-Wasa'il*, "Book of *as-Salat*," sec. on "Recitation," ch. 44, *hadith* 3.
[500] *Majma ul-Bayan*, vol. 1, p. 18.

SOME EXEGESIS OF
THE BLESSED *SURAH* OF *AT-TAWHID*
Chapter Six

Know that this noble *surah* is the lineage [*nasab*] of Allah, the Exalted, according to the noble *hadith*s, one of which is in the noble *al-Kafi*, on the authority of Imam as-Sadiq (a) who said: "The Jews inquired of the Messenger of Allah (*s*) and said: „Tell us your Lord's lineage [*nasab*].‟ The Prophet remained three days giving no reply. Then it was revealed to him: „Say: He is Allah, the One,‟ till the end."[501] Consequently, the human mind is incapable of understanding its facts, subtleties and secrets. Yet, though it is so, the share which the people of knowledge have of it, and what the hearts of the people of Allah know, cannot be understood by mere reasoning.

By the Beloved, this noble *surah* is one of the trusts which the heavens of the spirits, the lands of ghosts and the mountains of I-nesses, are incapable of carrying it. No one is fit to carry it other than the Perfect Man who has crossed the boundary of "the possible" and entered the realm of ecstasy. Nevertheless, there is the good news that would please the people of the End of the Time and offer safety to the people of knowledge. There is a *hadith* in the noble *al-Kafi*, which says that, asked about *at-Tawhid*, Imam Ali ibn Husayn (a) said: "Allah, the Almighty and Exalted, knew that in the End of the Time there would be people of deep knowledge. Therefore, Allah, the Exalted, revealed the *surah*: „Say: He is Allah, the One…‟ and some *ayah*s of the *Surah al-Hadid* up to „He knows what is in the breasts.‟ Whoever wanted other than that would perish."[502] From this noble *hadith* one deduces that to comprehend these noble *ayah*s and this

---

[501] *Usul al-Kafi*, vol. 1, p. 122, "Book of *at-Tawhid*," ch. on "Lineage," *hadith* 1.
[502] *Usul al-Kafi*, vol. 1, p. 125, "Book of *at-Tawhid*," ch. on "Prohibition of Talking on the Quality," *hadith* 4.

blessed *surah* is for the scrutinizers and the owners of deep insight. They contain the minute secrets of *at-Tawhid* and knowledge. The delicate divine knowledge is descended by Allah upon the worthy. Those who have no share of the secrets of *at-Tawhid* and divine knowledge, have no right to look into these *ayah*s. They have no right to interpret these *ayah*s according to the common and vulgar meanings which they know, and to which they confine them.

In the first noble *ayah*s of the blessed *surah* of *al-Hadid* there are delicate things of *at-Tawhid*, and great information of the secrets of divinity and abstraction, the like of which is unseen in the divine revelations, and the books of the people of knowledge and the owners of heart. Had there been nothing but these *ayah*s to confirm the truthfulness of the prophethood and the perfection of the religion of the Seal of the Prophets, they would have been sufficient for the people of insight and knowledge. The highest evidence proving that this knowledge is beyond the capacity of man and out of the limits of human thought is that till the revelation of these noble *ayah*s and the like, of the knowledge contained in the Quran, such knowledge had not been precedented among mankind, and there was no way to those secrets. Nowadays, there are the books and the writings of the great philosophers of the world, who took their knowledge from the source of divine inspiration—the highest and best of them maybe the noble book called *Ethology* [*Theologia*],[503] by the great philosopher and celebrated wise man, Aristotle, to whom great philosophers, such as the Master Avicenna, the rare wonder of the time, humbly bowed. Of the emanations of his mind was the logic and its rules, on which basis

---

[503] Dehkhuda's *Lexicon*, under the entry *Aristotle*, takes *Theologia* to be among the books written by Aristotle, and says: *Theologia* is a discourse about Divinity, explained by Porphyrius (Prophyry) of Tyre, and translated into Arabic by Abdul Masih ibn Abdullah the Naimi of Hims. Then Abu Yusuf Yaqub ibn Ishaq al-Kindi corrected it for Ahmad ibn al-Mutasim. It was printed in Berlin in the year 1882. It was also printed in Iran in the margin of *al-Qabasat* by Mirdamad, in the year 1314 H. (Lunar year). And under the entry *Theologia* it says: *Theologia* is derived from Greek, meaning "theology." *Mayamir* is a book by Plotinus, who is known by the Muslims as ash-Shaykh al-Yunani (the Greek Oldman). This book covers the 4th to 6th book of the "*Enneades.*" Some of the ancients mistakenly ascribed this book to Aristotle. In the year of 1314 H. the book of *Theologia*, was printed in the margin of *al-Qabasat*, by Abu 'l-Qasim ibn Akhund Mulla Rida Kamarbuni. The date of composing the book is mistakenly stated in Dehkhuda's *Lexicon* to be the date of its printing.

he was named "The First Teacher." Avicenna says that ever since this great scholar composed the rules of logic, no one has been able to object to even a single one of his rules or add to them. Despite what has been said, and although he had written that honorable book in order to prove the state of divinity, yet, could the whole of that noble book prove it as the noble *ayah* at the beginning of the *Surah al-Hadid* could do, or even something near it with a scent of the great secret of monotheism? Has it anything like the saying of Allah, the Exalted: **"He is the First and the Last and the Manifest and the Hidden,"**[504] or the noble saying: **"And He is with you wheresoever you may be."**[505]

Nowadays the deep thinkers and the people of insight and knowledge do know what secrets there are in these *ayah*s, and with what noble words and a great secret Allah, the Exalted, has honored and favored the people of the End of the Time! Whoever refers to the knowledge of the religions of the world and to the knowledge common among the great philosophers of each religion, and compares them, in respect of the Beginning and the Return, with the knowledge of the upright religion of Islam and of the great philosophers of Islam and of the well-versed gnostic teachers of this *ummah*, will certainly admit that the source of the Islamic knowledge is the light of the Quran and the *hadith*s of the Seal of the Prophets and his *Ahl al-Bayt* (a), all of whom receive their knowledge from the light of the Quran. Only then will he realize that the philosophy and gnosticism of Islam are not taken from the Greek, rather, they have no resemblance to theirs. Yes, some of the philosophers of Islam did imitate the method of the Greek philosophers, such as the Master Shaykh Avicenna. Yet, the Shaykh"s philosophy is not so prosperous in the market of the people of knowledge, and it has little value with them, as far as the knowledge about Divinity, the Beginning, and the Return is concerned.

In short, ascribing today"s philosophy of the Islamic philosophers, and the great knowledge of the people of knowledge to the Greek philosophy denotes the ascribers" lack of information about the Islamic writings, such as the writings of the great Islamic philosopher, Sadr ul-Mutaallihin (may his soul be sanctified) and his great tutor, Muhaqqiq Damad (may his soul be sanctified), and his

---

[504] *Surah al-Hadid* 57:3.
[505] *Ibid.* 57:4.

great student, Fayd Kashani (may his soul be sanctified), and the great student of Fayd, the great gnostic faithful, Qadi Said Qummi (may his soul be sanctified). It also shows their ignorance of the knowledge of the Divine Book and the *hadith*s of the infallibles (a), and that is why they ascribed every philosophy to the Greek, and regarded the Islamic philosophers as the followers of the Greek philosophy.

We have related a part of the delicate points of the noble *surah* of *at-Tawhid* and some hints about those noble *ayah*s in our book on explaining *The Forty Hadiths*. Furthermore, we also gave a brief explanation of this noble *surah* in our book *The Secret of the Salat*. Relying on Allah, we give here another short explanation, and so we say:

If the *bismillah* of this *surah* belongs to this *surah*—as we supposed it so when explaining the blessed *surah* of *al-Hamd*—it may be a hint at the fact that to explain the lineage [*nasab*] of Allah and the secrets of *at-tawhid* through our selfishness and our own language is not possible. Actually, unless the *salik* steps out of his veil, realizes the state of the Absolute Will and of the Holy Emanation and perishes in the Absolute Ipseity [*huwiyyat*], he will not be able to comprehend the secrets of *at-tawhid*.

"Say" is a command from the Collective Oneness [*hadrat-i ahadiyyat-i jam*] to the state of the big isthmus [*barzakhiyyat-i kubra*] and the mirror of Collectivity [*jam*] and distinctness [*tafsil*]. That is, "Say, O Muhammad, mirror of the appearance of the Collective Oneness, in the state of essential proximity [*tadalli-yi dhati*], or the sacred state of **"even nearer"**—which can be a reference to the state of the Most Holy Emanation—with a tongue self-perishing, and subsisting by Allah"s subsistence: **"He is Allah, the One."**

Do know, O traveler on the road of knowledge and *tawhid*, and ascender to the heights of transcendence and abstraction, that Allah"s Sacred Essence, in itself, is innocent of external and internal manifestations, and of mark, form, attribute and name. The hands of the hopes of the people of knowledge are short of His Majesty"s skirt, and the traveling legs of the people of heart are too slow to reach the threshold of His Holiness. The ultimate knowledge of the Perfect Friends is "We knew You not," and the end of the journey of the people of secrets is "We worshipped You not."[506] The head of the circle of the people of knowledge, the prince of the people of *at-Tawhid*, Imam Ali (a), in this lofty stance says: "...the perfection of sincerity is to deny Him attributes."[507] And the leader of the people of *suluk*, the master of the worshippers and the gnostics, at His mighty threshold says: "The attributes lost their way to You, and the descriptions fell into contradiction about You."[508]

The people of the scholarly *suluk* and terms, call His Holy Essence "The Immune *Ghayb*" [*ghayb-i masun*], "The Hidden Secret," "The Wonderful Unknown," [*anqa-i mughrib*] and "The Absolute Unknown" [*majhul-i mutlaq*]. They say that His Essence would appear in no mirror without the veil of Names and Attributes, and would be manifested in no one of the creations nor in any one of the invisible and visible worlds. But according to **"Every day He is in a state,"**[509] there are, for His Holy Essence, Names, Attributes and states [affairs =*shuun*] of "Beauty" and "Majesty." There are for Him Essential Names in the state of Oneness [*ahadiyyat*], which is the unseen state. They are to be called "the Essential Names," and, by the individuation [*taayyun*] of the Essential Names, He would be manifested through the Holy Emanation. From this manifestation in the apparel of the Essential Names, there would be the individuation [*taayyun*] and the appearance [*zuhur*] of the state of "Unity" [*wahidiyyat*] and "Names and Attributes," and the state of "Divinity."

So, it has become known that after the Holy Essence, as such, there are other three states and scenes: the state of the Unseen "Oneness" the state of the manifestation of "the Holiest Emanation," which may be referred to by the word *ama* in the noble Prophetic *hadiths*;[510] to the state of "Unity" [*wahidiyyat*], which, according to the

---

[506] This refers to a narrative quoted from the Messenger of Allah (*s*), saying: "We knew You not as You should be known, and we worshipped You not as You should be worshipped." *Mirat ul-Uqul*, vol. 8, "Book of Faith and Disbelief," ch. on "Thank-Giviing," p. 146.

[507] *Nahj al-Balaghah*, edited by Fayd ul-Islam, Sermon 1.

[508] *As-Sahifah as-Sajjadiyyah*, Invocation 32.

[509] *Surah ar-Rahman* 55:29.

[510] When the Prophet (*s*) was asked, "Where was our Lord before creating the heavens and the earth?" he said, "He was in the *ama*" [high]." *Awali al-Laali*, vol. 1, p. 54, ch. 4, *hadith* 79.

Collective Oneness [*ahadiyyat-i jam*], is the state of the Greatest Name, and, according to the "distinct multiplicity" [*kathrat-i tafsili*], is the state of Names and Attributes. To go into the details of these states requires an expansion that is out of the capacity of these papers.

Having understood this preliminary, we say that **"He"** [*huwa*] may be a reference to the state of the "Most Holy Emanation," which is the manifestation of the Essence in the individuation of the "Essential Names." **"Allah"** points to the state of the Collective Oneness [*ahadiyyat-i jam*] of the Names, which is the Greatest Name. *"Ahad"* (the One) is a reference to the state of the "Oneness" [*ahadiyyat*]. Therefore, the noble *ayah* intends to prove that these three states which, in the instance [*maqam*] of nominal multiplication, possess plurality [*kathrat*], actually possess utmost unity at the same time. The manifestation in the "Most Holy Emanation," according to the state of appearance, is **"Allah,"** and according to the state of interiority [*butun*], is the "One" [*Ahad*].

Perhaps **"He"** [*huwa*] points to the state of the Essence. And, as it is an invisible reference, it is actually a reference to the unknown. **"Allah"** and **"Ahad"** are references to the state of "Unity" [*wahidiyyat*] and "Oneness" [*ahadiyyat*]. So, He introduces the Essence—which is the Absolute Unknown—through the Names of Essence, and the Names of the Unitary Attributes. In fact, it points to the fact that the Essence is invisible and the hands of hopes are short of reaching it, and that spending the life in thinking about Allah''s Essence leads to going astray, and that what is known to the people of Allah and to the knowledge of those who know Allah, is related to the states of "Unity" [*wahidiyyat*] and "Oneness" [*ahadiyyat*], the "Unity" being for the common people of Allah, whereas "Oneness" is for the special people of Allah.

A Philosophic Note:

Do know that there are for Allah "Positive Attributes" [*sifat-i thubutiyyah*] and "Negative Attributes" [*sifat-i salbiyyah*], as the philosophers believe. By the "Negative Attribute" they mean the negation of the negative, i.e. negation of imperfection. Some say that the "Positive Attributes" are the Attributes of "Beauty" [*jamal*] and the "Negative Attributes" are the Attributes of "Majesty" [*jalal*], and that "The Owner of Majesty and Generosity" includes all the Negative and the Positive Attributes. But this talk, in both stages, is contrary to certainty [*tahqiq*].

Now the first stage: The "Negative Attributes" are certainly not of the attributes, since concerning the Essence of Allah, there can be neither any negative nor negation of the negative. Allah, the Exalted, is not attributed with negative attributes, because attributing with negative attributes is a privative proposition [*qadiyyat-i madulah*], and forming a privative proposition is not allowed in respect of Allah, the Exalted, since it is modification of the possible aspects and it requires admission of composition [*tarkib*] in the Holy Essence. Rather, the negative attributes are through the simple absolute negation, which is a negation of the attribute, not a confirmation of the attribute of negating the negation. In other words, Allah, the Exalted, is deprived of all imperfections in a simple negation, not that the negation of imperfections be confirmed for Him by way of affirmation of privation [*ijab-i uduli*]. So, as a matter of fact, the attributes of purification [*tanzih*] are not "attributes." Allah, the Exalted, is only attributed with the positive attributes.

As regards the second stage, the people of knowledge regard the "Attributes of Beauty" to be those which bring intimacy and affection. The "Attributes of Majesty" are those which bring fear, bewilderment and anxiety. So, whatever is affiliated to kindness and mercy is of the "Attributes of Beauty," such as "Compassionate," "Merciful," "Tender," "Affectionate," "Lord," and the like. And that which belongs to sovereignty and grandeur is of the "Attributes of Majesty," such as "Owner," "King," "Forceful," "Avenger," and the like, although in the inside of every Beauty there is a Majesty, too, because every beauty has, in the inside, bewilderment and anxiety, appearing in the heart with the secret of greatness and power, and, every majesty has, in the inside, mercy, and the heart feels, with it, intimacy inside. That is why as the heart naturally is attracted to beauty and the beautiful, it, at the same time, is attracted to power, greatness, the powerful, and the great. Therefore, both of these kinds of attributes are positive, not negative, attributes.

Now, as this subject has been understood, do know that although "Allah" is "The Greatest Name" and that the attributes of "Beauty" and "Majesty" are of its manifestations and are under its custody [*hitah*], yet sometimes it is used for the attributes of "Beauty" [*jamal*] in opposition to the attributes of "Majesty" [*jalal*], such that "divinity" [*ilahiyyat*] and "godhead" [*uluhiyyat*] categorically belong to the attributes of "Beauty," particularly if they are thought to oppose the attribute of "Majesty." In the noble *ayah*: **"Say: He is Allah, the One,"** **"the One"** may be a reference to one of the important attributes of "Majesty," which is the state [*maqam*] of the perfect simplicity of the Holy Essence, while "Allah" is a reference to the Name of "Beauty." Thus, the lineage [*nasab*] of Allah, the Exalted, has been explained in this noble *ayah,* in respect of the states of "Oneness" [*ahadiyyat*], "Unity" [*wahidiyyat*] and manifestation through "The Holiest Emanation"—the three of which are [covering] all the divine affairs [*shuun*]—according to the first possibility which has already been referred to in the previous "Note." In accordance with the possibility stated in this "Note," the lineage [*nasab*] of Allah, the Exalted, is explained in accordance with the states of the Names of Beauty and Majesty, which encompass all the Names. And Allah is the Knower.

A Gnostic Note

Know that the words of every speaker are a demonstration of his self in accordance with the state of appearance. It is the emergence of his inner faculties on the mirror of words, in proportion to the capacity of the composition of words. If a heart becomes luminous and purged of the pollutions and evils of the world of nature, its words will also become luminous, or, rather, it becomes light itself, and the very luminosity of the heart is manifested in the clothing of words. Concerning the Imams of guidance it is said: "Your words are light."[511] It is also said: "He manifested in His talk to His servants."[512] In *Nahj al-Balaghah* it is said: "His words are but His act."[513] Action is the appearance of the doer's self [*dhat*] without "words." If a heart becomes dark and polluted, its act and words will become dark and polluted, too: **"A good word is like a good tree...;"**[514] **"And the likeness of a bad word is as a bad tree."**[514a]

[511] *Uyunu Akhbar ar-Rida*, vol.2, p. 277, quoted from the invocation of "*Al-Jamiah al-Kabirah.*"
[512] *Bihar al-Anwar*, vol. 89, p. 107.
[513] *Nahj al-Balaghah*, edited by Fayd ul-Islam, p. 737, sermon 228.
[514] Derived from *Surah Ibrahim* 14:24.
[514a] *Surah Ibrahim* 14:26.

The Holy Essence of Allah, the Most High, according to "**Every day He is in a state [*shan*],**"⁵¹⁵ appears to the hearts of the prophets and the guardians [*awliya*] in the clothing of the Names and Attributes, and His manifestations differ in accordance with the differences of their hearts. Similarly, the heavenly Books, which descended upon their hearts by revelation through the Revelation Angel, Gabriel, are different according to the differences of these manifestations and of the Names which are the origins of them—as the difference of the prophets and their *Shariah*s is according to the kingdoms of the Names. So, the more the Name is comprehensive and embracing, the more comprehensive and embracing its kingdom, its relevant prophethood and its revealed Book, and the more comprehensive and permanent its *Shariah*. And, as the Seal of Prophethood, the Glorious Quran and the Islamic *Shariah* are of the phenomena, or of the manifestations and appearances of the Collective State of the One and of the Greatest Name of Allah, consequently, they are the most comprehensive prophethood, Book and *Shariah*, and the most all-inclusive ones, and nothing can be imagined more perfect and more honorable than them, and from the world of the unseen a knowledge loftier than that, or like it, would no longer come down to the expanse of nature. That is, the last appearance of a scientific perfection, concerning religions, is this, and there is no possibility of the descension of a better one to this world. Hence, the very person of the Seal of the Messengers (*s*) is the most honored one of the beings and is the complete manifestation of the Greatest Name, and his prophethood is also the most possible complete one, and is the image of the Kingdom of the Greatest Name, which is everlasting and eternal, and the Book revealed to him is also from the stage of the unseen through the manifestation of the Greatest Name. For this reason, this noble Book has its "oneness of collectivity and distinctness" [*ahadiyyat-i jamu tafsil*], and it is of "The Collective Words" [*jawamiul-kalim*].⁵¹⁶ The words of the Prophet himself were of the Collective Words, too. By saying that the Quran, or the Prophet"s words, are Collective Words we do not mean to refer to their general instructions and collective principles—although considering this, his

---

⁵¹⁵ *Surah ar-Rahman* 55:29.
⁵¹⁶ It is a reference to a Prophetic *hadith*, saying: "I have been given the Collective Words." *Al-Khisal*, ch. 5, *hadith* 56.

hadiths are also collective and of the principles, as is known to the science of jurisprudence. The Quran is collective because it is revealed for all the human classes, during all the stages of the human life, and it meets all the needs of the human race. The reality of this race is the same as the reality of the society, with all its stations, from the lowest earthly ones up to the highest spiritual, heavenly and mighty ones. Therefore, the individuals of this species in this low, mundane world are so different, and they are so diverse that the like of it is not seen in any other species. It is this species that includes the completely wretched and the completely happy. It is this species in which there are some individuals who are lower than all kinds of animals, while there are some others who are more honored than all the favored angels. In short, as the individuals of this species are different in respect of their understanding and knowledge, the Quran has been revealed in such a way as to be benefited by everybody in accordance with the degree of the perfection or weakness of his understanding and knowledge. For example, the noble *ayah*: **"Had there been in them [the heavens and the earth] any gods except Allah, they would have surely been in [a state of] disorder."**[517] As the common people, the people of letters, and the lexicographers understand, each a certain concept, the theologians understand something else, similarly the philosophers, men of wisdom understand a different meaning, as well as the gnostics and the godly men who benefit from it differently. The common people take it to be a speech addressed to them according to their own tastes. They say, for example, two kings cannot rule a single kingdom, or two chieftains in a tribe cause corruption, or two headmen in a village would lead to disputes and quarrels. So, had there been two gods in the world there would have been corruption, disputes and litigation. But as there is one God, this difference of the heavens and the earth and their systematic order are preserved. So, the Manager of the world is One. The theologians use this as mutual antagonistic demonstration, while the philosophers and the wise men use it for establishing a decisive reasoning argument based on: "The one does not issue but the one, and the one is not issued but by the one."[518] The people of knowledge [*ahl-i marifat*] get to recognize Unity, in a

---

[517] *Surah al-Anbiya"*21:22.
[518] A philosophic principle. *Al-Isharat wat-Tanbihat*, (explained by Khajah Nasir), vol. 3, p. 122. *Al-Asfar al-Arbaah*, vol. 2, p. 204, ch. 13.

different way through it, by way of knowing that the world is the mirror of appearance [*zuhur*] and the place of manifestation of the *Haqq* (Allah); and so on, which makes it too lengthy to expand on each of those ways.

Now that this introduction is understood, you may know that the noble *surah* of **"Say: He, Allah, is One"** is, like the other parts of the Quran, of "Collective Words," and, being so, every one makes use of it in a way. The men of letters and of form take "He" to be a pronoun of state, and "Allah" to be a proper noun, and "*ahad*" to mean "the One," or an exaggeration of "Oneness," i.e. Allah is One, or He has no partner in Divinity, or **"There is nothing like Him,"**[519] or in the divinity and Essential Eternity He has no partner, or His Acts are One, that is, all of them are based on practicality and benevolence, with no benefit for Himself. Allah is *as-Samad*, i.e. He is the Great Master who is sought by the people for their wants to be fulfilled, or He is *as-Samad*, meaning that He has no inside, and, being such, nothing can be born of Him, nor can He be born of anything, and no one is like Him or comparable to Him. This is a statement on the part of the common people intended to counter the disbelievers who had many gods, all of which had possible attributes. The Messenger of Allah (*s*) was ordered to tell them that his God was different from theirs, and His attributes are those which have been mentioned.

That was the explanation of this *surah* in a traditional and common way, and suitable for one group, and it is not incompatible with this fact that there may be another meaning or other scrupulous meanings, as we have already mentioned some of them.

A Philosophic Explanation

It is possible that for the blessed *surah* of "*at-Tawhid*"—which was revealed for the deep thinkers of the end of the Time—there may be a wise explanation based on theological criteria and philosophic proofs. This explanation has been revealed to me by the great gnostic Shaykh Shahabadi (may he live longer):[520]

So, **"He"** [*huwa*] is a reference to mere existence and absolute Ipseity [*huwiyyat*]—a fact which proves, in the blessed *surah*, six lofty philosophic subjects:

---

[519] *Surah ash-Shura* 42:11.
[520] Refer to footnote 97.

First: The state of "Divinity" [*uluhiyyat*], which is the state of containing all perfections, and the "Collective Oneness" [*ahadiyyat-i jam*] of "Beauty" and "Majesty," as in the relevant states of philosophic findings it has been proved that pure existence and absolute Ipseity are pure perfection, otherwise it would not be pure existence, either. As explaining these subjects require lengthy expansion and further preliminary steps, I suffice myself with the above-mentioned hints.

Second: The state of "Oneness" [*ahadiyyat*], which is a reference to complete intellectual, external and existential essential simplicity, and to being above all intellectual compositions, whether genus and differentia, or matter and mental image, or external, whether matter and external image or measured parts. The evidence proving this subject is the same proof of pure existence and absolute Ipseity, because if the "pure" [*sirf*] is not one in itself, it will by necessity quit its being pure and part with its identity [*dhatiyyat*].

Third: The state of "being the One sought for help" [*samadiyyat*] which points to negation of quiddity [*mahiyyat*]. Having no inside and being not empty also point to having no quiddity and no possible imperfection, for in all the possible beings, their essential degree—which is their inside—is empty. But as the Holy Essence is the pure existence and absolute Ipseity, He has no possible shortcoming, whose origin is quiddity, since quiddity is extracted from the existential limit, and its conventional status is derived from the existential individuation, whereas the pure existent is free from limit and individuation [*taayyun*], because every limited is a fixed [*muqayyad*] identity [*huwiyyat*] and a mixed existence. It is not absolute nor pure.

Fourth: Nothing separates from Him, because the separation of something form something denotes materiality, or even measured parts, which is contrary to absolute identity [*huwiyyat*] and pure existence. The existence of the caused from the cause does not happen, however, by way of separation, but by way of manifestation, appearance, consequence and issue. And it happens in such a way that nothing is reduced from the cause, and nothing is added to the cause by its return to it.

Fifth: He (Allah) has separated from nothing, which, besides the formerly stated depravity, is contrary to pure existence and absolute identity, as otherwise it would necessitate that there should be something prior to the pure existence, while high philosophy has already proved that "purity" [*sirf*] is the most ancient, and that individuation comes later than the absolute.

Sixth: Having no match and no equal, and negating His resemblance and like, which is proved by the proof that the pure existence has no repetition. So, no dual absolute identity can be imagined, and the absolute and the limited are neither equals nor matches.

To each of these subjects there are preliminaries and principles which cannot be explained in these few papers.

An Illuminative Wisdom

Know that this blessed *surah*, so brief as it is, includes all the Divine Affairs [*shuun*] and the stages of praising and glorification. In fact, it is the correlation between Allah, the Exalted, and whatever can be put into the mould of words and the construction of expressions, such as: **"He, Allah, is One"** which covers all the Attributes of Perfection, as well as the Positive Attributes. And from the word "*as-Samad*" up to the end of the *surah*, the words cover the "Attributes of purity" and denote negation of shortcomings. Furthermore, the *surah* proves being out of "the two limits": *tatil* (devesting Allah of all Attributes), and *tashbih* (assimilation), both of which are going beyond the limit of moderation and the reality of *at-tawhid*. The first noble *ayah* refers to the negation of *tatil*, and other parts of the *surah* refer to the negation of *tashbih*. It also includes the Essence as it is, and the state of "Oneness" [*ahadiyyat*], which is the manifestation by the Names of Essence, and the state of "Unity" [*wahidiyyat*], which is the manifestation by the Names of Attributes, a suitable explanation of which has already been related.

Completion

Shaykh as-Saduq (may Allah be pleased with him) quotes Abu l-Bukhtari, Wahab ibn Wahab al-Qurashi, quoting Imam as-Sadiq (a), quoting his great father, Imam al-Baqir (a), that in Allah's saying: **"Say: He, Allah, is One," "Say"** means: "Make known what We revealed to you and informed you about it by the constructed letters recited to you, so that he may be guided by them whoever lends his ears and sees. "*Huwa*" (He) is a pronoun of indication referring to the third person, in which "*ha*" [ﻫ] denotes an affirmed concept, and the "*waw*" [و] refers to what is absent from the senses, unlike "*hadha*" [this] which refers to what is present before the senses. This pointing to the absent is because the disbelievers pointed to their gods by the pronoun indicating a thing present and perceivable. They said: "*These are our gods, who are tangible and perceivable by the eyes. So, you too, Muhammad, point out to your god that we may see him and understand him, so that we may not feel bewildered about him.*" Hence, Allah sent down that: "**Say, He,**" in which the "*ha*" [ه] confirms what is affirmed, and the "*waw*" [و] points out to what is absent from sight and other senses, for Allah is the Most High, or rather, He is the Conceiver of the eyes and the Creator of the senses."[521]

Imam al-Baqir (a) said: "Allah is a Worshipped Diety about Whom the creatures are perplexed as unable to understand His truth and how He is. The Arabs, when confused about someone and lack concrete knowledge about him, say: *Aliha-r-rajul* (The man became a deity). They also say: *Walaha* when they try to take refuge in something from a frightening thing, while *al-ilah* denotes that which is covered from the human senses."

He also said: "*Ahad* means the One, and *Ahad* and *wahid* both have the same meaning, which is the One Who is unique and has no match. *At-tawhid* means the acknowledgement of monotheism, that is, uniqueness. One is a heterogeneous [*mutabayyin*] which does not issue from anything and does not unite with anything. Thus, it is said that the number is formed of the one, while the one is not a number, as it is not called a number, but two is a number. So, the meaning of Allah"s saying: "*Allahu ahad*" is that the Worshipped, Whom the human beings are confusedly incapable of understanding and of getting comprehensive knowledge about Him, is Unique in divinity and far above the creatures" attributes."[522]

Imam al-Baqir (a) has also said: "My father Zayn ul-Abidin (a) told me, quoting his father al-Husayn ibn Ali (a), that *as-Samad* is that which has no inside, and *as-Samad* is the one whose mastery has reached its maximum, and *as-Samad* is the one who neither eats nor drinks, and *as-Samad* is the one who does not sleep, and *as-Samad* is a permanent that has always been and will always be."

---

[521] *At-Tawhid*, p. 88, ch. on "Commentary on: "**Say, He, Allah, is One,**" *hadith* 1.
[522] *Ibid., hadith* 2.

Imam al-Baqir (a) said that Muhammad ibn al-Hanafiyyah used to say: *"As-Samad* is that which is self-existent and self-sufficient." Someone else said: *"As-Samad* is above becoming and decaying. *As-Samad* is that which does not change."

Imam al-Baqir (a) further said: *"As-Samad* is the commanding chief above whom there is no commander to bid and forbid." He said: "Ali ibn al-Husayn, Zayn ul-Abidin (a), asked about *as-Samad*, said: *"As-Samad* is the One who has no partner, and preserving of nothing is difficult or heavy for Him, and nothing is concealed from Him."[523]

Wahab ibn Wahab al-Qurashi says that Zayd ibn Ali said: *"As-Samad* is the One Who when desires a thing, He says to it „Be" and there it is. *As-Samad* is the One Who innovates the things, then creates them in forms unlike each other, or similar to each other, and in pairs, while He alone is the One Who has no antonym, no shape, no equal and no likeness."[524]

Wahab ibn Wahab further quotes Ali ibn al-Husayn (a) explaining *as-Samad*. He also reports Imam al-Baqir's explanations concerning the secrets of the letters of *as-Samad*. He says that Imam al-Baqir (a) said: "Had I found bearers for the knowledge which Allah has bestowed upon me, I would have spread knowledge about *at-Tawhid*, Islam, faith, religion, and the laws out of *as-Samad*. But how can I find bearers of such knowledge, while my grandfather, Amir al-Muminin, could find none to carry his knowledge, such that he used to painfully sigh and tell his followers, on the *minbar* (pulpit): „Ask me before you miss me. Behind the ribs of my bosom is a great knowledge. Alas! That I can find no carriers for it."[525]

Conclusion

In concluding this chapter, we relate some noble *hadiths* concerning the merits of this blessed *surah*, as they are too many to be all contained in these few pages.

The noble *al-Kafi* quoting Imam al-Baqir, says: "Whoever recites „Say: He, Allah, is One" once, will be blessed. Whoever recites it twice, he and his family will be blessed. Whoever recites it thrice, he, his family and his neighbors will be blessed. Whoever

---

[523] *Ibid., hadith* 3.
[524] *Ibid., hadith* 4.
[525] *Ibid., hadith* 6.

recites it twelve times, Allah will build for him twelve palaces in Paradise, such that the keepers [*hafazah*] say: „Take us to the palaces of our brother so-and-so to see them." Whoever recites it a hundred times, Allah will forgive his sins for twenty-five years, except [sins concerning] blood and property. Whoever recites it four hundred times, his will be the rewards of four hundred martyrs, the horses of all of whom were killed and their blood shed. Whoever recites it a thousand times in a day and a night, will not die unless he sees his seat in Paradise, or it is shown to him."[526]

In the same noble *al-Kafi*, on the authority of Imam al-Baqir (a) it is said that the Messenger of Allah (s) said: "Whoever recites „**Say: He, Allah, is One**" a hundred times on his going to bed, Allah will forgive his sins of fifty years."[527]

Imam as-Sadiq (a) is quoted to have said that his father said: "[The *surah* of] „**Say: He, Allah, is One**" is one-third of the Quran, and [the *surah* of] „**Say: O you, disbelievers**" is a quarter of the Quran."[528]

He also is quoted to have said that the Messenger of Allah (s) performed the *salat* over [the body of] Sad ibn Maadh, then said: "Seventy thousand angels, including Gabriel, came down and performed the *salat* over Sad's body. I asked Gabriel: „What for did Sad deserve that you performed the *salat* over him?" He said: „Because he used to recite: „**Say: He, Allah, is One**", standing, sitting, riding, walking on foot, in coming and going."[529]

Wasail ash-Shiah, quoting *al-Majalis wa Maaniy al-Akhbar*, on the authority of Imam as-Sadiq (a), says that the Imam has quoted his great fathers on the authority of Salman (al-Farsi—may Allah be pleased with him) that he heard the Messenger of Allah (s) say: "Whoever recites [the *surah* of] „**Say: He, Allah, is One**" once will be as if he has recited one-third of the Quran. Whoever recites it twice, he will be as if he has recited two-thirds of the Quran. And whoever

---

[526] *Usul al-Kafi*, vol. 4, p. 425, "Book of the Merit of the Quran," ch. on "The Merit of the Quran," *hadith* 1.
[527] *Ibid., hadith* 4.
[528] *Ibid., hadith* 7.
[529] *Ibid., hadith* 13.

recites it three times, he will be as if he has completed reciting the Quran."[530]

In *Thawab al-Amal* it is said: "If a Friday [a week] passes over somebody without his reciting [the *surah* of] „**Say: He, Allah, is One**," and he dies, he dies on the religion of Abu Lahab."[531]

In *al-Mustadrak* there are many lengthy *hadith*s relating the merits of this noble *surah*. For further information refer to it and to the *Wasail*.[532] And praise is for Allah.

---

[530] *Wasa'il ash-Shiah*, vol. 4, p. 868, "Book of the *Salat*," chs. on "Reciting the Quran," ch. 31, *hadith* 5. *Maaniy al-Akhbar*, p. 234, ch. on "The Meaning of Salman's Saying."

[531] *Thawab al-Amal*, p. 156, "The Reward of Reciting **Say: He, Allah, is One**," *hadith* 2."

[532] *Wasa'il ash-Shiah*, vol. 4, pp. 866 and 870, "Book of the *Salat*," sec. on "Reciting the Quran," chs. 31 and 33; *Mustadrak al-Wasa'il*, "Book of the *Salat*," sec. on "Reciting the Quran," chs. 24 and 26.

SOME COMMENTS ON
THE BLESSED *SURAH* OF *AL-QADR*
AS MUCH AS THEY SUIT THESE PAPERS
Chapter Seven

He, the Exalted, says: **"We revealed it on the night of *al-Qadr.*"** Lofty matters are there in this noble *ayah*, to refer to some of which is not without advantage.

The first matter is that this *ayah* and many of noble *ayah*s ascribe the revelation of the Quran to the Sacred Essence of Allah Himself, as He says: **"We have revealed it in a blessed night,"**[533] **"We have revealed the Reminder and We will be its guardian,"**[534] and similar noble *ayah*s. In some other *ayah*s it is ascribed to Gabriel, the Faithful Spirit, as He says: **"The Faithful Spirit descended with it."**[535]

The literalist scholars in these instances say that this is metaphorical, similar to: **"...O Haman! Build for me a tower..."**[536] Ascribing the revelation, for example, to Allah is because His Sacred Essence was the cause and the one who commanded it to be revealed, or the ascription of the revelation to Allah is real, and as the Faithful Spirit is the means, it is metaphorically ascribed to him. This is because they regard ascribing Allah''s act to the creatures to be like ascribing a creature''s act to another creature. Thus, the tasks of Izrael and Gabriel are ascribed to Allah, the Exalted, as the task of Haman is ascribed to Pharaoh, and the tasks of the builders and the constructors to Haman. But this is an analogy that is completely false and differential. Comprehending ascribing (a creature''s) creation to Allah, and the act of a creature to the Creator is among the important branches of theology and philosophy, through which a lot of problems

---

[533] *Surah ad-Dukhan* 44:3.
[534] *Surah al-Hijr* 15:9.
[535] *Surah ash-Shuara"* 26:193.
[536] *Surah Ghafir* 40:36.

are solved, including fatalism and free will, of which this matter is a branch.

It must be noted that it has been proved and confirmed in the high sciences that all the House of Realization and phases of existence are the image [*surat*] of the Holy Emanation, which is the luminous manifestation of Allah. As the Luminous Relation [*idafa-i ishraqiyyah*] is mere relation and pure dependence [*faqr*] its individuations and images are mere relations, too, having neither identity [*haythiyyat*] nor independence of their own. In another expression, the whole House of Realization is, essentially, attributively and actually, vanished in Allah, because if a being was independent in a personal affair of his, whether in the existential identity or in any of its other affairs, he would be out of the limits of possibility, and would be changed into essential necessity, which is an obvious falsity. If this divine grace is implanted in the heart and the heart tastes it as it deserves, a secret of *Qadar* (fate, predestination) will be exposed to him, and a delicate aspect of the truth of "a matter between two matters" (*amr-un bayn al-amrayn*) will be disclosed to him.

So, the effects and the acts of perfection can be attributed to the creature as they similarly can be attributed to Allah, without resorting to metaphor on either side, and this is realized in the view of Unity [*wahdat*] and multiplicity [*kathrat*] and joining between the two matters. But, the one who is in mere multiplicity [*kathrat*] and veiled off Unity, ascribes the act to the creature, heedless of Allah, as we, the veiled, are. The one in whose heart Unity [*wahdat*] is manifested, will be veiled against the creatures, and will ascribe all acts to Allah, while the gnostic researcher joins between "Unity" and "multiplicity." At the same time of attributing the act to Allah, without resorting to the blemish of metaphor, he also attributes it to the creature, without the blemish of metaphor. The noble *ayah*: "**...And you threw not when you did throw, but Allah threw,**"[537] in which, while confirming the throwing, negates it, and while negating the throwing, confirms it, is a reference to the way of the great gnostics and their strict faithful method. Our referring to the acts and effects of perfection, excluding the shortcomings, was because the shortcomings" recourse is to the privations, which are of the individuations [*taayyunat*] of existence,

---

[537] *Surah al-Anfal* 8:17.

and are not attributed to Allah, except accidentally [*bilarad*]. Going into the details of this subject is not possible in these papers.

Now that this introduction has been understood, the attribution of "revelation" [*tanzil*] to Allah and Gabriel, and the "bringing to life" [*ihya*] to Seraphiel and Allah, and the "bringing death" [*imatah*] to Izrael and the angels in charge of the souls and to Allah, can also be easily understood. There are many references to this matter in the noble Quran. It is part of the Quran's Knowledge [*maarif*] of which there was no trace in the books of the wise men and the philosophers before this Glorious Book, and the human family is indebted to the gift of this Divine Book in this respect, like other divine, Quranic Knowledge [*maarif*].

The second matter is the use of the plural pronoun: "We revealed." The point here is to aggrandize the state of Allah, the Exalted, as the revealer of this noble Book. It may be that this plurality refers to a nominal plurality denoting that Allah, the Exalted, with all the affairs of His Names and Attributes, is the originator of this noble Book. For this reason, this noble Book is the image of the Collective Oneness of all the Names and Attributes, and is the introducer of the Holy state [*maqam*] of Allah in all affairs [*shuun*] and manifestations. In other words, this luminous Book is the image of the Greatest Name, as is the Perfect Man, or rather, the truth of these two, in the Unseen [*hadrat-i ghayb*], is the same, while in the world of separation they separate in respect of the image, although in respect of concept they do not separate. This is a meaning of: "They would not separate until they come to me at the Pool."[538] As Allah, with the hands of Majesty and Beauty fermented the clay of the First Man, the Perfect Man, He, with the hands of Beauty and Majesty, revealed the Complete Book, the Comprehensive Quran. Probably it is for this reason that it was called the Quran, because the state of Oneness [*ahadiyyat*] is the Union of Unity and multiplicity, [*jam-i wahdat wa kathrat*], and it is for this reason that this Book can neither be abrogated nor ruptured, because

---

[538] "The Book of Allah and my *itrat* (progeny) will not be separated from each other until they come to me at the Pool (of *Kawthar*)." This is a part of a well-known and successively related *hadith* called *Hadith ath-Thaqalayn*. *Usul al-Kafi*, vol. 1, page 299, "The Book of Divine Proof," ch. "Concerning What Allah and His Messenger Imposed of Being with the Imams (a)," *hadith* 6; vol. 4, p. 141, "The Book of Faith and Disbelief," ch. "Concerning the Least by which a Servant may be a Believer," *hadith* 1.

the Greatest Name and its manifestations are eternal and everlasting, and all *Shariah*s call to this Muhammadan *Shariah* and guardianship [*wilayah*].

It is probable that as it is said: **"We revealed,"** on the same basis: **"We offered the trust..."**[539] is said in the first person plural, since **"the trust,"** according to its inside, is the truth of guardianship, and, according to its outside, is the *Shariah*, Islam, Quran or the *salat*.

The third matter is a brief about the revelation of the Quran. It is of the delicacies [*latayif*] of divine sciences [*maarif*] and of the secrets of religious facts that only few can scientifically get some information about them, except the perfect godly men, at the head of whom is the very person of the Seal of the Prophets (*s*), and then, with his assistance, the others of the godly men and the people of knowledge. No other one can, by way of intellectual intuition, know this divine delicacy [*latifah*], because this truth cannot be discerned except by attaining to the world of inspiration and getting out of the limits of the worlds of possibility. We shall, in this stage, refer to this truth by way of hints and expressive allegories.

It must be noted that the hearts which travel to Allah by way of spiritual *suluk* and internal journey, and migrate from the dark station of the self and from the house of I-ness and selfishness, are, generally, divided into two groups.

First, those who, after finishing their travel to Allah, death overtakes them, and they remain in the state of attraction, annihilation and death. The reward of this group is with Allah, and it is Allah. They are the beloved who perish under the "domes [*qibab*] of Allah." No one knows them, and they have connection to nobody. They know none but Allah: "My friends are under My domes, no one knows them other than Me."[540]

The second group is those who, having completed their journey to Allah and in Allah, became fit to return to themselves and be subject to a state of sobriety and intelligence. They are those whose aptitude, according to the manifestation by the Holiest Emanation, which is the secret of *qadr*, has been predetermined, and they have been chosen for perfecting the servants and engendering prosperity in the regions.

---

[539] *Surah al-Ahzab* 33:72.

[540] *Ihya'u Ulum 'ud-Din*, vol. 4, p. 256. A Divine utterance. In some editions it is "*qibabi*" (my domes) and in some other it is "*qiba'i*" (my cloak).

Having communicated with His knowledge [*hadrat-i ilmiyyah*] and returned to real entities, they disclosed the journey of the entities and their communication [*ittiSal*] with His Holiness [*hadrat-i quds*], and their travel to Allah and to happiness, receiving the honorable robe [*khalat*] of prophethood. This disclosure [*kashf*] is a divine revelation [*wahy*], before descending to the world of Gabrielic revelation. After turning from this world towards the descending worlds, they disclose what is in the High Pens and Holy Tablets, in proportion to their comprehension of knowledge and growth of perfection, which belong to the Names [*hadarat-i asmaiyyah*]. The difference of *Shariah*s and prophethoods, or rather all differences, stem from there.

In this stage it sometimes happens that the Unseen Truth and the Holy Secret, proved in His Knowledge [*hadrat-i ilmiyyah*] and the High Pens and Tablets, descend, by way of the unseen of their souls and the secret of their honorable spirits, by means of the Angel of Revelation, Gabriel, into their blessed hearts. Sometimes Gabriel appears in an "ideal image" [*tamaththul-i mithali*] in the "Ideal" [*hadrat-i mithal*] to them, and sometimes he takes a "worldly image," appearing from the hidden place [*makan*] of the Unseen, by that truth to the scene of the world of visibility, bringing down that divine delicacy [*latifah*]. The receiver [*sahib*] of the revelation, in each of the emergences [*nashaat*], understands and discerns in a certain way: in a way in His Knowledge [*hadrat-i ilmiyyah*], and in different ways in the entities [*hadrat-i ayan*], in the Pens [*hadarat-i aqlam*] in the Tablets [*hadrat-i alwah*] in the "Ideal" [*hadrat-i mithal*], in the Common Sense, and in the absolute visibilities [*shahadat*]. These are the seven stages of descension, which may be related to the *hadith* that the Quran has descended on "seven letters,"[541] which does not contradict the *hadith*: "The Quran is one, revealed from the One,"[542] as is known. This state, however, requires to be expanded upon, but not here.

The fourth matter concerns the secret of the third person singular pronoun "it" [*ha*] in **"We revealed it."** As is known, the Quran has passed, before being descended to this emergence [*nashah*] through stages and entities [*kaynunat*]. Its first stage was its entity in

---

[541] *Bihar al-Anwar*, vol. 89, p. 83.
[542] *Usul al-Kafi*, vol. 4, p. 438, "The Book of the Merits of the Quran," ch. "The Rarities," *hadith* 12.

the Knowledge [*kaynunat-i ilmiyyah*] in the Unseen by the speaking of His Essence and by His Self-Arguing [*muqariat-i dhatiyyah*] by way of the "Collective Oneness" [*ahadiyyat-i jam*]. And the said pronoun may be a reference to that state, as, in order to show that precept, He used the third person pronoun, as if to say that this very Quran which was revealed on "the night of *qadr*" is the same scholarly Quran, in the unseen secret hidden in the emergence of Knowledge [*nashat-i ilmiyyah*], and which was descended from those stages, in one of which it was united with the Essence and was of the manifestations of the Names. This apparent truth is that divine secret, and this Book, which has appeared in the uniform of words and expressions, in the stage of Essence is in the image of the Essential manifestations, and, in the stage of Action, is the very manifestation of Act, as the Commander of the Believers (Ali) (a) said: "His words are His act."[543]

The fifth matter concerns "the night of *qadr*," about which there are many discussions and uncountable pieces of information, which have been expanded upon by the great scholars (may Allah be pleased with them) according to their diverse ways and methods. In these pages we shall briefly relate some of them. As to the matters that they did not mention, we shall refer to them within our relating other matters.

As regards the naming of "the night of *qadr*," the scholars have different opinions. Some say that as it is honorable and great, and as the Quran is great, brought down (in it) by a great angel, to a great Messenger, for a great *ummah,* it was called "*Laylat ul-Qadr*" (the Night of Majesty).

Some say that it is called "the Night of Measure" because the affairs, the life-terms and the provisions of the people are "measured" in that very night.

Some say that as the angels on that night are so numerous (in the earth) that it is as if the earth is strictly "measured" for them, it is called *al-Qadr*, and that is like: **"and he whose provision is measured."**[544]

These are some of the opinions concerning this subject. About each of them there have been researches, a hint at which is not without advantage.

---

[543] *Nahj al-Balaghah*, edited by Fayd ul-Islam, p. 737, sermon 228.
[544] *Surah at-Talaq* 65:7.

As to the first opinion, i.e. that night being honorable and great, know that many things are said in this respect, to the effect that, as regards time and place in general, some are honorable and some are not, some are lucky and some are unlucky. But is this a natural and intrinsic characteristic of time and place, or is it because happy and unhappy events happen in them, and, consequently they are so described? Although this is not a noble and important topic, and to expand upon it is not advantageous, yet, we shall briefly refer to it. What gives priority to the first possibility is that some narratives and *ayah*s which apparently regard time and place either honorable or unlucky, confirm this to be intrinsic, not a characteristic belonging to the particular condition. So, as there is no rational objection, they can be taken according to their apparent meanings.

What gives priority to the second possibility is that the truth of time and place is a single one, or even their entity (personality) is one, too. Such being the case, it will not be possible that a single person can be divided and be different in status [*hukm*]. Therefore, it is inevitable to take what is said about time and place as lucky or unlucky as caused by the events and happenings taking place in them. But this is not provable, because although time is a single entity, yet, as it gradually expands and is measurable, there can be no objection that some part of it is different in status and effect from another part. There is no evidence that a person, whoever he may be, cannot enjoy two statuses and two effects, rather the contrary is apparent. For example, the human beings, although every one of them is a single person, yet, there are many differences in their corporeal features, like the skin, the brain and the heart, as these are more delicate and honored than the other organs. Similarly, some of the internal and external powers are more honorable than others. This is because man, in this world, is not apparently known as having a complete unity, though single in person. But as apparently he is known of multiplicity, he can have different statuses.

The priority of the first possibility is not, however, an agreeably correct one, because this opinion is based, for example, on "the originality of appearance" [*isalat uz-zuhur*] and "the originality of the truth," [*isalat ul-haqiqah*], whereas methodically it is known that "the originality of the truth" and "the originality of appearance" are used when there is a doubt in the objective for the purpose of making sure of the objective, not that they should confirm the objective after that it had already been known. So, consider.[545]

Therefore, both aspects are possible, but the second aspect seems preferable. Consequently, "the night of *qadr*" was described as "the honored night" because it was the night of the meeting of the Sealing Prophet, the night on which the real lover reached his Beloved. In the former discussions it was noted that the descension of the angels and the revelation was after the annihilation and the real proximity. From many narratives and noble *ayah*s it can be gathered that the luckiness and unluckiness of times and places are because of the events which take place in them. This can be realized by referring to them, although some of them also denote their intrinsic honor.

The other possibility for naming "the night of *qadr*" is because the affairs of the days of the year are measured on that night. So, know that the truth of "Fate" [*qada*] and "Destiny" (Divine Decree = *qadar*), its quality and its stages of appearance, are of the greatest and noblest divine knowledge, and it is because of their extreme exactness and nicety that deeply thinking about them is not allowed for the human race as it causes bewilderment and straying. Therefore, this truth is to be regarded of the religious secrets and the deposits of Prophethood, and one is to refrain from conducting scrutinizing research about it. We refer here only to a subject suiting this stage. That is, although the measurement of the affairs has been estimated from the very beginning in the knowledge of Allah, the Exalted, and it is not of the gradual matters in respect of the pure state of the divine knowledge, then, what does "*taqdir*" in every year and in a particular night mean?

Know that "Fate" and "Divine Decree" are of degrees, and according to those degrees and emergences [*nashaat*] they differ in their status. The first degree is the facts that are judged (evaluated) and measured in His Knowledge by the manifestation in "The Holiest Emanation" in the wake of the appearance of the Names and Attributes. Afterwards, by the High Pens and in the High Tablets, according to the appearance, and by the manifestation of the Act, they

---

[545] It demands consideration because this allegation can be claimed here from another aspect, and it is that the appearance in ascribing a predicate to a proposition is that the proposition itself has the same status and it is the proposition in complete, as the Shaykh, our teacher in the conventional sciences used, concerning generalization [*itlaq*], to call this statement, without needing preliminaries, to prove the generalization.

are ordained and confirmed. No changes and alterations may happen in these degrees. The inevitable and unchangeable decrees [*qada*] are the abstract facts happening in the entities [*hadarat-i ayan*] and in the emergence [*nashah*] of His Knowledge and descending to the abstract Pens and Tablets. Afterwards, the facts appear in isthmus [*barzakhiyyah*] and ideal [*mithaliyyah*] images in other Tablets and in a lower world, which is the world of "the distinct imagination" [*khiyal-i munfasil*] and "the universal imagination" [*khiyal ul-kull*]—the world which, according to the method of the illuminationist philosophers, is called "The World of the Suspended Ideas" [*alam-i muthul-i muallaqah*]. In such a world changes and differences are possible to happen, or actually they do happen. After that, the evaluations [*taqdirat*] and measurings take place by means of the angels in charge of the world of nature. In this Tablet of Fate there are continual changes and alterations, or rather it is, in itself, a flowing form and a passing, gradual fact. In this *lawh* (Tablet) the facts can be strong or weak, and the movements may be swift, slow, accelerated or decreased. Nevertheless, the "near-to-Allah" [*yalillahi*] aspect, the unseen aspect, of these very things—which is the aspect of *tadalli* (suspension) to Allah, and it is the form of the appearance of the "Spread Emanation" [*fayd-i munbasit*] and the "Extended Shade" [*zill-i mamdud*], and the truth of Allah's "Active Knowledge"—there can occur in it no change or alteration.

In short, all the changes, alterations, additions to the lives, and measuring (the peoples') provisions are, as the philosophers believe, in the *lawh* of "the *qadr* of knowledge" [*qadr-i ilmi*], which is "the world of ideas"—while to the writer, they are in the *lawh* of "the *qadr* of objectivity" [*qadr-i ayni*], which is the very place of the measurements—done by the angels in charge of it. Therefore, there is no objection [*mani*] that, as "the night of *qadr*" is the night of full attention of the "perfect guardian" [*waliyy-i kamil*] and of the appearance of his heavenly sovereignty, changes and alterations may happen in it, in the world of nature through the honorable person of the "perfect guardian" and the Imam of each era and the pole [*qutb*] of the time—who, in our time, is "Allah's Remainder" [*baqiyyatullah*] in the worlds (earths, lands = *aradin*), our Master, Patron, Imam, and Guide, the Proof, the son of al-Hasan al-Askari, may our souls be ransom for his coming. So, he may accelerate or slow any individual part of nature that he desires, and enlarge or straiten any provision he wills. And this will is that of the *Haqq*, and is the shadow and the rays of the Eternal Will and follows the Divine commands, as the angels of Allah, too, can do (change) nothing by themselves. Every act (change = *tasarruf*), rather every particle of existence, is of Allah and of His unseen grace [*latifah*]: **"So keep straight as you are commanded."**[546]

As to what has been said concerning the other possibility of naming "the night of *qadr*," i.e. it was so called because the earth seems too much narrow with the throng of the angels on that night, this point is a far-fetched one, despite the fact that Khalil ibn Ahmad,[547] the wonder of the time, may Allah's pleasure be upon him, says that what can be discussed is that the angels are not of the kind of the world of nature and matter, so what does it mean to say that the earth seemed narrow? However, such matters have been related in some noble narrations, like the case of the funeral procession of Sad ibn Muadh,[548] may Allah be pleased with him, or the angels" spreading their wings for the students of knowledge.[549] This is when the angels appear in the assimilation [*tamaththul*] of "Ideal Images," descending from the unseen world to the "World of Ideals" [*alam-i mithal*] and narrowing the dominion of the earth, or it is probably their worldly assimilation in the kingdom of the earth, although this still cannot be seen by the natural animal eyes. However, the narrowing is on the basis of "Ideal" [*mithaliyyah*] or "worldly" [*mulkiyyah*] assimilation.

The second matter concerns the truth of "the night of *qadr*." Know that every spiritual grace has a reality, and for every worldly form there is a heavenly and unseen interior. People of knowledge say

---

[546] *Surah Hud* 11:112.

[547] Khalil ibn Ahmad ibn Umar ibn Tamim, Abu Abdur-Rahman al-Bahili, al-Basri, the grammarian and prosodist, born in the year 100 or 105 AH in al-Basrah, and died in 160, 170 or 175 AH. He was a famous linguist and a writer. He discovered the meters of poetry. He was an *Imami* and, as some say, he was a companion of Imam Jafar as-Sadiq (a) and quoted him in his narrations. He wrote many books on diverse arts, including *Zubdat 'ul-Arud* (the Gist of Prosody), *al-Ayn*, a book on Imamate, *al-Iqa* (rhythm), *an-Num* (tone or softness), *al-Jumal* (*syntax*), *ash-Shawahid* (ancient verses as evidences), *an-Nuqat wash-Shikl* (dots and form), and a book on the meanings of the alphabetic letters. For further information bibliographies and books on *rijal* such as *Ayan ash-Shiah*, vol. 30, p. 50, may be consulted.

[548] *Furu al-Kafi*, vol. 3, p. 236, the "Book of Funerals," ch. on "Questioning in the Grave," *hadith* 6.

[549] This concept is referred to Imam as-Sadiq (a) through several channels in *Maalim al-Usul*, p. 7.

that the stages of the descension of the truth of the existence, in respect of the setting of the sun of the truth in the horizon of individuations, are "nights," whereas the stages of ascension, in respect of the rising of the sun of the truth in the horizons of individuations, are "days." Hence, the honor and the unluckiness of the "days" and the "nights" are, accordingly, clearly known.

According to another aspect, the arch of descension is the Muhammadan "Night of *Qadr.*" and the arch of ascension is the Ahmadian "Resurrection Day," because these two arches are the extension of the light of the "Expanded Emanation" [*fayd-i munbasit*], which is "the Muhammadan Truth" [*haqiqat-i muhammadiyyah*], and all the individuations [*taayyunat*] are of the First Individuation of "the Greatest Name." So, from the point of view of Unity [*wahdat*], the world is the "Night of *Qadr*" and the "Day of Resurrection," and it is no more than a single night and day, which is the entire House of Realization, the Muhammadan "Night of *Qadr*" and the Ahmadan "Day of Resurrection." The one who is assured of this truth will always be in the "Night of *Qadr*" and in the "Day of Resurrection," and these two become united.

From the point of view of multiplicity, there will be nights and days. Some nights have *qadr* (greatness, dignity) and some have not. Among all the nights, the Ahmadan constitution [*bunyah*], the Muhammadan individuation (*s*)—into whose horizon has set the light of the truth of existence, with all the affairs, Names and Attributes, and with full luminosity and entire truth—is the absolute night of *qadr*, as the Muhammadan day is the absolute Day of Resurrection. Other days and nights are limited ones. The Quran's revelation [*nuzul*] to this noble constitution [*bunyah*] and pure heart, is the revelation [*nuzul*] in the "night of *qadr*." So, the Quran was revealed both in full in "the night of *qadr*," by way of complete and absolute disclosure, and in parts along twenty-three years in "the night of *qadr*."

The gnostic Shaykh, the Shahabadi[549a] (may he live longer), used to say that the Muhammadan period is "the Night of *Qadr*," that is, all the periods of existence are the Muhammadan period, or it is because in this period the perfect Muhammadan poles, the infallible guiding Imams (a), are "the nights of *qadr*." What proves our

---

[549a] Refer to footnote 97.

suggested possibility concerning the truth of "the night of *qadr*" is the lengthy noble *hadith* which is quoted in *al-Burhan Exegesis* from the noble *al-Kafi*, in which it is said that when a Christian asked Imam Musa ibn Jafar about the hidden explanation of **"Ha Mim! (I swear) By the explaining Book. We revealed it on a blessed night—Surely We are ever warning. There in every wise affair is made distinct,"**[550] he replied: "As to **"Ha Mim,"** it is Muhammad (*s*) "The explaining Book" is Amir al-Muminin Ali (a), and "the night" is Fatimah (a)."[551]

In another narrative it is said that "the ten nights" are interpreted to be the pure Imams from al-Hasan to al-Hasan.[552] This is one of the degrees of "the night of *qadr*" to which Imam Musa ibn Jafar referred, testifying that "the night of *qadr*" was the entire Muhammadan period.

In *Al-Burhan Exegesis* there is a narrative from Imam al-Baqir (a). Being a noble *hadith* referring to several pieces of information, disclosing important secrets, we, owing to its blessedness, relate it in full:

The author (may Allah have mercy upon him), quoting Shaykh Abu Jafar at-Tusi, from his men, from Abdullah ibn Ajlan as-Sakuni, said: "I heard Abu Jafar (a) say: The house of Ali and Fatimah is the room of the Messenger of Allah (*s*), and the roof of their house is the *Arsh* of the Lord of the worlds. And at the bottom of their house there is an uncovered opening to the *Arsh*, the *miraj* of revelation; and the angels bring down revelation upon them in the morning and in the evening and every hour and twinkle of an eye. The angels are in ceaseless groups, some descending and some ascending. And Allah, the Blessed and Exalted, disclosed to Ibrahim the heavens till he saw the *Arsh* and He increased his seeing power. And Allah increased the seeing power of Muhammad, Ali, Fatimah, al-Hasan and al-Husayn (a). They used to see the *Arsh* and they found no roof over their houses except the *Arsh*. Their houses were roofed with the *Arsh* of the Beneficent, and the ascensions of the angels and the Spirit in them, with the permission of their Lord, for every affair in peace. ,I said:

---

[550] *Surah ad-Dukhan* 44:1-4. *Al-Burhan Exegesis*, vol. 4, p. 158.
[551] *Usul al-Kafi*, vol. 2, p. 326, the "Book of the Proof," ch. on "The Birth of the Prophet (*s*), *hadith* 4.
[552] *Al-Burhan Exegesis*, vol. 4, "*Surah al-Fajr*," *hadith* 1, p. 457.

"for every affair"." He said: „In every affair." I said: „Is that revelation?" He said: „Yes"."[553]

Contemplating on this noble *hadith* will open doors of knowledge in the face of the deserving people and discloses parts of the truth of guardianship and of the hidden inside of "the night of *qadr*."

The third matter: Know that as "the night of *qadr*" has a truth and an inside, as it has been mentioned, it also has a form and an appearance, or even appearances in the world of nature. But as appearances can differ in respect of their shortcomings and perfections, from the narratives and *hadith*s about specifying "the night of *qadr*" can be deduced that all the noble nights specified in those narratives are of the appearances of "the night of *qadr*," except that they differ from one another in respect of their honor and perfection of appearance, while that noble night, which is the full appearance of "the night of *qadr*," the night of the complete joining [*wasl*] and the perfect attainment [*wusul*] of the Last Prophet, is hidden in the whole year, in the blessed month of Ramadan, in its last ten (nights) or in the "three nights." The narratives of the Elite [*khassah*] and the public [*ammah*] also differ. The Elite narrate, with uncertainty, that it is on the nights of the nineteenth, twenty-first and twenty-third (of Ramadan), and sometimes they waver between the night of the twenty-first and the twenty-third.

Shihab ibn Abdu Rabbih says: I asked Imam Jafar as-Sadiq (a) to tell me about "the Night of *Qadr*." He said: "the night of the twenty-first and the night of the twenty-third."[554]

Abdul Wahid ibn al-Mukhtar al-Ansari says: "I asked Imam al-Baqir (a) about „the night of *qadr*." He said: „it is on two nights: the night of the twenty-third and the night of the twenty-first," I said: „Name only one of them."He said: „What if you do something on the two nights of which one is „the Night of *Qadr*?"""[555]

---

[553] *Al-Burhan Exegesis*, vol. 4, "Surah al-Qadr," hadith 25, p. 487.
[554] *Majma ul-Bayan*, vol. 10, p. 519; *Nur ath-Thaqalayn*, vol. 5, p. 628, "Surah al-Qadr," hadith 71.
[555] *Bihar al-Anwar*, vol. 95, p. 149.

Hassan ibn Abu Ali says: "I asked Imam as-Sadiq (a) about „the Night of *Qadr*". He said: "Get it on the nineteenth, twenty-first and twenty-third.""[555a]

The devotee and pious "Sayyid" (may Allah be pleased with him) in *Iqbal* says: "Know that it is the night of the twenty-third of the month of Ramadan. There are explicit narratives that it is „the Night of *Qadr*" by revelation and declaration. Of that I relate, on my authority up to Sufyan ibn as-Sit (or as-Simt) who said: "I asked Imam Jafar as-Sadiq (a) to tell me which was „the Night of *Qadr*" exactly." He said: "The night of the twenty-third." Another is to narrate, on my authority up to Zurarah, quoting Abdul Wahid ibn al-Mukhtar al-Ansari, who said: "I asked Imam al-Baqir (a) about „the Night of *Qadr*." He said: "By Allah I tell you with no ambiguity, it is the first night of the last seven nights." Zurarah was further quoted to have said that the month which the Imam mentioned had twenty-nine days.[556] After that other narratives are related to the effect that "the Night of *Qadr*" is the night of the twenty-third (of Ramadan), such as the case of Juhani,[557] which is well known.

A Gnostic Note

As it has been said in respect of the two previously explained blessed *surah*s, it is more obvious that the *bismillah* of each *surah* belongs to it. Therefore, in the blessed *surah* of al-Qadr it means: "We revealed the noble Quranic truth, the Sacred Divine Grace [*latifah*], in the Name of Allah, which is the „Collective Truth of the Names" and the Greatest Name of the Lord, individuated by the absolute mercy of *Rahman* and *Rahim*, on the Muhammadan night of *qadr*." That is, the appearance of the Quran follows the "Collective Appearance" [*zuhur-i jami*] of the Divinity and the "Contraction" [*qabd*] and "Expansion" [*bast*] of "Mercifulness" [*rahimiyyat*) and "Beneficence" [*rahmaniyyat*]. Rather, the truth of the Quran is the state of the appearance of the Greatest Name of Allah through the appearance of the "Beneficence" and the "Mercifulness," and is the "collector of the union and distinctness" [*jami-i jamu tafsil*]. Consequently, this noble

---

[555a] *Majma ul-Bayan*, vol. 10, p. 519; *Wasa'il ash-Shiah*, vol. 7, p. 263, "Book of Fasting," ch. 32, *hadith* 21.

[556] *Iqbal al-Amal*, p. 206.

[557] *Ibid.*, p. 207.

Book is "Quran" and "Furqan" (distinguisher), similar to the spirituality of the Seal of the Prophets and his sacred state of guardianship, which are also *"Quran"* and *"Furqan"* and the state of the "Oneness of Collectivity and Distinctness" [*ahadiyyat-i jam wa tafsil*].

So, it seems that the Sacred Essence, according to this possibility, says: "We have—with the manifestation of the state of the Greatest Name, which is the state of the "Oneness of Collectivity and Distinctness" [*ahadiyyat-i jam wa tafsil*], with the appearance of the mercy of the Beneficent and the Merciful—revealed the Quran on the Muhammadan night of *qadr*. And as in the world of distinction [*farq*], or rather, the distinction of distinction, there was a distinction [*furqaniyyat*] between the two "Qurans," i.e., the revealed and written Quran, and the Quran revealed to him, that is, the "Divine Book" and the "Muhammadan truth," we united between the two Qurans and joined the two *Furqan*s in the night of union [*wisal*], and on this consideration, this night was called „the night of *qadr*," but its actual meritorious status, as it is, cannot be recognized by anybody except by the very Seal of the Prophets (*s*), who is the owner of „the night of *qadr*" in person, as well as his infallible successors, who are its owner, too, through him."

Completion
Some Narratives Concerning the Merits of "the Night of Qadr"

Among them are those narrated by the knower of Allah, Sayyid ibn Tawus (may Allah be pleased with him) in his noble Book *Iqbal al-Amal*. He says: "I found in the book, called *Yawaqit*, by Abu l-Fadl ibn Muhammad al-Hirawi, some narratives on the merits of "the night of *qadr*." Then he quotes from it a narrative from the Messenger of Allah (*s*) as to have said: "Moses said: „O Allah! I desire Your proximity." Allah said: „My proximity is for the one who keeps awake on „the night of *qadr*." He said: „O Allah! I wish for your mercy." Allah said: „My mercy is for the one who shows mercy to the poor on `the night of *qadr*." He said: „O Allah! I want to cross the *Sirat* [the (Right) Path]". He said: „That is for the one who gives out a *sadaqah* on „the night of *qadr*." He said: „O Allah." I want of the trees and fruits of Paradise." Allah said: „They are for the one who glorifies (Me) on „the night of *qadr*." He said: „I want to be delivered." Allah said: „From the Fire?" „Yes," he said. Allah said: „It is for the one who asks forgiveness on „the night of *qadr.*" He said: „O Allah! I ask for Your pleasure." Allah said: „I would be pleased with the one who performs two *rakah*s of *salat* on „the night of *qadr*"."

The same book, quoting the Messenger of Allah (*s*), also says: "The doors of the heaven are opened on „the night of *qadr*. No servant may perform the *salat* on it unless Allah, the Exalted, writes down for him, for every *sajdah* a tree in Paradise, such that if a horseman rides under its shadow for a hundred years he will not finish it, for every *rakah* (or *ruku*) a house, in Paradise, made of quartzes, rubbies, chrysolites and pearls, for every *ayah* a paradisiac crown, for every glorifying one of the precious birds, for every sitting one of the paradisiac degrees, for every *tashahhud* a paradasiac room and for every *taslim* a garment from paradise. And when the column of dawn bursts out, Allah will grant him (in Paradise) sociable women (wives) whose bosoms bulge out from behind the dress, educated and good-behaving maids, eternal boys, noble birds, fragrant flowers, flowing rivers, pleasing graces, gifts, presents, coats of honor, wonders and whatever the heart desires and pleases the eye, in which you will eternally live."

Quoting Imam al-Baqir (a), the same book says: "Whoever remains in „the night of *qadr*" awake, his sins will be forgiven, even if as many as the stars of the sky, and as heavy as the mountains or the weight of the seas."[558] The narratives about its merits are too many to be included in these papers.

* * * * * * *

His saying: "And how do you know what the night of *qadr* is!" is a construction intended to denote honoring, tributing and paying homage to the greatness of the subject and the truth, especially when considering the addresser and the addressee. Although the addresser is Allah, the Exalted, and the addressee is the Messenger of Allah (*s*), yet, the subject is sometimes so glorious that it is impossible to contain it with the construction of words and expressions. It is as if He says, "You know not how great the truth of the night of *qadr* is!" It cannot be explained in arranged words and letters, as they are incapable of containing it. Therefore, He just used "How" [*ma*] to denote that

---

[558] *Bihar al-Anwar*, vol. 98, p. 168.

greatness, trying not to describe it, only saying that "the night of *qadr* is better than a thousand months," that is, He introduces it by referring to its characteristics and effects, since telling its truth is not possible. Hence, one may well guess that the truth of the night of *qadr* and its inside are different from its external form, though its external form is great and important, too, but not to the extent of addressing the Messenger of Allah, the absolute guardian and the informed of all worlds, in this way.

If you say: On the basis of the said possibility that the inside of "the night of *qadr*" is the very truth and constitution of the Messenger of Allah (*s*), in which the sun of truth, in all its affairs, is hidden, then the objection will be higher, because it will not be possible to tell him: "How do you know what ,,the night of *qadr*," which is your own visible form, is?"

I will say: This subject has a secret. This delicate point has an inner meaning **"for him who has heart or gives ear and is a witness."**[559] Know, dear, that in the inside of the real "night of *qadr*," i.e., the constitution and the visible form, or the immutable essence of Muhammad [*ayn-i thabit-i muhammadi*] (*s*), there is manifested the Greatest Name and the Divine Collective Oneness. Therefore, as long as the traveling-to-Allah servant, that is, the Sealing Messenger (*s*), is still inside his own veil, he will not be able to witness that inside and truth, as the same was said about Moses, the son of ,,Imran, (a) in the Glorious Quran: **"You will never see Me,"**[560] despite the fact that Moses witnessed the manifestation in Essence or in Attributes, as in: **"When his Lord manifested (His glory) to the mountain, He made it crumble to dust, and Moses fell down in a swoon,"**[561] or in the great noble invocation of *Simat,* as is quite obvious. There is also the note: "O Moses, as long as you are in your Musawiyan veil and in your concealment [*ihtijab*], you will have no chance of witnessing. Witnessing the Beauty of the Beautiful is possible for the one who has come out of himself, because having come out of himself, he would see with the *Haqq*"s eye, and the *Haqq*"s eye would be seeing the *Haqq*. So, the manifestation of the Greatest Name, which is the perfect form of "the night of *qadr*," cannot be seen through one"s concealment

---

[559] *Surah Qaf* 50:37.
[560] *Surah al-Araf* 7:143.
[561] *Ibid.*

[*ihtijab*]. Therefore, this expression is, according to the mentioned verification, correct and fitting.

If you say: "the night of *qadr* is the very Ahmadan constitution in view of the fact that in him the sun of the truth is hidden, not the sun itself" that the said justification may be correct.

I will say: "According to the people of insight, the thing-ness of a thing depends on its form of perfection, and that the things with reasons, [*asbab*] especially divine reason [*sabab*], their truth cannot be recognized without recognizing their reasons. In view of the people of knowledge, the correlation between the outside and the inside, manifestation and the manifesting, is not like that of two separate matters, because a truth may sometimes have an external manifestation, and sometimes an internal manifestation, as the well-known gnostic says:

We are non-existents showing existence,
You are the Absolute Being and our existence.

As the gnostic Rumi says, this talk has no end and it is better to forgo it.

* * * * * * *

His saying: **"The night of *qadr* is better than a thousand months."** If we note the worldly appearance of the external form of the night of *qadr*, we realize that its goodness is more than a thousand months which have no night of *qadr* in them, or the night of *qadr* and the acts of devotional worship on it are better than thousand months in which the Israelites used to carry their weapons and fight for the sake of Allah, or the night of *qadr* is better than the thousand months of the rule of the Umayyads (may Allah curse them), as is stated in the noble narratives.[562]

If we note the truth of the night of *qadr*, "a thousand months" may be an allusion to all beings, as "a thousand" is a complete number, and by "months" the kinds are intended. That is, the respected Muhammadan constitution, who is the perfect man, is better than the thousand kinds which cover all beings, as has been said by some people of gnosticism.[563]

---

[562] *Bihar al-Anwar*, vol. 94, p. 8, quoting *Majalis-i Shaykh*, the *Tafsir* of Ali ibn Ibrahim, p. 732; *Al-Burhan Exegesis*, vol. 4, p. 486; *Rawdat al-Kafi*, hadith 280, p. 222.
[563] Reference unknown.

Another possibility occurs to the writer, that is, the night of *qadr* may be a hint at the manifestation of the Greatest Name, i.e., the complete Muhammadan (*s*) mirror, and "a thousand months" may be the manifestations of the other Names. And, as Allah, the Exalted, has one thousand and one Names, and as one Name is especially hidden in the unseen world, similarly, the night of *qadr* is hidden, too, and the night of *qadr* of the Muhammadan constitution is also a hidden name. Thus, this especially hidden name is known to nobody except to the sacred essence of the Sealing Messenger (*s*).

A Gnostic Note

It must be noted that as the perfect guardian, the Seal of the Prophets (*s*), is the night of *qadr* because of the interiority [*butun*] of the Greatest Name in him and the occultation [*ihtijab*] of the *Haqq* with all affairs in him, likewise he is the day of *qadr,* too, since the appearance of the sun of the truth and the projection of the all-embracing Name appear from the horizon of his individuation. Similarly, the "Day of Resurrection" is his person, too.

In short, that sacred essence is the day and night of *qadr,* and the Day of Resurrection is the day of *qadr,* too. Therefore, the point that, out of all phenomena, the "month" is referred to, and from this complete and sacred phenomenon it is referred to "the night," is, perhaps, because the beginning of the months and years is the day and night, like the "one" which is the beginning of the numbers. That master [*sarwar*] in the inside [*batin*] of the truth, the Greatest Name, is the beginning of the other names; and, in his individuation [*taayyun*] and immutable essence [*ayn-i thabit*], he is the root (origin = *asl*) of the "Good Tree" [*shajarat-i tayyibah*] and the beginning of the individuations [*taayyunat*]. Consider, so that you may know, and seize the opportunity!

* * * * * * *

His saying: **"The angels and the Spirit descend in it, by the permission of their Lord, for every affair."** In this noble *ayah* there are points, to some of which we shall refer briefly.

The first point is about the ranks of the angels of Allah, the Exalted, and their reality in general. Know that there are differences among the traditionists and researchers concerning the angels whether they are abstract or corporeal. All the philosophers and researchers,

389

and many of the juristic researchers, believe in their abstraction and in the abstraction of the rational soul, which they prove by strong evidences. There are also many noble narratives and *ayah*s from which (their) abstraction can be understood, as the traditionist and researcher, our master Muhammad Taqi Majlisi, the great father of the late Majlisi, says, in *Sharh ul-Faqih,* commenting on some relevant narratives, that they confirm the abstraction of the rational soul.[564]

On the other hand, some of the great traditionists believe in their non-abstraction. Their utmost proof is that to believe in their abstraction is contrary to religion, and they add that there is no abstract except the Sacred Essence of Allah, the Exalted. This, however, is a very weak argument, because their most attention is probably directed to only two points: the first is the case of the temporal contingency [*huduth-i zamani*] of the world, as they think that the existence of an abstract other than Allah contradicts it. The second point is the case of the free will of Allah, the Exalted, in His acts, as they think that this contradicts the abstraction of the world of intelligence and the angels of Allah, the Exalted. Both these cases are of the insane [*manunah*] affairs within the High Sciences. The non-contradiction of such cases with an abstract being is quite obvious. Even to believe in the non-abstraction of the rational souls, the world of intelligence and the angels of Allah, is contrary to many divine affairs and true beliefs, which cannot be explained for the time being. The temporal contingency of the worlds, as is interpreted by this group, is contrary to the principle of the temporal contingency, besides being in opposition to many divine rules, too.

To the writer, the truth, which agrees with reason [*aql*] and tradition [*naql*], is that the angels of Allah are of different types. Many of them are abstracts and many are intermediate [*barzakhi*] corporeal: **"No one knows the host of your Lord save Him."**[565] As to their types, according to their general division, it is said that the heavenly beings are of two types: Type one has nothing to do with the corporeal

---

[564] Such as the narrative quoted from Imam as-Sadiq (a) to the effect: "When the soul is taken (in death), it remains hovering over the body..." On this he comments: "This narrative and the one after it, and the many other similar narratives, and the other successive narratives, as well as the apparent literal meanings of the Quranic *ayah*s, all prove the spiritual resurrection, i.e. the survival of the soul after the destruction of the body..." *Rawdat 'ul-Muttaqin,* vol. 1, p. 492.
[565] *Surah al-Muddaththir* 74:31.

world, belonging to neither incarnation [*hulul*] nor management [*tadbir*]. The other type belongs to one of the said two aspects.

The first type consists of two groups.

The first group are those who are called "the Passionate [*muhayyimah*] Angels." They are those who are infatuated with the Beauty of the Beautiful, absorbed in the Essence of His Majesty, unaware of all other creatures, paying no attention to other beings.

Among the friends of Allah [*awliyaullah*] there is a group like them. While we are indulged in the dark sea of nature, and are completely unaware of the unseen world and the Essence of His Majesty, despite the fact that He is apparent by His Essence [*bi dh-dhat*] and that every appearance is a reflection of His Appearance, they are unaware of the world and of whatever is in it, and are engaged only in the *Haqq* and His Beautiful Beauty. A narrative says that Allah has some creatures who know nothing of His creating Adam and *Iblis*.[566]

The second group are those whom Allah, the Exalted, has made the means of the mercy of His Being. They are the beginning of the series of the beings and the goal of their longings. They are called *ahl al-jabarut* (the Owners of Power), and their chief and leader is "the Greatest Spirit." It may be that **"The angels and the Spirit descend,"** is a reference to this group of the angels of Allah. Describing him as "the Spirit," though he is an angel, is a hint at his greatness, as is in the noble *ayah*: **"On the day when the angels and the Spirit stand arrayed."**[567] From a point of view, the Spirit is called "the Highest Pen" [*qalam-i ala*], as it is said: "The first that Allah created was the Pen."[568] According to another point of view, it is called "the First Intellect" [*aql-i awwal*], as it is also said: "The first that Allah created was the Intellect."[569] Some others take "The Spirit" to be Gabriel. Some philosophers consider Gabriel to be the last of the Cherubic angels; some call him "The Holy Spirit;" and they regard the "Spirit" to be the first of the Cherubic angels. The noble narratives also state that "the Spirit" is greater than Gabriel. The noble *al-Kafi*, quotes Abu Basir, who said: "I asked Abu Abdullah, as-Sadiq, (a) about the words of Allah, the Exalted" „**They will ask you concerning the Spirit. Say:**

---

[566] *Ilm al-Yaqin*, vol. 1, p. 250; *Al-Kafi* (*ar-Rawdah*, hadith 301), p. 231.
[567] *Surah an-Naba"* 78:38.
[568] *Nur ath-Thaqalayn Exegesis*, vol. 5, hadith 9, p. 389; *Ilm al-Yaqin*, vol. 1, p. 154.
[569] *Bihar al-Anwar*, vol. 1, p. 97.

The Spirit is of the bidding of my Lord" (*Surah al-Isra* 17:85). He said: „(It is) a creature [*khalq*] greater than Gabriel and Michael. It was with the Messenger of Allah (*s*), it is with the Imams (a), and it is from the heavenly kingdom"."[570] Some narratives say that the Spirit is not of the angels, it is greater than them.[571]

Probably "The Spirit" has two meanings in terms of the Quran and the Traditions, as it has its meanings in other terms. A Spirit is of the angels" type, since it was said to be of "the heavenly kingdom." Another Spirit is that of the holy men [*awliya*], which is not of the angels, but greater than them. Therefore, the Spirit in the noble *surah* of *al-Qadr* may refer to "the Faithful Spirit" [*ruh al-amin*] or "the Greatest Spirit," because the *surah* was revealed on "the night of *qadr*." In the noble *ayah*: **"They will ask you about the Spirit,"**[571a] the reference may be to the spirit of the human beings, which, in its perfect degree, is greater than Gabriel and other angels. It is of "the World of Command" [*alam-i amr*], and sometimes combined with His "Will" [*mashiyyat*], which is absolute command.

Another group of the angels of Allah are those who are in charge of the corporeal beings and of managing them. These are of so many types and uncountable kinds, because for every being, high or low, celestial or terrestial, there is a heavenly aspect [*wijhah*] through which it is connected to the world of the angels and the host [*junud*] of Allah, the Exalted, as Allah refers to the heavenly domain of the things in the noble *ayah*: **"Therefore, glory be to Him in Whose hand is the dominion of all things, and to Him you shall be brought back."**[572]

The Messenger of Allah (*s*), concerning the host of the angels, say (as it has been narrated): "The heaven clamored, and it had the right to do so, as there was no place for a foot without there being an angel bowing or kneeling down."[573] Noble narratives speak much of the multitude of the angels and their numerous ranks.[574]

---

[570] *Usul al-Kafi*, vol. 2, p. 18, "The Book of Divine Proof," ch. on "The Spirit by which Allah Directs the Steps of the Imams" (a), *hadith* 3.

[571] *Bihar al-Anwar*, vol. 25, "Book of the *Imamah*," sec. on "Their Creation, Nature and Spirits," ch. 3, *hadith* 45, p. 64.

[571a] *Surah Isra"* 17:85.

[572] *Surah Ya-Sin* 36:83.

[573] *Ilm al-Yaqin*, vol. 1, p. 259.

[574] *Bihar al-Anwar*, vol. 56, ch. on "The Angels," p. 144.

The second point concerns the descent of the angels upon the *waliyy al-amr* (the legal guardian).

Know that the Greatest Spirit is the greatest creature among the angels of Allah, i.e. it is placed in the first rank of the angels of Allah, and is the greatest and most honorable of all. The immaterial (abstract) angels of Allah, confined to the world of power [*alam-i jabarut*], would not forsake their states, as for them ascending and descending, as done by the material bodies, is impossible, because the immaterial (abstract) is innocent of the material requisites. Therefore, their descending will be in heavenly or worldly resemblance [*tamaththul*], whether in the heart, the bosom and the common sense of the guardian [*wali*], or in edifices of the earth, in the *kabah*, around the grave of the Messenger of Allah (*s*), or in the Populous House [*bayt al-mamur*]. Allah, the Exalted, concerning the descending of "The Faithful Spirit" to Mary (a), says: **"...it assumed for her the likeness of a perfect man."**[575] It is also possible for the holy men [*awliya*] and the perfect to assume heavenly resemblance and spiritual likeness of sovereignty. Therefore, the angels of Allah have the power and ability to enter the visible and invisible worlds assuming likenesses, and the perfect holy men [*awliya*] have the power to enter the heavenly world [*malakut*] and the world of power [*jabarut*] assuming spirituality, and to return from the exterior to the interior. To believe in this is quite easy for the one who understands the realities of the abstracts, whether heavenly and powerly abstracts or the rational souls, which are also abstracts of the worlds of *jabarut* and *malakut*, and who can imagine the stages of their existence and appearances, and the correlation [*nisbat*] of the outside to the inside, and the inside to the outside.

One must know that the assumption [*tamaththul*] of the "beings of *jabarut*" and the "beings of *malakut*" in the heart, bosom and sense of the human being is not possible except after his coming out of the apparel of humanity and being connected with those worlds. Otherwise, as long as the soul is engaged in the mundane preparations and is unaware of those worlds, it is impossible for it to witness those scenes or assumptions. Yet, it is sometimes possible that, with a gesture of a holy man, the soul comes out of this world, and, according to its deservedness, it may get a spiritual or formal [*suri*] understanding of the unseen world. And sometimes it happens that,

---

[575] *Surah Maryam* 19:17.

due to some stupendous event, the soul is directed away from nature and perceives an example of the invisible world, such as the episode of that naïve man who, on his pilgrimage, received an acquittal from the fire of Hell, as related by Avicenna. The gnostic Shaykh, Muhyi d-Din, also relates a story like this one.[576] Such stories are due to the soul‟s turning away from the *mulk* to the *malakut.* It sometimes happens that the souls of the perfect holy men [*awliya*] after detachment from the worlds and witnessing the Greatest Spirit or other angels of Allah through the power of soul, come to themselves, keeping the power of witnessing the invisible and the visible. In such a case they simultaneously, and in all emergences (growths = *nashaat*), witness the truths of the beings of *jabarut.* It may also happen that the perfect *wali*, through his personal power, will be able to have the angels descend. And Allah is the Knower!

The third point is that since the night of *qadr* is the night of disclosure [*mukashafah*] to the Messenger of Allah (*s*) and the Imams of guidance (a), all the worldly affairs are uncovered by the unseen *malakut* to them, and the angels in charge of every affair appear to them in the invisible world and the world of the heart, and all the affairs which are prescribed for the creatures during the year in the high and low *lawh*s (tablets), appear to them, heavenly writ and covertly existed, in a disclosure. And it is a *malakuti* exposure [*mukashafah*] covering every particle of the world of nature, and no affair of the people‟s is hidden from the *waliyy al-amr.* There is no discrepancy in their knowing, in a single night, the affairs of a whole year, or, in an instance, the entire affairs of the world, or, in a single moment, all the measured assignments [*muqaddarat*] of *mulk* and *malakut.* Also during the days of the year, all the daily affairs may gradually be disclosed to them, both in general and in details. For example, it is in the *hadith,* concerning the revelation of the Quran, that it was revealed in general (in the whole) in "The Populous House" [*bayt al-mamur*], then it was revealed to the Messenger of Allah in details within twenty-three years.[577] And its revelation in "The Populous House" was a revelation to the Messenger of Allah (*s*), too.

---

[576] Reference unknown.
[577] *Usul al-Kafi*, vol. 4, p. 437, "The Book of the Merits of the Quran," ch. on "Rarities," *hadith* 6.

In short, sometimes the *waliyy al-amr* may become connected to the High Council [*mala-i ala*], the High Pens and the abstract *lawh*s, where to him will be exposed all the beings, from the beginning to eternity. Sometimes the connection is with the low *lawh*s, and for a period he uncovers the assignments [*muqaddarat*], and the whole page of the universe is present before his guardian-like presence, and whatsoever affair happens will pass before his eyes.

Some narratives refer to the exposition [*ard*] of the acts to *waliyy al-amr*. They are exposed every Thursday and Monday to the Messenger of Allah and the Imams of guidance (a). Other narratives say that the acts are exposed every morning, or every morning and night. These exposures are also in general and in details, collectively and distinctly. In this respect, there are noble narratives from the infallible and pure *Ahl al-Bayt*, mentioned in the books of exegeses, such as *al-Burhan* and *as-Safi*.[578]

* * * * * * *

His saying: **"Peace it is till the break of the dawn,"** means that this blessed night is safe from Satanic evils, calamities and misfortunes till the break of the dawn. Or it is peace upon Allah'ʼs friends [*awliyaullah*] and the worshipping people [*ahl-i taat*]. Or the angels of Allah who meet Allah'ʼs friends and the worshipping people greet them on the part of Allah, the Exalted, till the break of the dawn.

A Gnostic Note

As it has formerly been said concerning the truth of "the night of *qadr*," the degrees of existence and the visible and invisible individuations [*taayyunat*] are regarded "night" because the sun of the truth has set in their horizon. Consequently, "The night of *qadr*" is the night in which the *Haqq* (Allah), the Exalted—according to all the affairs and the "Collective Oneness of the Names and Attributes," which are the truth of the "Greatest Name"—is veiled [*muhtajib*]. That is the individuation [*taayyun*] and the constitution [*bunyah*] of the perfect *wali*, who was the Messenger of Allah (*s*) in his life, and then the Imams of guidance, one after another. Therefore, "the dawn" of "the night of *qadr*" is when the first rays of the rising sun of the truth shine from behind the veils [*hujub*] of the individuations [*taayyunat*].

---

[578] *Bihar al-Anwar*, vol. 23, pp. 338, 346 and 347; *as-Safi*'ʼs *Exegesis*.

The rise of the sun from the horizon of the individuations is "the dawn" of the Day of Resurrection, too. As from the time of the setting and veiling [*ihtijab*] of the sun of the truth in the horizon of the individuations of these perfect *wali*s [*awliya*], till the time of the break of the dawn, which is the period of "the night of *qadr*," that night full of honor is absolutely safe from the Satanic intrusions, and since the sun rises as it had set, blemishless and free from the Satanic intrusion, thus, He says: **"Peace it is till the break of the dawn."** As to the other nights, they are either completely peaceless, such as the nights of the Umayyads and their like, or they have no peace in all its concepts, and these are the nights of the common people.

Conclusion

From the gnostic statements and faithful revelations [*mukashafat*], which, with the help of the great *wali*s (a), dawned upon the luminous hearts of the "people of knowledge" [*ahl-i marifat*], it is obvious that if the noble *surah* of *at-Tawhid* is related to the Sacred Essence of Allah, the noble *surah* of *al-Qadr* is related to the great *Ahl al-Bayt*, as is stated in the narratives concerning the *miraj*.

Muhammad ibn Yaqub, on the authority of Abu Abdullah [as-Sadiq] (a), concerning the performance of the Messenger of Allah (*s*) his *salat* in the heaven, in the *hadith* of *al-Isra*, said: "...Then Allah, the Most High, revealed to him: Read, O Muhammad, the lineage [*nisbat*] of your Lord, the Blessed and Most High: „He is Allah, the One. He is Besought by all. He begets not, nor is He begotten. And none is comparable to Him." This is in the first *rakah*. Then, Allah, the Exalted and Most High, revealed to him: Read: „All praise is for Allah." He read it as he did first. Then Allah revealed to him: Read: „We revealed it" which is your lineage [*nisbat*] and your offspring"s till the Day of Resurrection."[579]

The noble narratives concerning the merits of the blessed *surah* of *al-Qadr* are numerous. Among them is a narrative in the noble *al-Kafi*, from Imam al-Baqir (a) who said: "Whoever recites „We revealed it on The Night of *Qadr'* openly (with a loud voice), he is like the one who unsheathes his swords for the sake of Allah. And whoever recites it secretly, is as if he rolls in his blood shed in the way of Allah, and whoever recites it ten times, a thousand of his sins will

---

[579] *Al-Burhan Exegesis*, vol. 4, p. 487, "*Surah al-Qadr*," hadith 22.

be forgiven."[580] In *Khawass al-Quran*, the Messenger of Allah (*s*) is quoted to have said: "Whoever recites this *surah*, he will have the reward of the one who has fasted the month of Ramadan, attaining "The night of *qadr*," and he will have the reward of a fighter in the way of Allah."[581] Praise is for Allah, at the beginning and at the end.

An Apology

Despite the fact that the writer's intention in this thesis was to refrain from referring to those gnostic topics unfamiliar to the common people, and keep only to the hearty disciplines of the *salat*, yet, I realize now that the pen has exceeded the proper bounds, and particularly in commenting on the noble *surah* I have surpassed my own decision. Now I have but to apologize to my brothers in religion and spiritual friends. At the same time, if they found in this thesis a subject not conforming with their taste, they may not unthoughtfully label it as false, because each knowledge has its people, and each road has its treaders. "May Allah have mercy on the person who knows his worth and does not go beyond his status."[582]

It is also possible that some neglect the reality of the condition, and, as they have no information of the Quranic knowledge and of the minute details of the divine laws, they take some matters of this thesis as to be interpretation according to one's opinion. This is sheer mistake and a grave falsity, because:

Firstly, these knowledges [*maarif*] and subtleties [*lataif*] are all taken from the noble Quran and *hadith*s, and they are proved through heard [*samiyyah*] evidences, some of which have been referred to in the discussions, and most of them were left out for brevity.

Secondly, all, or most of them, agree with the rational or gnostic proofs, and such a thing cannot be interpretation according to one's opinion.

---

[580] *Usul al-Kafi*, vol. 4, p. 427, "The Book of the Merit of the Quran," ch. on "The Merit of the Quran," *hadith* 6.
[581] *Al-Burhan Exegesis*, vol. 4, p. 480, "*Surah al-Qadr*," *hadith* 1. From *Khawass al-Quran*.
[582] *Ghurar al-Hikam*, ch. 3, letter R, *hadith* 1.

Thirdly, most of the subjects which we mentioned, or we relate in explaining the noble *ayah*s, are of the kinds of stating the "evidences of the concepts" [*masadiq-i mafahim*]; and explaining the evidences and degrees of the facts has nothing to do with interpretation, let alone its being according to one"s opinion.

Fourthly, after all stages, we tried with utmost religious precaution—though unnecessarily— to relate any unnecessary subject by way of being possible and as one of the possibilities. It is clear that the door of possibility is not shut, and it can have no connection to interpretation on one"s opinion. Here there are other subjects that we refrain from mentioning, in our attempt to be short.

SECTION FIVE

Some Disciplines and Secrets of the *Ruku*

Discussed in Five Chapters

ON THE *TAKBIR* BEFORE THE *RUKU*
Chapter One

Apparently, this *takbir* (saying: *Allahu Akbar* = Allah is the Greatest) belongs to the *ruku* (obeisance = genuflection) in order to be prepared for the stage of *ruku*. Its relevant discipline is to bring to mind Allah''s status of Greatness and Majesty and the Lord''s Might and Sovereignty, and considering, at the same time, one''s weakness, inability, poverty, humility and servitude. In such a condition, and according to one''s knowledge of the Lord''s Might and the servant''s humility, one will say the *takbir* of the *Haqq* (Allah), the Exalted, being above all description.

The description [*tawsif*] which the *salik* servant makes of the *Haqq* (Allah), the Exalted, and his glorifying and extolling, should be out of pure obedience, and taking them to be by the permission of the *Haqq* (Allah), the Exalted, to describe and worship Him. Otherwise he would dare not to vaunt of his describing and glorifying in the presence of the Lord, weak a servant as he is, and, actually, having nothing of his own, for whatsoever he has is from his Great Worshipped. When Ali ibn al-Husayn, with such sweet and authoritative a tongue as he had, being the tongue of Allah, says: "How, with this feeble tongue as I have, can I thank you?,"[583] "what a thin gnat can do?"[584]

So, when the *salik* servant wants to enter the grave stage of *ruku*, he has to prepare himself for that stage, throwing behind, with his own hand, his describing, glorifying, worshipping and conduct [*suluk*]. He then has to raise his hands beside his ears, facing his empty palms towards the *qiblah*, and, empty-handed, with a heart full of fear and hope—fear of failure and deficiency in observing the state of servitude; and assured hope in the Holy state of Allah Who honored

---

[583] *Misbah al-Mutahajjid*, an extract from Abu Hamzah''s invocation, p. 534.
[584] Refer to footnote 272.

him into such situations, which belong to the bosom friends of Allah and the perfect lovers—he enters the stage of *ruku*. Probably, raising the hands in this way denotes leaving the *qiyam* (standing) position and the stand [*wuquf*] in that stage—a sign indicating taking no provision from the stage of *qiyam*. *Takbir* denotes glorifying and aggrandizing the descriptions done in the stage of *qiyam*. As *ruku*, to the people of knowledge, is the stage of the Unity of Attributes, the *takbir* of *ruku*, to them, is aggrandizing this Unity, and raising the hands is a sign of rejecting the attributes of the creatures.

CONCERNING THE DISCIPLINES OF BOWING IN *RUKU*
Chapter Two

Know that the principal positions of the *salat* are three. The other acts and deeds are preliminary and preparatory:

First: *qiyam*;

Second: *ruku*;

Third: *sujud.*

The people of knowledge regard these three positions to be a hint at the three Unities [*tawhidat*]. We, in *The Secret of the Salat*, referred to these stages in terms of the gnostic taste. Now, we explain them in other terms suitable to the common people.

So, we say that as the *salat* is the believer's perfective *miraj*, and the bringer of the pious people to Allah's proximity, it stands on two bases, the one is the preliminary to the other.

The first is abandoning self-conceit and selfishness, as it is the truth and the inside of *taqwa* (piety).

The second is seeking Allah and being in quest of the *Haqq*, as this is the truth of the *miraj* and proximity. Hence, it is in the noble narratives that: "The *salat* is the means of proximity for every pious person,"[585] the same as the Quran is a light of guidance, but for the pious: **"This is the Book, there is no doubt in it. It is a guide for the *muttaqin* (the pious)."**[586]

In short, in these three states: the states of *qiyam*, *ruku*, and *sujud*, the said two states (bases) take shape gradually. So, in the state of *qiyam*, self-conceitedness is forsaken according to the state of Activity [*failiyyat*], and regarding Allah to be the Absolute Factor and

---

[585] *Furu al-Kafi*, vol. 3, p. 265, "The Book of *as-Salat*," ch. on "The Merit of *as-Salat*," hadith 6.

[586] *Surah al-Baqarah* 2:2.

Eternal. In the state of *ruku*, self-conceitedness is forsaken according to the state of Attributes and Names, considering the state of Allah's Attributes and Names. In the *sujud*, the self-conceitedness is forsaken altogether, and it is entirely Allah—seeking and being in quest of the *Haqq*. All the stages of the *salik*s are of the affairs [*shuun*] of these three states, as it is quite obvious to the people of insight, the gnostics and the *salik*s.

When the *salik* along these three states realizes that the secret of these acts is the three Unities, he will have to pay more attention to that state which is nicer and more delicate. Naturally, the danger of the state is greater and it is more slippery. Then, in the state of *ruku*, the *salik* claims that in the house of existence [*dar-i wujud*] there is no knowledge, power, life nor will except from Allah—a claim so great and a state so delicate, which we are not (qualified) to put forth. We should inwardly turn to the Holy Threshold of Allah, showing supplication, distress and humility, asking forgiveness for our faults and failures, and, with seeing eyes and witnessing conscience, admitting our shortcomings, that perhaps His Sacred Holiness may show kindness to, and care for, us, and may He, in the time of necessity, extend a hand of help to us. **"Or, Who answers the distressed one when he calls upon Him, and removes the evil...?"**[587]

---

[587] *Surah an-Naml* 27:62.

THE *RUKU* OF THE *SALAT* OF
THE MESSENGER"S *MIRAJ*
Chapter Three

In respect of the *miraj salat* of the Messenger of Allah (*s*) it is stated that after the *ruku*, the Almighty addressed him, saying: "Look at My *Arsh*." The Messenger of Allah said: "I looked at a greatness which astounded my soul and I went in a swoon. I was inspired to say: „Glory be to my Great Lord and praise be to Him" because of the greatness which I saw. As I said that, I came to myself. I continued to say it for seven times till I came to myself as before..."[588] as the *hadith* goes.

Consider, dear, the state of the greatness of the *suluk* of the "Universal Master" [*sarwar-i kull*] and the Guide to the Paths (*s*), who, while in the state of *ruku*, which is a looking down at one"s inferior, sees the light of the *Arsh*; and, as the light of *Arsh* to the *wali*s [*awliya*] is the manifestation of the Essence, without mirror, the self individuation is gone, and a mood of swoon and shock takes place. So, the Holy Essence, with eternal care, helped that honorable being, and with affectionate inspiration taught that noble personality how to "glorify," "aggrandize" and "praise," until after seven times—the number of the veils and the number of man"s ranks—he came to himself and to wakefulness. This condition prevailed throughout the *miraj salat*.

But as we have no admission into the privacy of intimacy, nor into a place of Holy State, it is good to use our incapability and humility as a capital for the attainment of the objective, and as a pretext to reach the goal. We have to keep clinging to the skirt of the intended until we get what we desire. Or, at least, if we are not the men

---

[588] *Ilal ash-Shara'i* , p. 315. A part of the *hadith* concerning *al-miraj salat*.

for the job, we are to seek guidance from the guides of the road, and find help with the perfect spiritual men, so that a smell of fragrant of knowledge may reach the smelling sense of our souls, and a breeze of the graces may blow into our dead corpses, because Allah, the Exalted, is accustomed to being beneficent, and His habit is to be graceful and generous.

It must be noted that *ruku* consists of "glorifying," "aggrandizing" (magnifying) and "praising" the Lord, Almighty and Most High. Thus, "glorifying" is purifying Allah, the Exalted, from description and definition. "Aggrandizing" and "praising" are refraining from limits of assimilation and devesting Allah from attributes, because "praising" denotes the appearance in the mirrors of creation, and "aggrandizing" negates limitation. Thus, He is apparent and there is no appearance in the world more apparent than Him. He is not clothed in the apparel of the individuations of the creation.

DELICACIES AND SECRETS OF THE *RUKU*, *SUJUD* AND THEIR CORDIAL DISCIPLINES
Chapter Four

It is stated in *Misbah ash-Shariah* that as-Sadiq (a) said: "No servant bows in the *ruku* for Allah, in a true way, unless Allah adorns him with the light of His Brilliance, and shades him with the shade of His Majesty, and clothes him with the gown of His chosen friends. The *ruku* is first and the *sujud* is second. The one who performed the first is fit for the second. The *ruku* is politeness, and the *sujud* is proximity. So, the one who is not well-mannered, is unfit for proximity. Therefore, perform the *ruku* like the one who is submitting to Allah with his heart, humble and afraid under His Sovereignty, drooping to Him his limbs like the one who is afraid and grieved for what one loses of the benefit of those who perform the *ruku*. It is narrated that ar-Rabi ibn Khuthaym used to keep indulged in a single *ruku* all the night till dawn. In the morning he would raise his head and say: „Oh, the sincere ones have passed us and we are left behind." Complete your *ruku* by levelling your back, and rebuke yourself for being vigilant in serving Him except with His help. Protect your heart against Satan''s whispers, deceits and traps. Allah, the Exalted, raises His servants as much as they show humility to Him, and He guides them to the principles of humility and submission as much as His Greatness knows of their secrets."[589]

This noble *hadith* contains signs, good tidings, disciplines and instructions, as "adorning" with the "light of Allah''s Brilliance," being under the "shade of Allah''s Majesty" and wearing the "gown of Allah''s chosen ones" are good tidings of attaining to the state of learning the Names: **"And He taught Adam all the names."**[590] Of

---

[589] *Misbah ash-Shariah*, p. 12; *Bihar al-Anwar*, vol. 89, p. 108.
[590] *Surah al-Baqarah* 2:31.

that state is the taking of the state of attributive annihilation and the state of wakefulness, because Allah"s adorning the servant with the state of "the light of His Brilliance" means taking him to the state of Names, which is the reality of teaching man. Taking him under the shade and shadow of "Majesty," which is of the Names of Power, and placing him in His Court, refer to annihilating the servant of himself. After this state, clothing him in "the gown of the chosen ones" is survival after annihilation. From this it is realized that the *sujud* is self-annihilation, as is said by the people of knowledge. The *ruku* is first, and it is these states, and the *sujud* is second, which is nothing but the state of annihilation in the Essence.

It is also realized that the Absolute Proximity, which happens in the *sujud*, is not accessible except through the true *ruku*. Whoever wants to be fit for the second, must acquire the discipline of the *ruku* and its proximity.

After stating the delicacies and secrets of the *ruku* and *sujud*, he refers to their hearty disciplines to suit the middle class. These are among the general matters, which we have referred to in the Preliminaries; and some of them belong to *ruku*. Now, as most of these things have already been stated, we leave out further explanation.

CONCERNING RAISING THE HEAD FROM THE *RUKU*
Chapter Five

Its secret is the return from *wuquf* (standing) in the multiplicity of names, as it is said: "The perfect monotheism is the negation of ascribing attributes to Him,"[591] because after the awakening from the annihilation in the Names [*fana-i asmai*], the *salik* servant witnesses his failure and shortcoming, since the beginning of Man"s sin—which is to be compensated for by his offspring—is the inclination toward the multiplicities of names, which is the inside of the "tree." Having understood the sin of himself, who is Adam"s offspring, and the sin of Adam, who is his origin, he would recognize his state of humility and need, and get ready to remove the sin by way of behaving with humility in „the presence of Allah"s Majesty. He would then stand erect out of this state, and with the *takbir* after the *ruku* he would remove the multiplicities of names, and, empty-handed, he would comprehend the state of humility, helplessness and the earthly origin. The important discipline in this respect is to find out the state"s great significance, and to have the heart to taste it through complete remembrance, and strive to attend [*tawajjuh*] to His Essence, forsaking attending [*tawajjuh*] to oneself, even to one"s state of humility.

Know, dear, that complete remembrance of the *Haqq* (Allah), and absolute turning, with the inside of the heart, to the Holy Essence, will open the heart"s internal eye, through which meeting Allah—the pleasure of the eyes of the *walis* [*awliya'*]—takes place: **"And those who strive hard for Us, We will most certainly guide them in Our ways."**[592]

---

[591] *Usul al-Kafi*, vol. 1, p. 191, "The Book of Monotheism," ch. on "General *Hadiths* on Monotheism," *hadith* 6.
[592] *Surah al-Ankabut* 29:69.

SECTION SIX

A Brief Explanation of the Secrets and
Disciplines of the *Sujud*

Discussed in Four Chapters

GENERAL SECRET OF THE *SUJUD*
Chapter One

According to the people of gnosticism and of heart, this secret is to be forsaking oneself and closing one"s eyes against anything except Him; and, with a Jonahian *miraj*—which took place by sinking into the stomach of the fish—one can pay attention to his origin without seeing the veil. And, in putting the head on the dust, there is a hint at seeing the Beauty of the Beautiful in the inner heart of the dust and the origin of the world of nature.

Its hearty disciplines are to find one"s reality and the original root of one"s existence, and to place the brain, which is the center of the sovereignty of the soul and the *Arsh* of the spirit, at the lowest threshold of the State of Holiness, and to consider the world of dust as the threshold of the Master of the Kings.

Thus, the secret of the position of the *sujud* is to give up oneself, and the discipline of putting the head on the dust is to debase one"s most high position, regarding it to be lower than the dust. Should there be in the heart a cause for these claims, in respect of the states of the *salat*, which are a reference to them, they are, to the people of knowledge, hypocrisy. And, as this state is the most dangerous one, the *salik* to Allah will have to cling to the skirt of the care of Allah, the Most High, by means of his personal disposition and innermost nature, humbly and meekly asking forgiveness for the shortcomings. But this is a dangerous state that is out of the obligations of people like us.

As we have explained in *The Secret of the Salat* these states in details, we refrain from repeating them in this thesis, satisfying ourselves with relating the *hadith* narrated in *Misbah ash-Shariah* concerning the relevant discipline.

DISCIPLINES OF THE *SUJUD*
Chapter Two

It is stated in *Misbah ash-Shariah* that Imam as-Sadiq (a) said: "By Allah he will not be a loser, the one who performs the *sujud* as it really should be, even if for a single time in his life. No one will be successful if he takes to privacy with his Lord, in a similar position resembling the deceiver of himself, unaware of, and neglecting, what Allah has arranged for the *sajidin* (the prostrate worshippers) of immediate intimacy and adjourned comfort. The one who is good at approaching (Allah) in the *sujud*, will never be far from Him, whereas the one who observes not the discipline of, and loses the respect for, the *sujud*, can never be near Him by longing for other than Him in his *sujud*. So, let yours be the *sujud* of a submissive and humble to Allah, the Exalted, knowing that you have been created from the dust which is trodden upon by the creatures, and that He has made you of a *nutfah* (semen) which is regarded filthy by everybody, and was brought into existence though not existed before. The concept of the *sujud* has been made by Allah, the Exalted, a cause for getting near Him with the heart, the inside and the spirit. So, whoever nears Him turns away from other than Him. Do you not realize that in the external form the position of the *sujud* is not complete except by hiding oneself from everything, and turning away from all things visible to the eyes? Similar is the question of the internal position. Whoever his heart is attracted, during the *salat*, to other than Allah, the Exalted, he will be near to that which attracted him, and far from the reality of that which Allah wanted him to be in his *salat*. Allah, the Exalted, says: **"Allah has not made for any man two hearts within him,"**[593] and the Messenger of Allah (*s*) said that Allah, the Exalted, told him: „Whenever I look into the heart of a servant and find in it his love to be

---

[593] *Surah al-Ahzab* 33:4.

sincere in obeying Me for My sake and for obtaining My pleasure, I undertake setting him aright and managing his affairs. But whoever is indulged in other than Me, he is among those who mock themselves, and his name is registered in the Book of the Losers."[594]

This noble *hadith* explains both the secrets and the disciplines, and, by contemplation, it opens ways of knowledge in the face of the *salik* to Allah, and destroys the obstinacy and the denial of the deniers, and supports and praises the godly men of knowledge and the people of certainty, and attracts attention to the reality of privacy and intimacy with Allah, and forsaking other than Allah, the Exalted.

---

[594] *Misbah ash-Shariah*, ch. 16, on "The *Sujud.*"

CONTENTS AND MEANING OF THE FORM, MOOD AND INVOCATION OF THE *SUJUD*
Chapter Three

It is stated in a narrative that when the *ayah*: **"Therefore, glorify the Name of your Lord, the Great,"**[595] was revealed, the Messenger of Allah (*s*) said: "Recite this in your *ruku*," and when the *ayah*: **"Glorify the Name of your Lord, the Most High"**[596] was revealed, he said: "Recite this in your *sujud*."[597]

It is in the noble *hadith* of *al-Kafi* that "... the first and foremost name He assumed for Himself was *al-Aliyy* (the High) *al-Azim* (the Great).[598] It may be that *"al-Aliyy"* was the first of the names of Essence, and *"al-Azim"* was the first of the names of Attributes.

Know that the *sujud*, like the other positions of the *salat* has its form, mood, recitation [*dhikr*] and secret. These matters, in relation to the Perfect Ones, are as have formerly been related in this thesis, but to go into the details is not suitable. For the middle class the form is showing humbleness and forsaking arrogance and self conceit. Pressing the nose onto dust—which is of the confirmed supererogations, or even neglecting it is contrary to precaution—is a token of showing complete submission, humility and modesty. It also means being aware of one"s origin and creation. And putting the tops of the exposed organs—which are the places of sensation and of the appearance of mobility and power, being the very seven or eight organs—on the dust of humility and helplessness, is a sign of complete surrender, of offering one"s entire powers, and getting out of Adam"s sin.

---

[595] *Surah al-Waqiah* 26:74.
[596] *Surah al-Ala* 87:1.
[597] *Majma ul-Bayan*, vol. 9, p. 224, commenting on *ayah* 74 of *Surah al-Waqiah*.
[598] *Usul al-Kafi*, vol. 1, p. 153, "The Book of *at-Tawhid*," ch. on "The Originality of the Names (of Allah), *hadith* 2.

By strengthening the remembrance of these concepts in the heart, it becomes affected by them and it acquires a mood of running away from oneself and from self-conceit. This mood results in a mood of pleasure, which, in turn, results in a mood of complete privacy and there will be full love.

As regards the recitation [*dhikr*] during the *sajdah*, it is based on *tasbih*, which is glorifying (purifying) Allah from description and observance of the command (*amr*), or it is purifying (glorifying) Him from multiplicity of names, or purifying (glorifying) Him from unification [*tawhid*], which is "*tafil*," moving from multiplicity to unity, and it is not free from the blemish of multiplying [*takthir*] and associating with Allah [*tashrik*], as describing Him with the Essential highness and praising Him are also not free from the blemishes of these concepts.

"*Al-Aliyy*" is of the Names of Essence, and, according to the narrative of *al-Kafi*, it is the first name adopted by Allah for Himself. That is, the first manifestation of the Essence is for Himself. When the *salik,* in this state, becomes annihilated out of himself and forsakes the world and what is in it, he will have the honor of this Essential manifestation.

Know that as the *ruku* is first and the *sujud* is second, glorification and praising in them differ a great deal. Also *rabb* is different in those two states, because *rabb* as the people of knowledge say, is of the Names of Essence, Attributes and Acts in three aspects. Therefore, *rabb* in *al-hamdu lillahi rabbil-alamin* may be of the Names of Act in accordance with the state of standing, which is the state of the Unity of Acts. In the *ruku* it is of the Names of Attributes in accordance with the fact that the *ruku* is the state of the Unity of Attributes. In the *sujud* it is of the Names of Essence in accordance with the fact that *sujud* is the state of the Unity of Essence. The "glorifying" and "praising" in each one of these states are related to that particular state.[599]

---

[599] In the MS (manuscript), before starting "Chapter Four," the Imam has scribed nearly two pages under the title "A Gnostic Note," then these were crossed out as to be deleted, and in the margin he wrote: "This note is not needed and it is to be completely effaced." In the book's latest MS (manuscript) this part is omitted. But it appears in the former editions of this book. In this edition that passage is not printed.

THE MOODS OF THE *SAJID* DURING THE *SUJUD*
Chapter Four

The *sajdah*, as described in the *salat* of the *miraj*, is a swoon and a shock resulting from witnessing the lights of the Greatness of Allah. When the servant feels being raptured and he undergoes a fit [*hal*] of annihilation [*mahw*] and shock [*saq*], he will be covered by the eternal care and will receive inspiration from the Unseen [*ghayb*].

The recitation [*dhikr*] in the *sujud* and repeating it are for one to come to himself and turn to the state of wakefulness [*sahw*]. So, when one comes to himself, the fire of longing for seeing the light of Allah kindles in his heart, and he raises his head from the *sujud*. When he finds in himself residues of his selfishness, he leaves them by a sign with his hand. Thus, the light of Majesty is manifested to him once again and the remnants of selfishness are burnt off, and he becomes annihilated [*fani*] from the annihilation [*fana*], and, while repeating *Allahu Akbar*, a state of complete and absolute annihilation and full real swooning [*saq*] happens to him. So, the unseen help, by the inspiration of the recitations, makes him firm in his state, and he will attain to a state of sobriety [*sahw*], which is the sobriety of the state of guardianship [*wilayat*] and is free from any sort of veiling and creational [*khalqi*] blemish. The states of *tashahhud* and *taslim*, which are of the status of multiplicity, also happen during this sobriety after annihilation [*mahw*]. Up to this point, all the circle of man''s journey has been full and complete.

SECTION SEVEN

General Notes on the Disciplines of *Tashahhud*

Discussed in Two Chapters

MEANING AND EFFECT OF TESTIFYING TO THE *TAWHID* AND THE MESSENGERSHIP (OF THE PROPHET)
Chapter One

Know that testifying to the Oneness (of Allah) and to Prophethood in the *adhan* and *iqamah*—which belong to the *salat* and prepare the situation to enter in it—and in the *tashahhud*—which is going out of annihilation [*fana*] to subsistence [*baqa*], and out of unity [*wahdat*] to multiplicity [*kathrat*], at the end of the *salat*—remind the *salik* servant of the fact that the reality of the *salat* is the taking place of the real Unity [*tawhid*], and that testifying to the Oneness (of Allah) is of the inclusive states, which accompany the *salik* from the beginning of the *salat* till its end. There is also in it the secret of the "Firstness" and "Lastness" of Allah, the Glorified and Most High. Further, there is the great secret of the *salik*'s journey from Allah to Allah: **"...as He created you at first, so shall you return."**[600]

Therefore, the *salik* must pay attention to this object at all states, bringing the truth of Allah's Oneness and Divinity to his heart, making it a divine ascending journey so that his testimonies may become real and purified from hypocrisy and polytheism.

In testifying to the Prophethood there may be a hint at the fact that the support of the Absolute Guardian and the Seal of the Prophets in this *miraj* of behavior [*miraj-i suluki*] is of the inclusive states, to which the *salik* must pay attention in all states, so that the secret of the appearance of the "firstness" and the "lastness," which are of the states of guardianship, becomes clear to the worthy people.

It must be noted that there is a difference between the *shahadah* (testifying) at the beginning of the *salat* and the testifying in the *tashahhud*, because the former is a testimony before the *suluk*, a

---

[600] *Surah al-Araf* 7:29.

devotional [*taabbudi*] or a contemplative [*taaqquli*] testimony, whereas the latter is after the return, and it is either a realizational [*tahaqquqi*] or a confirmative [*tamakkuni*] testimony. So, the testimony in the *tashahhud* is of great danger, because it includes the claim of realization [*tahaqquq*] and confirmation [*tamakkun*], and of returning to multiplicity unveiled. And as this lofty state is not possible for persons like us, nor is it expected under our present condition, behaving ourselves in the presence of the Creator is to remember our shortcomings, humility, failure, inability and distress, and, in a state of shamefulness, we are to face the Holy threshold and plead:

O Allah! Of the states of the holy men [*awliya*], the steps [*madarij*] of the Chosen [*asfiya*], the perfection of the sincere and the *suluk* of the *salik*s we have no share but a few words. Instead of striving for high states we are satisfied with idle talk, of which there avails nothing in quality nor in spirituality. O Lord! Loving this world and its attractions bars us from the Holy Court and the presence of Your intimacy, unless You, with Your hidden kindness help us, the helpless, so as to make up for what has passed, that we may rise from our sleep of negligence and find our way to Your Holy Presence.

THE DISCIPLINES OF *TASHAHHUD*
Chapter Two

It is stated in *Misbah ash-Shariah* that Imam as-Sadiq (a) said: "The *tashahhud* is extolment of Allah, the Most High. So, be His servant in your inside and submit to Him in your act, as you are His servant in (your) saying and claim. Join the truthfulness of your tongue to the purity of the truthfulness of your inside, as He has created you a servant and ordered you to worship Him with your heart, tongue and organs, and to carry out your servitude by His being your Lord, believing that He has in His grip all the creatures; so, they take no breath nor a glance except by His power and will, and they are incapable of performing the least act in His Domain except by His permission and will. Allah, Almighty and Glorious, says: **"And your Lord creates what He wills and chooses. They have not the choice. Glorified is Allah and Exalted above all that they associate (with Him)."**[601] So, be a thankful servant by act, as you are a remembering servant by word and claim. Join the truthfulness of your tongue to the purity of the truthfulness of your inside, for He has created you. He is High above being a volition and will to anybody except with His own prior volition and will. So, use servitude to be contented with His judgment, and use worship to perform His commands. He has ordered you to send blessing upon His Prophet (s). So, join blessing Him to blessing him, and obeying Him to obeying him and testifying Him to testifying him. Take care not to miss the blessings of admitting his sanctity, in which case you will be deprived of the benefit of his blessings, as He ordered him to ask forgiveness for you and intercede for you, if you performed your duty concerning the obligatory and the

---

[601] *Surah al-Qasas* 28:68.

forbidden acts, the laws and good manners, knowing his great position with Allah, Almighty, Most High."[602]

There are, in this noble *hadith*, hints at the cordial disciplines of worshippings and their truths and secrets, as he says that the "*tashahhud*" is praising Allah, Almighty and Most High. Formerly, however, we have said that all worshippings in general are praising Allah, either by a Name or Names, by one of the manifestations or by the origin of the Ipseity [*asl-i huwiyyat*].

At the head of the disciplines he refers to the fact that since you apparently show servitude and claim to be a worshipper, in your secret you are also to be serving so that the secret cordial servitude may spread to the acts of the organs, and that the word and act be the plan of the secret and the inside, and the truth of servitude may spread through all the organs, internal and external, and each of the organs, may have a share of the *tawhid*. The tongue of the praiser of Allah conveys the praising to the heart, and the sincere and monotheist heart conveys the *tawhid* and sincerity to the tongue. He seeks Lordship inside the truth of servitude, forsaking egotism and conveying Allah's divinity to the heart. He knows that the control of the servants is in the hands of Allah, the Exalted, that they have no power to breathe and to see except through the power and will of Allah, the Exalted, and that they are unable to do anything in the domain of Allah, however slight, except with the permission and will of His Holy Essence, as He has said: **"And your Lord creates what He wills and chooses. They have not the choice. Glorified is Allah and Exalted above all that they associate (with Him)"** (28:68). On conveying this grace [*latifah*] to the heart, your thanking Allah will be implemented and it will spread through your organs and acts. And, as the tongue and the heart should, in servitude, be coordinating, the truthfulness of the tongue and the purity of the secret of the heart should, in this unity of acts, be joined together, because Allah, Almighty and Most High, is the Creator and there is no effective factor but He, and all wills and volitions are shadows of His prior eternal will and volition.

After observing the disciplines of testifying to the Oneness and Divinity of Allah, one turns to the holy state of the absolute servant, Last of the Prophets, paying attention to the priority of the state of "servitude" to the state of "prophethood," since the state of servitude is

---

[602]*Misbah ash-Shariah*, ch. 17, on *"The Tashahhud."*

the preliminary to all the states of the *salik*s, and the prophethood is a branch of servitude. As the Final Messenger is a true servant annihilated in the *Haqq* (Allah), to obey him is to obey Allah, and testifying to his prophethood is connected to testifying to Allah''s Oneness. The *salik* servant should take care not to fall short of obeying the Messenger, as it is obeying Allah, lest he may be deprived of the blessings of worshipping, which is attainment to the Holy Court, with the help of the Absolute Guardian. And let him know that there will be no admission to the Holy Court and the place of intimacy without the help of the Patron, the Messenger of Allah (*s*).

SECTION EIGHT

On the Disciplines of the *Salam*

Discussed in Two Chapters

STATE OF THE *MUṢALLI* DURING UTTERANCE OF THE *SALAM*, AND THE CONDITION FOR THE *SALAM* TO BE TRUTHFUL
Chapter One

Know that when the *salik* comes out of the state of *sujud*, whose secret is "annihilation," and comes to himself, and into a state of wakefulness and attentiveness, returning from the state of being absent from the world to the state of being present, he offers his *salam* (peace) to the beings—the *salam* of the one who has come back from a journey, from an occultation. So, as he returns he sends peace upon the noble Prophet, because after returning from unity [*wahdat*] to multiplicity [*kathrat*], the first manifestation will be that of the truth of guardianship: "We are the first preceding ones"[603] Thereafter, he will pay attention to the essences [*ayan*] of other beings, distinctly and collectively.

The one who has not kept away, in the *salat*, from the creatures [*khalq*] and has not become a traveler to Allah, to him the *salam* has no meaning and is nothing but a chattering of the tongue. So, the cordial discipline of the *salam* depends on the discipline of the *salat* as a whole. If in this *salat*, which is the truth of the *miraj*, there was no ascension, and he did not come out of the house of the soul, he would actually have no *salam*. Furthermore, if in this journey there was safety from the intrusions of Satan and the evil-commanding soul, and, if the heart had no ailment during this real *miraj*, his *salam* would be truthful; if not, he would have no *salam*. Yes, the *salam* upon the

---

[603] *Bihar al-Anwar*, vol. 15, p. 15: "We are the first and we are the last;" Muslim's *Sahih*, vol. 2, p. 585; Al-Bukhari's *Sahih*, vol. 1, p. 36: "We are the last and we are the preceding ones."

Prophet (*s*) is, therefore, a *salam* with truthfulness, because, in this ascending journey, in this travel to Allah, in both ascending and descending, he enjoys peace, and, along his journey, he is free from the conducts [*tasarrufat*] of other than the *Haqq* (Allah), to which we have referred in our commentary on the *surah* of *al-Qadr*.

CONCERNING THE MEANING AND THE SECRET OF THE *SALAM* AND ITS DISCIPLINES
Chapter Two

It is stated in *Misbah ash-Shariah* that Imam as-Sadiq (a) said: "The meaning of the *salam* at the end of each *salat* is „security," that is, whoever obeys the command of Allah and the tradition of His Prophet (s), with a submissive heart, will be secured from the trials of this world and exempted from the tortures of the Hereafter. „*Salam*" is one of the names of Allah, the Exalted. He trusted it to His creatures so that they may use its concept in their transactions, trusts and annexations, exemplifying reciprocal companionship among themselves and the correctness of their association. If you wish to use the *salam* in its proper place and according to its meaning, you must fear Allah, and your religion, heart and mind should be secured on your part. So, do not make them filthy by the darkness of sinning, and do not cause your protectors (angels) to be vexed, tired and disgusted with your maltreating them. Both your friend and, your enemy should be secured from you, as the one whose close friends are not secured from him, the strangers are certainly more expected not to be so. And whoever does not put the *salam* in those proper places, his will be no *salam* and no *taslim*, and his *salam* will be a false one, even if he shows it off before the people.[604]

Being secured from the trials of this world means to be secured from Satanic intrusions, because obeying the commands of Allah secures one against the intrusion of Satan: **"Surely prayer forbids indecency and dishonor."**[605]

---

[604] *Misbah ash-Shariah*, ch. 18, "On *Salam*"; *Bihar al-Anwar*, vol. 82, p. 307.
[605] *Surah al-Ankabut* 29:45.

Then, he refers to one of the secrets of the "*salam*" and says: ",*salam*" is one of the Names of Allah. He trusted it to His creatures." This is a hint at the appearance of beings from the Divine Names. The *salik* servant should declare this divine grace, which has been trusted in the inside of his essence and nature, and use it in all of his dealings, associations, trusts and relationships, and spread it throughout his inside and outside domains. He should use it in his dealings with Allah and His religion so as not to betray the divine trust. Thus, he is to spread the truth of "*salam*" in all his worldly and heavenly powers as well as in his customs, beliefs, morals, and actions, so that he may be secured from all intrusions.

The way to this security is, thus, said to be *taqwa*. It should be realized that *taqwa* is of many degrees and stages:

The external *taqwa*: It means protecting the outside against the pollution and the darkness of formal sinning. This is the *taqwa* of the common people.

The internal *taqwa*: This means protecting the inside and purifying it from extravagance and shortcoming and exceeding the limit of moderateness in morality and spiritual instincts. This is the *taqwa* of the elite.

The *taqwa* of the mind: It is protecting and purifying the mind from being spent on the non-divine sciences. The divine sciences are those that deal with the divine laws and religion. Other natural sciences and the like which are required for knowing the manifestations of Allah, are also divine. But if they are not for that, they are not divine, even if they are discussions about the Beginning and the Resurrection. This is the *taqwa* of "the choice of the elite" [*akhass-i khawass*].

The *taqwa* of the heart: It is protecting the heart against seeing or discussing other than Allah. This is the *taqwa* of the *walis* [*awliya'*]. The noble *hadith* in which Allah, the Exalted, says: "I am the co-sitter to the one who sits with Me,"[606] refers to this hearty privacy, which is the best privacy, and the other ones are preliminaries to this one.

So, the one who acquires all these degrees of *taqwa*, his religion, intellect, spirit, heart and all his internal and external powers

---

[606] *Al-Mawahib as-Saniyyah*, p. 77; *Al-Mahajjat al-Bayda'*, vol. 8, p. 58 (with a slight difference).

will remain sound and safe, and the angels in charge of protecting him will not be vexed, tired or disgusted with him. The dealings and the company of such a person with both the friend and the enemy will be done in peace, or, actually, enmity will be uprooted from his heart, no matter how much his enemies are hostile to him. But the one who has not acquired all the degrees of *taqwa*, would proportionally be deprived of the emanation of *salam*, and would be nearer to the horizon of hypocrisy, from which we take refuge in Allah. With peace! [*was-salam*].

CONCLUSION OF THE BOOK

Concerning Some Disciplines of
the Inside and Outside of the *Salat*

In Three Chapters

THE SECRETS AND THE CORDIAL DISCIPLINES OF THE FOUR *TASBIH*S
Chapter One

There are four *rukns* (pillars) in the *Tasbihat*:

The first *rukn* concerns the *tasbih* (glorification), which is purifying Allah from descriptions by *tahmid* (saying: *al-hamdu lillah* = praise is for Allah) and *tahlil* (saying: *la ilaha illallah* = there is no god but Allah), which is of the inclusive states. The *salik* servant should, in all his worshippings, pay attention to that, and prevent his heart from the claim of describing and seeking a eulogy on the *Haqq* (Allah). He should not think that a servant is able to offer the due servitude to Allah, let alone paying the due homage to the Lord, which is not hoped for even by the perfect *wali*s [*awliya*], and from reaching which the hands of the great ones of the people of knowledge are short:

> No one can net the phoenix, so undo the net,
> Since there can be nothing but wind in it,[607]

That is why it has been said that the perfect knowledge of the people of knowledge is their knowing their own inability.[608]

Yes, it is because of the vast mercy of Allah, the Exalted, which covers us, the weak servants, that He vests us, the helpless, with serving Him and permits us to enter such a holy and pure state which bent the backs of even the Cherubim to get near it. This is of the greatest favors and graces of the Holy Essence, The Provider that bestowed upon His servants. The people of knowledge, the perfect *wali*s [*awliya*] and the godly men value it in proportion to their personal knowledge. We—the veiled, left short of all states, the

---

[607] Poetry from Hafiz Shirazi.
[608] *Bihar al-Anwar*, vol. 94, p. 150, "Supplication Eighteen," "The Supplication of the Gnostics."

deprived of and kept at a distance from any perfection and knowledge—are completely unaware of that, and regard the divine commands, which are, in fact, the highest, big unlimited blessings, as imposition and duty, performing them lazily and with boredom, and that is why we are completely deprived of and veiled from its luminosity.

It must be realized that as *tahmid* and *tahlil* include Unity of Acts, in which there is the blemish of limiting and decreasing, or even the blemish of assimilation and mixing, the *salik* servant, to be prepared for entering it, has to enter first the strong fortress of glorification and purification, telling his inner heart that Allah, Great and Most High, is innocent of all creational [*khalqiyyah*] individuations [*taayyunat*] and of the apparels of multiplicities, so that the entering into praising Him can be free from the blemish of multiplication.

The second *rukn* is *tahmid*, which is the state of Unity of Acts, suitable for *qiyam* and recitation. In this respect, these glorifications in the last *rak,,as* take the place of the *surah* of al-Hamd, as the *musalli* is free to recite the *surah* of al-Hamd (the Opening) instead. The Unity of Acts—as has already been explained in "*al-Hamd*"—is to be used to exclusively assign praising to Allah, completely cutting short the hand of the servant from praisings. We should convey: **"He is the First and the Last and the Manifest and the Hidden"**[609] to the ears of the heart, and let: **"And you threw not when you did, but Allah threw"**[610] reach the taste of our spirit, treading upon selfishness and self-conceit by the foot of behavior [*suluk*], in order to take ourselves to the state of *tahmid*, and out of the burden of being indebted to the creatures.

The third *rukn* is the *tahlil*, which is of many states:

One is the state of negating the divinity of act, that is "There is no effecter in the (world of) existence but Allah," which is a confirmation of confining the *tahmid* (to Allah) as its cause and factor, because the stages of the possible beings are the shadow of the Real Existence of Allah, Almighty, and mere connection. No one of them, in any way, is independent or self-sustaining. Thus, effecting existence can never be ascribed to them, since effectiveness requires

---

[609] *Surah al-Hadid* 57:3.
[610] *Surah al-Anfal* 8:17.

independence in bringing into existence, and being independently effective in bringing into existence necessitates being independent in existing. According to the terms of the people of (gnostic) taste, the reality of the shadow-beings is the appearance of the Power of the *Haqq* (Allah) in the mirrors of creation. The meaning of *la ilaha illallah* (There is no god but Allah) is witnessing the *Haqq*"s (Allah"s) effectiveness and power upon the creatures, and negating the individuations [*taayyunat*] of creation, and annihilating the state of their activity [*failiyyat*] and their effect in the *Haqq* (Allah).

The other is the negation of any worshipped other than Allah, and *la ilaha illallah* means: There is no worshipped except Allah. Therefore, the state of *tahlil* is the result of the state of *tahmid*, as when the *tahmid* is exclusively confined to the Holy Essence of Allah, servitude places its burden in that Holy State, and all the servitudes, which people do to one another for the purpose of being praised, become negated. So, it is as if the *salik* says that since all praises are exclusively for Allah, servitude must also be exclusively for Allah, Who is to be the worshipped, and all the idols are to be broken to pieces. There are other states for *tahlil*, which do not suit this situation.

The fourth *rukn* is the *takbir*, which also means that Allah is greater than any description. The servant, by commencing the *tahmid* and the *tahlil*, denies the description of Allah, and, having finished that, he again denies describing Allah, and glorifies Him, accompanying his *tahmid* and *tahlil* with humbleness and confession of shortcomings. Probably the *takbir*, in this instance, is a *takbir* of *tahmid* and *tahlil*, as they contain the blemish of multiplicity, as has already been said. Probably in *tasbih* there is *tanzih* (purification) of *takbir* and in the *takbir* there can be *takbir* of *tanzih*, where the servant"s claims turn to be completely invalid, and he becomes in command of the Unity of Acts, and the state of obeying Allah becomes a habit in his heart, getting out of changing colors into a state of stability.

The *salik* servant, in these noble recitations, which are the spirit of knowledge, should create in his heart a mood of devotion, supplication, dedication and humility, and by continual repetition give to his inner heart the form of remembrance, fixing the truth of remembrance into his heart such that the heart would be clothed with the clothes of remembrance, taking off its own wear, which is the wear of remoteness [*bud*] (from Allah). Then, the heart becomes divine, truthful, in which will be fulfilled the reality and spirit of: "**Surely Allah has bought from the believers their lives.**"[611]

[611] *Surah at-Tawbah* 9:111.

CONCERNING THE CORDIAL DISCIPLINES
OF THE *QUNUT*
Chapter Two

Know that the *Qunut* (supplication in the *salat* with the hands raised) is one of the recommended supererogations, which is not becoming to neglect, but to perform it is of precaution, such that some companions say that it is obligatory. Some narratives also confirm that, although from the juristic point of view it is not obligatory, as is common among the great scholars. It is performed as is particularly common among the Imamis [*imamiyyah*] (may Allah be pleased with them), i.e., by raising the hands near to the face, with the palms open towards the sky and reciting common or uncommon invocations. It is allowed to recite them in any language, Arabic or non-Arabic, though the Arabic is better and is according to precaution.

The jurisprudents say that the best *dua* (invocation) in this respect is *dua al-faraj*,[612] though its preference has not been proved to the writer by an authentic juristic evidence. Yet, the contents of the *dua* confirm its preference, because it includes *tahlil*, *tasbih* and *tamhid*, which are the spirit of *tawhid* as has been explained. It also includes the great Names of Allah, such as: Allah, *al-Halim*, *al-Karim*, *al-Aliyy*, *al-Azim*, and *ar-Rabb*, besides the *dhikr* (the wordings to be recited) in the *ruku* and the *sujud*, and the Names of Essence, Attributes and Acts, as well as the stages of the manifestations of Allah, Almighty and Most High, and sending *salam* to the Messengers though to neglect this is of the acts of precaution, but upon a stronger opinion it is allowed. It also includes sending blessings upon the

---

[612] The *dua*"that begins with: "*La ilaha illallah al-Halim al-Karim*" (There is no god but Allah, the Clement, the Generous). *Wasa'il ash-Shiah*, vol. 4, p. 906. "The Book of the *Salat*," sec. on "The *Qunut*," ch. 7, *hadith* 4; *Mustadrak al-Wasa'il*, "The Book of the *Salat*," sec. on "The *Qunut*," ch. 6, *hadith* 4 and 9.

Prophet and his offspring (a). It seems that this noble *dua*, short as it is, covers all the *salat*'s duties of remembrance.

Its merit can also be confirmed through the sayings of the jurisprudents (may Allah be pleased with them) or through "Tolerating the Proofs of the Traditions"[613]—although the writer has a second thought on that—or by means of discovering a creditable evidence—which has not occurred to us—regarded by the latecomers to be the basis of unanimity [*ijma*].

Among the noble *dua*'s of great merit, which includes the polite manners of supplication to Allah, and also numerates the full divine gifts, and completely suits the state of *qunut*, which is a state of supplication and devotion to Allah, and some great men (may Allah have mercy upon them) almost continually practiced it, is the *dua* called "*ya man azhar al-jamil*" (O, the One Who manifested the Beautiful), which is of the treasures of the *Arsh* and Allah's gift to His Messenger. Each one of its paragraphs has so much merits and rewards, as is stated in *at-Tawhid* by Shaykh as-Saduq (may Allah have mercy upon him).[614]

The best manner of servitude is that, in the state of *qunut*—which is a state of supplication and devotion to Allah in the *salat*, all of which is showing servitude and praising, and in this state the Holy Essence of Allah, the Exalted and Most High, specially opens the door of supplication and invocation to the servant and honors him so the *salik* servant must also observe the discipline of the Holy State of Lordship, and take care that his *dua* should include glorifying and purifying Allah, the Exalted, and His remembrance. He should ask Allah, in this noble state, to give him those things that are of the kind of divine knowledge [*maarif*], and to open for him the door of supplication, intimacy, privacy, and devotion to Him. He should avoid demanding this world, mean animal matters and selfish desires, so that

---

[613] There are many narratives, to the limit of prolixity [*istifadah*], to the effect that if somebody gets the information—by hearing or reading—that to perform a certain act results in getting a reward, and he performs that act, he will receive the promised reward, even if his information turned to be incorrect. Such narratives are known as "the narratives of the attainer" and their contents are called "Tolerating the Proofs of the Traditions." Refer to *Bihar al-Anwar*, vol. 2, p. 256, "The Book of Knowledge," ch. 30; *Usul al-Kafi*, vol. 3, p. 139, "The Book of Faith and Disbelief," ch. on "The One Who Attained a Reward from Allah for an Act."

[614] *At-Tawhid,* ch. on "The Names of Allah, the Exalted," ch. 29, *hadith* 14.

he may not feel ashamed in the presence of the pure ones, and not debase himself in the gathering of the pious ones.

O dear, *qunut* is giving up other than Allah, and completely turning towards the Lord"s Might, and extending the empty hand of demand to the Absolute Self-Sufficient. During such a state of devotion, to talk of the stomach, private parts and mundane matters is but a shortcoming and a loss.

Darling, now that you are far away from your homeland, blocked from neighboring the free people and captured in this dark house full of troubles and perils, do not spin around yourself, like a silkworm.

O dear, Allah, the Beneficent, has fermented your disposition with the light of knowledge and the fire of love, and supported you with the lights like the prophets, and the lovers like the *wali*s [*awliya*], so, do not extinguish this fire with the dust and ashes of this low world, and do not tarnish and darken that light with a world which is a place of exile. Probably if you pay attention to the original home, and demand from Allah to be devoted to Him, and expose before Him your deprivation and dislike of separation, in a painful tone out of your heart, displaying the conditions of your helplessness, weakness and distress, an invisible assistance will reach you and an inside hand of help will be extended to you, and your shortcomings will be done away with, as it is His habit to be charitable, and it is His custom to be benefactor.

If you recite parts of the *Shabaniyyah* supplication by the Imam of the Pious and the Commander of the Believers and his infallible offspring, who are the Imams of the people of knowledge and truths, in your *qunut,* especially the part in which he says: "O Allah, grant me „to be completely devoted to You","[615]etc., but in a state of necessity [*idtirar*], devotion and imploration, not with a dead heart, like the writer"s, it will be quite becoming of the condition.

In short, the state of the *qunut,* according to the writer"s opinion, is like the state of the *sujud.* The former is turning towards the humility of servitude and the remembrance of the state of the Lord"s Might, and the latter is turning towards the Lord"s Might and the remembrance of inability and the humility of servitude. This is in

---

[615] "*Munajat-i Shabaniyyah,*" *Bihar al-Anwar*, vol. 91, p. 99.

proportion to the state of the middle class. But according to the state of the perfect ones, since the *sujud* is the state of the servant"s annihilation, and neglecting the other [*ghayr*] and otherness, the *qunut* is the state of the exclusive devotion to Allah, and giving up depending on the other, which is the spirit of the state of "trust in Allah" [*tawakkul*]. In short, as *qiyam* is the state of the Unity of Acts, which is confirmed in the second *rakat*, he displays in the *qunut* its result, and extends his begging bowl before Allah, and completely parts with, and runs away from, all creatures.

AFTER-THE-*SALAT* INVOCATION
Chapter Three

It is one of the confirmed *mustahab*s (supererogatories), and to neglect it is abominable. It is most recommended after the *salat*s of the morning and of the afternoon. The after-the-*salat* invocations are so many, including the final three *takbir*s.

The great religious men take care to raise their hands in the *takbir*s, like the opening *takbir*s, to near their ears, with their palms open and facing the *qiblah*. To prove this is difficult, although some narratives refer to raising the hands three times. Probably raising the hands, saying the *takbir* three times and then reciting the *dua* which starts with: *la ilaha illallah, wahdahu wahdah ...*[616] (there is no god but Allah, alone, alone!) etc., will be enough. If raising the hands in the way the great men do is a supererogatory act, it confirms the same secrets which have already been stated, and maybe it refers to rejecting their *salat* and worshippings lest they may admit conceit and self-admiration into their hearts.

The three *takbir*s may be a reference to magnification(s) [*takbir*(s)] showing the shortcomings of the Three Unities which keep the spirit of the whole *salat*. So, the hearty discipline of these *takbir*s is to reject, with each raising of the hands, one of the three unities, and magnify and glorify Allah, Almighty and Most High, from his describings and unifications, displaying his inability, humility, failure and shortcomings before the Holy Presence of Allah, Almighty and Most High. In the *Sirr as-Salat* thesis we related, in a nice [*latif*] way, the spiritual secrets of these *takbir*s and raising the hands. It was of the graces of Allah, the Exalted, bestowed upon this helpless person. For Him are the thanks and praise.

---

[616] *Wasa'il ash-Shiah*, vol. 4, p. 1030, "The Book of the *Salat*," sec. on "After-the-*Salat* Invocation," ch. 14, *hadith* 2.

Of the other noble after-the-*salat dua*''s are the *tasbihat* of the Pure *Siddiqah* (Fatimah) (a), the daughter of the Prophet (*s*), which was taught to her by the Messenger of Allah (*s*). It is the best of the after-the-*salat dua*''s. It is in the *hadith* that had there been a better one, the Messenger of Allah (*s*) would have taught it to Fatimah (a).[617] Imam as-Sadiq (a) is quoted to have said that these *tasbihs* every day after every *salat* are more loved by me than a thousand *rakat*s of the *salat* every day.[618] It is known among the companions that these *tasbihs* are arranged as follows: *takbir* thirty-four times, *tahmid* thirty-three times and *tasbih* thirty-three times. It is most probable that this arrangement is the best, not positively imposed. One is free to change the successions of, say, the *tahmid* and the *tasbih*, or replace the *takbir* by the *tasbih*. But the best, and according to precaution, is the said known arrangement.

The relevant cordial disciplines are the same as have been stated concerning "the Four *Tasbihs*." Furthermore, as these noble recitations are for after the *salat,* and as their *tasbih* is magnification [*takbir*] and glorification [*tanzih*] showing failure in due servitude, and magnification [*takbir*] and glorification [*tanzih*] showing incapability in servitude before His Holy Presence, and magnification [*takbir*] and glorification [*tanzih*] showing the shortcomings of knowledge [*marifat*] (in knowing Him), which is the objective of servitude, the *salik* servant should, in the after-the-*salat* invocation, think about his shortcomings, his incomplete worship and his negligences during the state of presence, which are regarded to be sins in the school of love and affection. He is to think about his being deprived of his share of the Holy Presence of Allah, the Exalted, so that he may, in the after-the-*salat* recitations, which open a new door leading to the mercy of Allah, the Blessed and Exalted, compensate as much as possible, conveying those noble recitations to his heart and revive it with them, in which case his end may be sealed with goodness and happiness. In the *tahmid* (praising) of the *tasbihs* of the (pure) Siddiqah (a), he is to prove this praising, too, which is the performance of servitude, for the

---

[617] *Furu al-Kafi*, vol. 3, p. 343, "The Book of the *Salat*," ch. on "The After-the-*Salat* Dua''," *hadith* 14.

[618] *Bihar al-Anwar*, vol. 83, p. 332, quoting *Thawab al-Amal*, p. 149; *Wasa'il ash-Shiah*, vol. 4, p. 1024, "The Book of *as-Salat*," sec. on "After the-*Salat* Invocation," ch. 9, *hadith* 2.

Divine Ipseity [*huwiyyat-i ilahiyyah*], taking it to be a support, a power and a success from that Holy Essence. He is to convey the truths of these matters to the inside of his heart, letting it taste the secret of these graces, so that the heart may be enlivened with the remembrance of Allah, and get eternal life by it.

As the morning is the beginning of being engaged in the multiplicity and entering the world, where man is faced with the danger of getting busy with the creatures and neglecting Allah, the conscious *salik*, in this crucial situation of entering this dark house, has to turn to Allah, the Exalted, and be devoted to Him. And as he finds himself not so dignified in the Holy Presence, he is to resort to the guardians of the affairs, the guards of the times, the intercessors of *ins* and *jinn*, i.e., the Seal of the Messengers (*s*) and the infallible Imams (a), asking those honorable personalities to be his intermediates to, and his intercessors with, Allah. Now each day has its guard and shelterer: for Saturday it is the blessed being of the Messenger of Allah (*s*), for Sunday it is Amir al-Muminin, Ali (a), for Monday are the two magnificent Imams, the grandsons [of the Messenger of Allah (*s*), al-Hasan and al-Husayn (a)], for Tuesday Imams as-Sajjad, al-Baqir and as-Sadiq (a), for Wednesday Imams al-Kazim, ar-Rida, at-Taqi and an-Naqi (a), for Thursday Imam al-Askari (a), and for Friday *waliyy al-amr* (may Allah hasten his glorious advent) (The 12th Imam (a).[619] So, it is suitable for one, in the after-the-*salat* recitations in the morning, and for the purpose of entering this deadly dark sea, the awful Satanic trap-place, to resort to the guards of that day, and, with their intercession—as they are close to the Holy Court and are the favorite confidents at the door of intimacy—ask Allah, the Exalted, to remove the evils of Satan and the evil-commanding soul, and to have those great ones as his intermediates for the completion and acceptance of incomplete worshippings and unworthy rites. Naturally, if Allah, Highly Exalted, made Muhammad (*s*) and his offspring our means of guidance, and through their blessings He saved the *ummah* from ignorance and straying, He would, because of their intercession, amend our inability and complete our shortcomings, and accept our unworthy obediences and worshippings, "He is the Lord of grace and bounty." Other reported after-the-*salat dua*‛s are stated in the relevant

---

[619] *Bihar al-Anwar*, vol. 24, p. 239, quoting *al-Khisal*, vol. 2, ch.7, p. 394.

books of invocations. Everybody may select those which suit him best in order to bring this honorable journey to its good and happy destination.

CONCLUSION AND INVOCATION (*DUA*)

It was appropriate to finish this thesis by stating the *salat*'s moral obstacles, such as imposture, conceitedness and the like, but as I have given some explanations in the book *The Forty Hadiths*[620] about some *hadith*s connected to this subject, and also, now, being too much busy, and owing to distraction of mind, I apologize for not being able to offer this service. So, I end these papers by admitting my inability and shortcomings, and ask forgiveness from the people of pure insight for my mistakes, and request their good *dua* and generous attention.

O Allah, You Who have clothed us, Your weak servants, with the dress of existence through Your grace and favor and pure mercy and generosity, prior to any service and worship on our part, and without needing our worshipping and servitude. You have bestowed upon us diverse kinds of spiritual and corporeal favors, and different sorts of internal and external mercies, although our non-existence causes no flaw in Your power and strength, nor our existence adds anything to Your greatness and prestige. Now that the headspring of Your beneficence gushed forth, and the sun of Your Beautiful Beauty effulged, drowning us in the seas of mercy and illuminating us with the lights of Your Beauty, make up for our shortcomings, sins and failures with the light of internal success and Your secret help and guidance, and relieve our fully attached hearts from mundane attachments, and make them cling to Your Holy Might.

O Allah, our unworthy worshipping expands nothing of Your domain. Our disobedience decreases nothing of Your kingdom, and torturing and punishing the sinners benefit You not a bit, and forgiving the fallen and having mercy upon them lessen nothing of Your power. The immutable essences of the sinners implore for mercy, and the dispositions of the imperfect ask for perfection. You Yourself treat us with Your comprehensive kindness and disregard our inefficiency.

---

[620] Refer to footnote 63.

"O Allah, if I am unworthy to receive Your mercy, You are worthy of granting me of Your vast favor. O Allah, You have covered for me in this world sins which I need more to be covered in the Hereafter. O Allah, grant me to be completely devoted to You, and light our hearts" eyes with the light of witnessing You until the hearts" eyes penetrate the veils of light, to reach the source of greatness."[621]

Our talk has come to an end here, according to the *taqdir* of Allah, Almighty and Most High, with praises and thanks for His graces, asking Him to send His blessings upon Muhammad and his pure progeny, on the date of Monday, 2nd of (the month of) Rabiuth-Thani, thirteen-hundred and sixty-one of Lunar year (1361 L.H.).[622]

---

[621] "The Shabaniyyah Supplication," *Bihar al-Anwar*, vol. 91, p.99.
[622] Corresponds to 30th of Farvardin, 1321 Solar Hijri Year.

GLOSSARY

A

adhan: *announcement or the call announcing the arrival of the time for the* salat.

***Ahl al-Bayt*: the offspring of the Messenger of Allah (s).**

Ahl al-Jabarut: the owner of Power, the owners of power.

Ahl al-Allah: the people of Allah.

aynul jam: the very union, the essence of union (collectively).

al-amr bil-maruf wan-nahyanil-munkar: bidding unto honor and forbidding dishonor.

al-Baytul-Mamur: Allah"s Populous House.

Alim (pl. *ulama*): scholar, scientist, learned.

ama: a sufist term meaning "the truth of the truths;" heavy clouds, high.

amr: affair; order; sovereignty, rule, authority, power, ordinance decree.

(a):   *alayhis-salam* = Peace be upon him;
      alayhas-salam = Peace be upon her;
      alayhimus-salam = Peace be upon them.

asrar: (pl. of *sirr*): secret.

ayah (pl. *ayat*): a Quranic term use for one of the smaller portions of a chapter of the Quran usually called "verse;" a divine sign or communication.

B

barzakh: isthmus; the interval between death and the Day of Resurrection.

barzakhian (adj. of *barzakh*): intermediate.

basmalah: uttering "*bismillahir-rahmanir-rahim*," i.e. In the Name of Allah, the Beneficent, the Merciful.

batil: false, invalid, void, null, wrong.

batin: the inside, the inward, interior, hidden meaning.

bismillah: In the Name of Allah.
butun: interior.

D

dar-i tahaqquq: the House of Realization.
dar al-ghurur: the house of conceit, i.e. this world.
dar as-surur: the house of pleasure, i.e. the Hereafter world.
din (pl. *adyan*): religion, judgment.
dua (pl. *adiyah*): invocation, benediction, prayer.

F

faqih: (pl. *fuqaha*): jurisprudent, expert of *fiqh*.
fitrat: disposition, nature.

G

ghayb (pl. *ghuyub*): the unseen, the invisible.
ghusl (pl. *aghsal*): ritual bathing; the major ritual ablution.

H

hadath: a ritual impurity which requires either a *wudu* or a *ghusl* before performing *salat*.
hadith (pl. *ahadith*): the saying of the Prophet (*s*), the tradition of the Prophet (*s*); narrative relating deeds and utterances of the Prophet, the *Ahl al-Bayt*, the infallible Imams and the Companions.
hajj: the pilgrimage of the Muslims to Makkah (Mecca) during certain months.
halal: religiously lawful or allowed.
haram: religiously unlawful.

I

Iblis: Satan, the devil.
ihram: the state of being in the pilgrimage period; the special dress worn during pilgrimage.
ihtijaj: argumentation.
ins: the human beings as against the *jinn*.
inshaallah: an Islamic expression meaning: if Allah wills, Allah willing.
istiadhah: saying *audhu billah*, i.e. I take refuge in Allah.

istikharah: consulting the Quran or the rosary beads to do, or not to do, something.
ikhlas: sincerity.
iqamah: preliminary wordings said before entering the *salat*.

J

jabarut: of omnipotence; the possession of power.
janabah: the state of being ritually impure owing to seminal ejaculation or to a sexual penetration, though without ejaculation—a state requiring a ritual *ghusl*.
jawamial-kalim: comprehending many significations; the Quran; collective words.
jihad: struggle or exertion of effort for the sake of Islam.

K

kabah: a structure in the middle of the Holy Mosque in Makkah, to which the Muslims of the world direct their faces during the performance of *salat*.
khilafah: succession, successorship, vicegerency.
khums: a fifth of one"s net profit to be paid to a religious authority.

L

latifah: grace; subtlety, delicacy.
lawh (pl. *alwah*): a tablet, a slab, a Quranic term denoting "The Tablet" with Allah, the Exalted, in which everything is registered.

M

maad: resurrection.
mahdar: presence, company.
mahw: (self-)effacement, (self-)extinction, annihilation.
majdhub-i salik: the attracted one who is traveling to Allah.
malakut: heavenly kingdom.
masum: infallible.
minbar: a pulpit of several ascending steps in a mosque from which the speaker delivers his speech.
miraj: ascension to Allah.
muadhdhin: one who speaks out the *adhan*.
mufassir: one who writes exegesis on the Quran, an exegetist.
mukashafah: revelation, disclosure, apocalypse.

mulk: this transitory world.

muqarinat: affinities.

musalli (pl. *musallin*): a Muslim when performing the *salat*.

mustaadhun bihi: one with whom refuge is sought.

mustaadhun lahu: that for which refuge is sought; one for whom refuge is sought.

mustaadhun minhu: that from which refuge is sought; one from whom refuge is sought.

mustaidh: one who seeks refuge; refuge-seeker.

muttaqi (pl. *muttaqqin*): one who guards against Allah‟s wrath by obeying His commandments; God-fearing, pious.

N

nafilah (pl. *nawafil*): supererogatory *salat*s.

nutfah (pl. *nutaf*): sperm of human beings.

niyyah (pl. *niyyat*): intention.

Q

qadr: measure; predestination.

qibab (pl. of *qubbah*): domes.

qiblah: the direction to which the Muslims are to face when performing the *salat*, i.e. the *kabah* in Makkah.

qiyam: the standing position in the *salat*.

qunut: supplication recited in the *salat* after the second *rakah*, in the standing position, with the palms of the hands raised upwards.

R

rabb: the Lord, the Sustainer; One of Allah‟s Names.

rafraf: the name of one of the Messenger‟s heavenly mounts.

rakah (pl. *rakaat*): a complete section of the *salat*.

rijal: biographical books about the narrators of the *hadith*s, who sort them according to their authority, truthfulness and dependability; sources of information.

rukn (pl. *arkan*): one of the pillars of the *salat*.

ruku (pl. *rukuat*): the position of bowing in the *salat*; genuflection.

S

(s): *Sallallahu alayhi wa alih* = May Allah send His blessings upon him (the Prophet) and his offspring.

sadaqah: charity, alms.

sahw: sobriety.

sajdah: prostration in prayer, prostration in worship.

salam: peace, salutation, greetings.

salat (pl. *salawat*): the Muslim"s ritual prayer.

sajid (pl. *sajidin*): a prostrate worshipper; one who prostrates himself.

salik: a Gnostic term denoting the traveler to Allah.

salik-i majdhub: a *salik* attracted by Divine Grace.

sawm (or *siyam*): fasting.

shahadah (pl. *shahadat*): testimony.

shar: divine law.

shariah (pl. *sharai*): divine law.

shuhud: intuition, divine vision.

sujud: prostration.

suluk: a Gnostic term for the journey to Allah.

sunnah (pl. *sunan*): tradition; the Prophet"s tradition.

surah: a chapter of the Quran.

T

taala: a divine attribute meaning the Most High.

tafsir (pl. *tafasir* and *tafsirat*): explanation, commentary; an exegesis of the Quran.

tahlil (pl. *tahlilat*): saying *la ilaha illallah* = There is no god but Allah.

tahmid (pl. *tahmidat*): saying *al-hamdu lillah* = All praise is for Allah; Praise belongs to Allah.

taghut (pl. *tawaghit*): an ancient idol, anything worshipped other than Allah; a tyrant, a despot.

tajwid: a style of reciting the Quran with intonation; rules of correct recitation of the Quran.

takbir (pl. *takbiirat*): saying; *Allahu akbar* = Allah is the Greatest.

talqin: giving instructions; religious instruction recited to the dead as a funeral rite.

tanzih: purifying Allah from all blemishes and defects.

taqdir: measuring; Allah"s decree.

taqib (pl. *taqibat*): after-the-*salat* invocation.

taqwa: avoiding Allah"s wrath by precaution and obeying His commandments; fearing Allah, piety.

tartil: a style of reciting the Quran without intonation.

tasbih (pl. *tasbihat*): glorifying Allah by saying: *subhanallah* = Glory be to Allah.

tashahhud: the act of testifying the unity of Allah and that Muhammad is the Messenger of Allah (as part of the *salat*).

taslim: the greetings with which the *salat* is closed.

tasmiyah: naming; saying: In the Name of Allah, the Beneficent, the Merciful.

tawhid: believing in Allah's Oneness; monotheism.

U

ummah: people, nation.

ummul-qura: the Mother of the towns.

uruj: ascension.

W

wali (or *waliyy*) (pl. *awliya*): friend, patron, protector; holy man, saint.

waliyy al-amr (pl. *awliya al-umur* or *al-amr*): plenipotentiary, religious guardian, legal guardian, the religiously legal authority.

wasi (or *wasiyy*)(pl. *awsiya*): trustee, custodian; successor, vicegerent.

was-salam: and that is the end to the matter; and now good bye; with peace.

wilayah: guardianship.

wudu: ritual ablution (made before performing the *salat*).

Z

zakat: purity; alms tax; prescribed portion of one's wealth which is to be given to the religious authorities or to the poor according to certain conditions.

Know that for the salat, beside its form, there is a meaning, and apart from its exterior it has an interior; and as the exterior has its disciplines, neglecting which would render the outer form of the salat invalid or incomplete; likewise, its interior has cordial spiritual disciplines, neglecting which would render the spiritual salat invalid or incomplete; whereas observing them would inspire the salat with a heavenly spirit.

Imam Khomeini

www.ingramcontent.com/pod-product-compliance
Lightning Source LLC
Chambersburg PA
CBHW032014080526
44654CB00085B/40